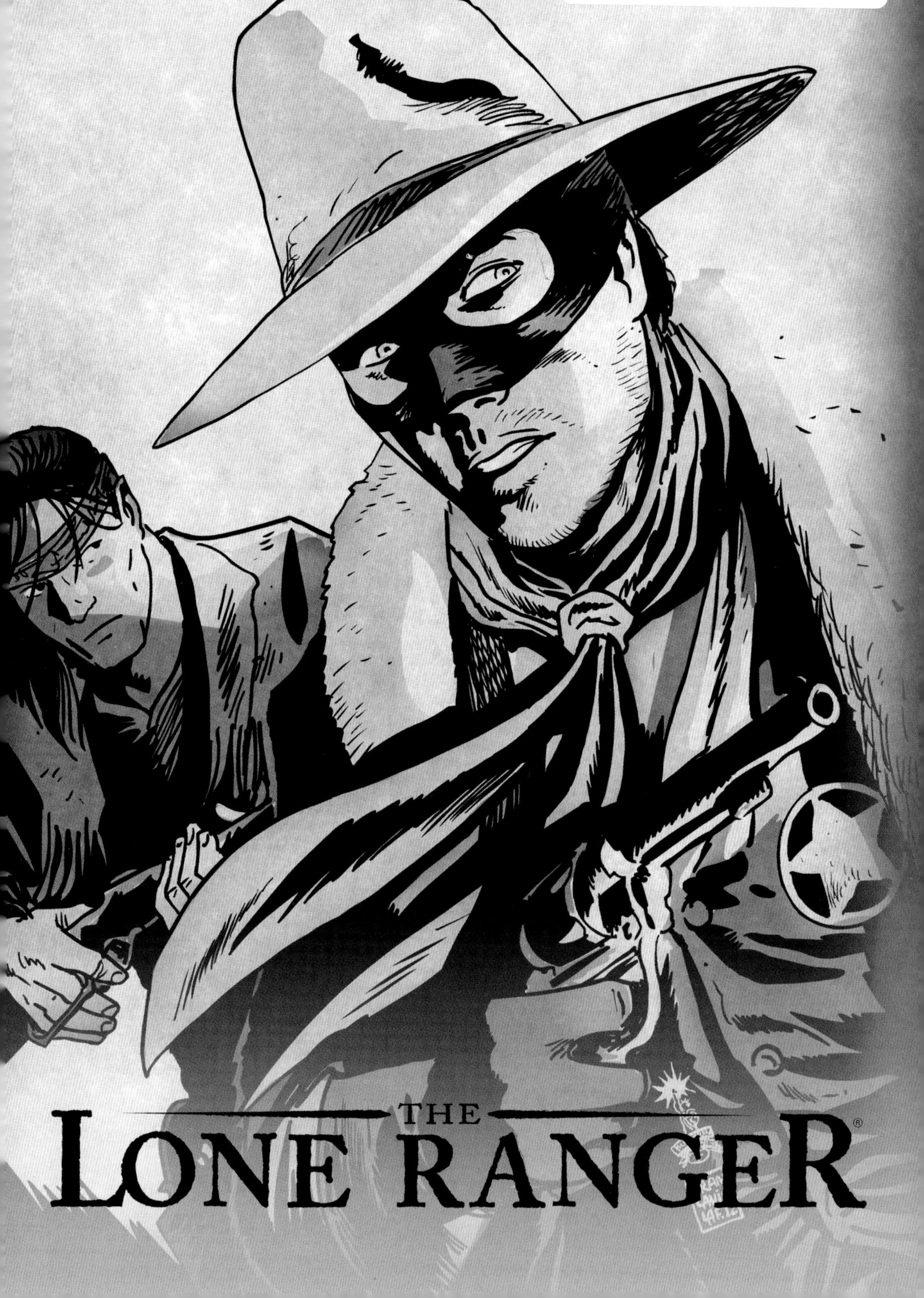

THE LONE RANGER®

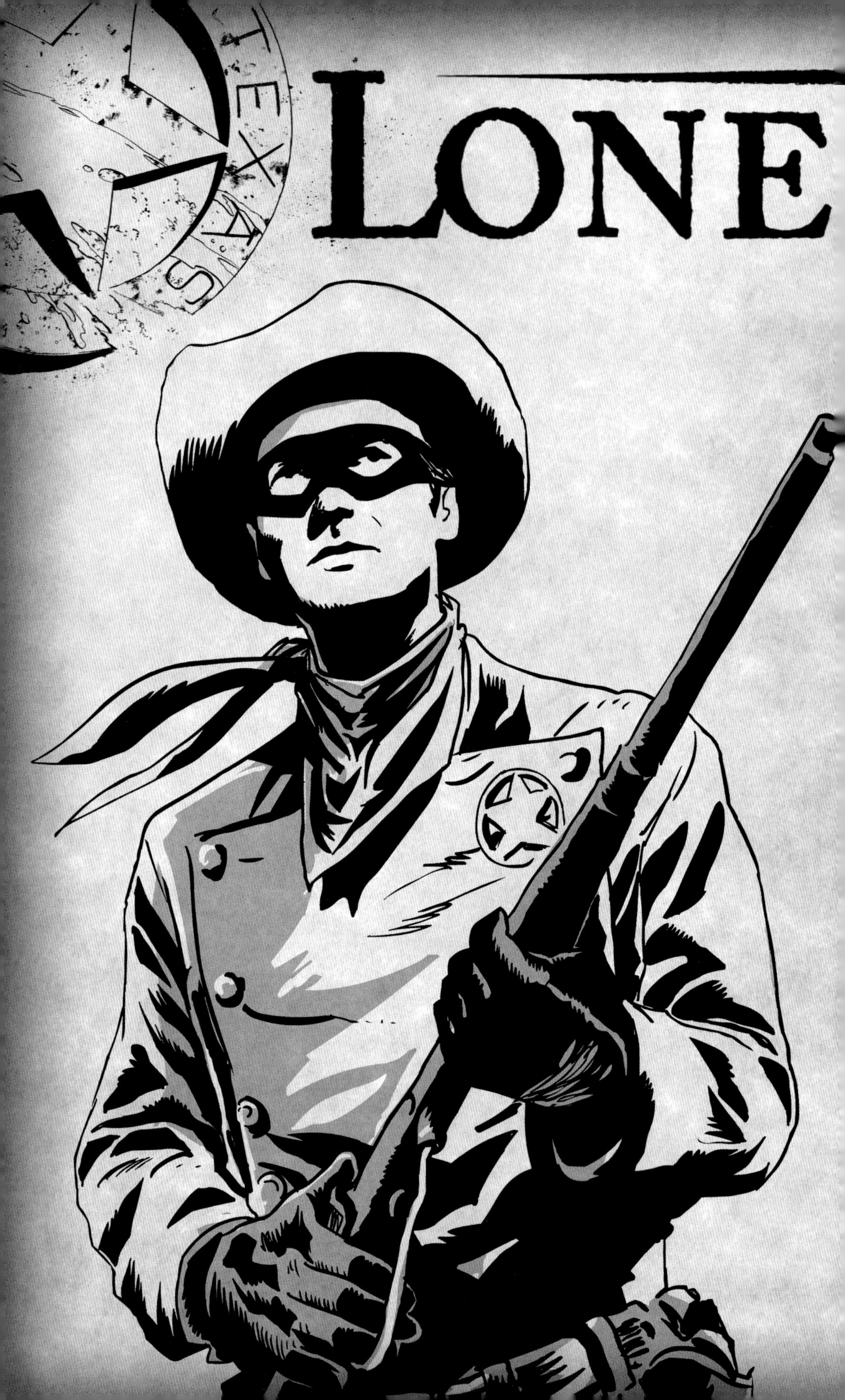
LONE

THE RANGER

★ VOLUME VIII: ★
THE LONG ROAD HOME

WRITER:
ANDE PARKS

ARTIST:
ESTEVE POLLS

COLORIST:
MARC RUEDA

LETTERER:
SIMON BOWLAND

COVER ARTIST:
FRANCESCO FRANCAVILLA

COLLECTION DESIGN:
KATIE HIDALGO

SPECIAL THANKS TO:
SCOTT SHILLET
COLIN MCLAUGHLIN
DAMIEN TROMEL

THIS VOLUME COLLECTS THE LONE RANGER VOLUME 2 ISSUES 19-25
BY DYNAMITE ENTERTAINMENT

DYNAMITE®

ck Barrucci, CEO / Publisher
an Collado, President / COO
h Young, Director Business Development
ith Davidsen, Marketing Manager

e Rybandt, Senior Editor
nnah Elder, Associate Editor
lly Mahan, Associate Editor

sh Johnson, Art Director
son Ullmeyer, Senior Graphic Designer
tie Hidalgo, Graphic Designer
ris Caniano, Production Assistant

Visit us online at www.DYNAMITE.com
Follow us on Twitter @dynamitecomics
Like us on Facebook /Dynamitecomics
Watch us on YouTube /Dynamitecomics

ISBN-10: 1-60690-563-5   ISBN-13: 978-1-60690-563-0   First Printing   10 9 8 7 6 5 4 3 2 1

THE LONE RANGER, VOL. 8: THE LONG ROAD HOME. This volume collects material originally published in The Lone Ranger Volume 2 #19-25. Published by Dynamite Entertainment. 113 Gaither Dr., STE 205, Mt. Laurel, NJ 08054. © 2014 Classic Media, LLC. THE LONE RANGER and associated character names, images and other indicia are trademarks of and copyrighted by Classic Media, LLC. All rights reserved. DYNAMITE, DYNAMITE ENTERTAINMENT and its logo are © & ® 2014 Dynamite. All rights reserved. All names, characters, events, and locales in this publication are entirely fictional. Any resemblance to actual persons (living or dead), events or places, without satiric intent, is coincidental. No portion of this book may be reproduced by any means (digital or print) without the written permission of Dynamite Entertainment except for review purposes. The scanning, uploading and distribution of this book via the Internet or via any other means without the permission of the publisher is illegal and punishable by law. Please purchase only authorized electronic editions, and do not participate in or encourage electronic piracy of copyrighted materials. Printed in China

For information regarding press, media rights, foreign rights, licensing, promotions, and advertising e-mail: marketing@dynamite.com

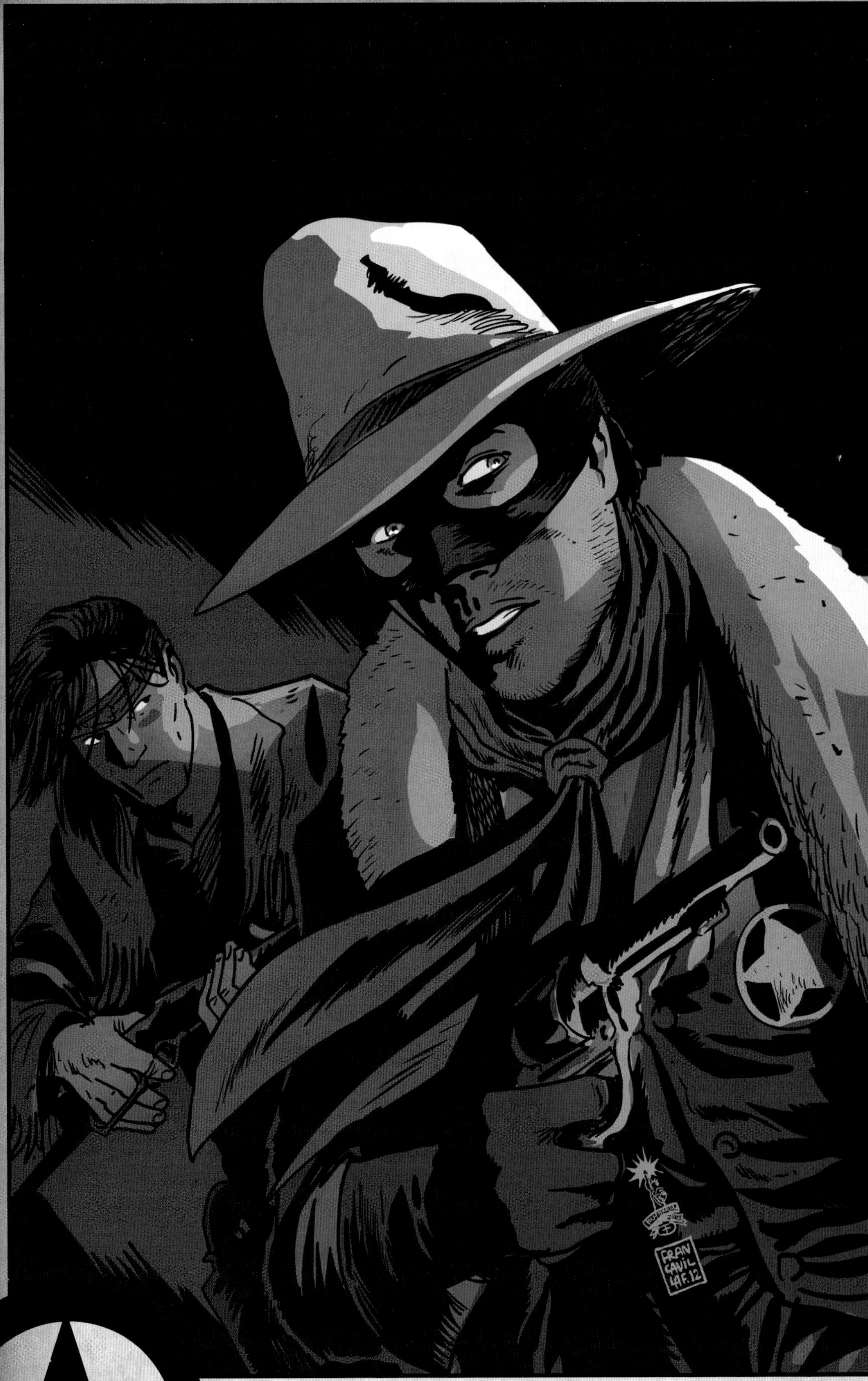

19

COVER BY **FRANCESCO FRANCAVILLA**

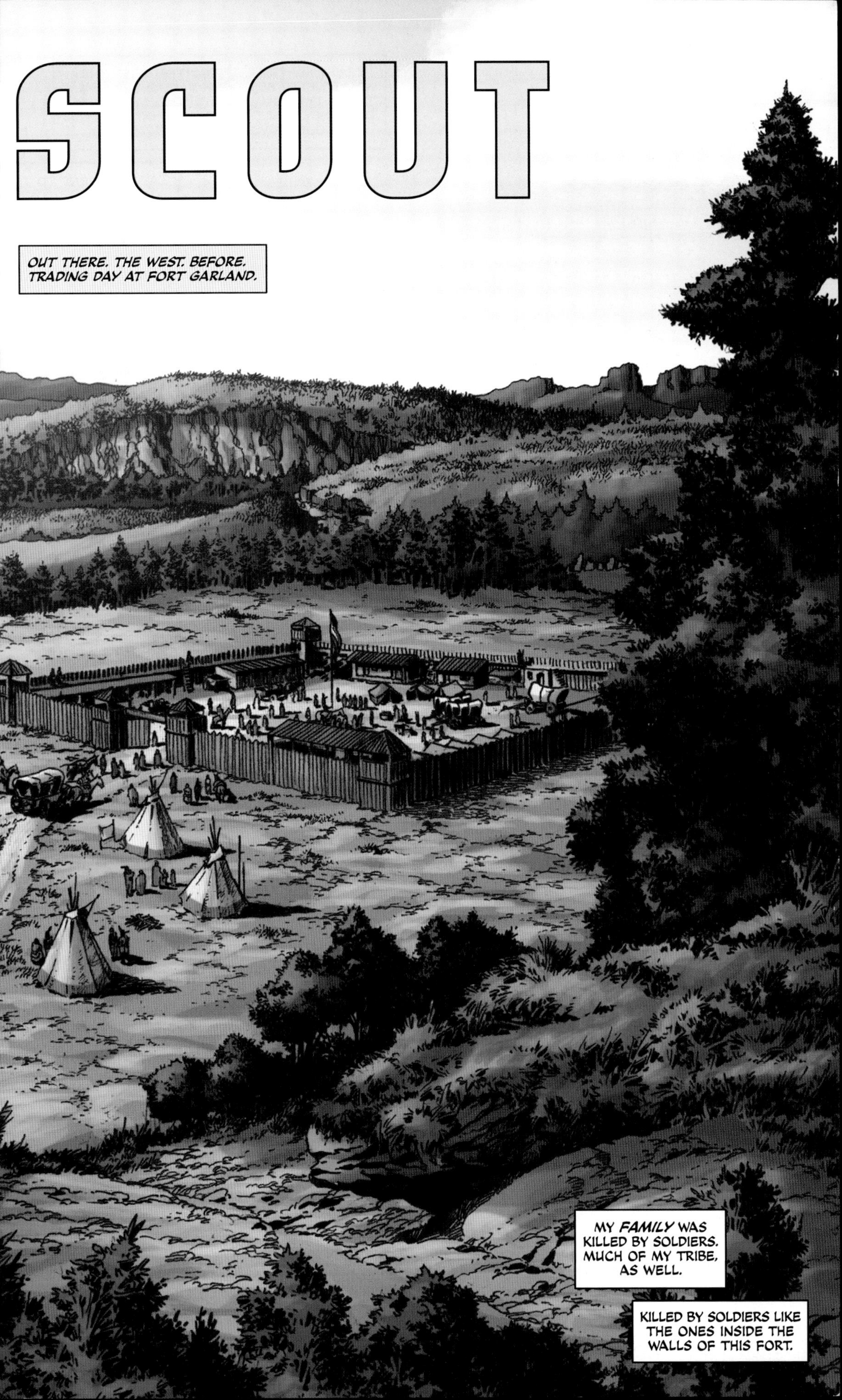
SCOUT
OUT THERE. THE WEST. BEFORE. TRADING DAY AT FORT GARLAND.
MY FAMILY WAS KILLED BY SOLDIERS. MUCH OF MY TRIBE, AS WELL.
KILLED BY SOLDIERS LIKE THE ONES INSIDE THE WALLS OF THIS FORT.

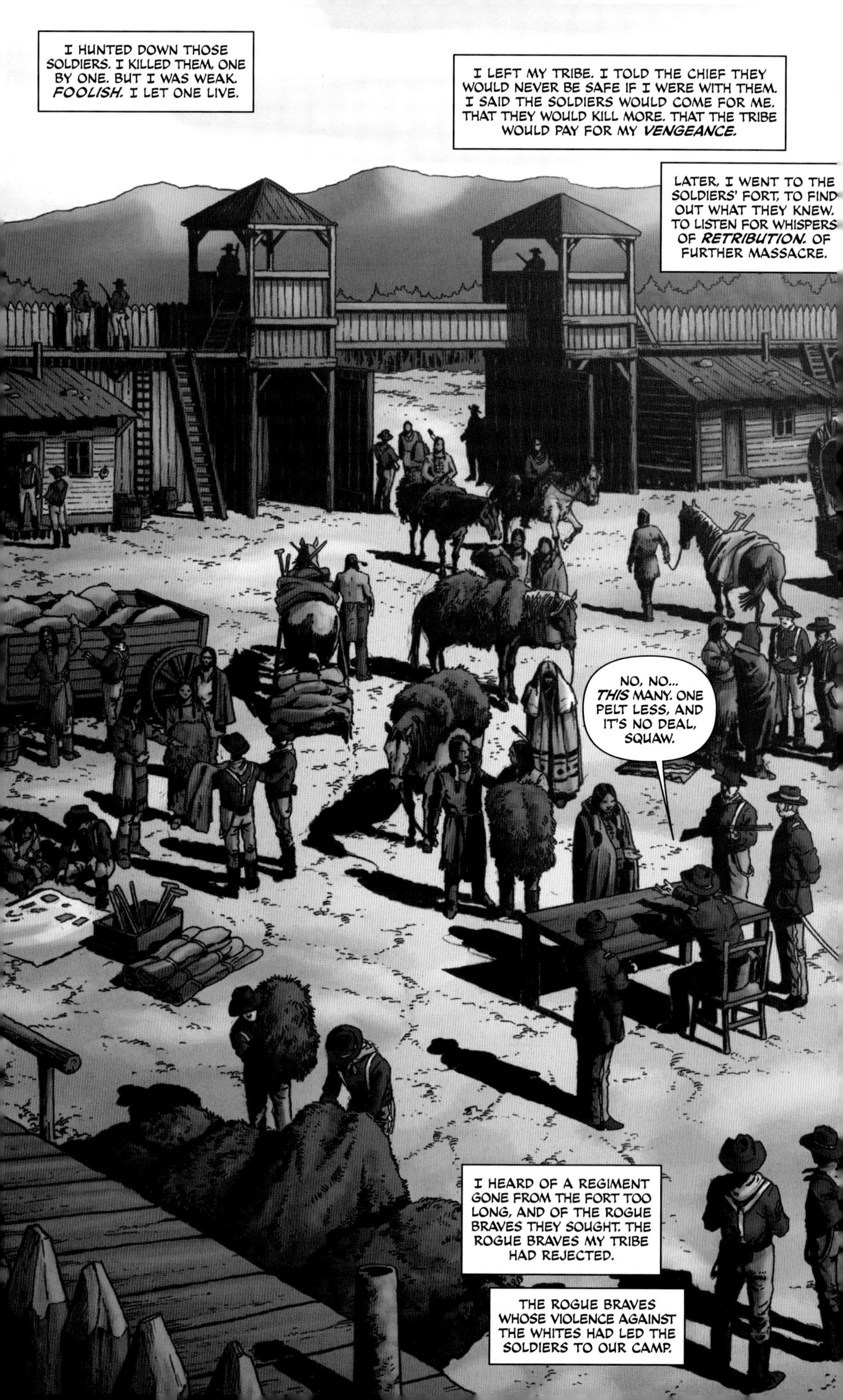

I HUNTED DOWN THOSE SOLDIERS. I KILLED THEM, ONE BY ONE. BUT I WAS WEAK. *FOOLISH.* I LET ONE LIVE.
I LEFT MY TRIBE. I TOLD THE CHIEF THEY WOULD NEVER BE SAFE IF I WERE WITH THEM. I SAID THE SOLDIERS WOULD COME FOR ME. THAT THEY WOULD KILL MORE. THAT THE TRIBE WOULD PAY FOR MY *VENGEANCE.*
LATER, I WENT TO THE SOLDIERS' FORT, TO FIND OUT WHAT THEY KNEW. TO LISTEN FOR WHISPERS OF *RETRIBUTION.* OF FURTHER MASSACRE.
NO, NO... *THIS* MANY. ONE PELT LESS, AND IT'S NO DEAL, SQUAW.
I HEARD OF A REGIMENT GONE FROM THE FORT TOO LONG, AND OF THE ROGUE BRAVES THEY SOUGHT. THE ROGUE BRAVES MY TRIBE HAD REJECTED.
THE ROGUE BRAVES WHOSE VIOLENCE AGAINST THE WHITES HAD LED THE SOLDIERS TO OUR CAMP.

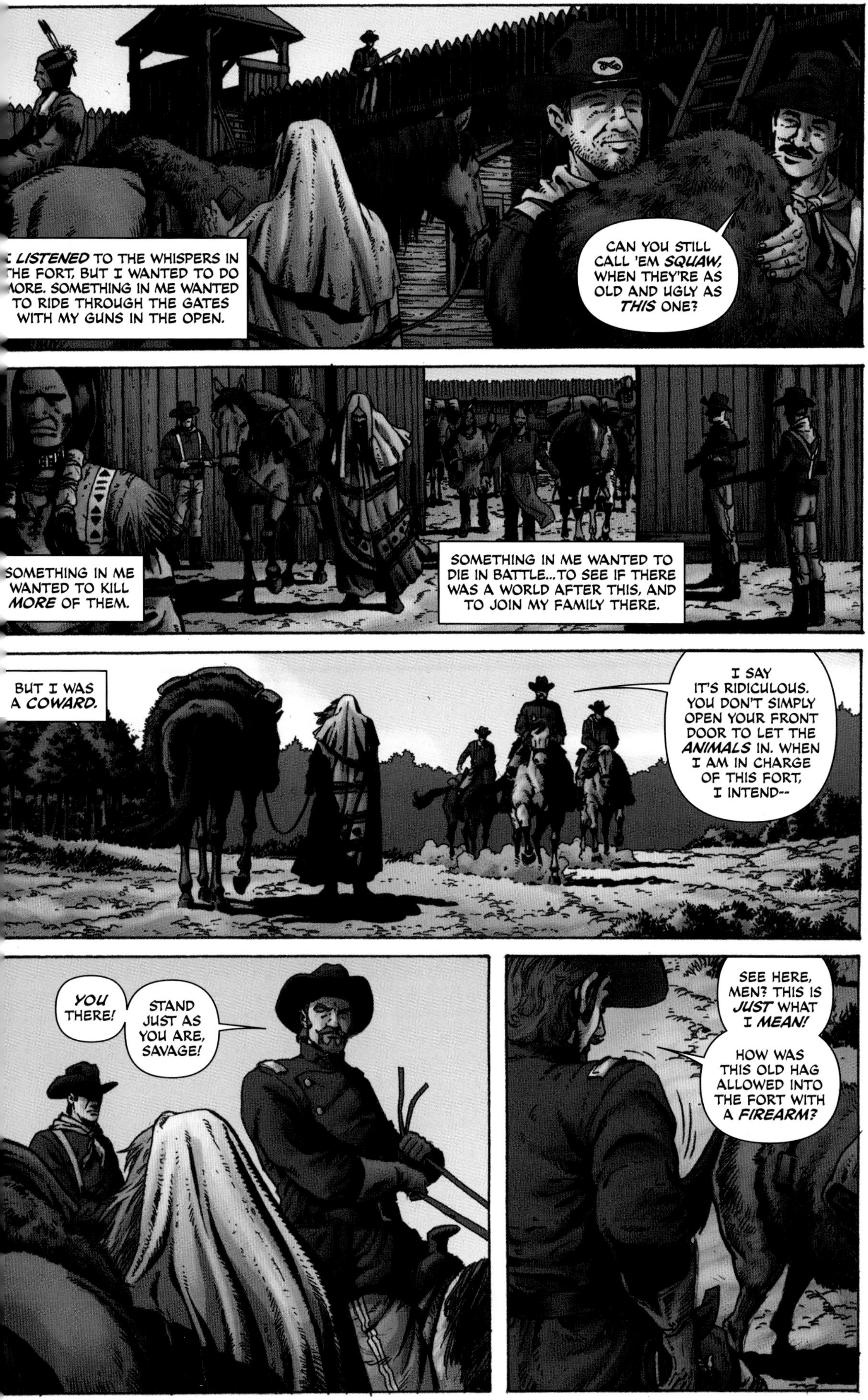

I LISTENED TO THE WHISPERS IN THE FORT, BUT I WANTED TO DO MORE. SOMETHING IN ME WANTED TO RIDE THROUGH THE GATES WITH MY GUNS IN THE OPEN.
CAN YOU STILL CALL 'EM SQUAW, WHEN THEY'RE AS OLD AND UGLY AS THIS ONE?
SOMETHING IN ME WANTED TO KILL MORE OF THEM.
SOMETHING IN ME WANTED TO DIE IN BATTLE...TO SEE IF THERE WAS A WORLD AFTER THIS, AND TO JOIN MY FAMILY THERE.
BUT I WAS A COWARD.
I SAY IT'S RIDICULOUS. YOU DON'T SIMPLY OPEN YOUR FRONT DOOR TO LET THE ANIMALS IN. WHEN I AM IN CHARGE OF THIS FORT, I INTEND--
YOU THERE!
STAND JUST AS YOU ARE, SAVAGE!
SEE HERE, MEN? THIS IS JUST WHAT I MEAN!
HOW WAS THIS OLD HAG ALLOWED INTO THE FORT WITH A FIREARM?

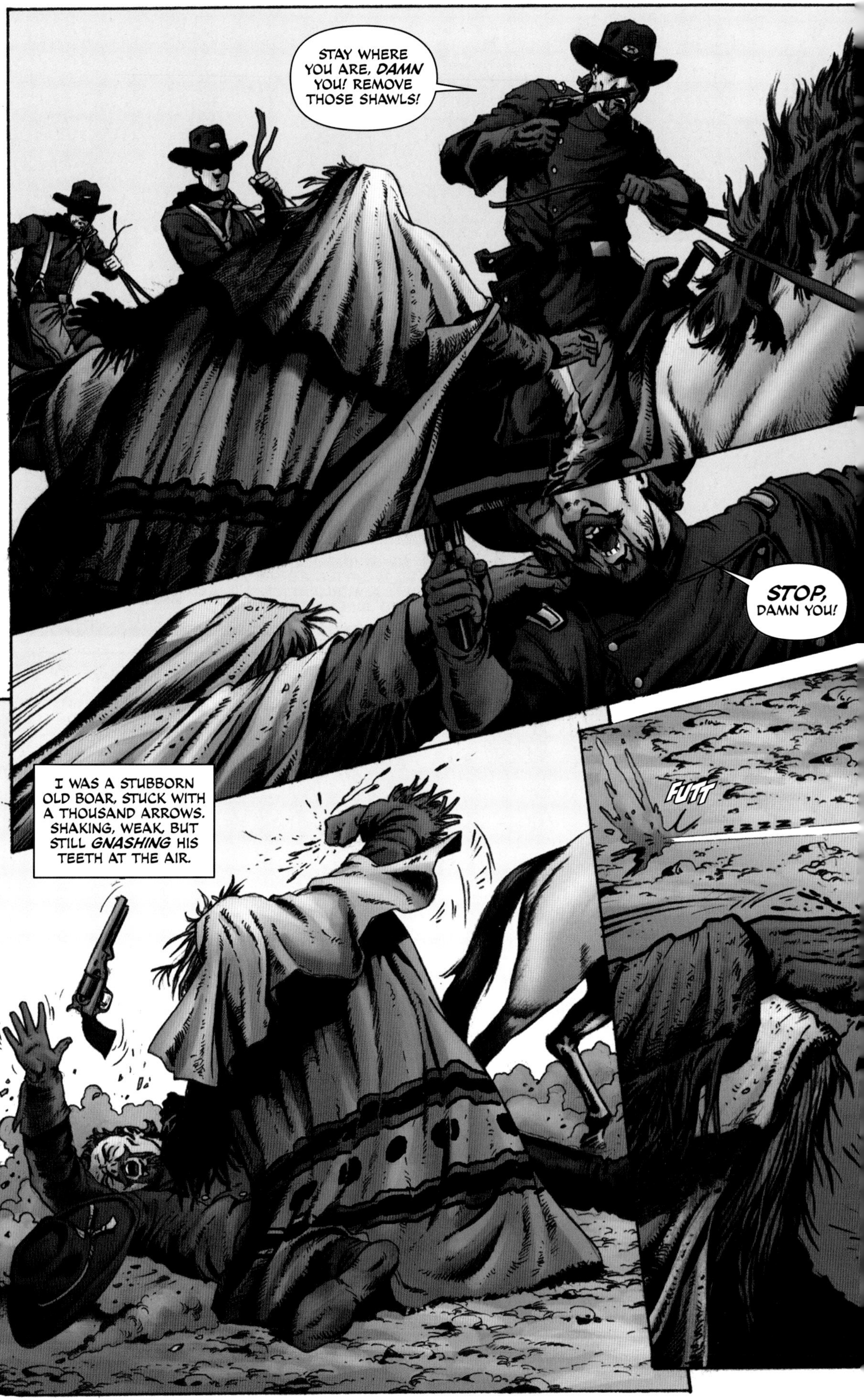
STAY WHERE YOU ARE, *DAMN* YOU! REMOVE THOSE SHAWLS!
STOP, DAMN YOU!
I WAS A STUBBORN OLD BOAR, STUCK WITH A THOUSAND ARROWS. SHAKING, WEAK, BUT STILL *GNASHING* HIS TEETH AT THE AIR.
FUTT

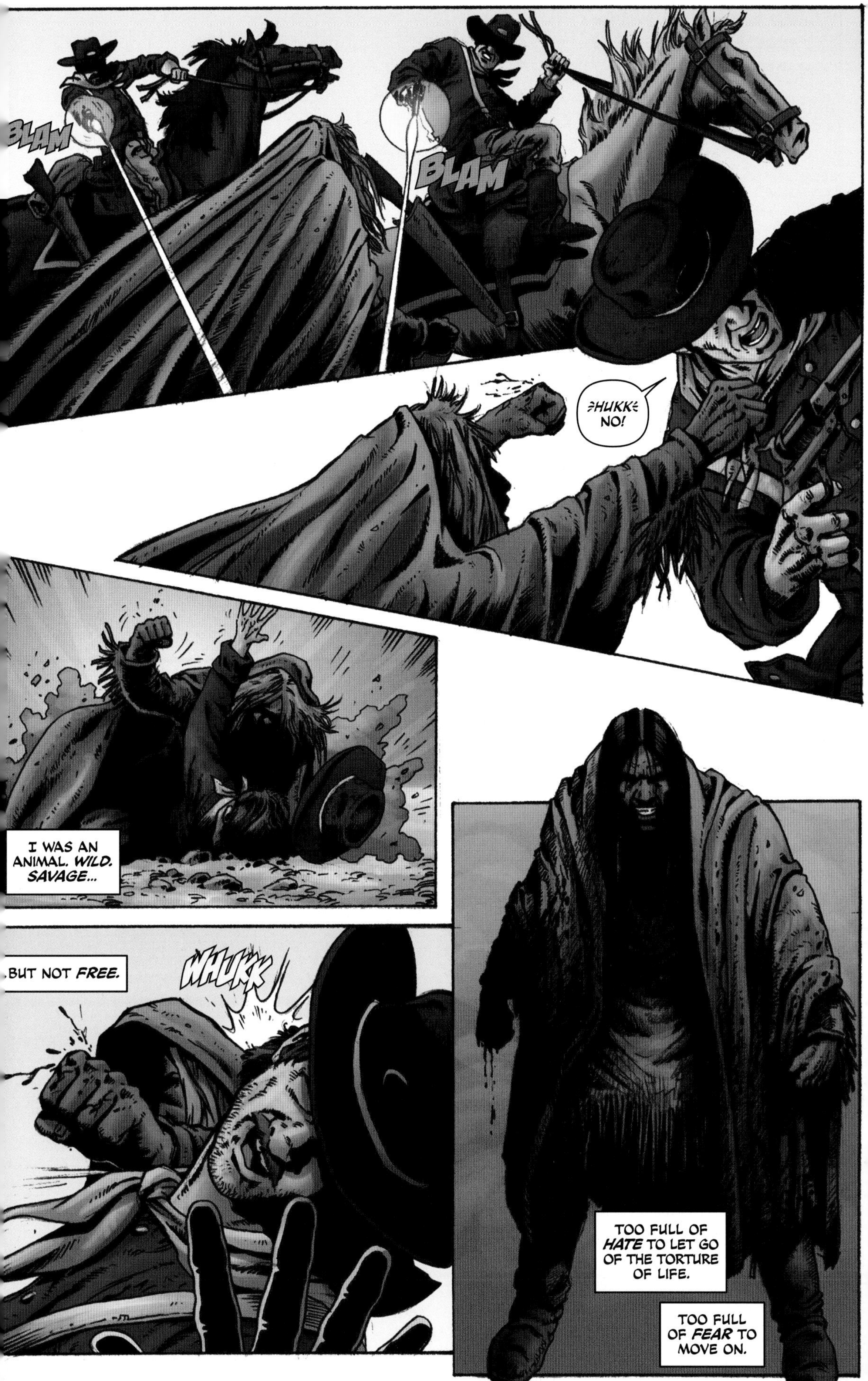
BLAM
BLAM
HUKK
NO!
I WAS AN ANIMAL. *WILD. SAVAGE...*
...BUT NOT *FREE.*
WHUKK
TOO FULL OF *HATE* TO LET GO OF THE TORTURE OF LIFE.
TOO FULL OF *FEAR* TO MOVE ON.

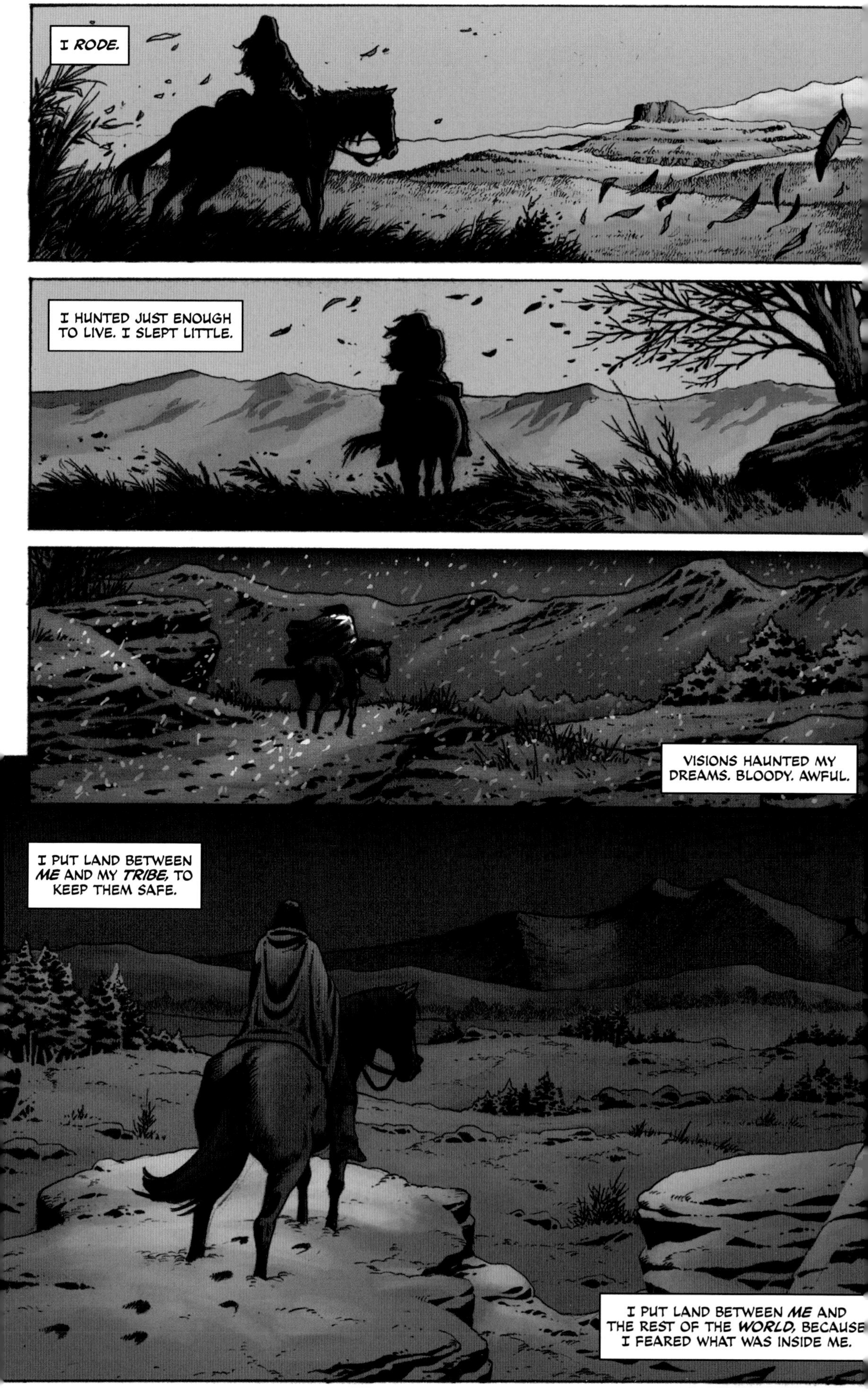
I RODE.
I HUNTED JUST ENOUGH TO LIVE. I SLEPT LITTLE.
VISIONS HAUNTED MY DREAMS. BLOODY. AWFUL.
I PUT LAND BETWEEN ME AND MY TRIBE, TO KEEP THEM SAFE.
I PUT LAND BETWEEN ME AND THE REST OF THE WORLD, BECAUSE I FEARED WHAT WAS INSIDE ME.

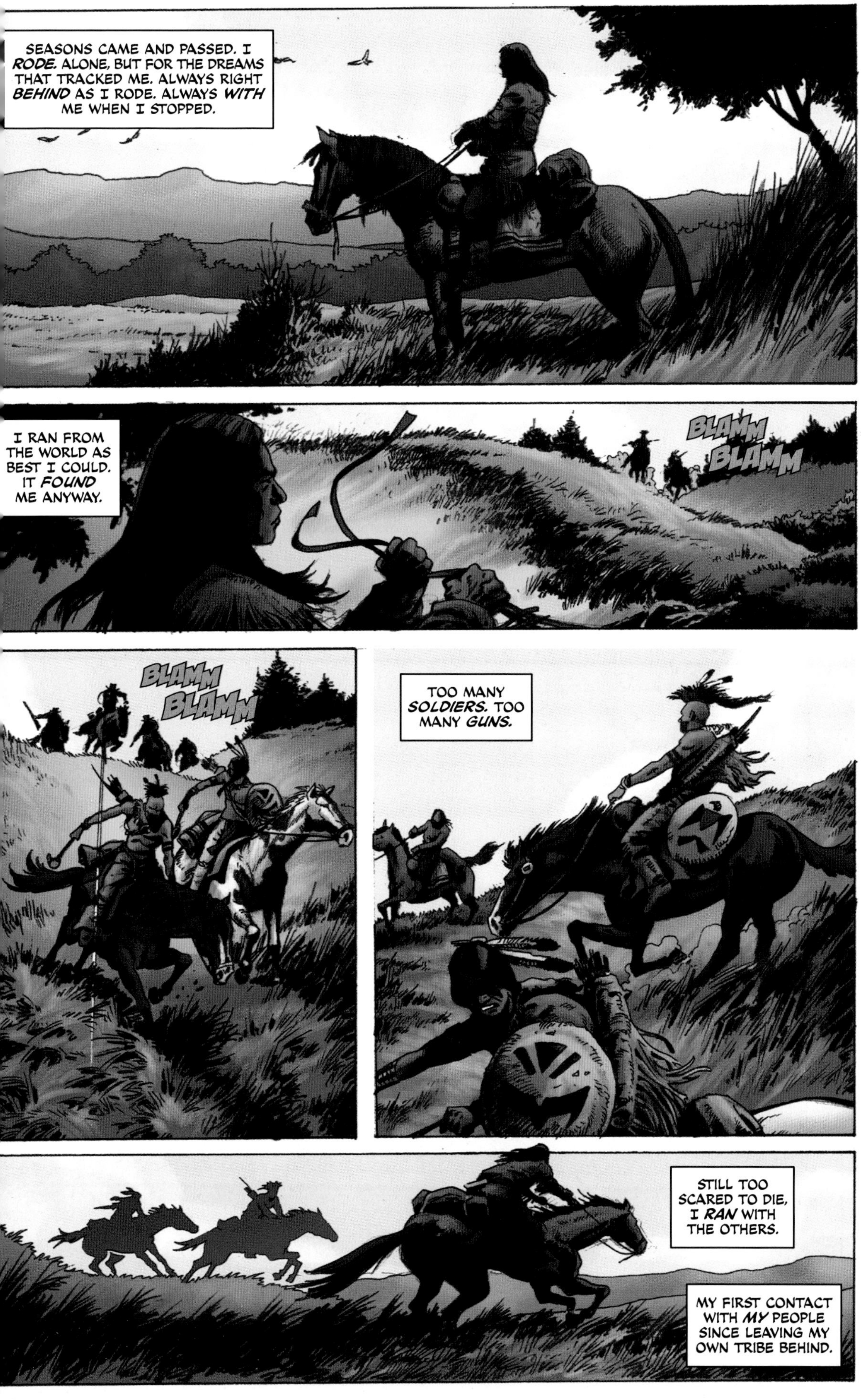
SEASONS CAME AND PASSED. I RODE. ALONE, BUT FOR THE DREAMS THAT TRACKED ME. ALWAYS RIGHT BEHIND AS I RODE. ALWAYS WITH ME WHEN I STOPPED.
I RAN FROM THE WORLD AS BEST I COULD. IT FOUND ME ANYWAY.
BLAMM BLAMM
BLAMM BLAMM
TOO MANY SOLDIERS. TOO MANY GUNS.
STILL TOO SCARED TO DIE, I RAN WITH THE OTHERS.
MY FIRST CONTACT WITH MY PEOPLE SINCE LEAVING MY OWN TRIBE BEHIND.

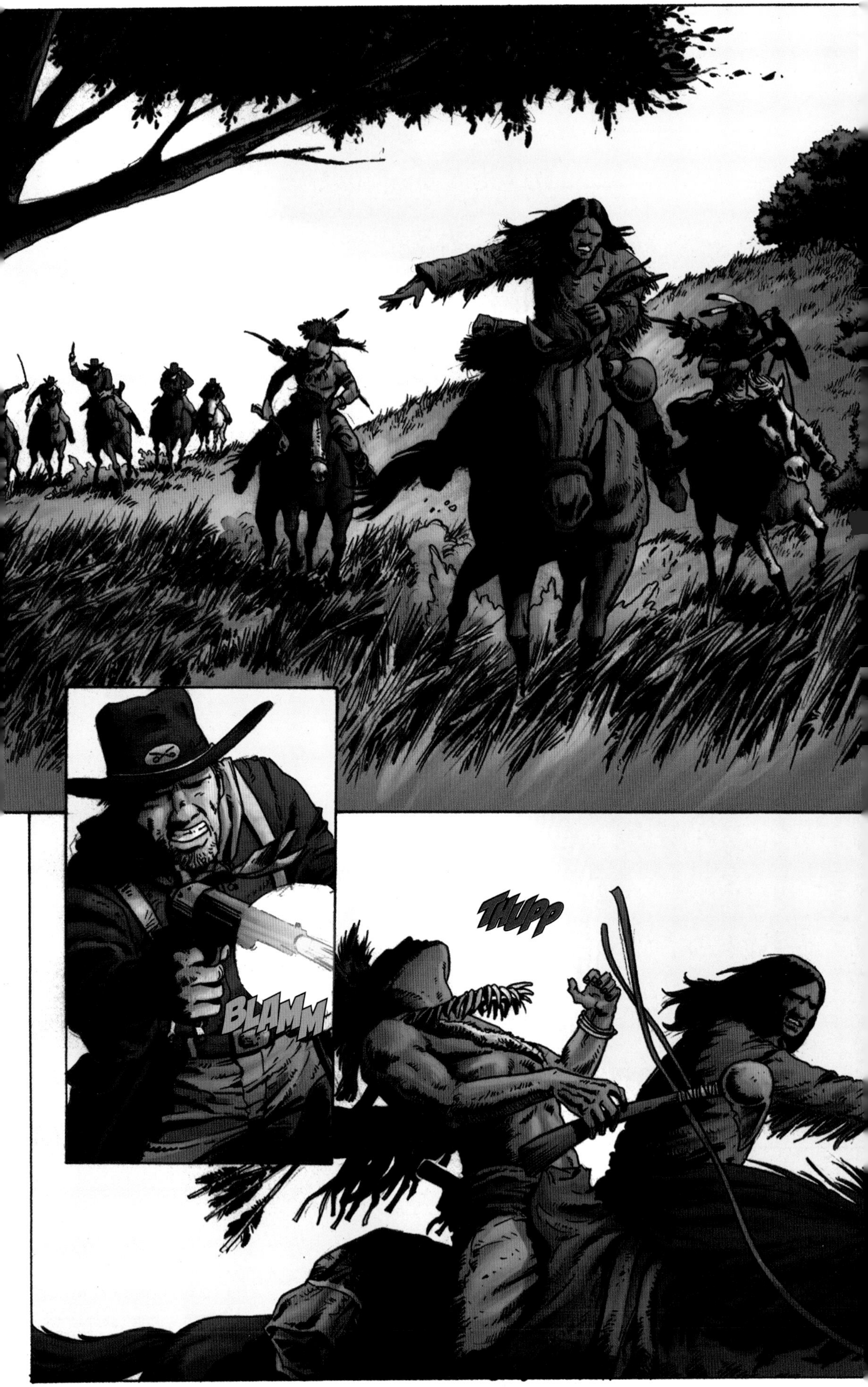
THUPP
BLAMM

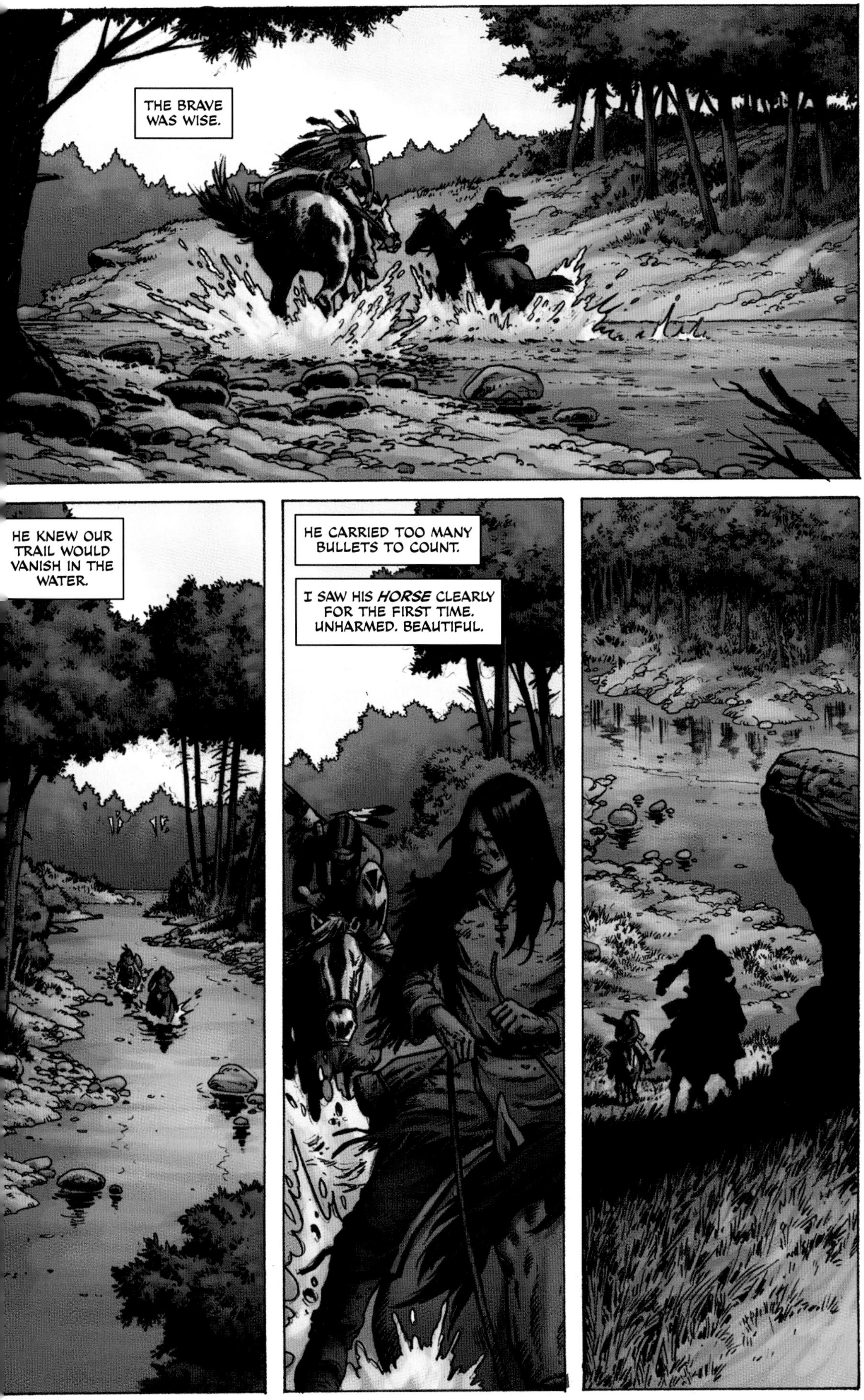
THE BRAVE WAS WISE.
HE KNEW OUR TRAIL WOULD VANISH IN THE WATER.
HE CARRIED TOO MANY BULLETS TO COUNT.
I SAW HIS *HORSE* CLEARLY FOR THE FIRST TIME. UNHARMED. BEAUTIFUL.

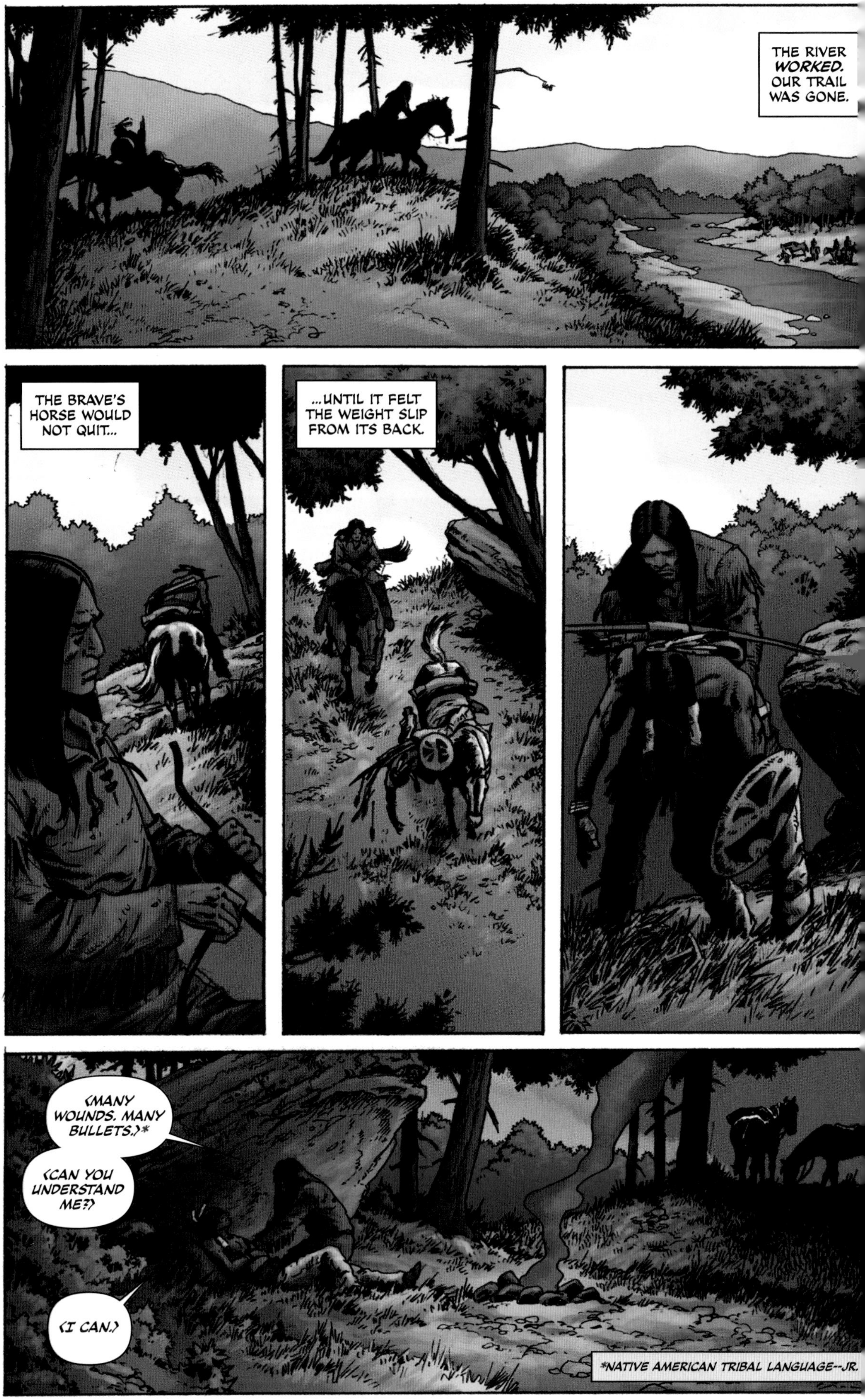
THE RIVER WORKED. OUR TRAIL WAS GONE.
THE BRAVE'S HORSE WOULD NOT QUIT...
...UNTIL IT FELT THE WEIGHT SLIP FROM ITS BACK.
‹MANY WOUNDS. MANY BULLETS.›*
‹CAN YOU UNDERSTAND ME?›
‹I CAN.›
*NATIVE AMERICAN TRIBAL LANGUAGE--JR.

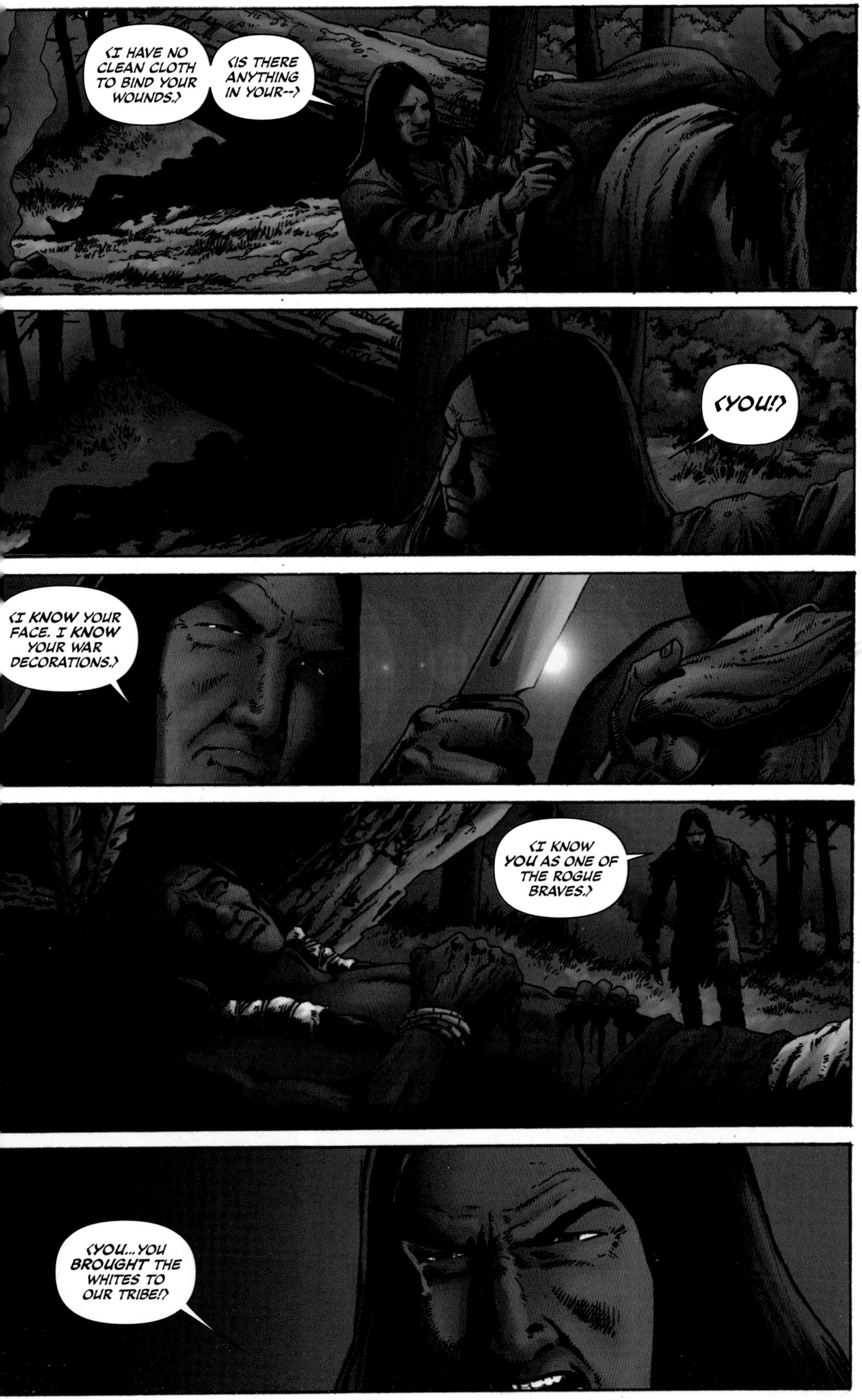
<I HAVE NO CLEAN CLOTH TO BIND YOUR WOUNDS.>
<IS THERE ANYTHING IN YOUR-->
<YOU!>
<I KNOW YOUR FACE. I KNOW YOUR WAR DECORATIONS.>
<I KNOW YOU AS ONE OF THE ROGUE BRAVES.>
<YOU...YOU BROUGHT THE WHITES TO OUR TRIBE!>

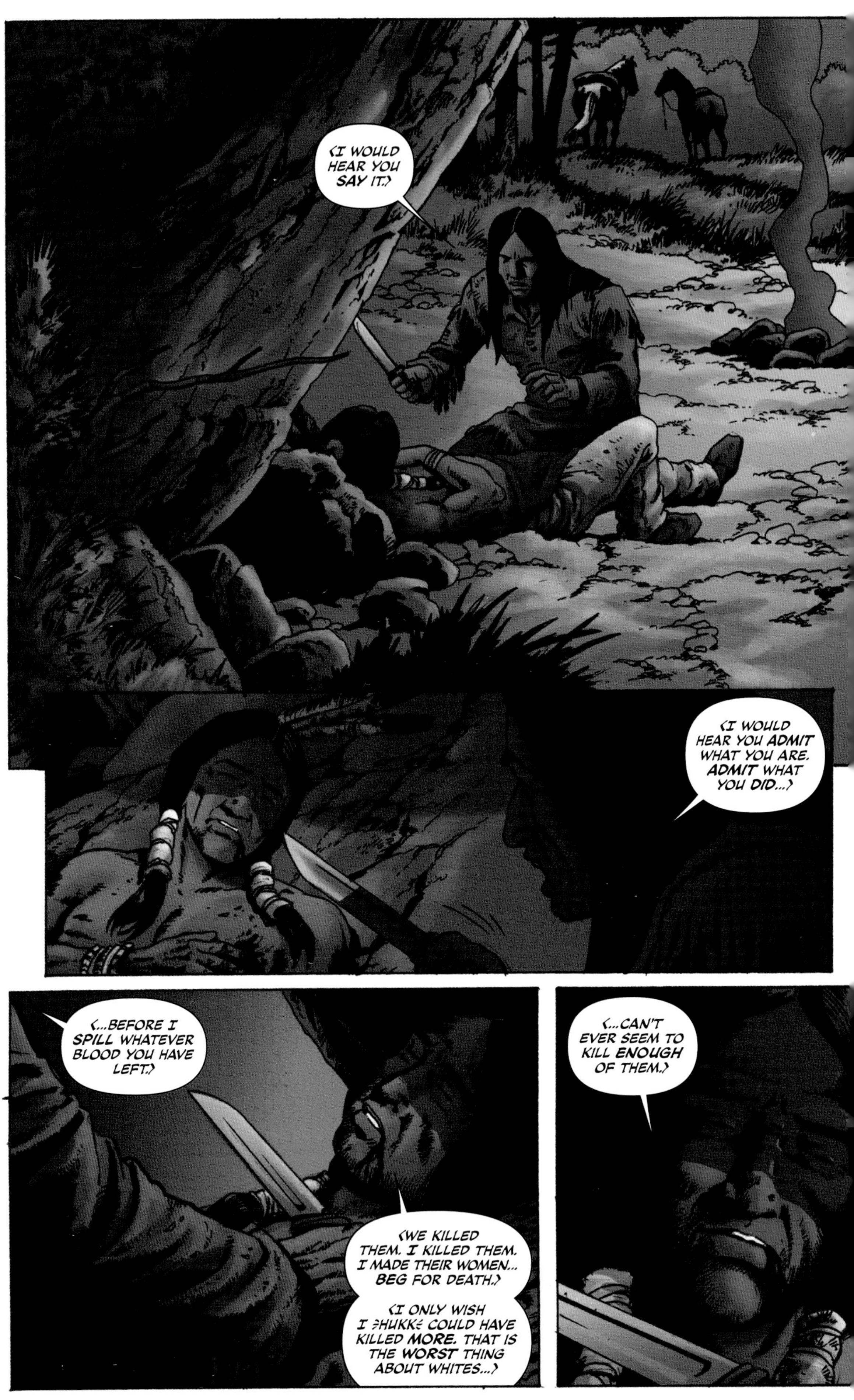

<I WOULD HEAR YOU SAY IT.>
<I WOULD HEAR YOU ADMIT WHAT YOU ARE. ADMIT WHAT YOU DID...>
<...BEFORE I SPILL WHATEVER BLOOD YOU HAVE LEFT.>
<WE KILLED THEM. I KILLED THEM. I MADE THEIR WOMEN... BEG FOR DEATH.>
<I ONLY WISH I >HUKK< COULD HAVE KILLED MORE. THAT IS THE WORST THING ABOUT WHITES...>
<...CAN'T EVER SEEM TO KILL ENOUGH OF THEM.>

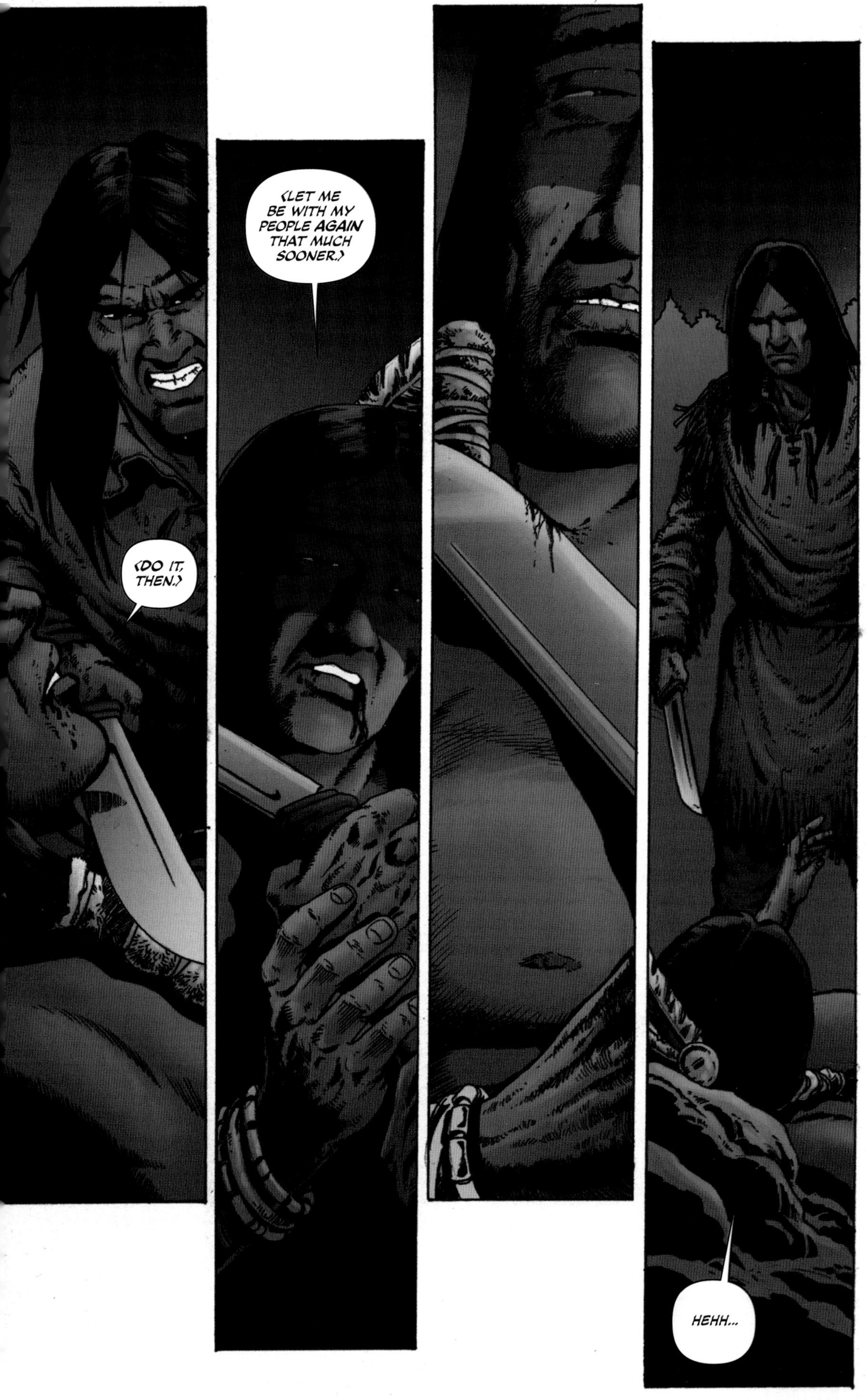

‹DO IT, THEN.›
‹LET ME BE WITH MY PEOPLE AGAIN THAT MUCH SOONER.›
HEHH...

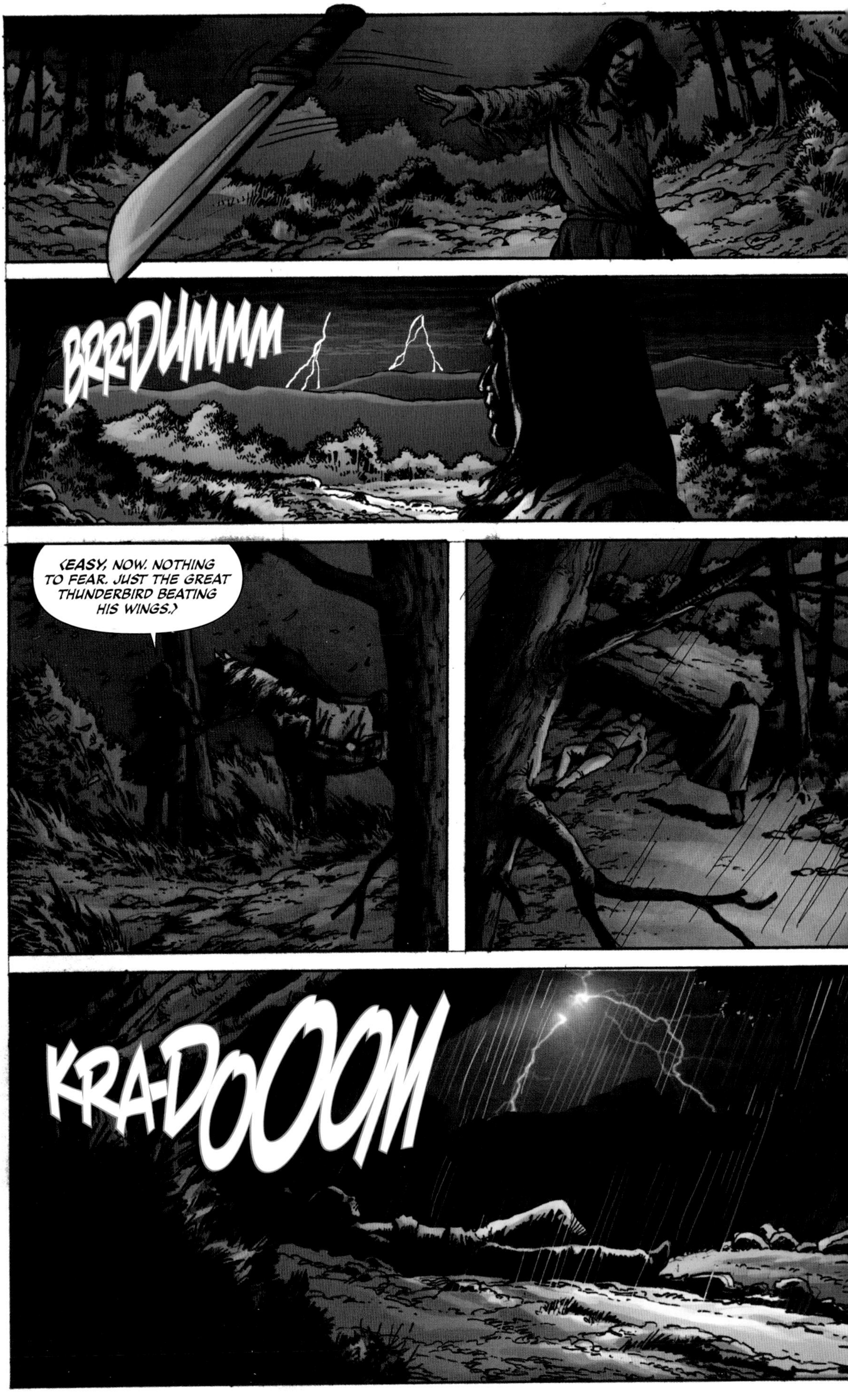
BRR-DUMMM
‹EASY, NOW. NOTHING TO FEAR. JUST THE GREAT THUNDERBIRD BEATING HIS WINGS.›
KRA-DOOOOM

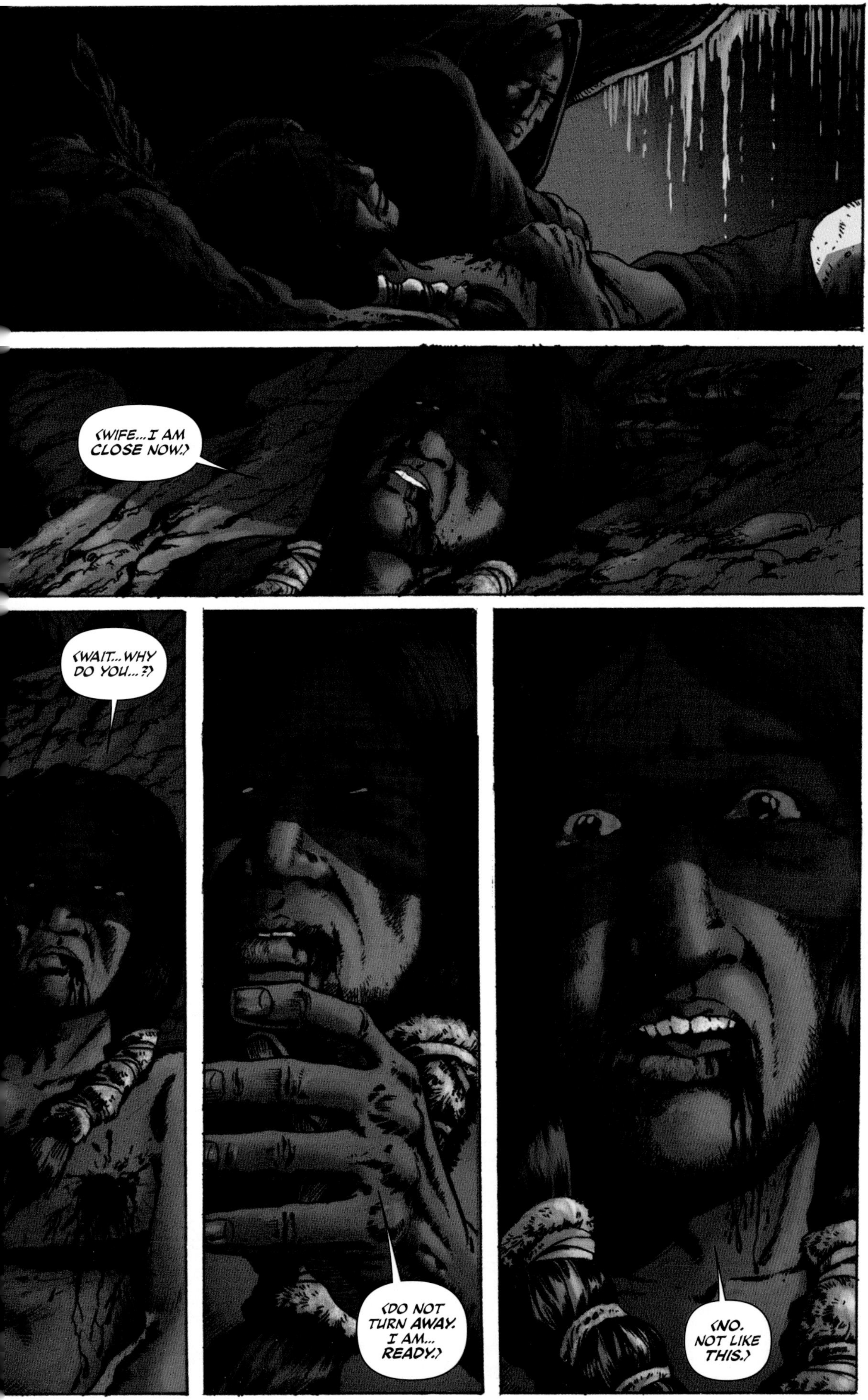
‹WIFE... I AM CLOSE NOW.›
‹WAIT... WHY DO YOU...?›
‹DO NOT TURN AWAY. I AM... READY.›
‹NO. NOT LIKE THIS.›

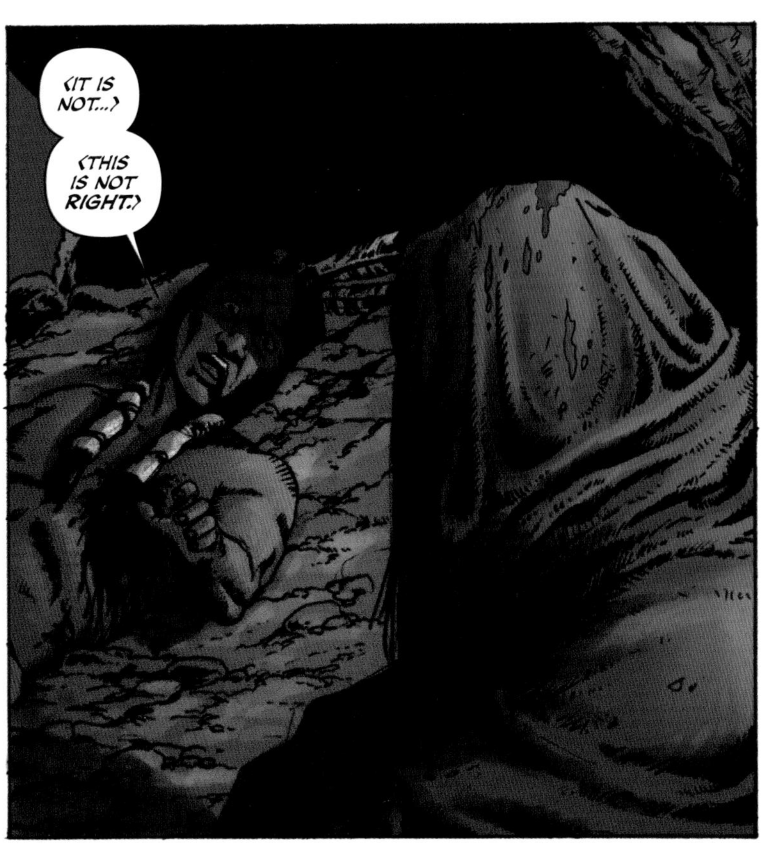

‹IT IS NOT...›
‹THIS IS NOT RIGHT.›

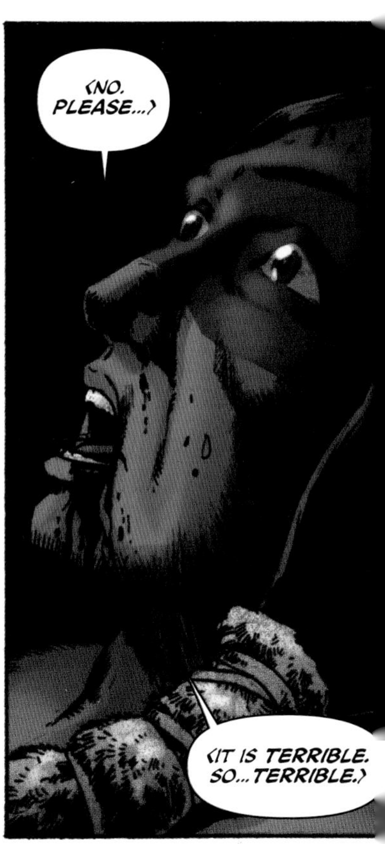

‹NO. PLEASE...›
‹IT IS TERRIBLE. SO...TERRIBLE.›

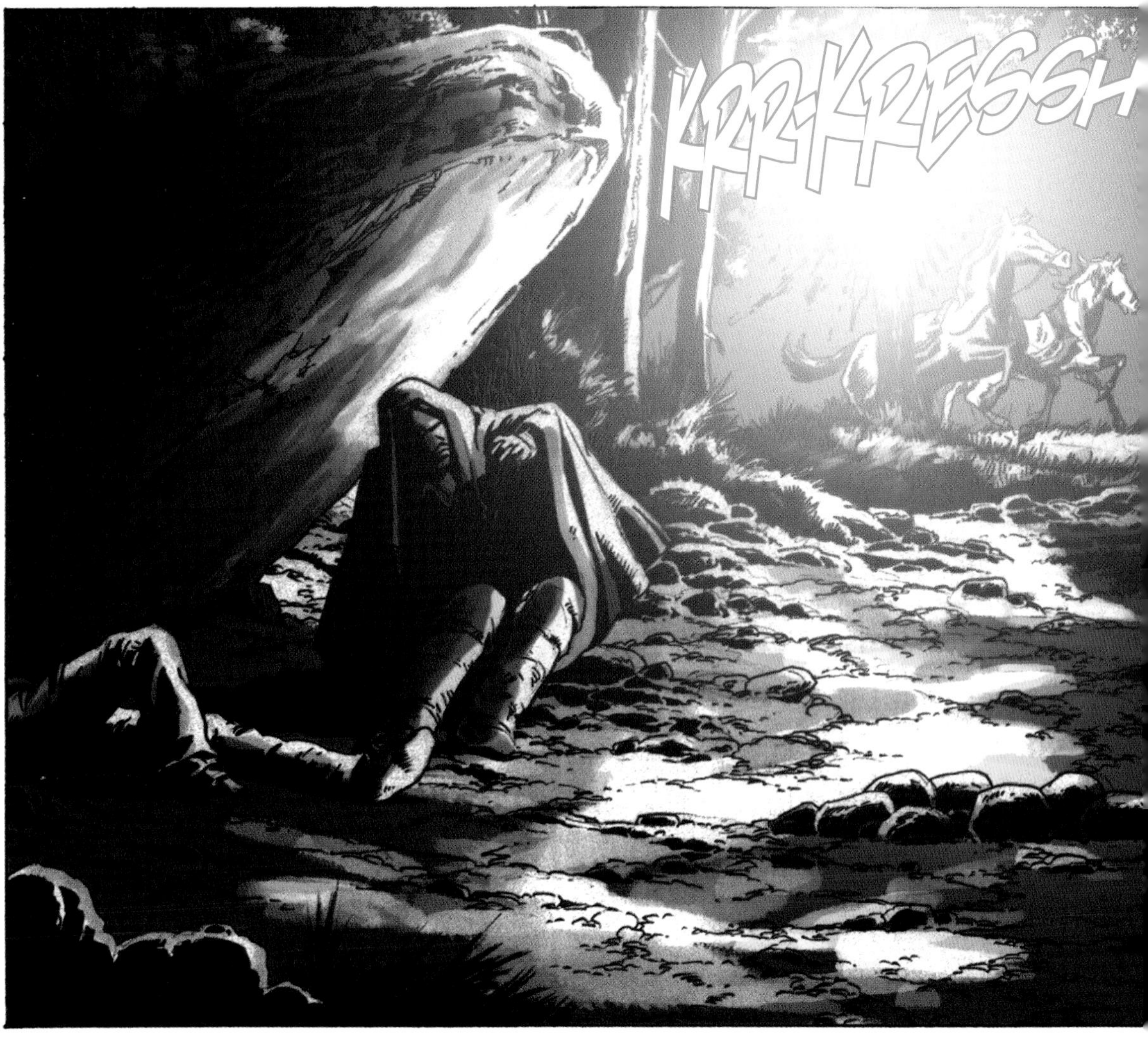

KRR-KRESSH

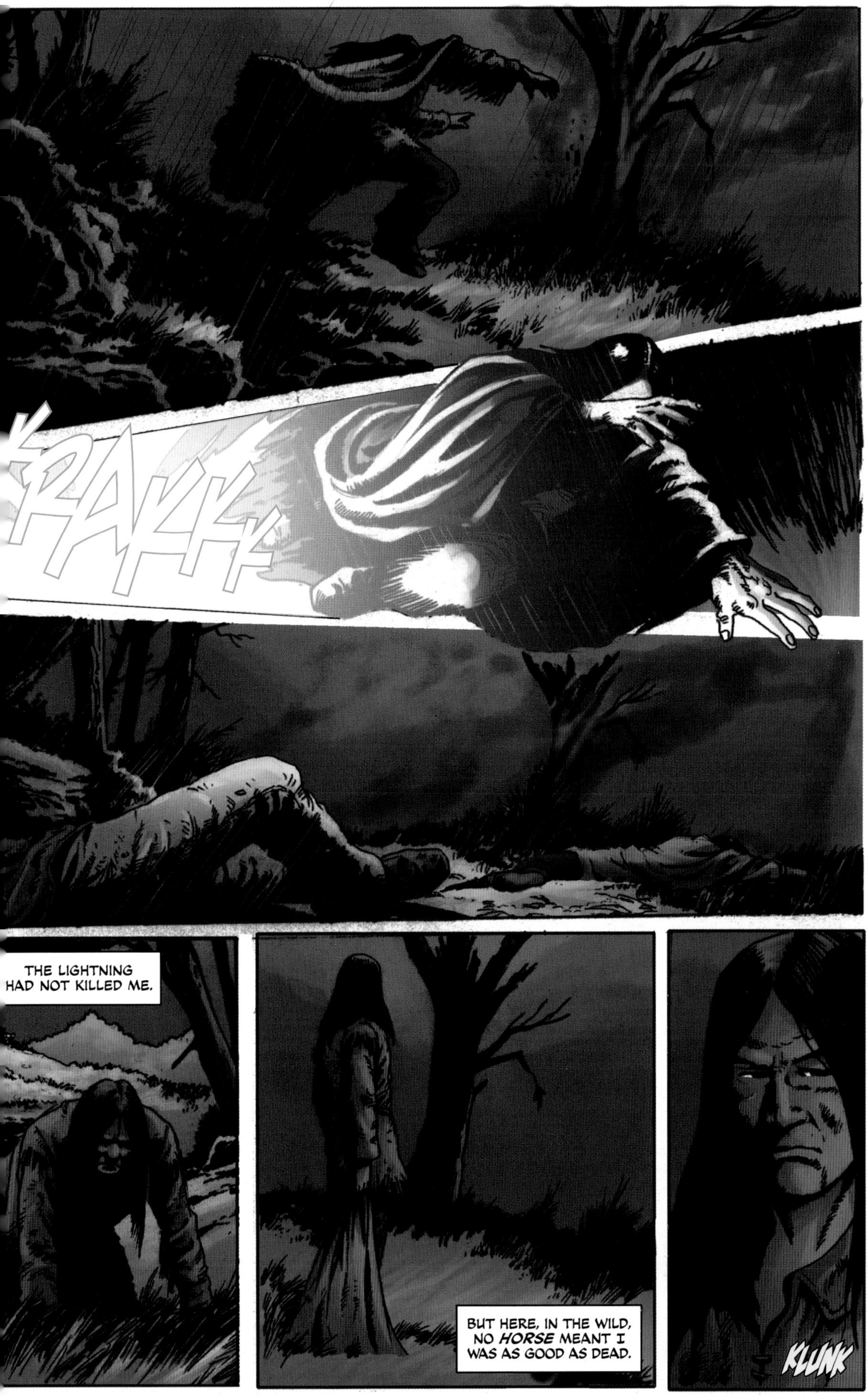
KRAKK
THE LIGHTNING HAD NOT KILLED ME.
BUT HERE, IN THE WILD, NO *HORSE* MEANT I WAS AS GOOD AS DEAD.
KLUNK

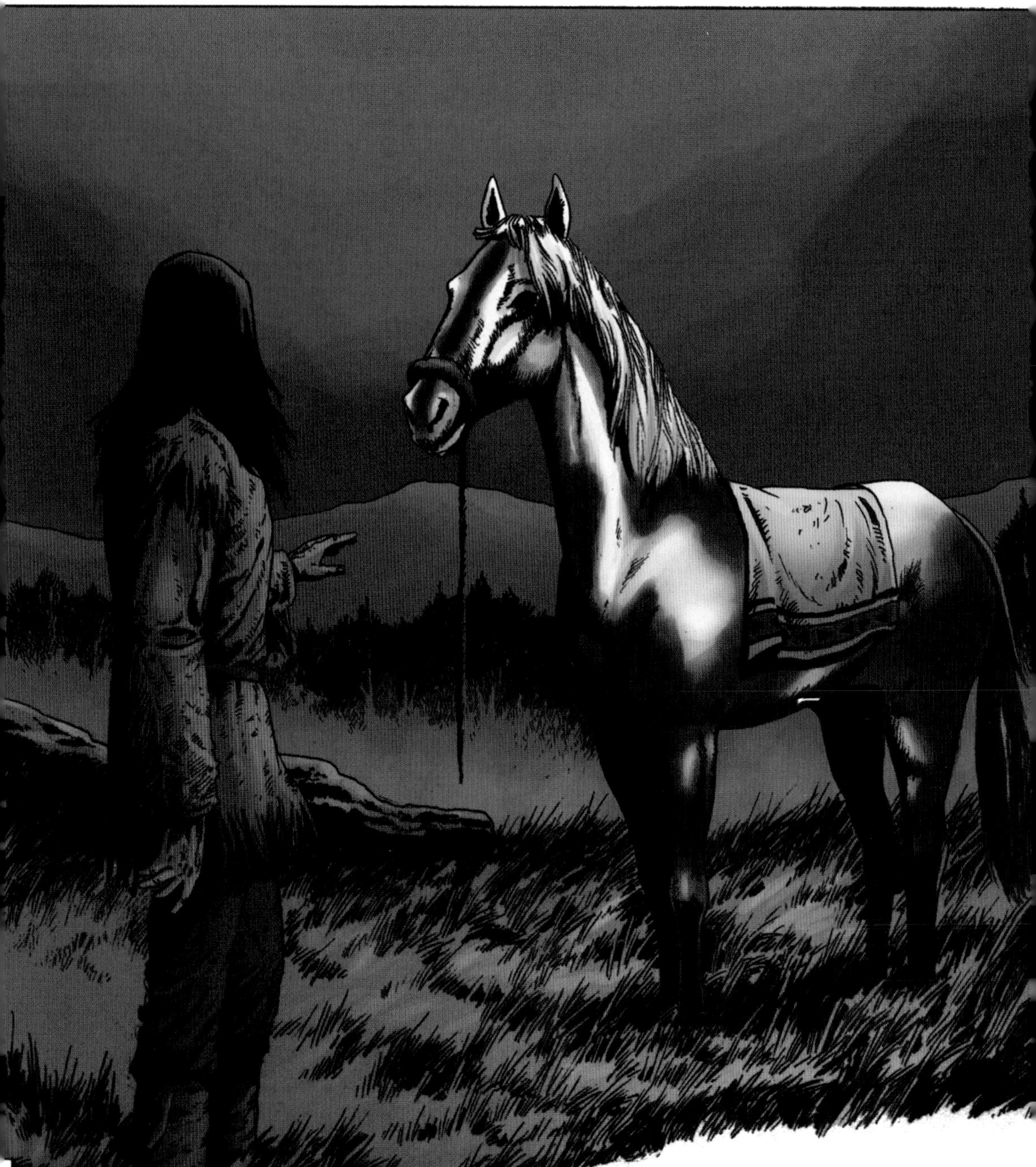

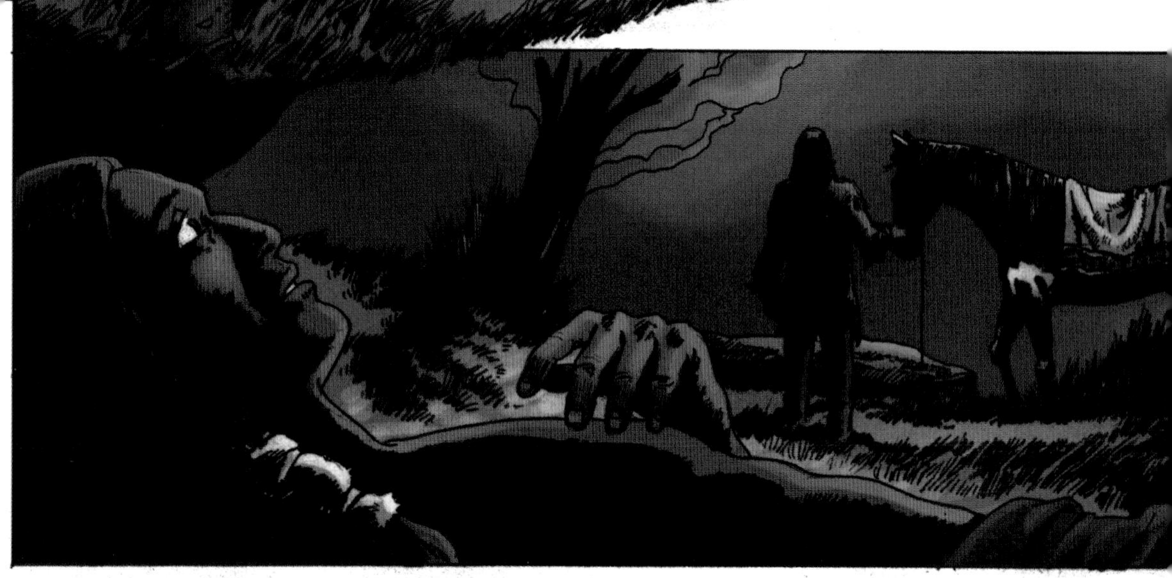

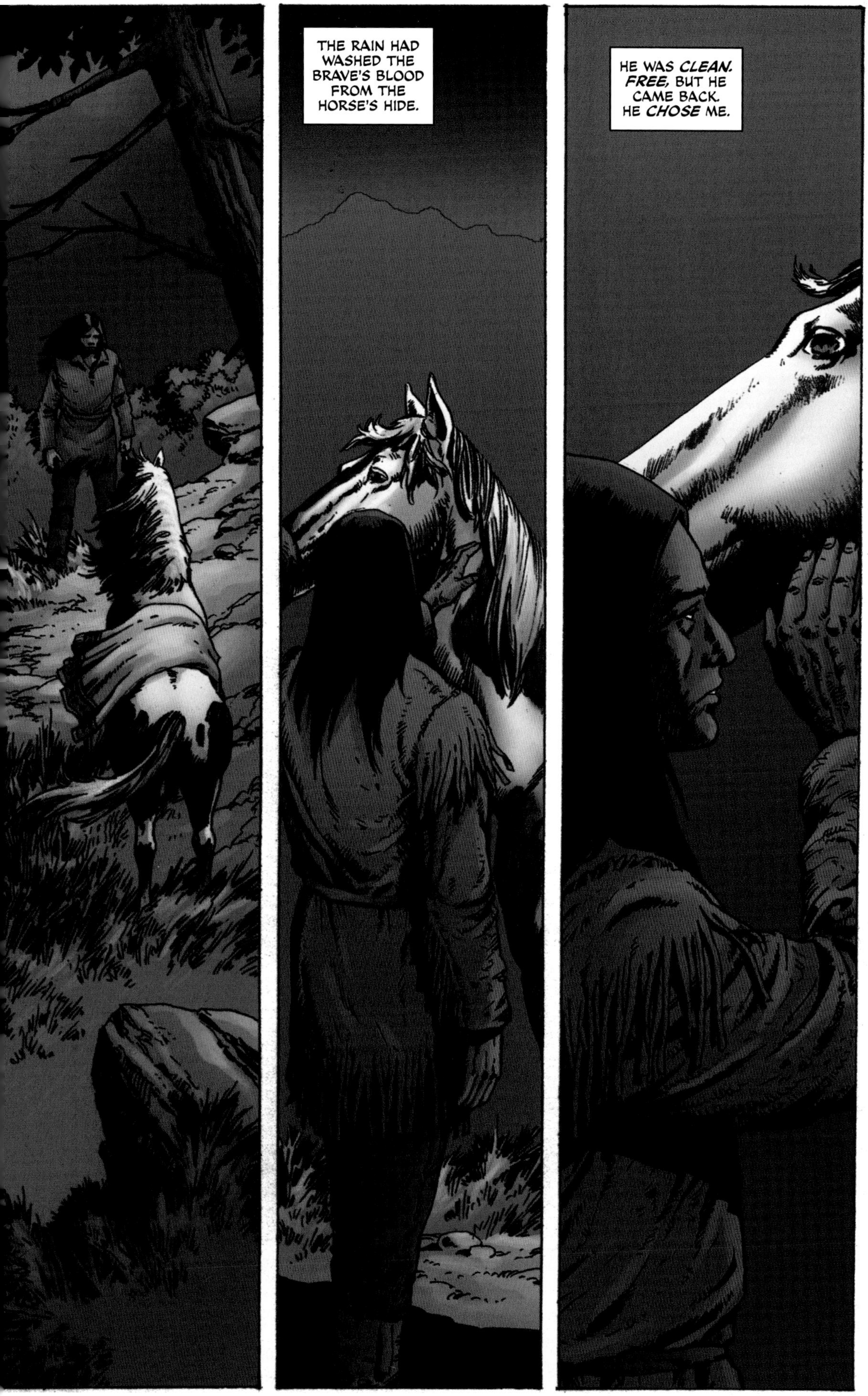
THE RAIN HAD WASHED THE BRAVE'S BLOOD FROM THE HORSE'S HIDE.
HE WAS *CLEAN.* *FREE,* BUT HE CAME BACK. HE *CHOSE* ME.

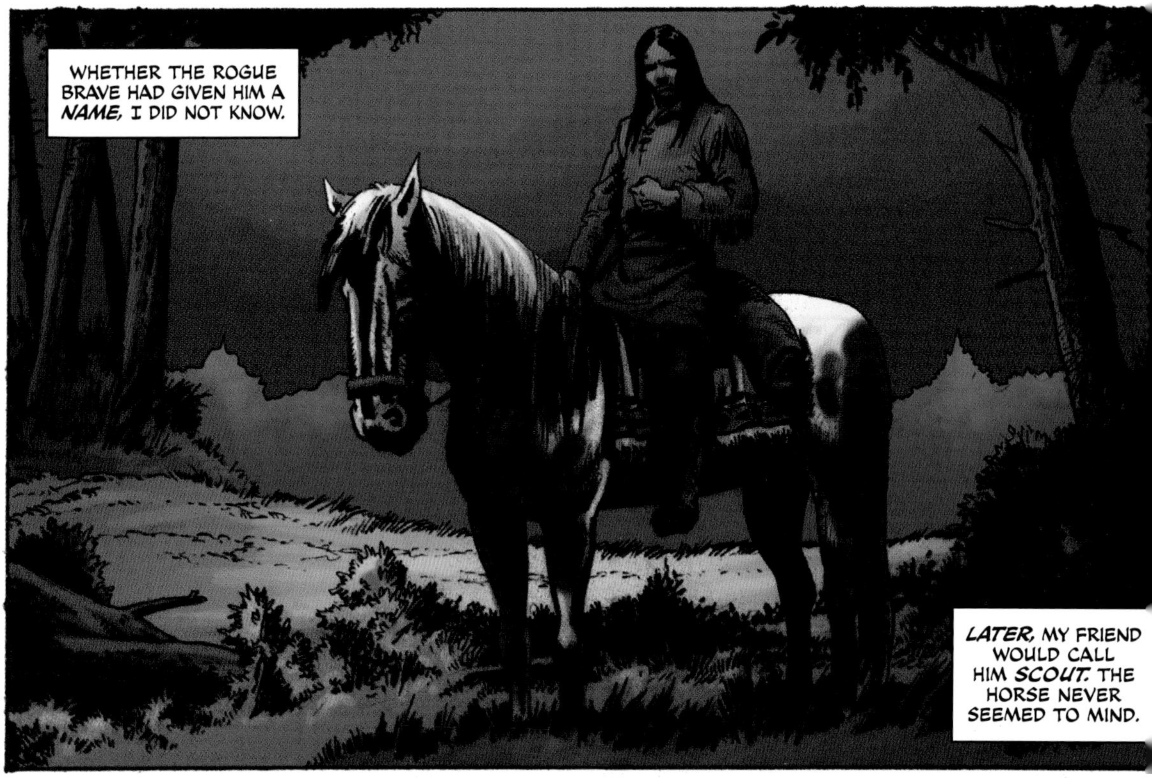
WHETHER THE ROGUE BRAVE HAD GIVEN HIM A NAME, I DID NOT KNOW.
LATER, MY FRIEND WOULD CALL HIM SCOUT. THE HORSE NEVER SEEMED TO MIND.

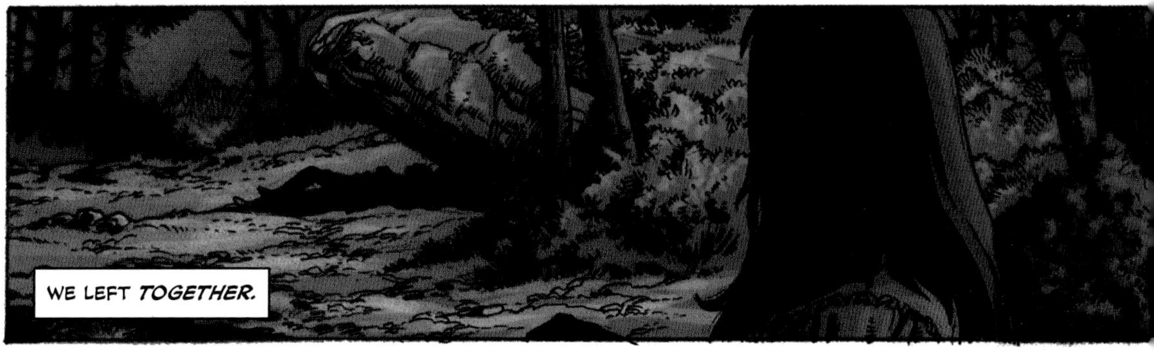
WE LEFT TOGETHER.

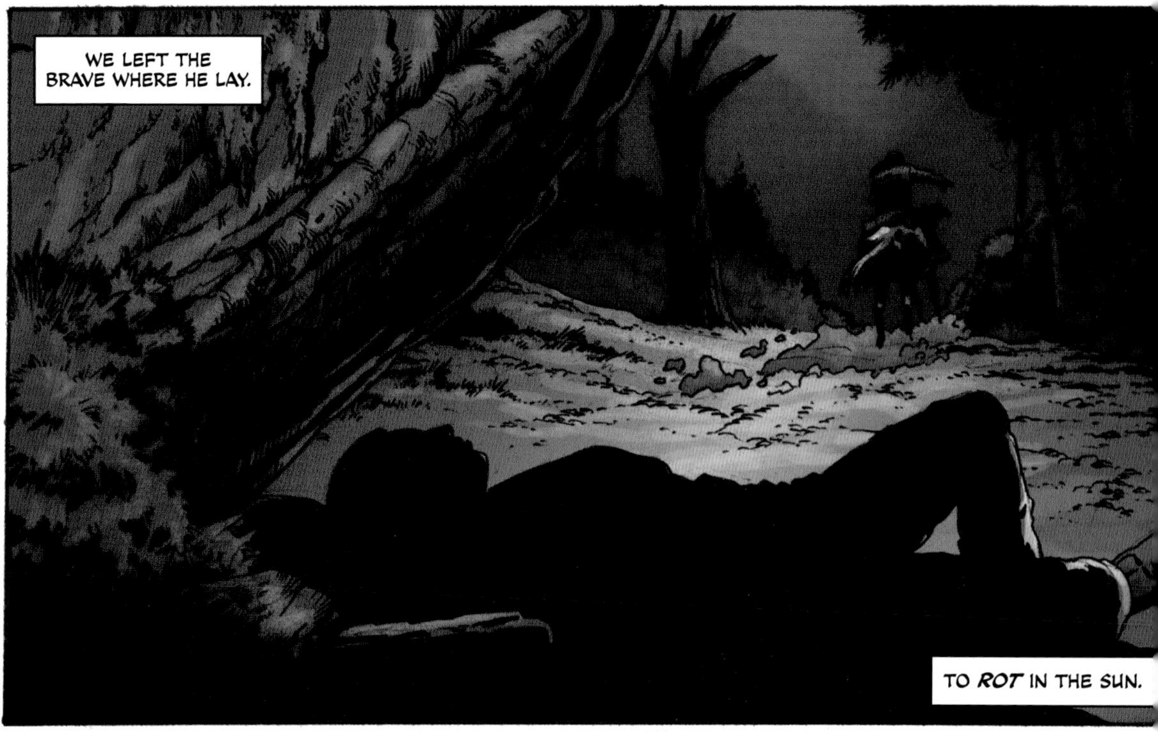
WE LEFT THE BRAVE WHERE HE LAY.
TO ROT IN THE SUN.

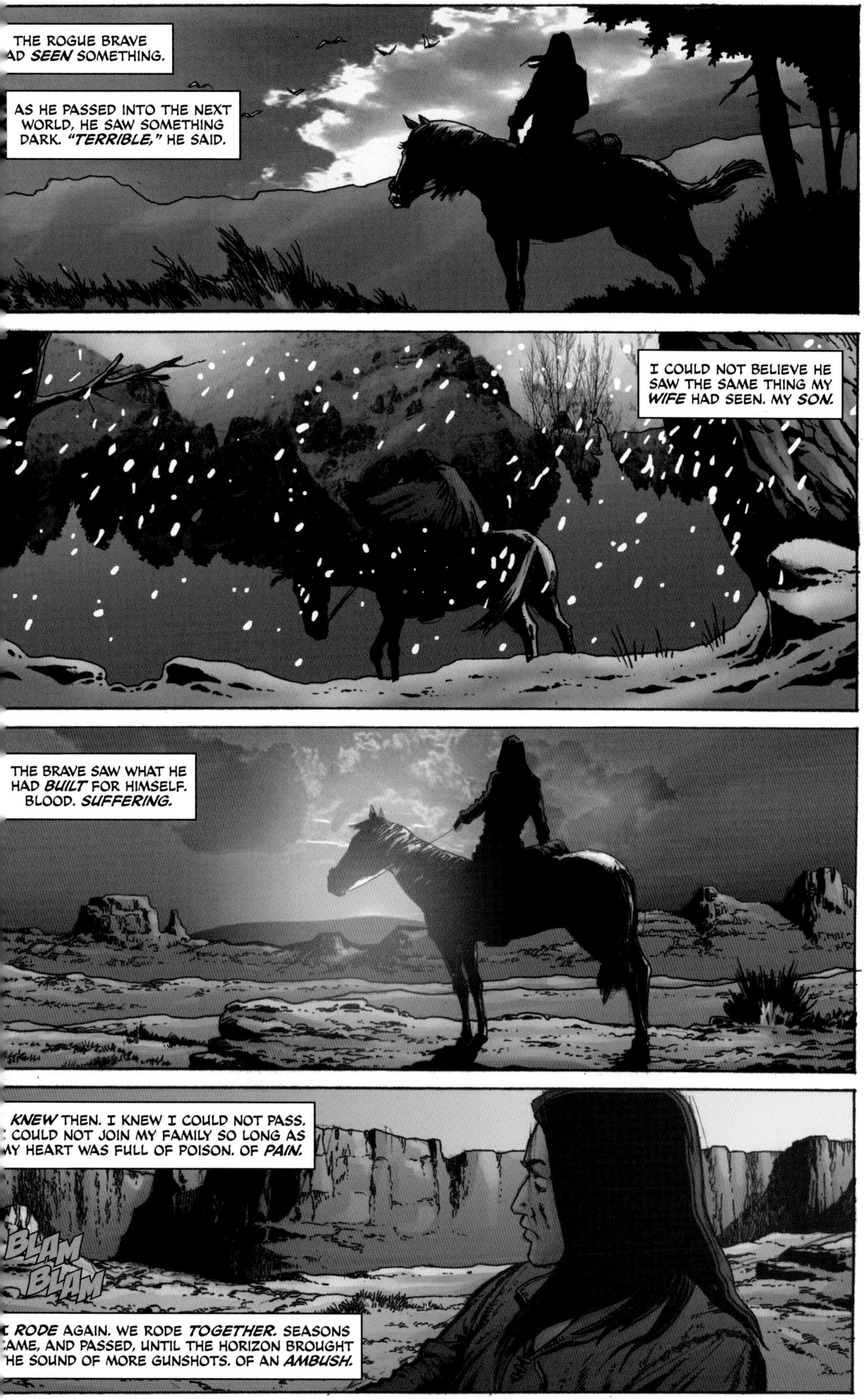

THE ROGUE BRAVE
AD SEEN SOMETHING.
AS HE PASSED INTO THE NEXT WORLD, HE SAW SOMETHING DARK. "TERRIBLE," HE SAID.
I COULD NOT BELIEVE HE SAW THE SAME THING MY WIFE HAD SEEN. MY SON.
THE BRAVE SAW WHAT HE HAD BUILT FOR HIMSELF. BLOOD. SUFFERING.
KNEW THEN. I KNEW I COULD NOT PASS. COULD NOT JOIN MY FAMILY SO LONG AS MY HEART WAS FULL OF POISON. OF PAIN.
BLAM
BLAM
RODE AGAIN. WE RODE TOGETHER. SEASONS AME, AND PASSED, UNTIL THE HORIZON BROUGHT HE SOUND OF MORE GUNSHOTS. OF AN AMBUSH.

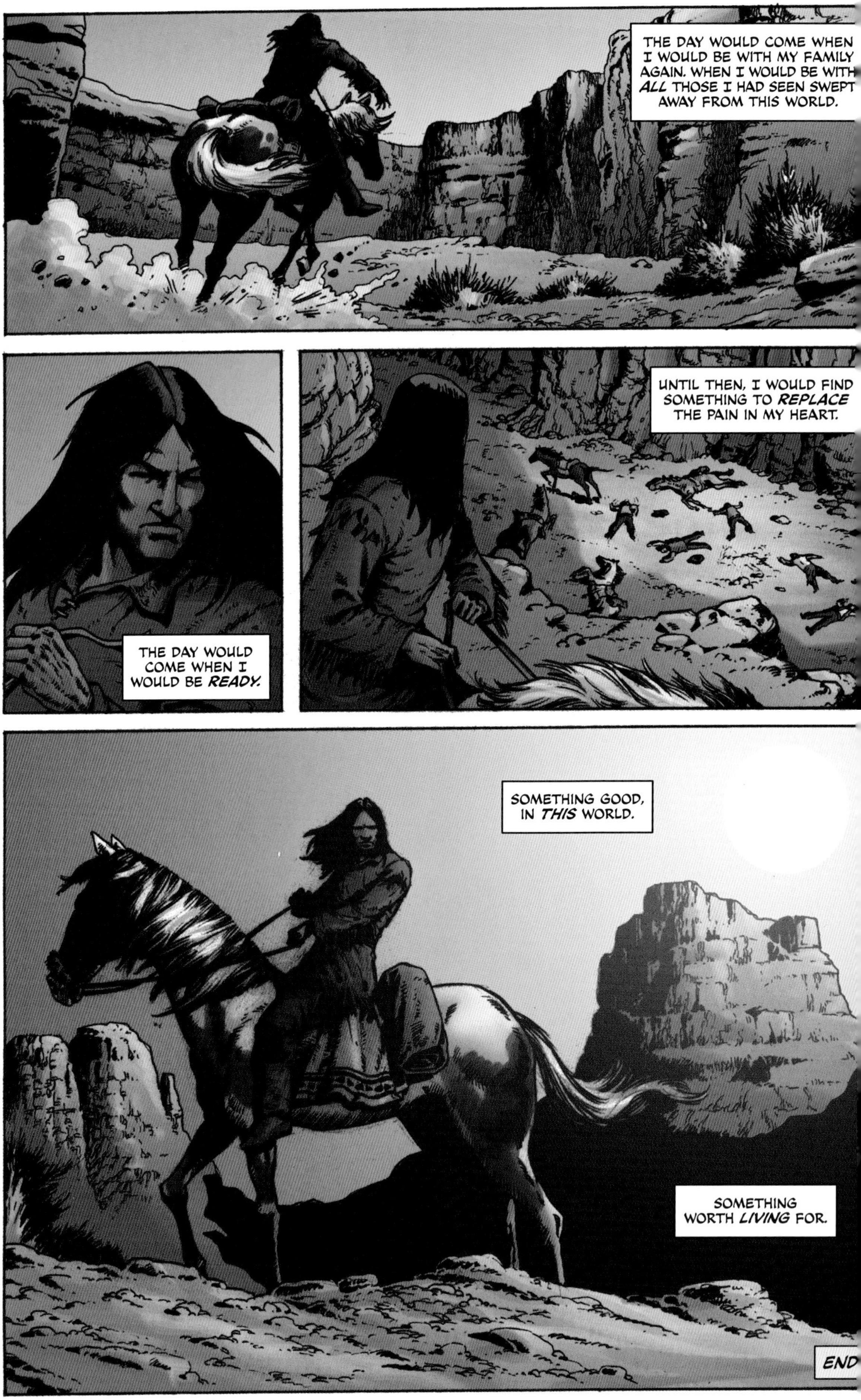

THE DAY WOULD COME WHEN I WOULD BE WITH MY FAMILY AGAIN. WHEN I WOULD BE WITH *ALL* THOSE I HAD SEEN SWEPT AWAY FROM THIS WORLD.
THE DAY WOULD COME WHEN I WOULD BE *READY.*
UNTIL THEN, I WOULD FIND SOMETHING TO *REPLACE* THE PAIN IN MY HEART.
SOMETHING GOOD, IN *THIS* WORLD.
SOMETHING WORTH *LIVING* FOR.
END

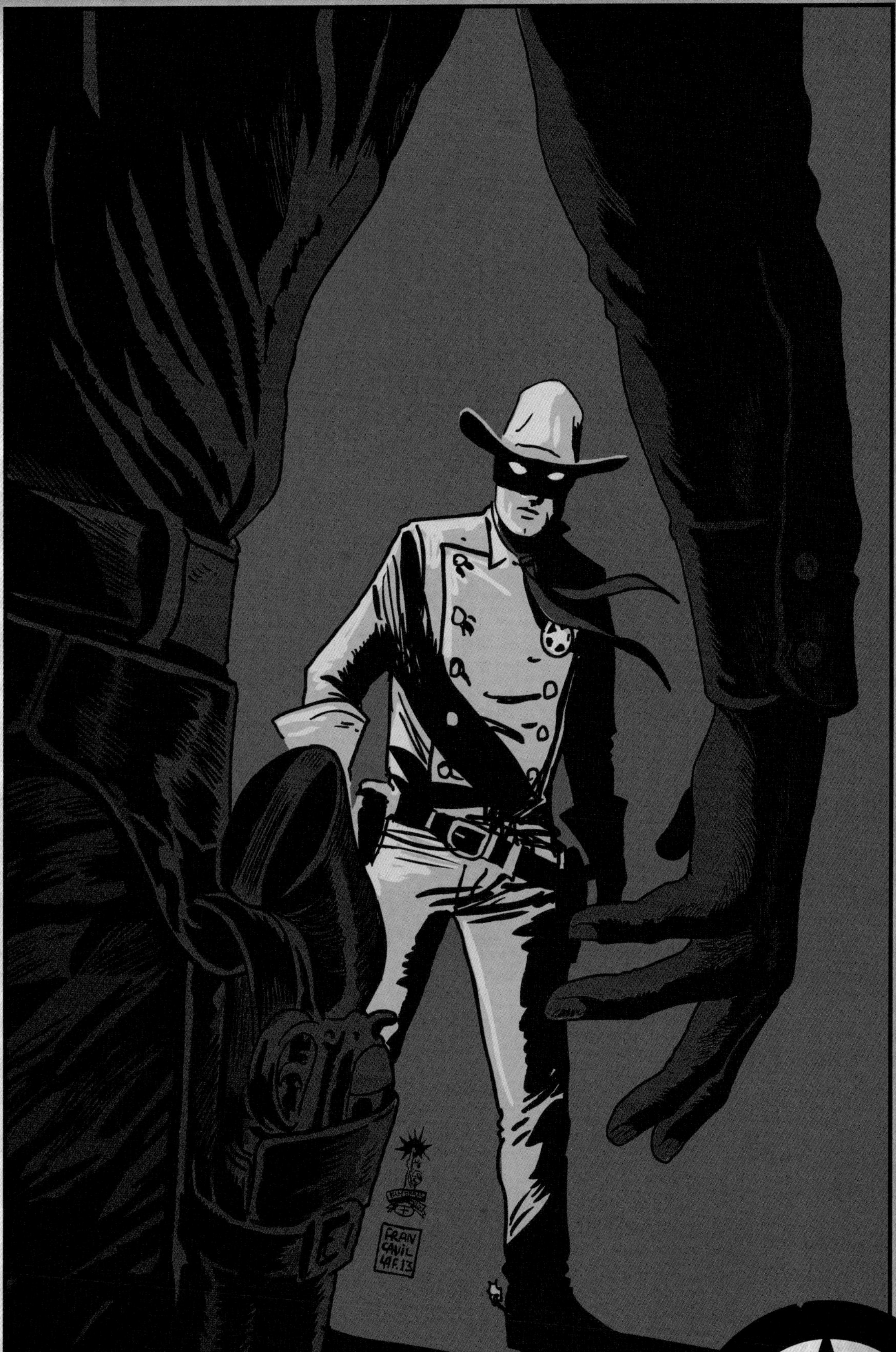

COVER BY **FRANCESCO FRANCAVILLA**

20

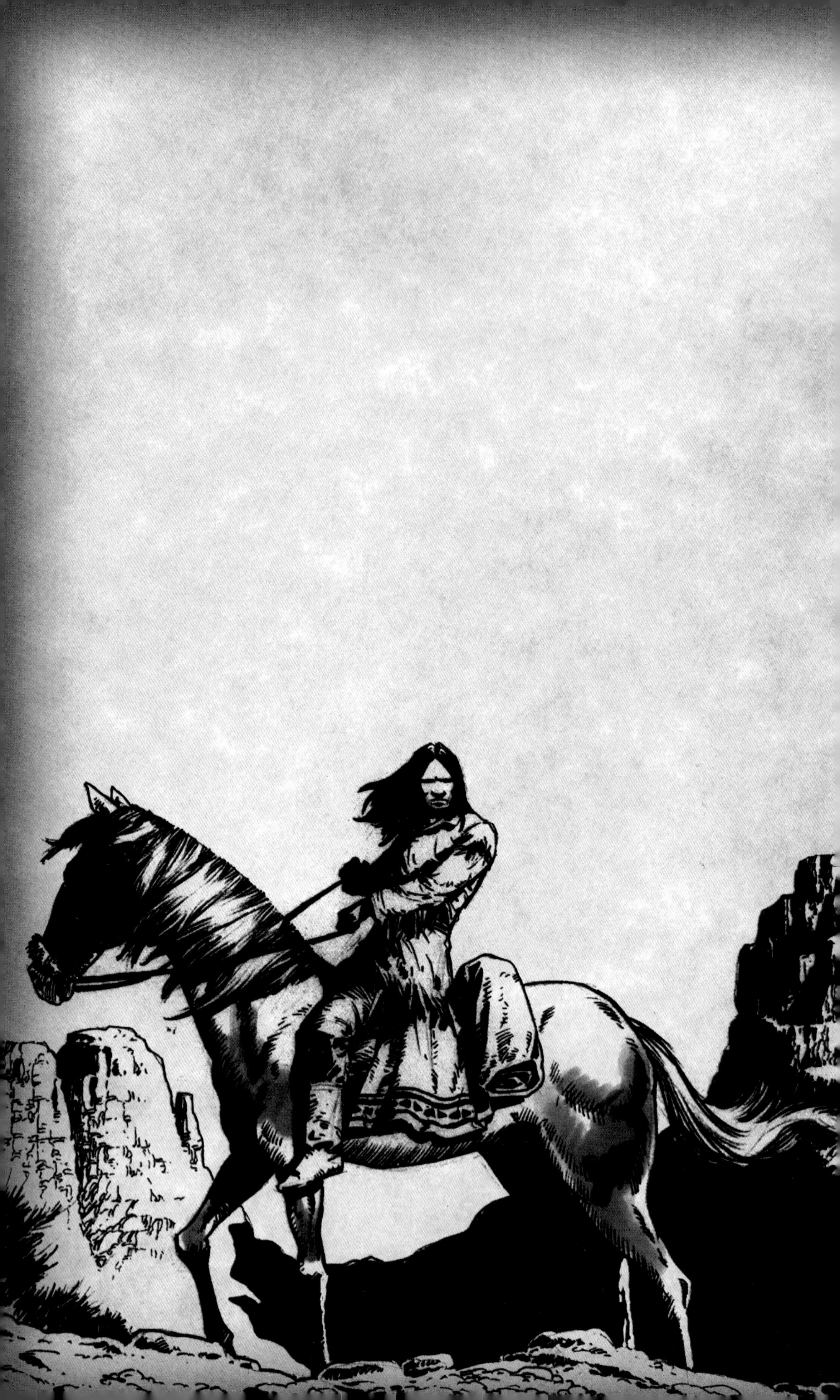

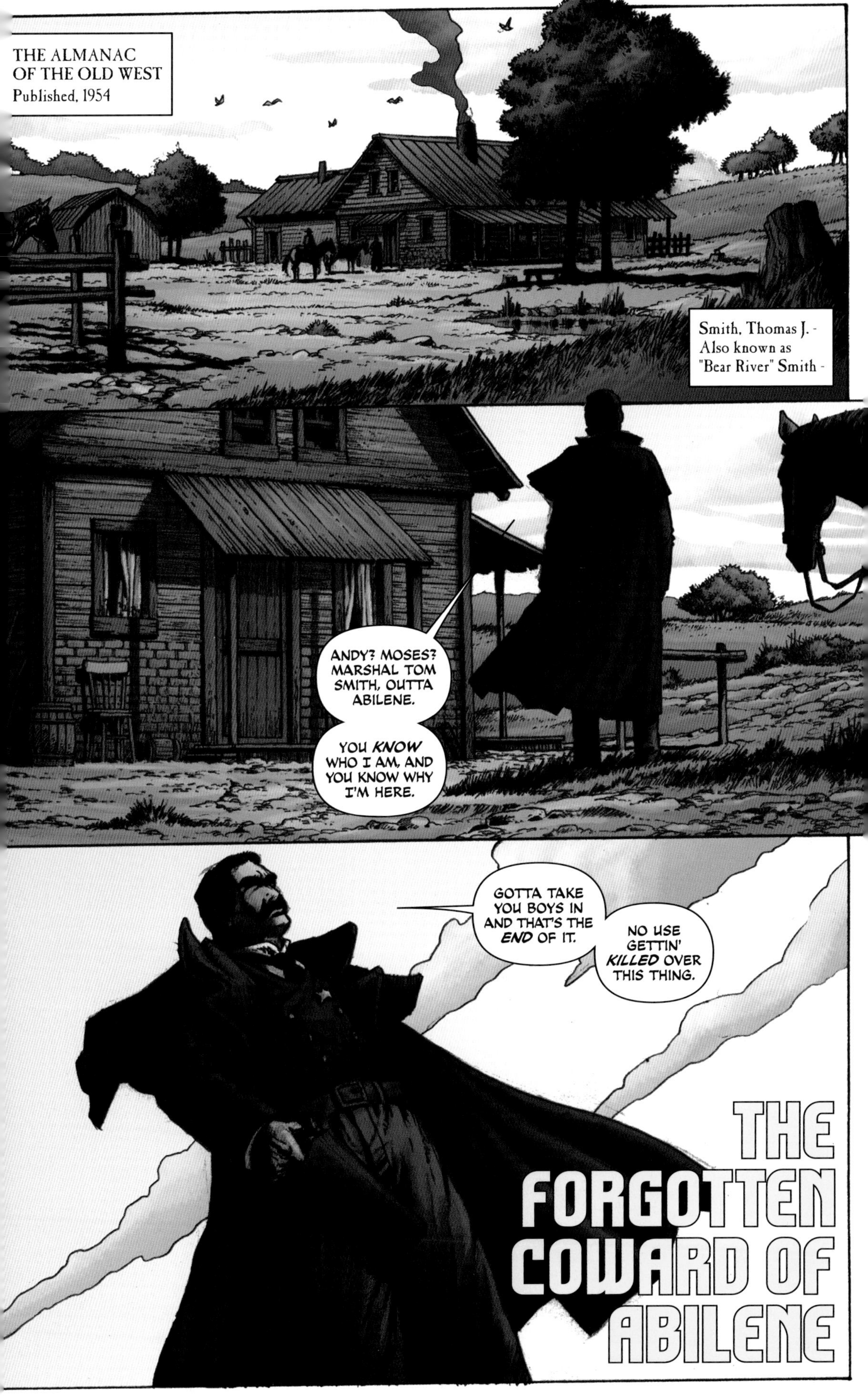
THE ALMANAC OF THE OLD WEST
Published, 1954
Smith, Thomas J. - Also known as "Bear River" Smith -
ANDY? MOSES? MARSHAL TOM SMITH, OUTTA ABILENE.
YOU KNOW WHO I AM, AND YOU KNOW WHY I'M HERE.
GOTTA TAKE YOU BOYS IN AND THAT'S THE END OF IT.
NO USE GETTIN' KILLED OVER THIS THING.
THE FORGOTTEN COWARD OF ABILENE

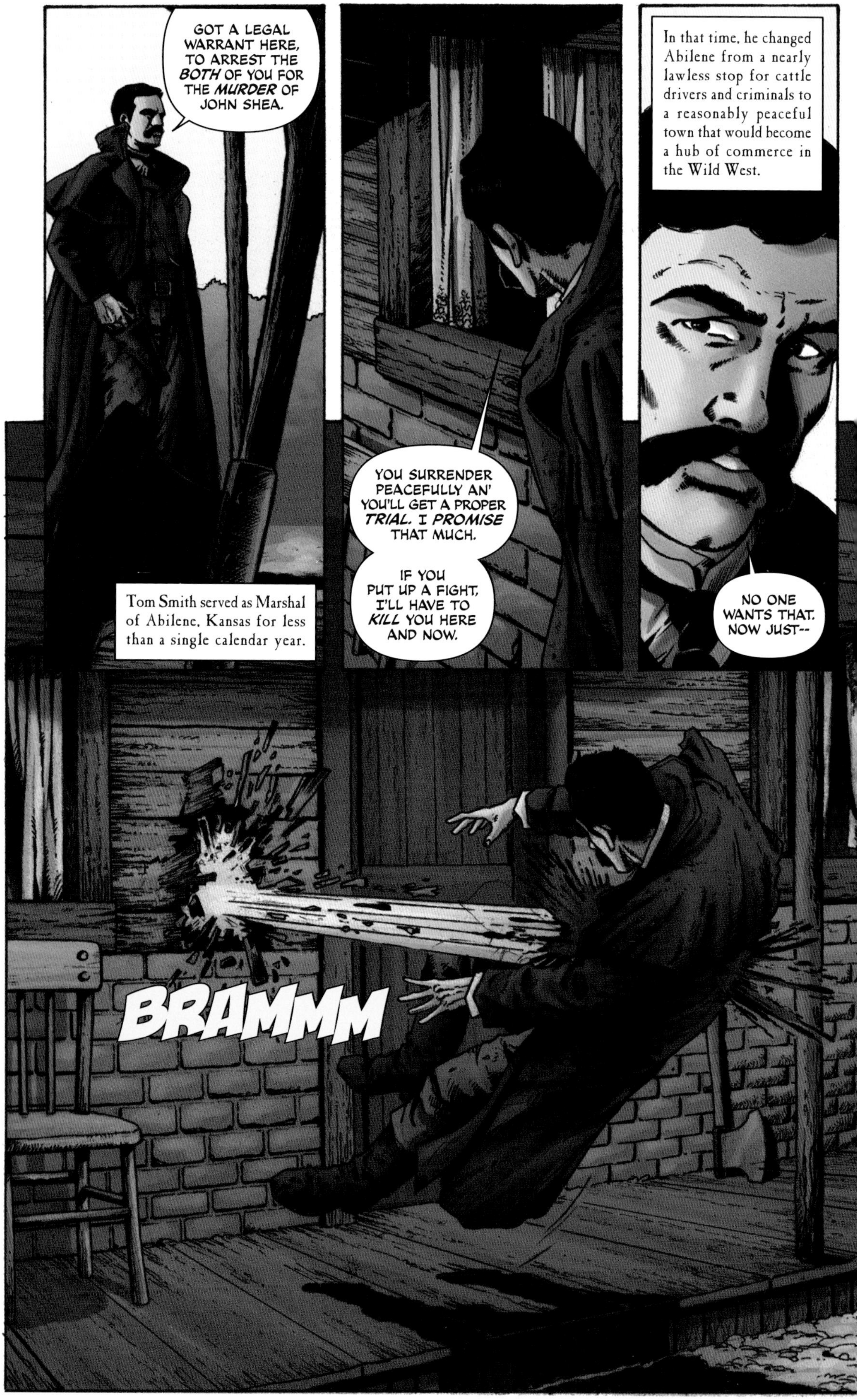
GOT A LEGAL WARRANT HERE, TO ARREST THE *BOTH* OF YOU FOR THE *MURDER* OF JOHN SHEA.
Tom Smith served as Marshal of Abilene, Kansas for less than a single calendar year.
YOU SURRENDER PEACEFULLY AN' YOU'LL GET A PROPER *TRIAL.* I *PROMISE* THAT MUCH.
IF YOU PUT UP A FIGHT, I'LL HAVE TO *KILL* YOU HERE AND NOW.
In that time, he changed Abilene from a nearly lawless stop for cattle drivers and criminals to a reasonably peaceful town that would become a hub of commerce in the Wild West.
NO ONE WANTS THAT. NOW JUST--
BRAMMM

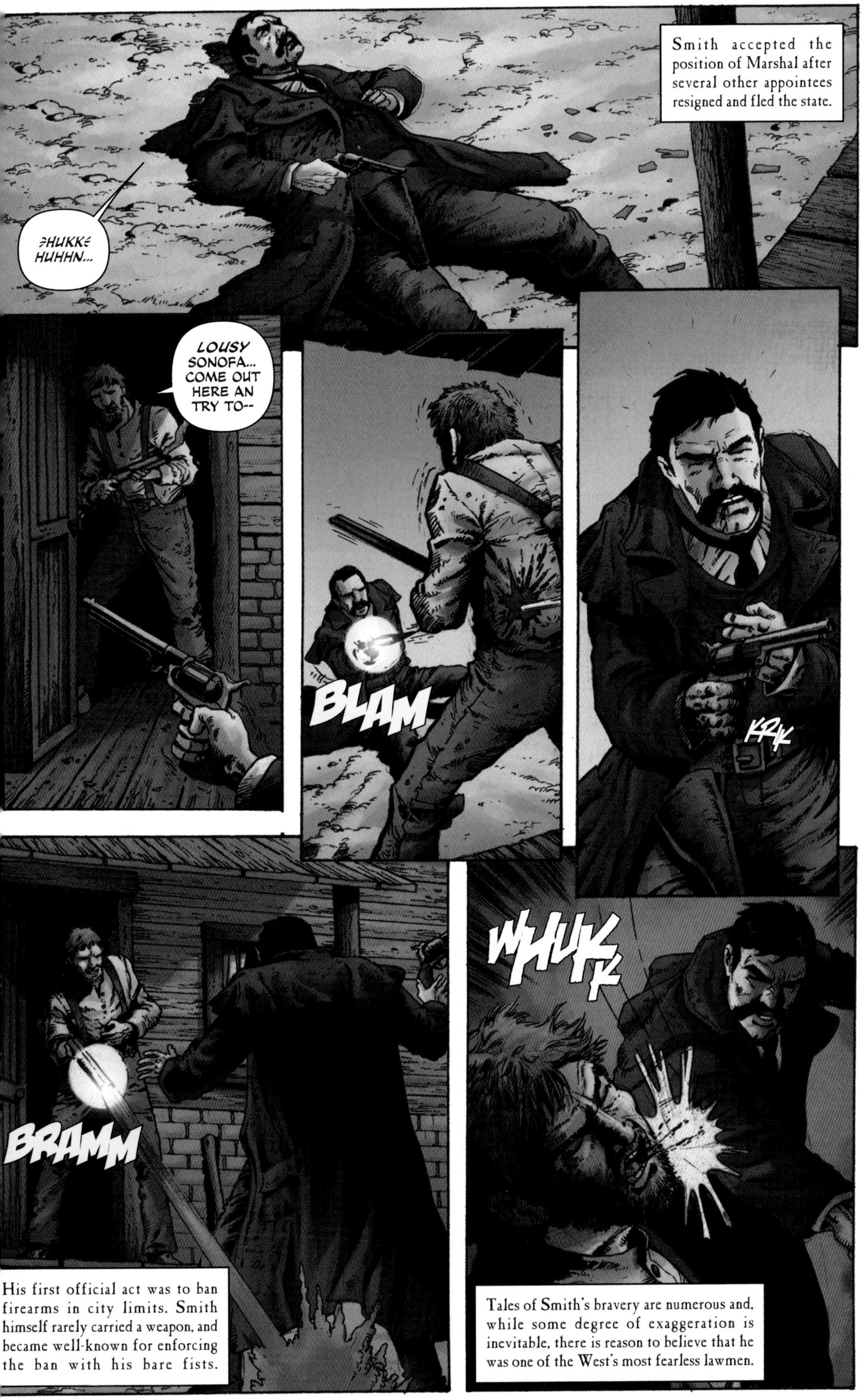

Smith accepted the position of Marshal after several other appointees resigned and fled the state.
≈HUKK≈ HUHHN...
LOUSY SONOFA... COME OUT HERE AN TRY TO--
BLAM
KRIK
BRAMM
WHUKK
His first official act was to ban firearms in city limits. Smith himself rarely carried a weapon, and became well-known for enforcing the ban with his bare fists.
Tales of Smith's bravery are numerous and, while some degree of exaggeration is inevitable, there is reason to believe that he was one of the West's most fearless lawmen.

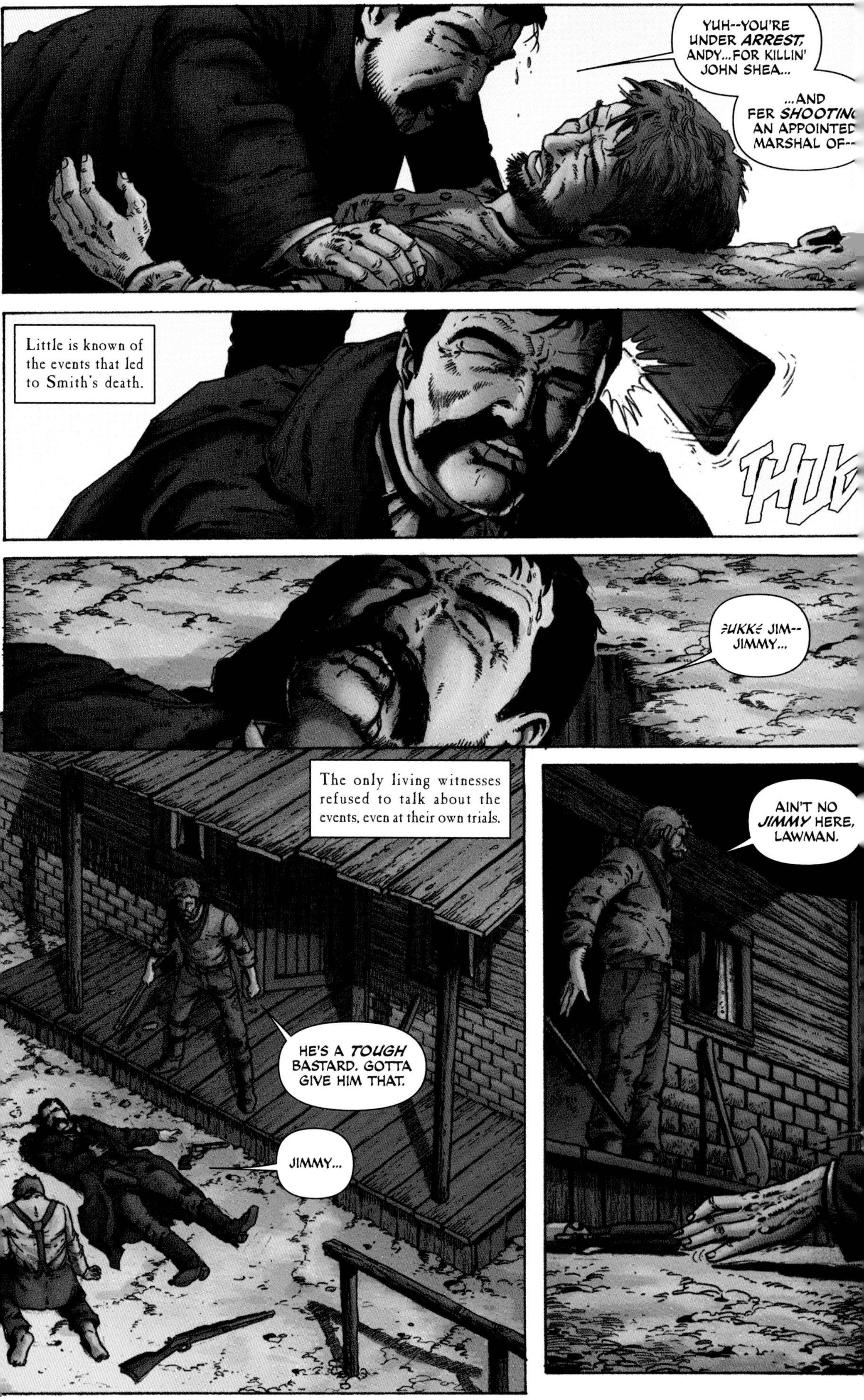
YUH--YOU'RE UNDER ARREST, ANDY...FOR KILLIN' JOHN SHEA...
...AND FER SHOOTIN AN APPOINTED MARSHAL OF--
Little is known of the events that led to Smith's death.
THUK
UKK JIM--JIMMY...
The only living witnesses refused to talk about the events, even at their own trials.
HE'S A TOUGH BASTARD. GOTTA GIVE HIM THAT.
JIMMY...
AIN'T NO JIMMY HERE, LAWMAN.

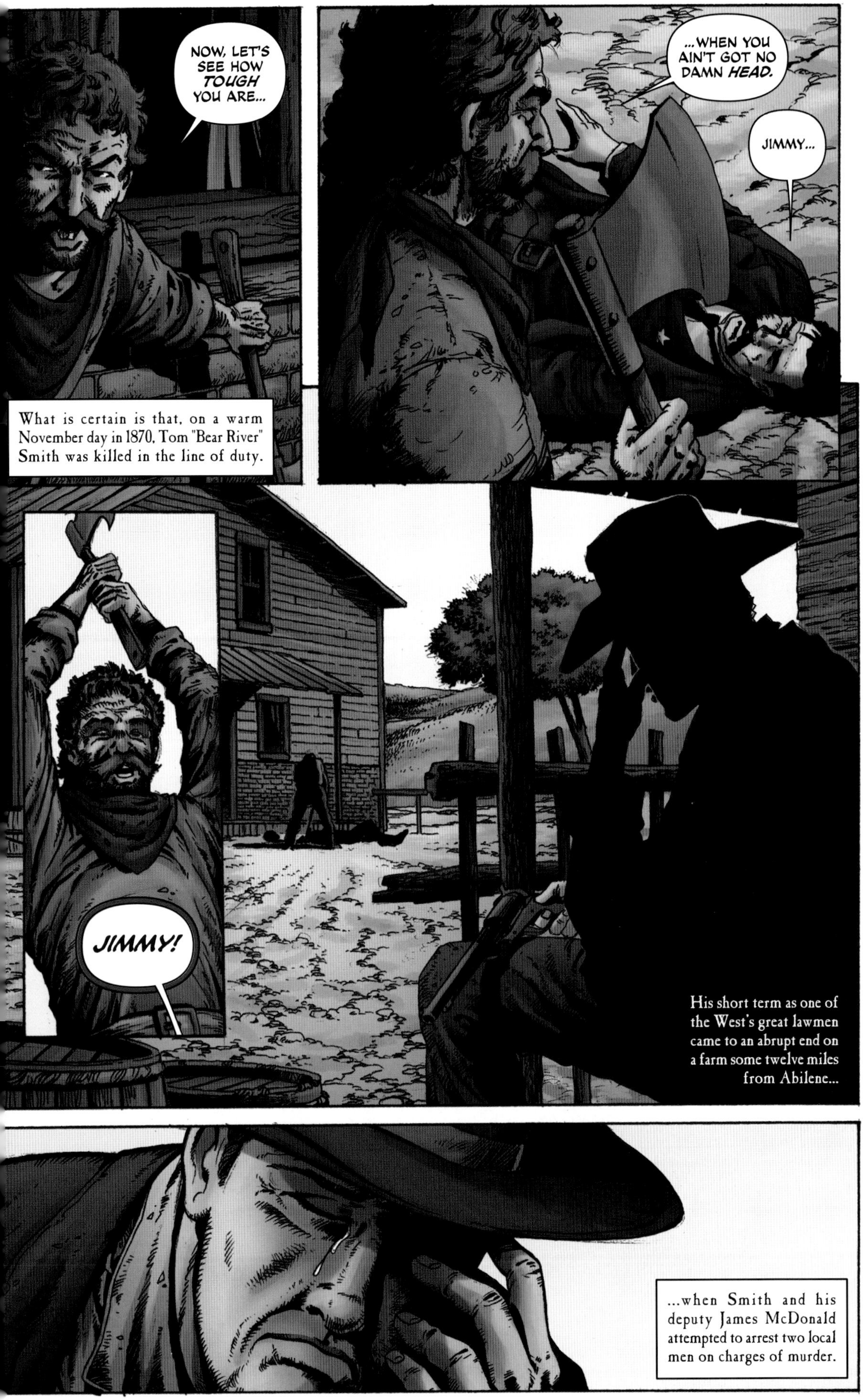
NOW, LET'S SEE HOW TOUGH YOU ARE...
...WHEN YOU AIN'T GOT NO DAMN HEAD.
JIMMY...
What is certain is that, on a warm November day in 1870, Tom "Bear River" Smith was killed in the line of duty.
JIMMY!
His short term as one of the West's great lawmen came to an abrupt end on a farm some twelve miles from Abilene...
...when Smith and his deputy James McDonald attempted to arrest two local men on charges of murder.

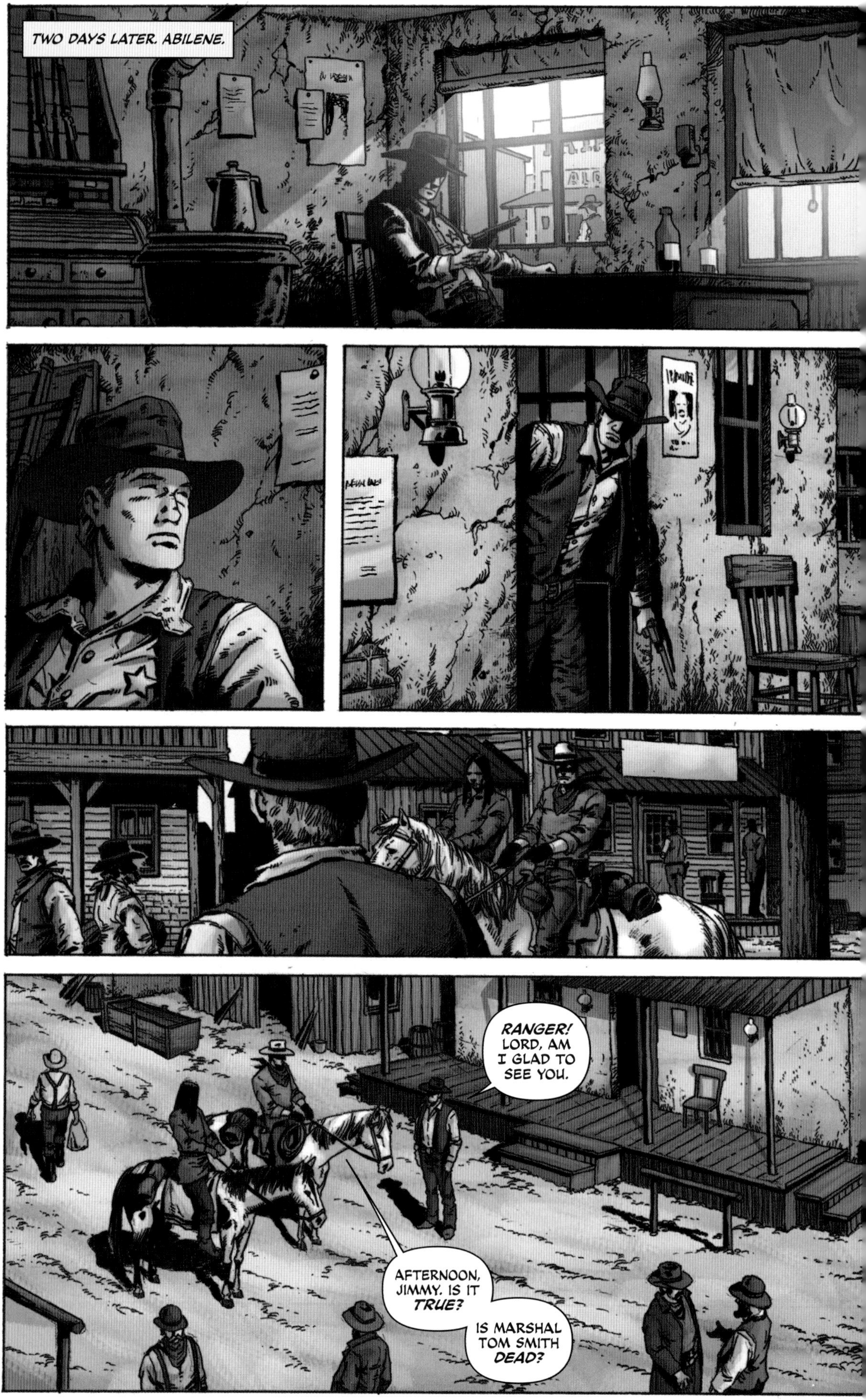

TWO DAYS LATER. ABILENE.
RANGER! LORD, AM I GLAD TO SEE YOU.
AFTERNOON, JIMMY. IS IT *TRUE?*
IS MARSHAL TOM SMITH *DEAD?*

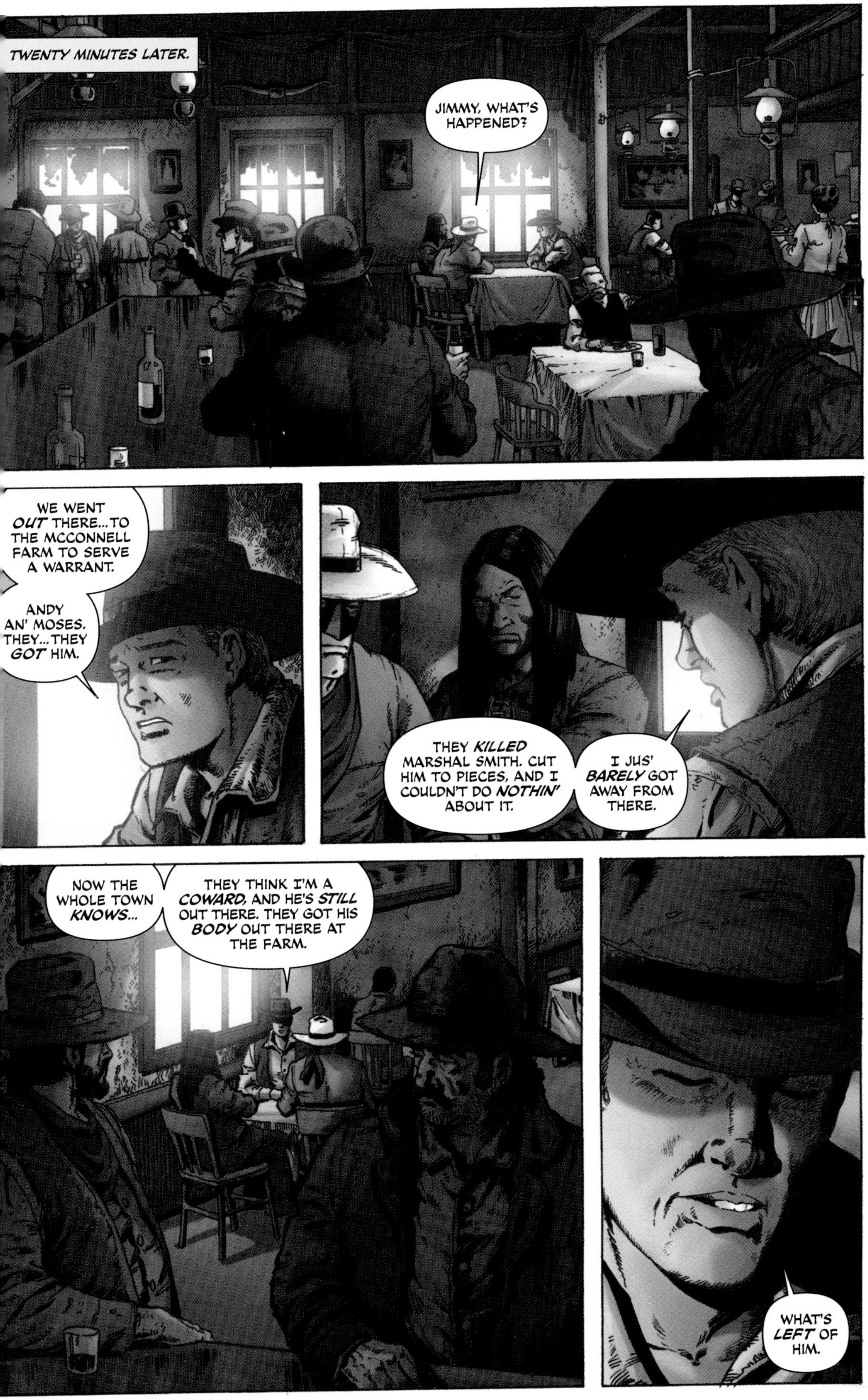
TWENTY MINUTES LATER.
JIMMY, WHAT'S HAPPENED?
WE WENT OUT THERE...TO THE MCCONNELL FARM TO SERVE A WARRANT.
ANDY AN' MOSES. THEY...THEY GOT HIM.
THEY KILLED MARSHAL SMITH. CUT HIM TO PIECES, AND I COULDN'T DO NOTHIN' ABOUT IT.
I JUS' BARELY GOT AWAY FROM THERE.
NOW THE WHOLE TOWN KNOWS...
THEY THINK I'M A COWARD, AND HE'S STILL OUT THERE. THEY GOT HIS BODY OUT THERE AT THE FARM.
WHAT'S LEFT OF HIM.

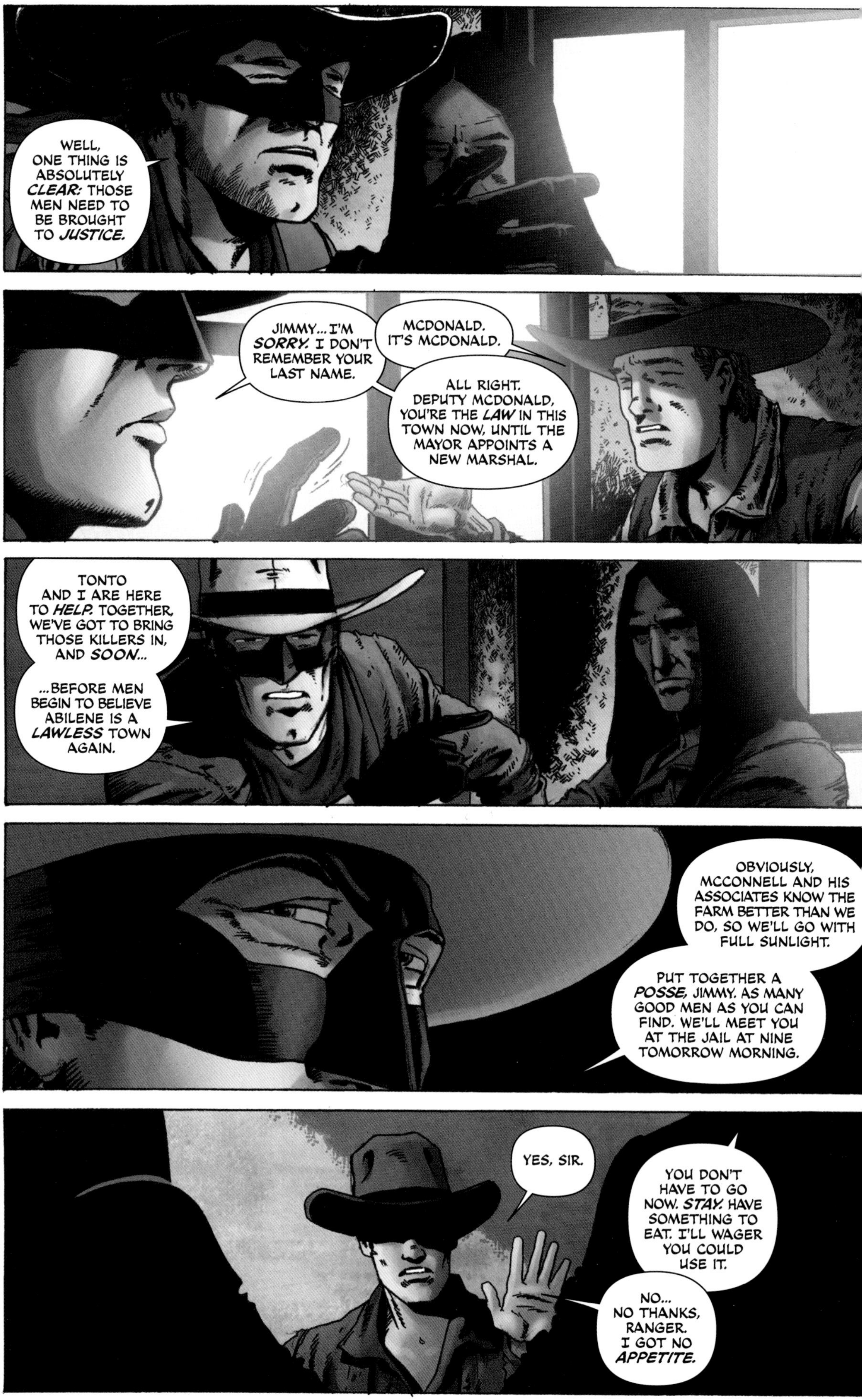
WELL, ONE THING IS ABSOLUTELY CLEAR: THOSE MEN NEED TO BE BROUGHT TO JUSTICE.
JIMMY... I'M SORRY. I DON'T REMEMBER YOUR LAST NAME.
MCDONALD. IT'S MCDONALD.
ALL RIGHT. DEPUTY MCDONALD, YOU'RE THE LAW IN THIS TOWN NOW, UNTIL THE MAYOR APPOINTS A NEW MARSHAL.
TONTO AND I ARE HERE TO HELP. TOGETHER, WE'VE GOT TO BRING THOSE KILLERS IN, AND SOON...
...BEFORE MEN BEGIN TO BELIEVE ABILENE IS A LAWLESS TOWN AGAIN.
OBVIOUSLY, MCCONNELL AND HIS ASSOCIATES KNOW THE FARM BETTER THAN WE DO, SO WE'LL GO WITH FULL SUNLIGHT.
PUT TOGETHER A POSSE, JIMMY. AS MANY GOOD MEN AS YOU CAN FIND. WE'LL MEET YOU AT THE JAIL AT NINE TOMORROW MORNING.
YES, SIR.
YOU DON'T HAVE TO GO NOW. STAY. HAVE SOMETHING TO EAT. I'LL WAGER YOU COULD USE IT.
NO... NO THANKS, RANGER. I GOT NO APPETITE.

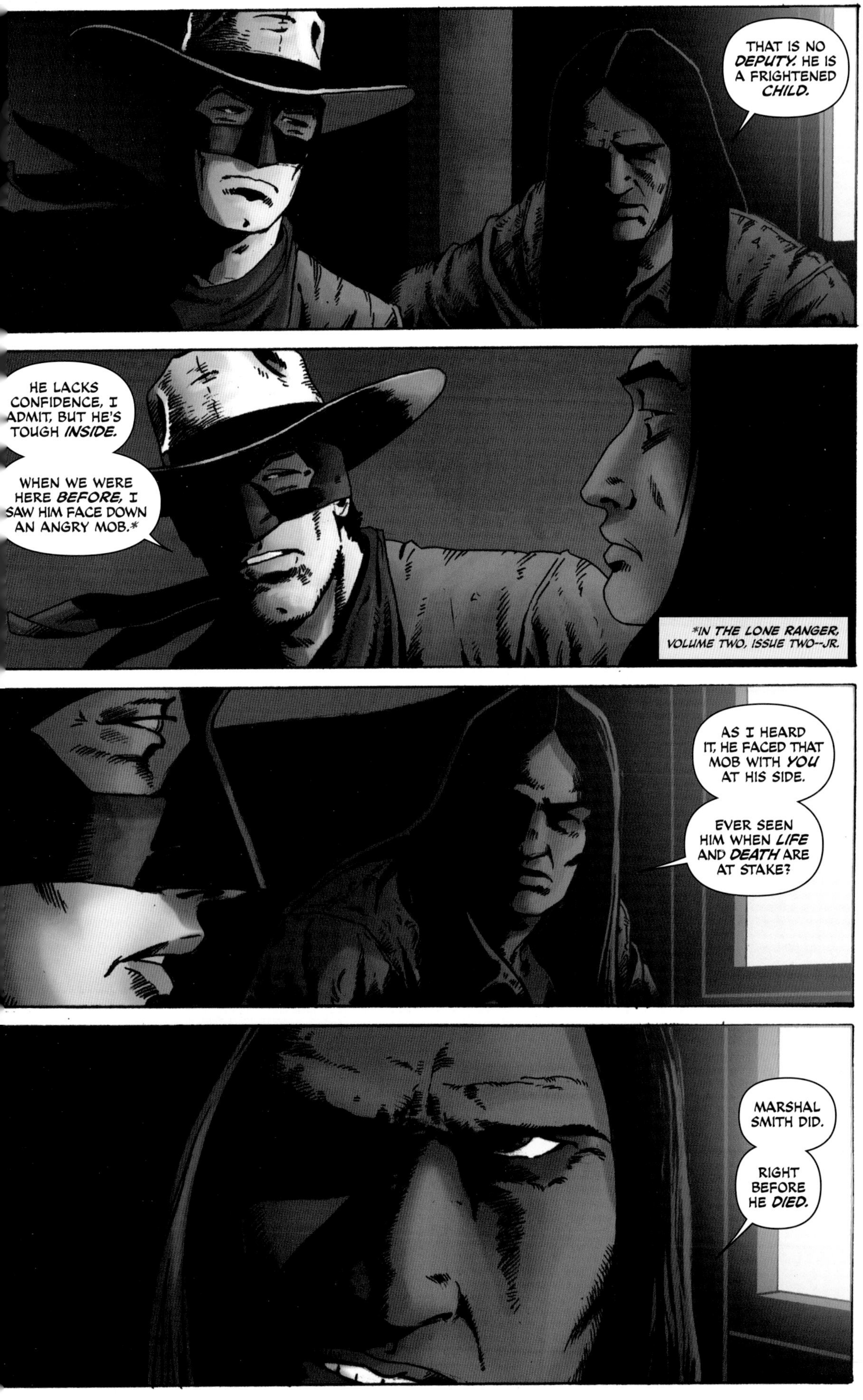
THAT IS NO *DEPUTY.* HE IS A FRIGHTENED *CHILD.*
HE LACKS CONFIDENCE, I ADMIT, BUT HE'S TOUGH *INSIDE.*
WHEN WE WERE HERE *BEFORE,* I SAW HIM FACE DOWN AN ANGRY MOB.*
*IN THE LONE RANGER, VOLUME TWO, ISSUE TWO--JR.
AS I HEARD IT, HE FACED THAT MOB WITH *YOU* AT HIS SIDE.
EVER SEEN HIM WHEN *LIFE* AND *DEATH* ARE AT STAKE?
MARSHAL SMITH DID.
RIGHT BEFORE HE *DIED.*

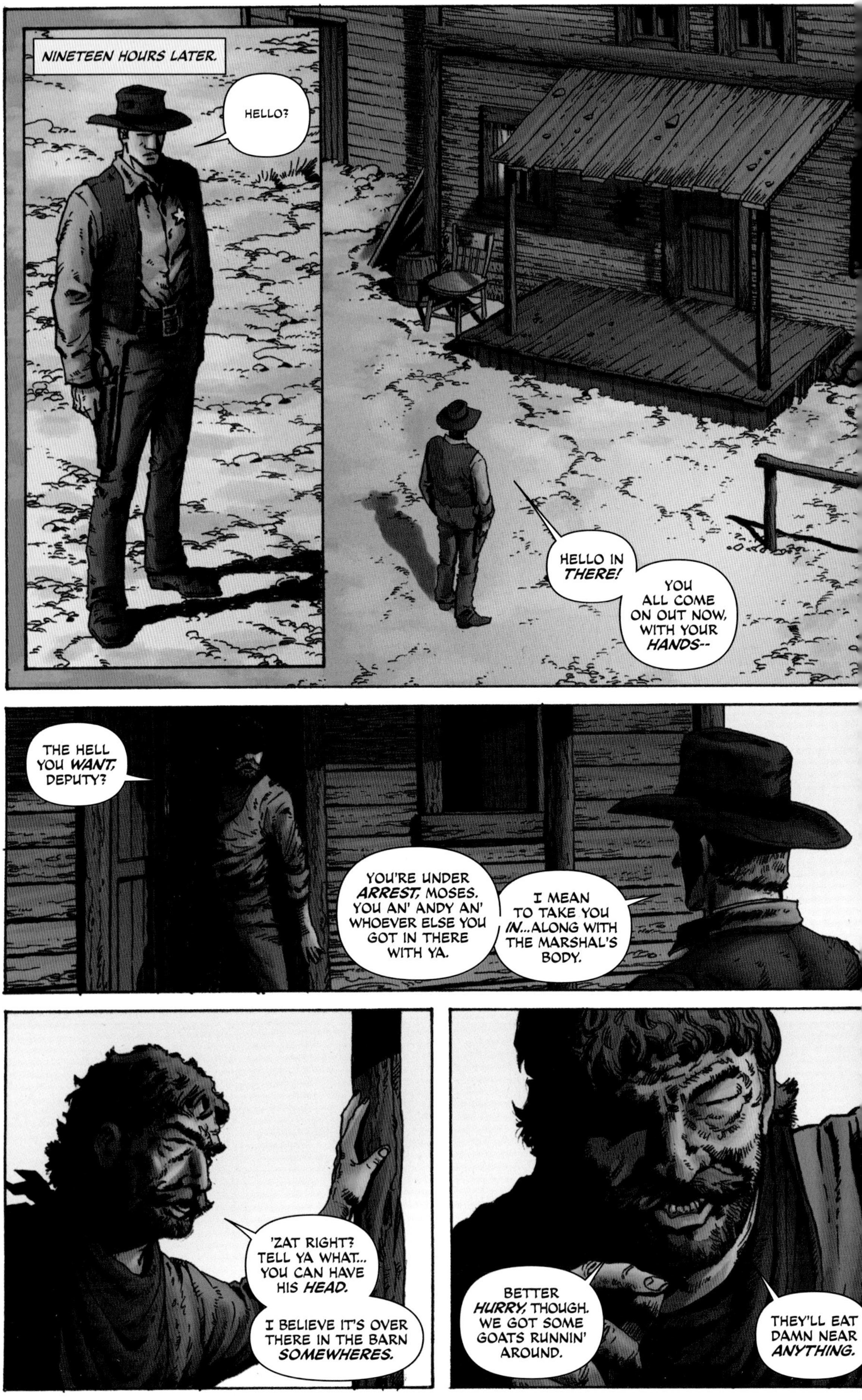
NINETEEN HOURS LATER.
HELLO?
HELLO IN THERE!
YOU ALL COME ON OUT NOW, WITH YOUR HANDS--
THE HELL YOU WANT, DEPUTY?
YOU'RE UNDER ARREST, MOSES. YOU AN' ANDY AN' WHOEVER ELSE YOU GOT IN THERE WITH YA.
I MEAN TO TAKE YOU IN...ALONG WITH THE MARSHAL'S BODY.
'ZAT RIGHT? TELL YA WHAT... YOU CAN HAVE HIS HEAD.
I BELIEVE IT'S OVER THERE IN THE BARN SOMEWHERES.
BETTER HURRY, THOUGH. WE GOT SOME GOATS RUNNIN' AROUND.
THEY'LL EAT DAMN NEAR ANYTHING.

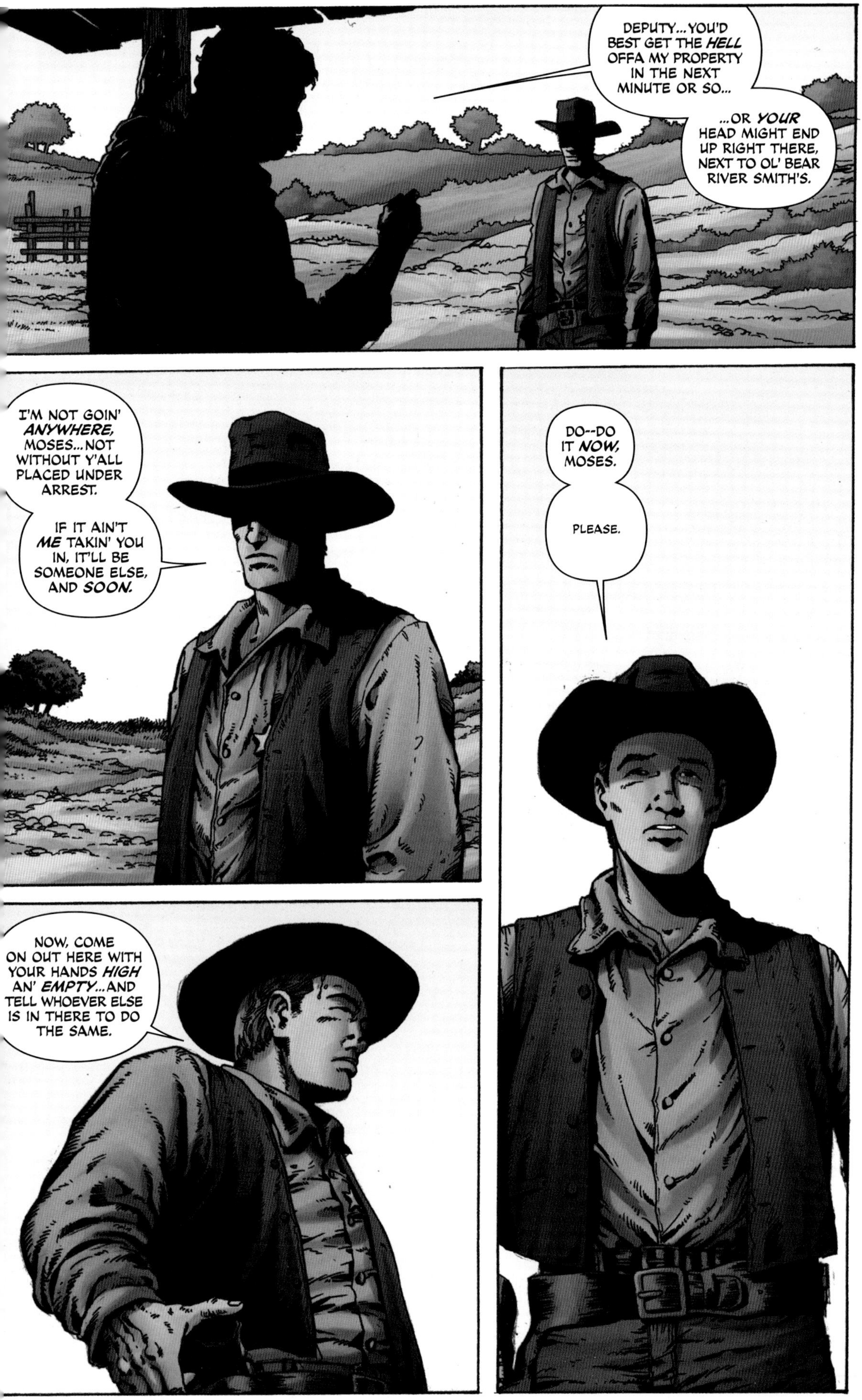
DEPUTY...YOU'D BEST GET THE *HELL* OFFA MY PROPERTY IN THE NEXT MINUTE OR SO...
...OR *YOUR* HEAD MIGHT END UP RIGHT THERE, NEXT TO OL' BEAR RIVER SMITH'S.
I'M NOT GOIN' *ANYWHERE,* MOSES...NOT WITHOUT Y'ALL PLACED UNDER ARREST.
IF IT AIN'T *ME* TAKIN' YOU IN, IT'LL BE SOMEONE ELSE, AND *SOON.*
NOW, COME ON OUT HERE WITH YOUR HANDS *HIGH* AN' *EMPTY*...AND TELL WHOEVER ELSE IS IN THERE TO DO THE SAME.
DO--DO IT *NOW,* MOSES.
PLEASE.

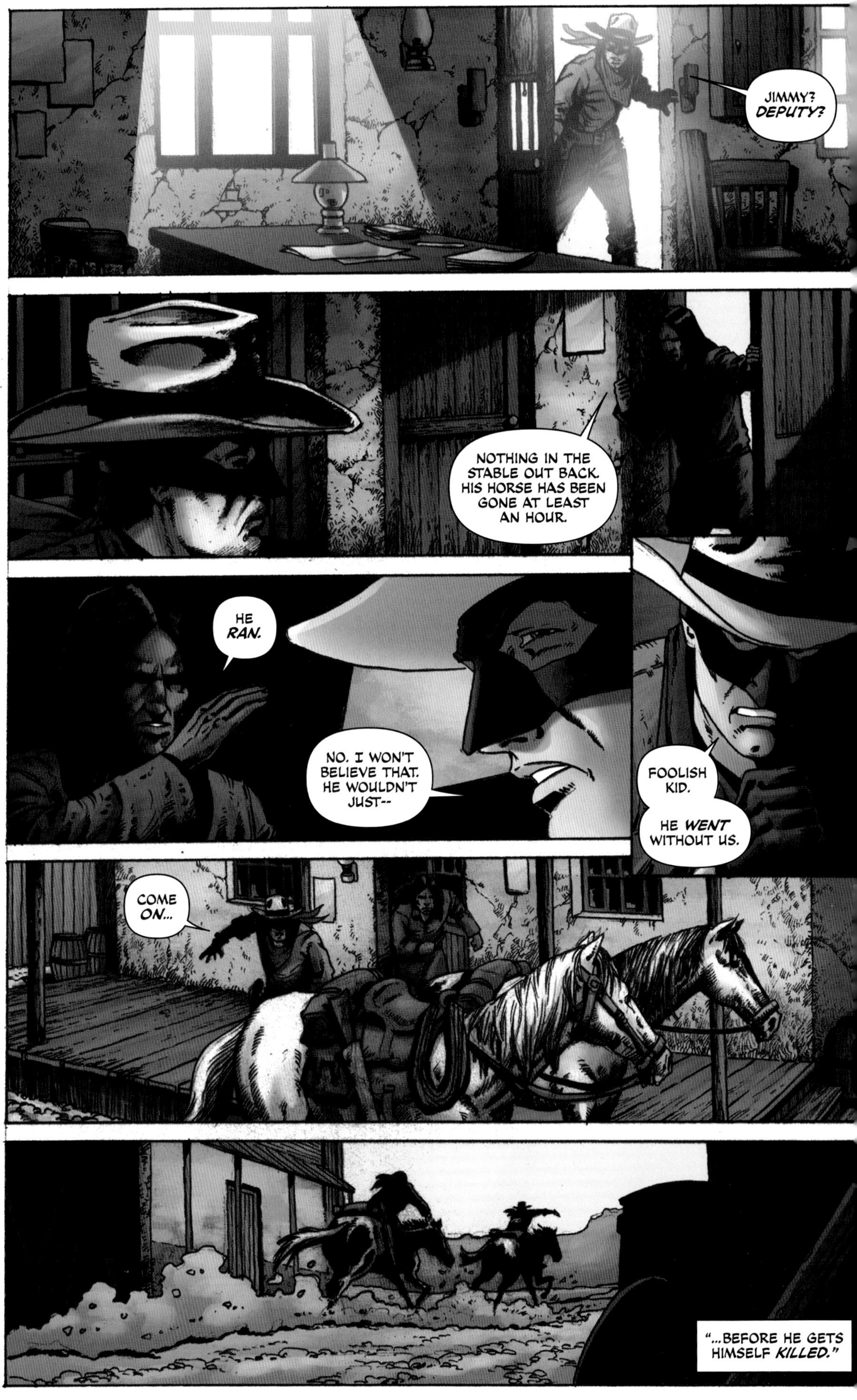

JIMMY? DEPUTY?
NOTHING IN THE STABLE OUT BACK. HIS HORSE HAS BEEN GONE AT LEAST AN HOUR.
HE RAN.
NO. I WON'T BELIEVE THAT. HE WOULDN'T JUST--
FOOLISH KID.
HE WENT WITHOUT US.
COME ON...
"...BEFORE HE GETS HIMSELF KILLED."

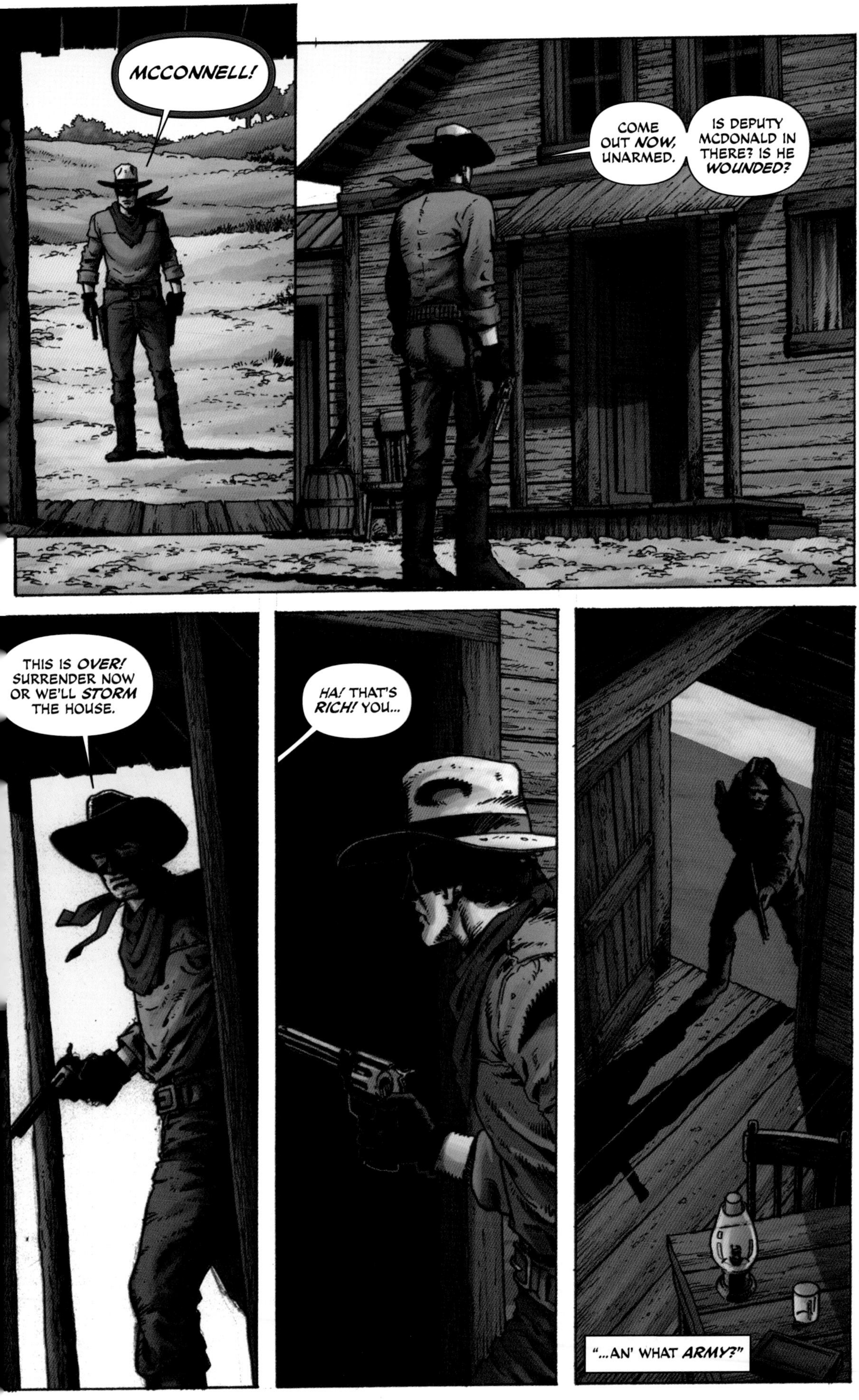
MCCONNELL!
COME OUT NOW, UNARMED.
IS DEPUTY MCDONALD IN THERE? IS HE WOUNDED?
THIS IS OVER! SURRENDER NOW OR WE'LL STORM THE HOUSE.
HA! THAT'S RICH! YOU...
"...AN' WHAT ARMY?"

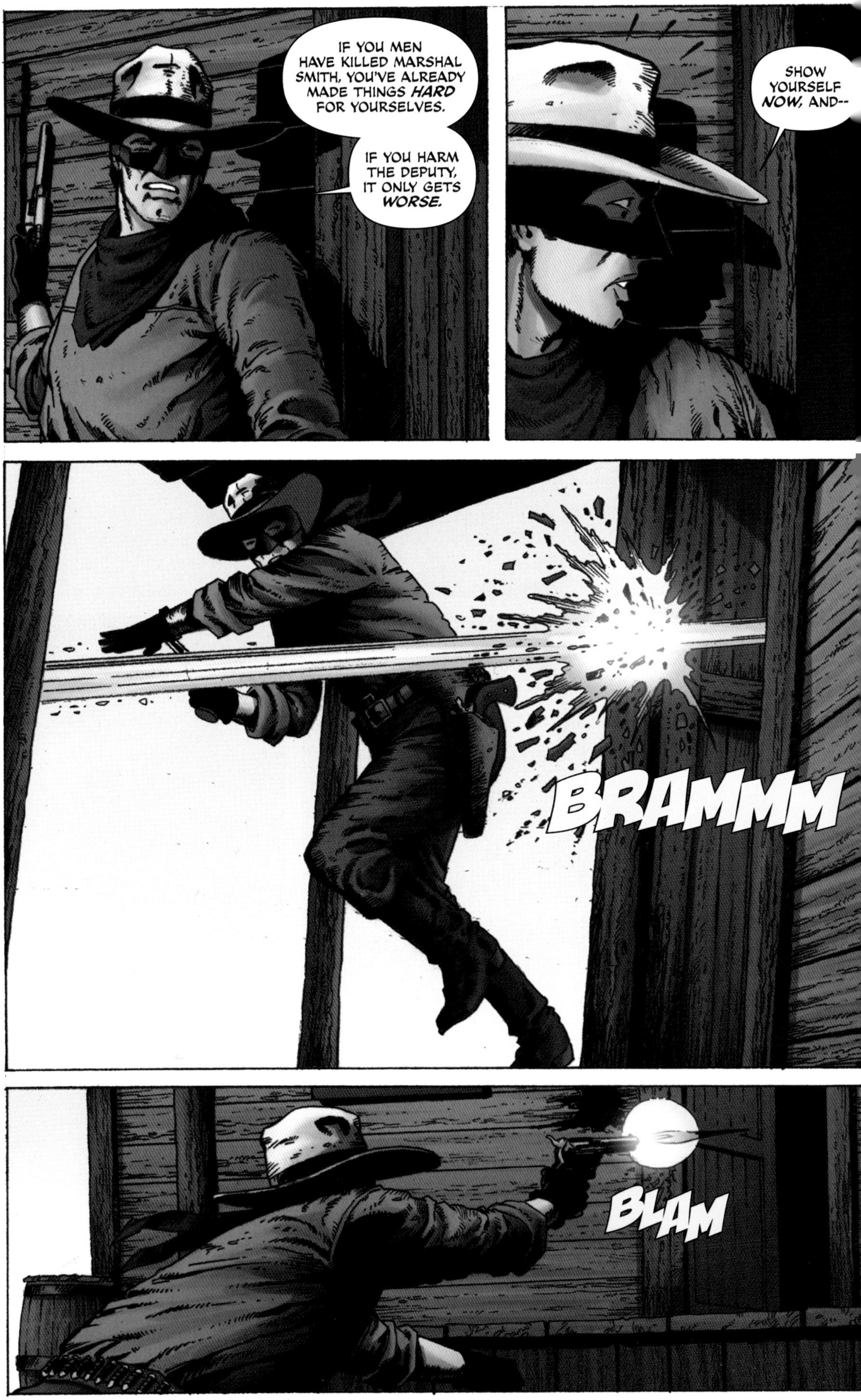
IF YOU MEN HAVE KILLED MARSHAL SMITH, YOU'VE ALREADY MADE THINGS *HARD* FOR YOURSELVES.
IF YOU HARM THE DEPUTY, IT ONLY GETS *WORSE.*
SHOW YOURSELF *NOW,* AND--
BRAMMM
BLAM

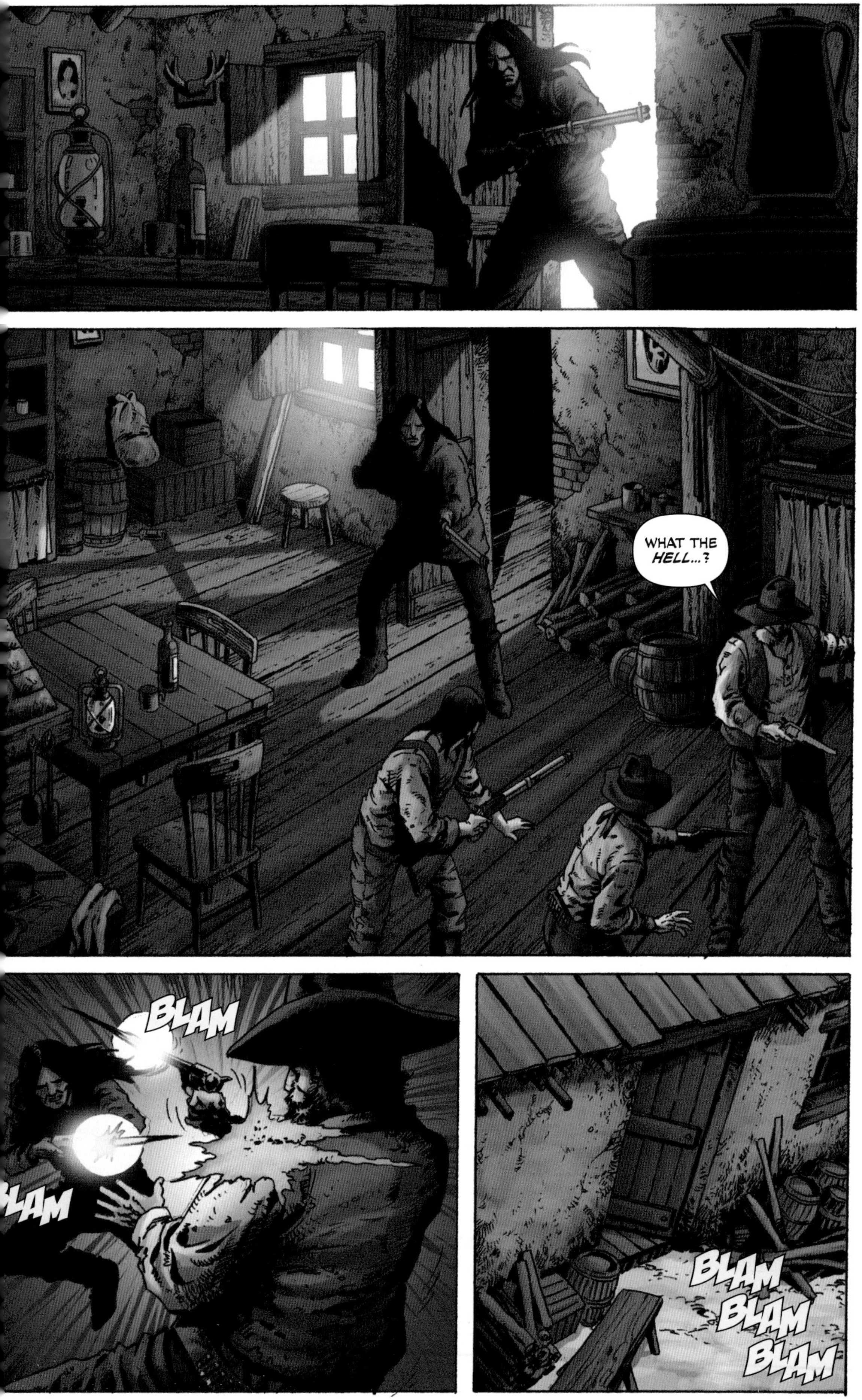
WHAT THE HELL...?
BLAM
BLAM
BLAM
BLAM
BLAM

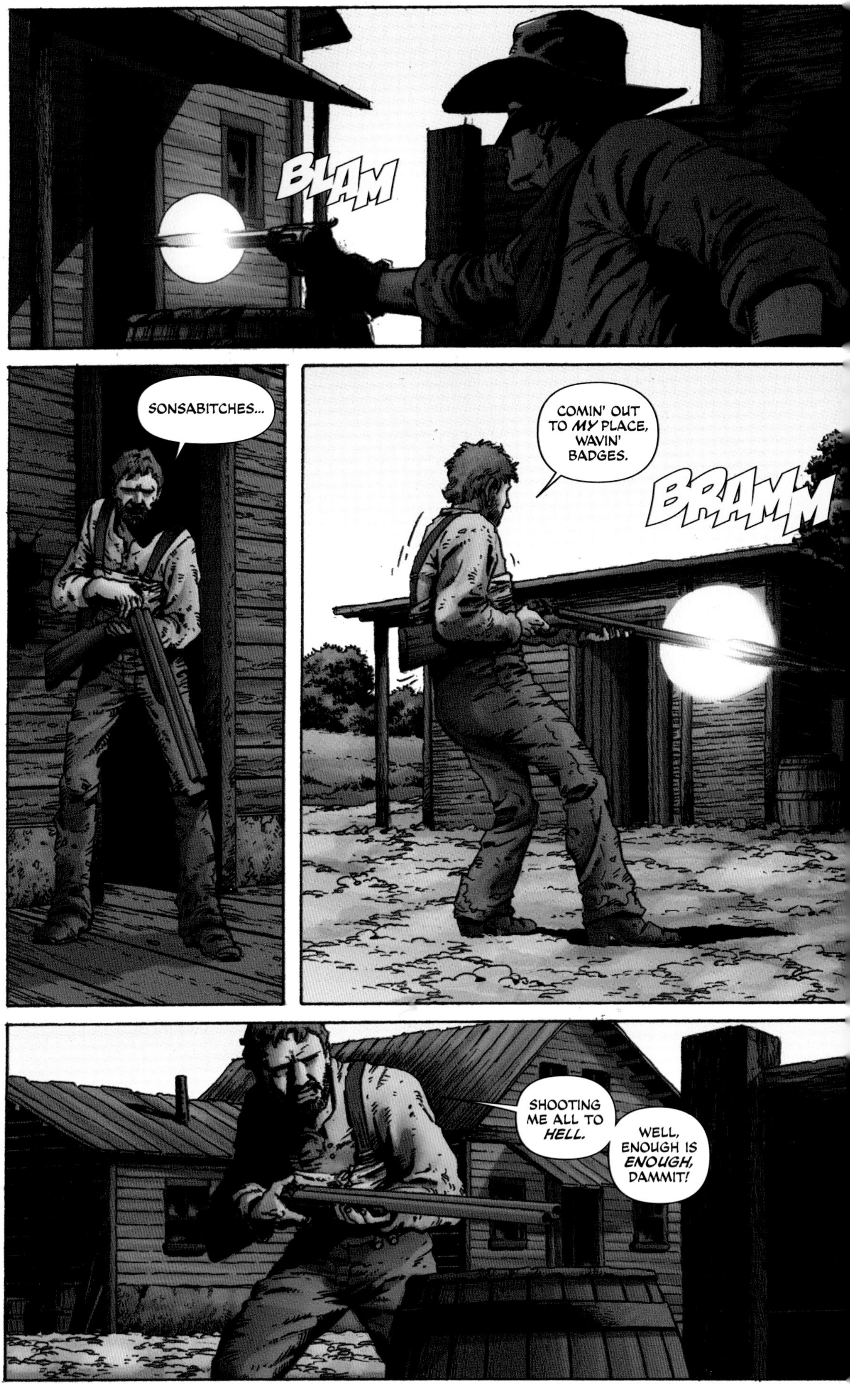
BLAM
SONSABITCHES...
COMIN' OUT TO MY PLACE, WAVIN' BADGES.
BRAMM
SHOOTING ME ALL TO HELL.
WELL, ENOUGH IS ENOUGH, DAMMIT!

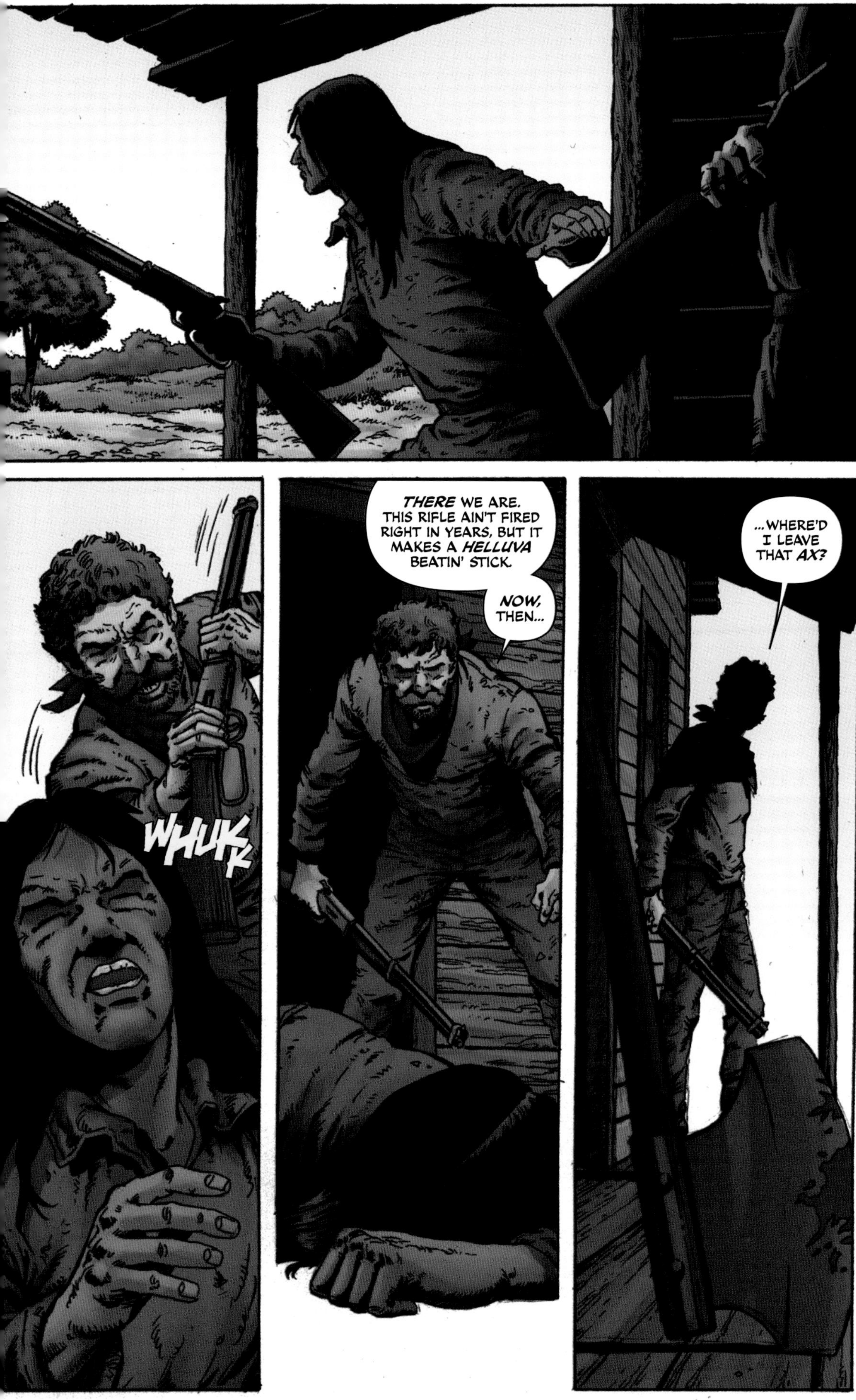
WHUKK
THERE WE ARE. THIS RIFLE AIN'T FIRED RIGHT IN YEARS, BUT IT MAKES A HELLUVA BEATIN' STICK.
NOW, THEN...
...WHERE'D I LEAVE THAT AX?

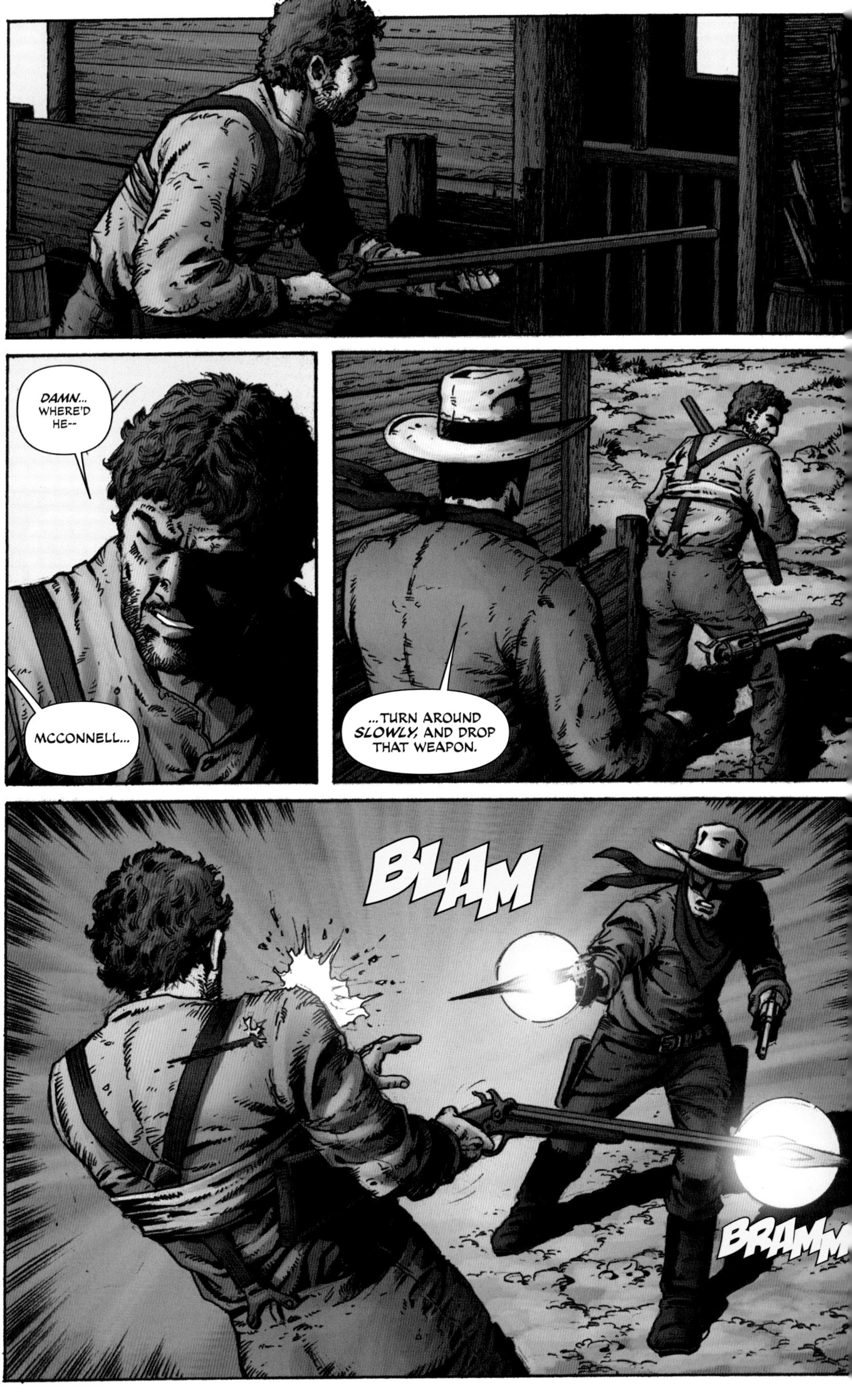
DAMN... WHERE'D HE--
MCCONNELL...
...TURN AROUND SLOWLY, AND DROP THAT WEAPON.
BLAM
BRAMM

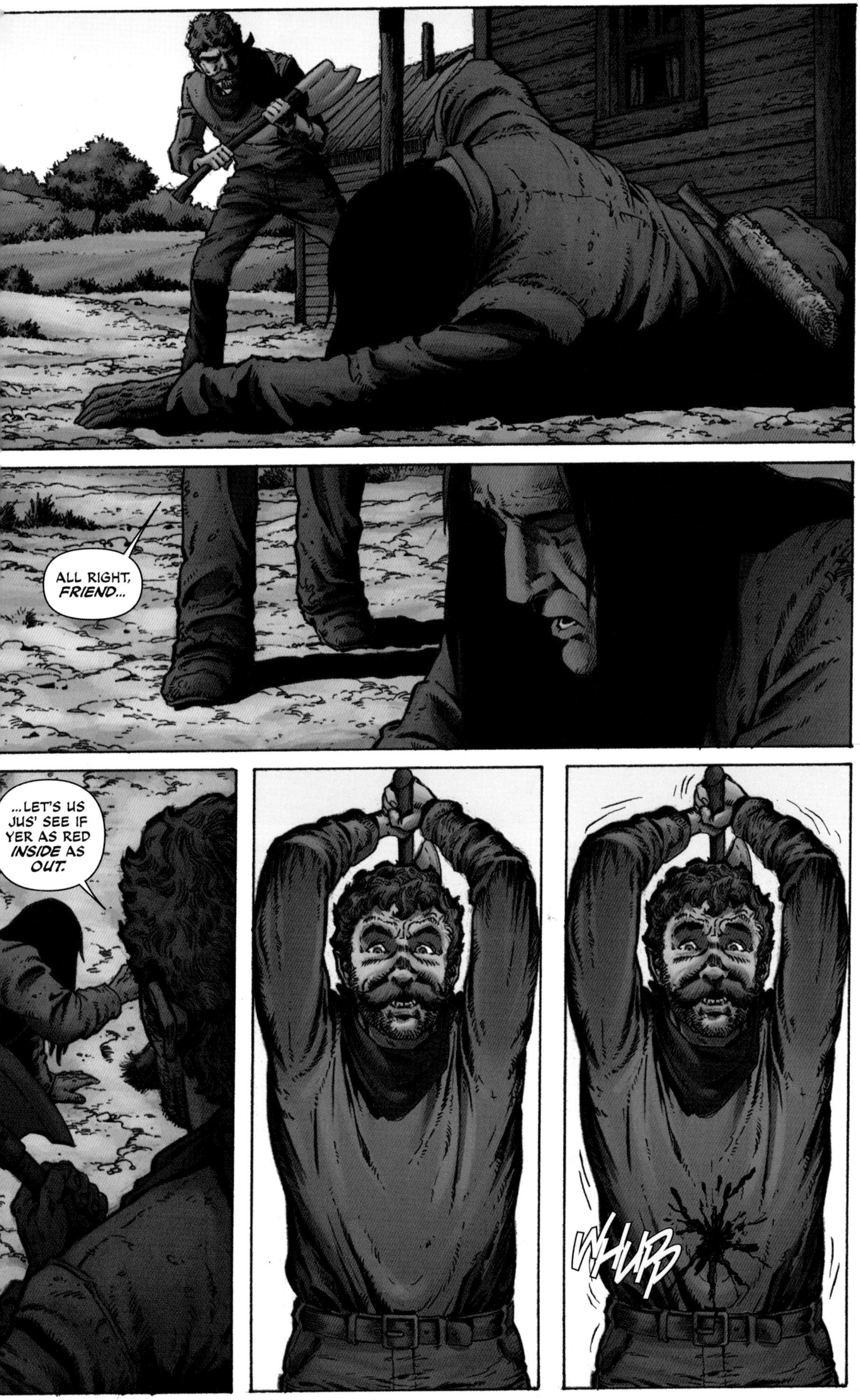
ALL RIGHT, *FRIEND*...
...LET'S US JUS' SEE IF YER AS RED *INSIDE* AS *OUT.*
WHUB

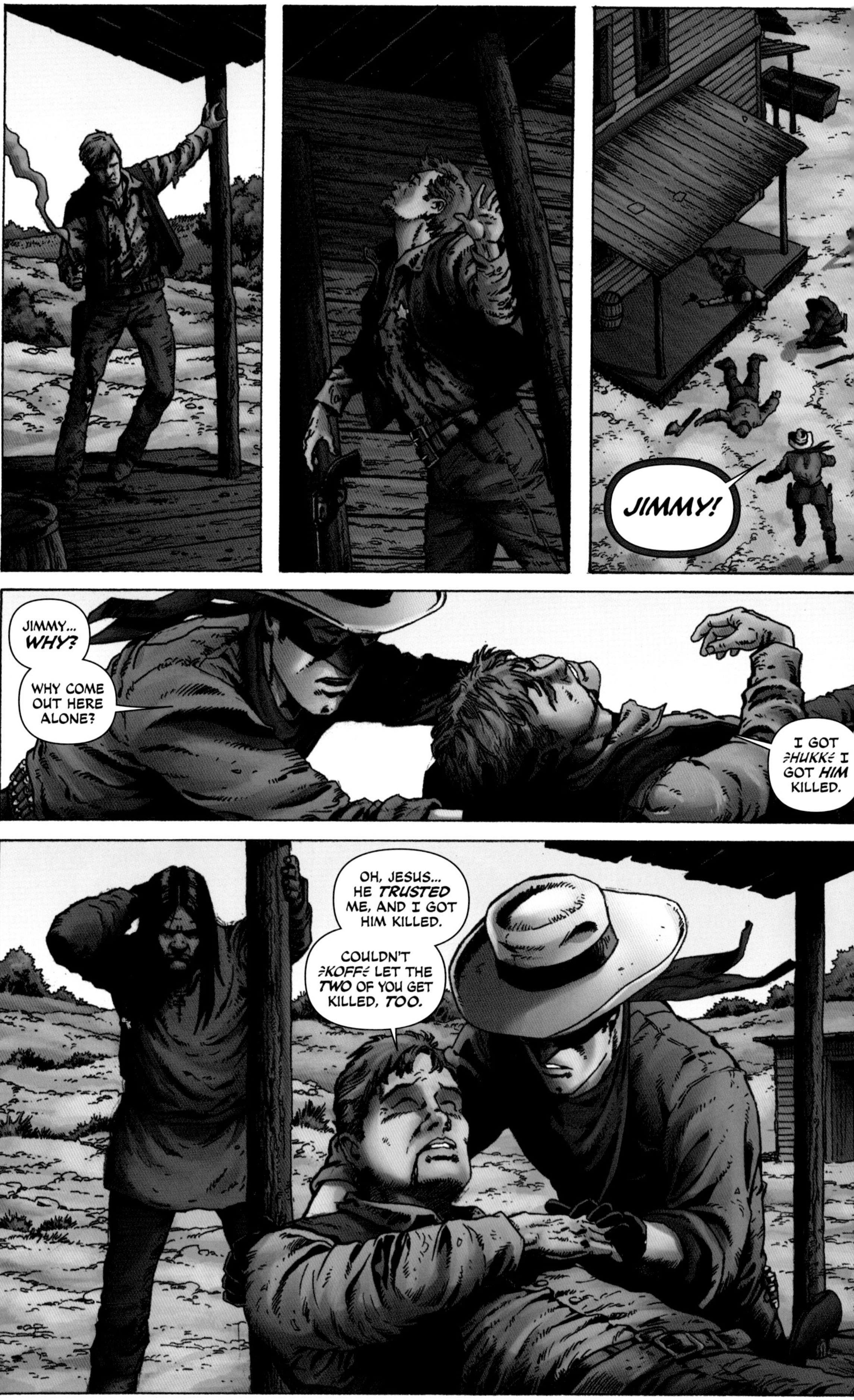
JIMMY!
JIMMY... WHY?
WHY COME OUT HERE ALONE?
I GOT HUKK I GOT HIM KILLED.
OH, JESUS... HE TRUSTED ME, AND I GOT HIM KILLED.
COULDN'T KOFF LET THE TWO OF YOU GET KILLED, TOO.

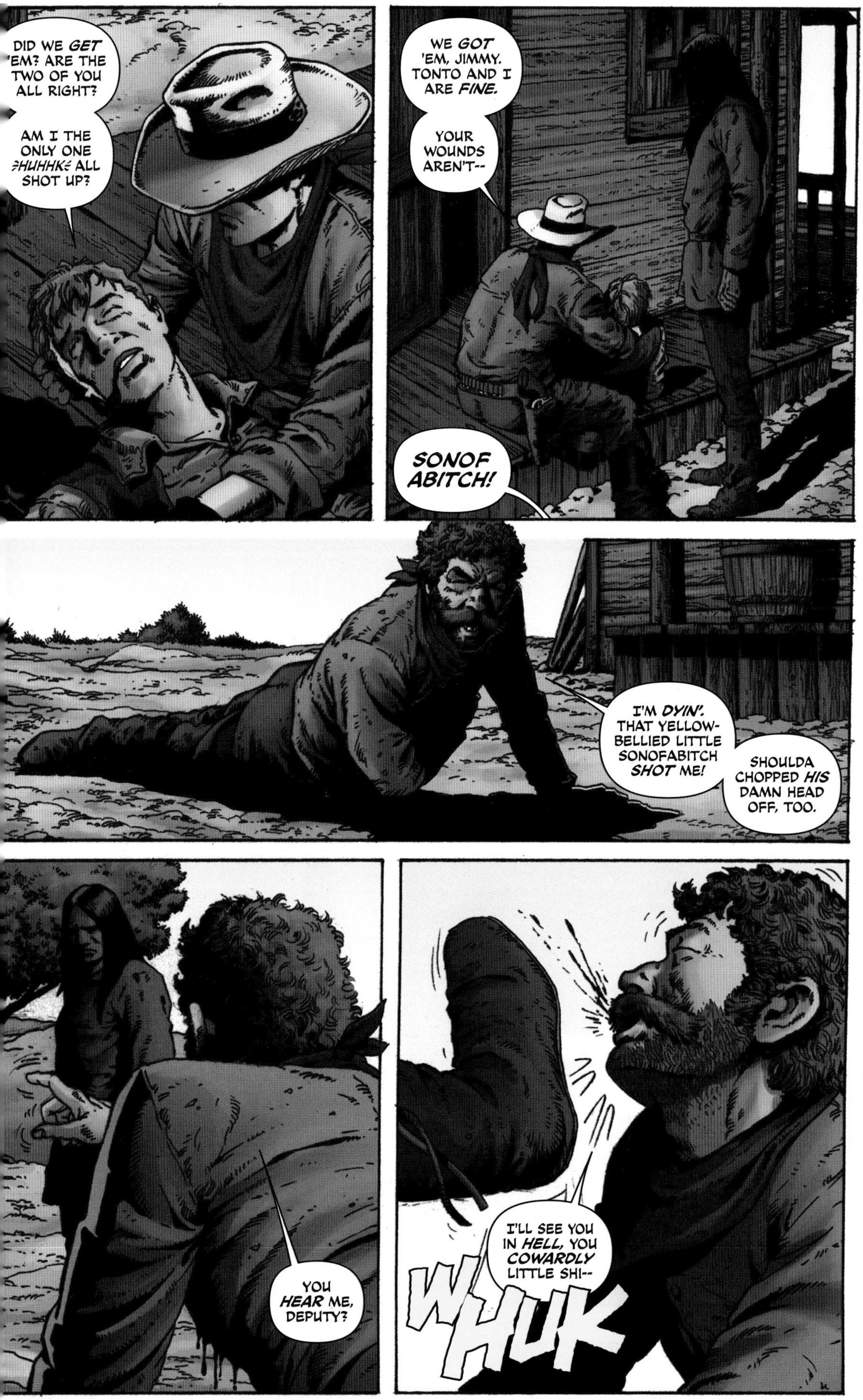
DID WE GET 'EM? ARE THE TWO OF YOU ALL RIGHT?
AM I THE ONLY ONE ≈HUHHK≈ ALL SHOT UP?
WE GOT 'EM, JIMMY. TONTO AND I ARE FINE.
YOUR WOUNDS AREN'T--
SONOF ABITCH!
I'M DYIN'. THAT YELLOW-BELLIED LITTLE SONOFABITCH SHOT ME!
SHOULDA CHOPPED HIS DAMN HEAD OFF, TOO.
YOU HEAR ME, DEPUTY?
I'LL SEE YOU IN HELL, YOU COWARDLY LITTLE SHI--
WHUK

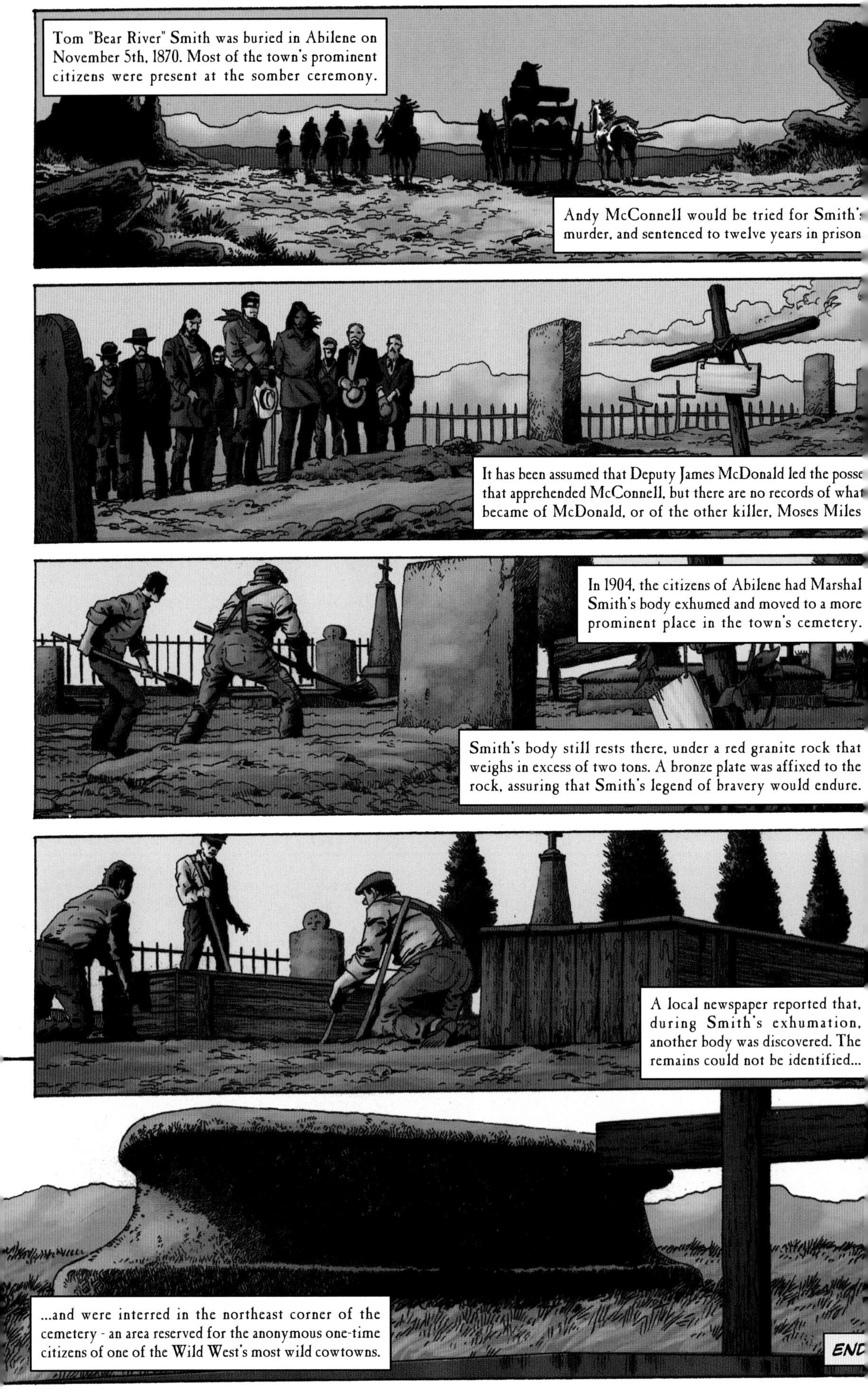
Tom "Bear River" Smith was buried in Abilene on November 5th, 1870. Most of the town's prominent citizens were present at the somber ceremony.
Andy McConnell would be tried for Smith' murder, and sentenced to twelve years in prison
It has been assumed that Deputy James McDonald led the posse that apprehended McConnell, but there are no records of what became of McDonald, or of the other killer, Moses Miles
In 1904, the citizens of Abilene had Marshal Smith's body exhumed and moved to a more prominent place in the town's cemetery.
Smith's body still rests there, under a red granite rock that weighs in excess of two tons. A bronze plate was affixed to the rock, assuring that Smith's legend of bravery would endure.
A local newspaper reported that, during Smith's exhumation, another body was discovered. The remains could not be identified...
...and were interred in the northeast corner of the cemetery - an area reserved for the anonymous one-time citizens of one of the Wild West's most wild cowtowns.
EN

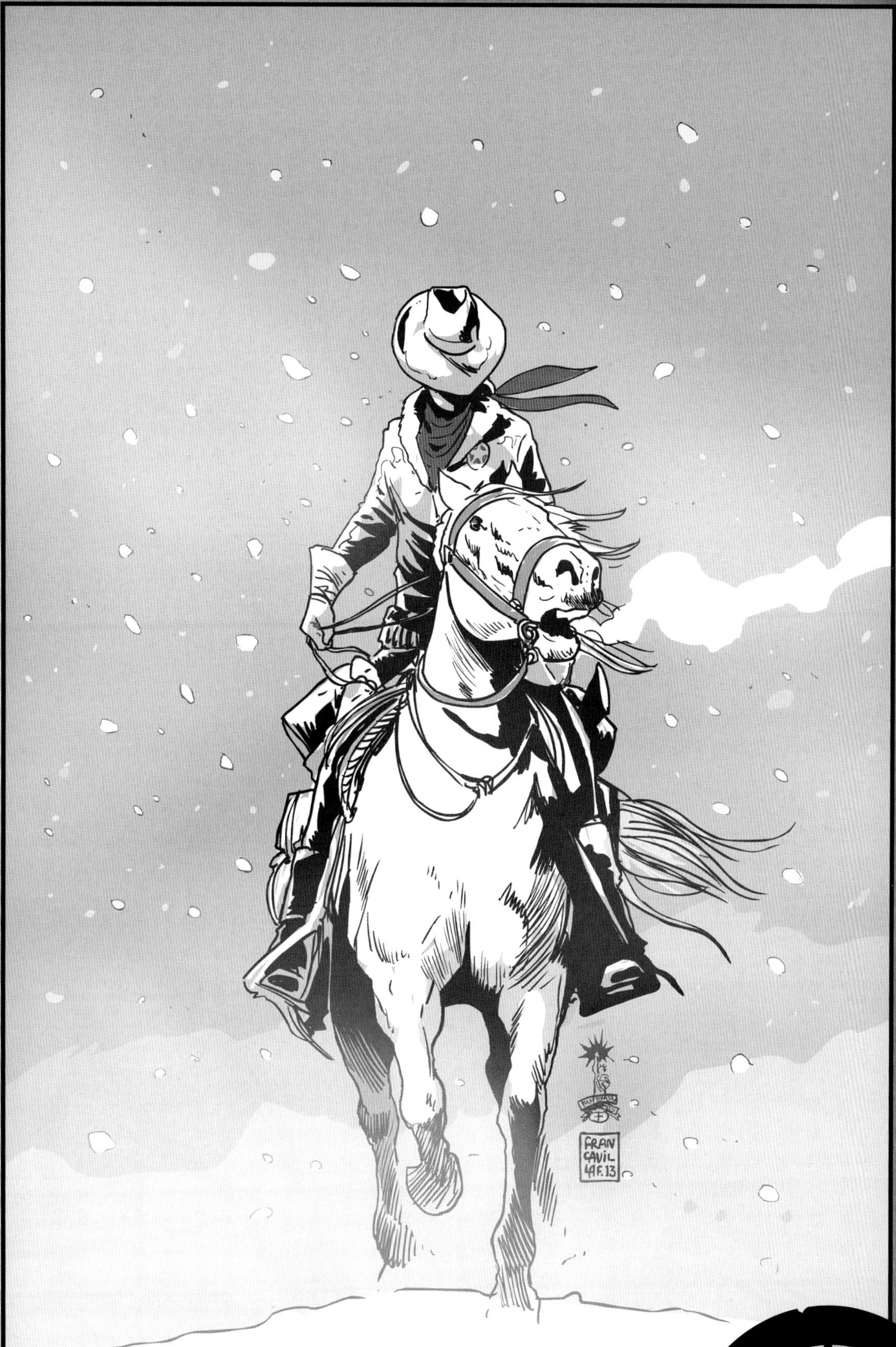
FRAN
CAVIL
LA F.13

COVER BY **FRANCESCO FRANCAVILLA**

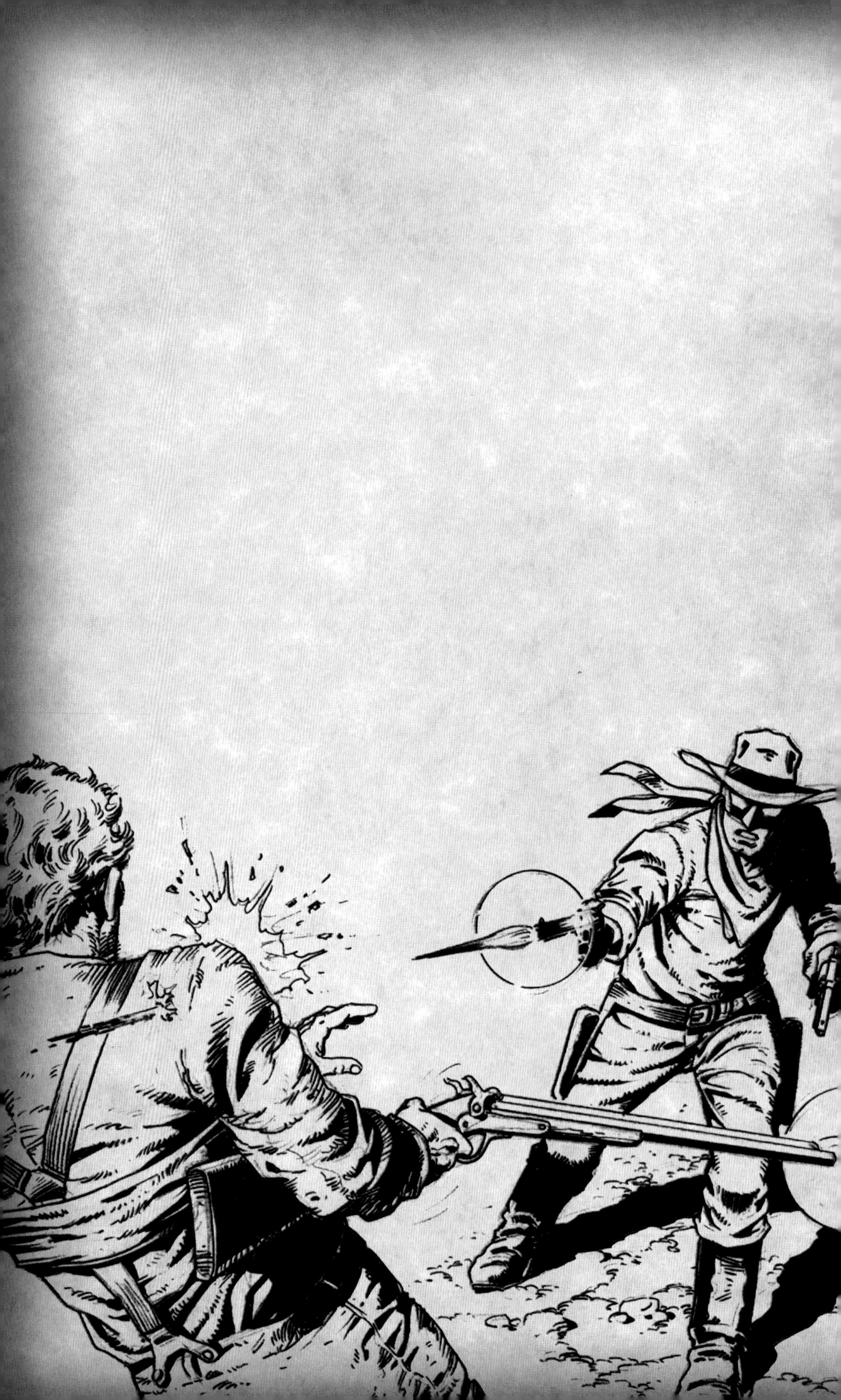

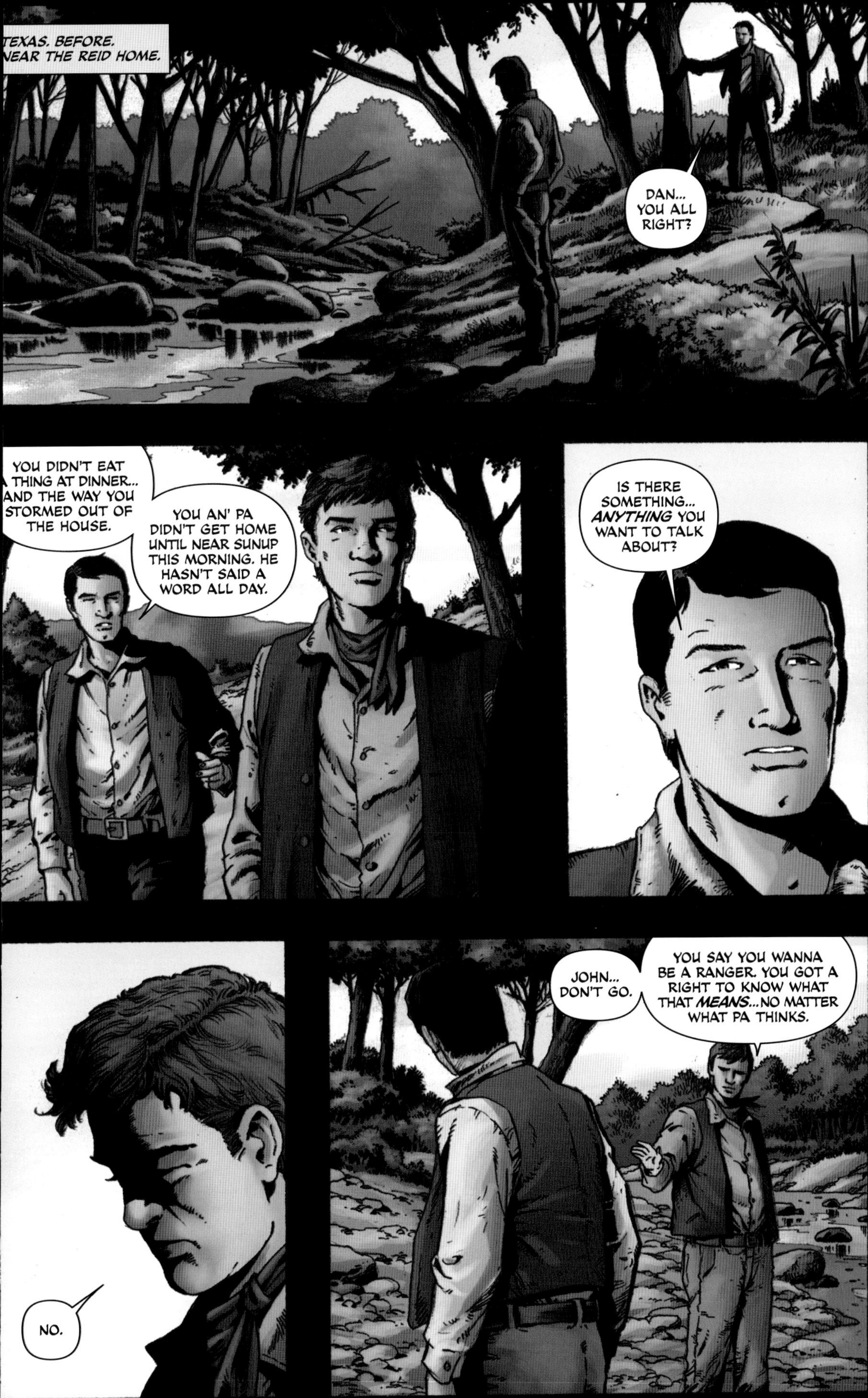
TEXAS. BEFORE. NEAR THE REID HOME.
DAN... YOU ALL RIGHT?
YOU DIDN'T EAT A THING AT DINNER... AND THE WAY YOU STORMED OUT OF THE HOUSE.
YOU AN' PA DIDN'T GET HOME UNTIL NEAR SUNUP THIS MORNING. HE HASN'T SAID A WORD ALL DAY.
IS THERE SOMETHING... ANYTHING YOU WANT TO TALK ABOUT?
NO.
JOHN... DON'T GO.
YOU SAY YOU WANNA BE A RANGER. YOU GOT A RIGHT TO KNOW WHAT THAT MEANS...NO MATTER WHAT PA THINKS.

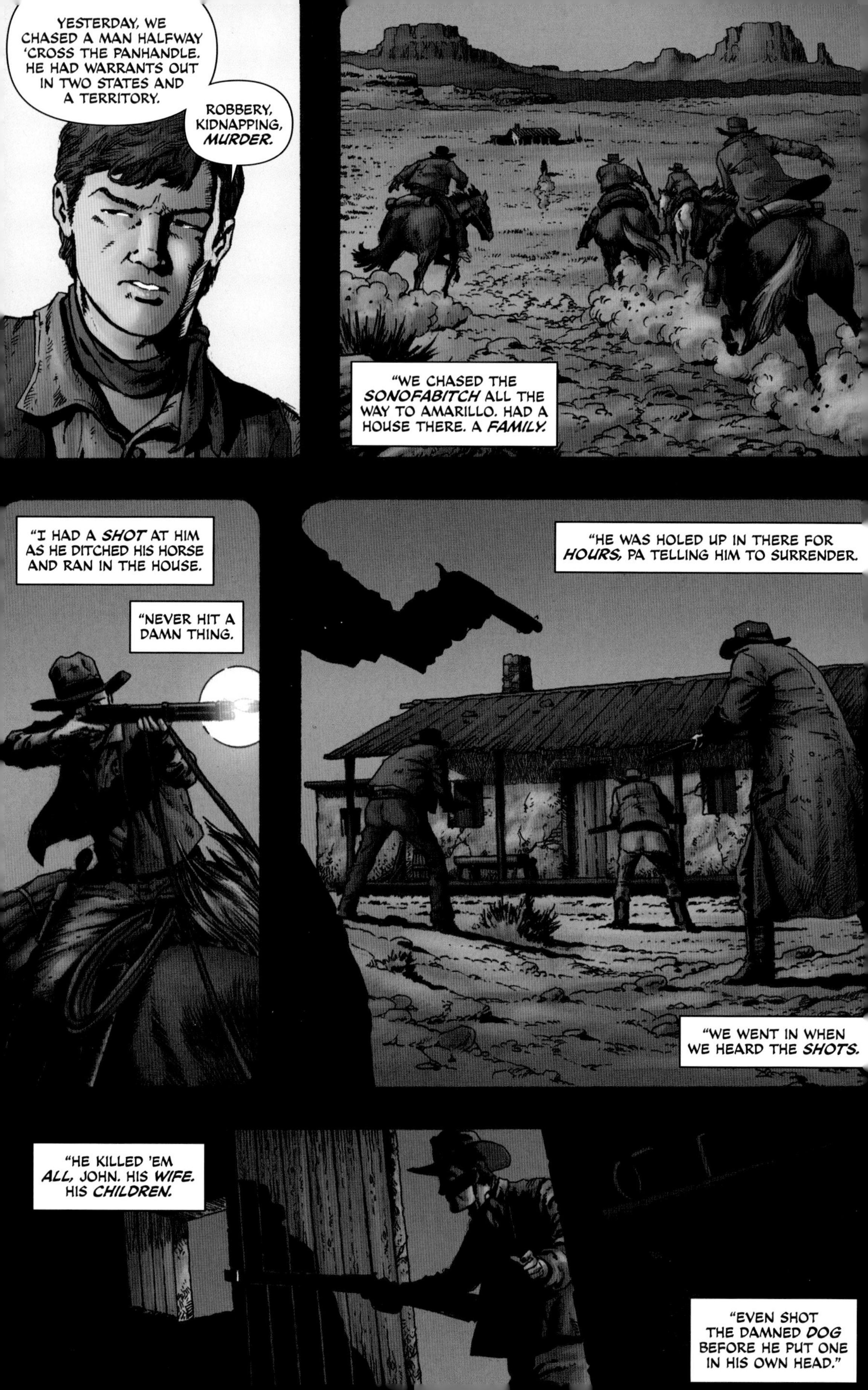
YESTERDAY, WE CHASED A MAN HALFWAY 'CROSS THE PANHANDLE. HE HAD WARRANTS OUT IN TWO STATES AND A TERRITORY.
ROBBERY, KIDNAPPING, MURDER.
"WE CHASED THE SONOFABITCH ALL THE WAY TO AMARILLO. HAD A HOUSE THERE. A FAMILY.
"I HAD A SHOT AT HIM AS HE DITCHED HIS HORSE AND RAN IN THE HOUSE.
"NEVER HIT A DAMN THING.
"HE WAS HOLED UP IN THERE FOR HOURS, PA TELLING HIM TO SURRENDER.
"WE WENT IN WHEN WE HEARD THE SHOTS.
"HE KILLED 'EM ALL, JOHN. HIS WIFE. HIS CHILDREN.
"EVEN SHOT THE DAMNED DOG BEFORE HE PUT ONE IN HIS OWN HEAD."

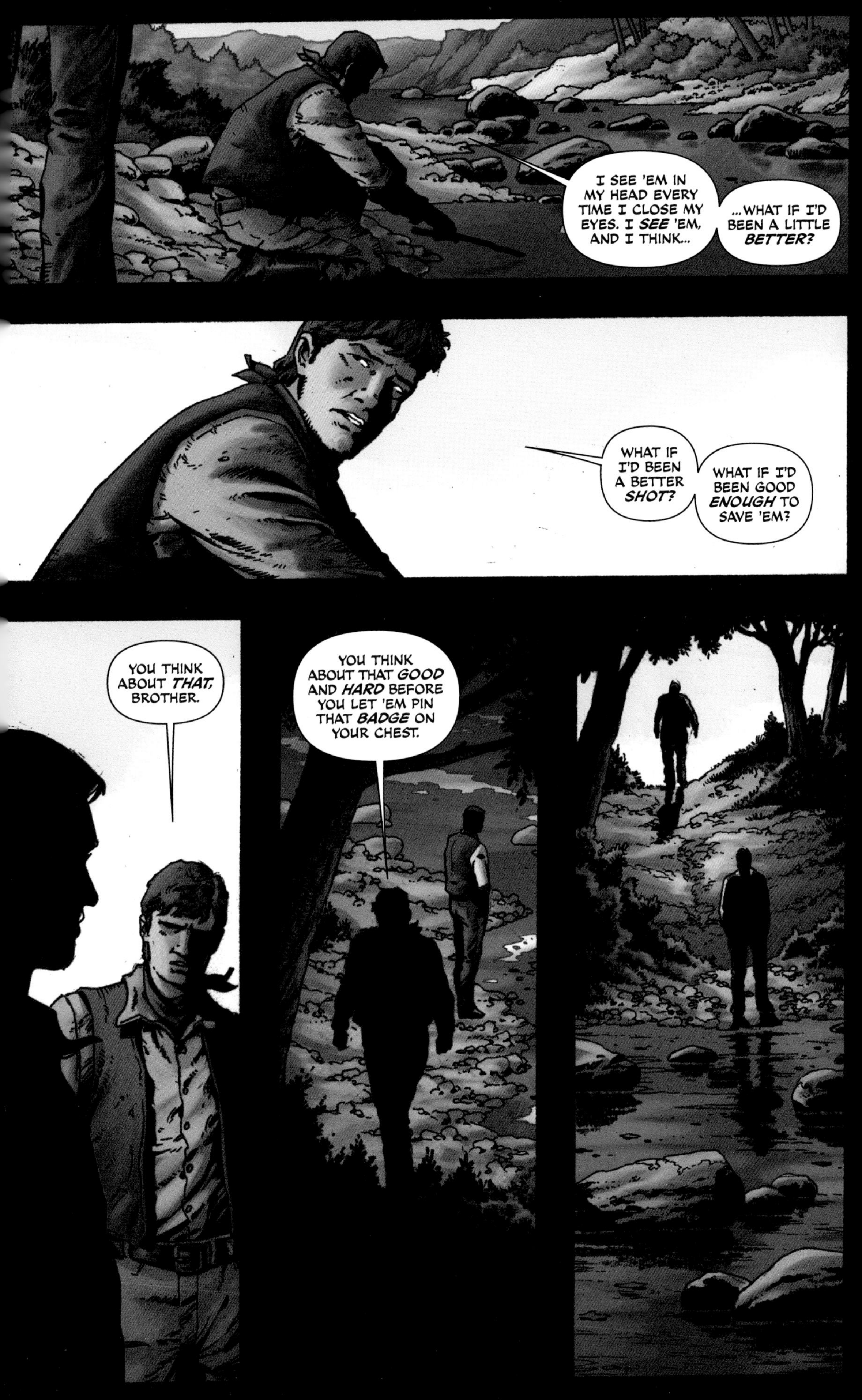
I SEE 'EM IN MY HEAD EVERY TIME I CLOSE MY EYES. I *SEE* 'EM, AND I THINK...
...WHAT IF I'D BEEN A LITTLE *BETTER?*
WHAT IF I'D BEEN A BETTER *SHOT?*
WHAT IF I'D BEEN GOOD *ENOUGH* TO SAVE 'EM?
YOU THINK ABOUT *THAT,* BROTHER.
YOU THINK ABOUT THAT *GOOD* AND *HARD* BEFORE YOU LET 'EM PIN THAT *BADGE* ON YOUR CHEST.

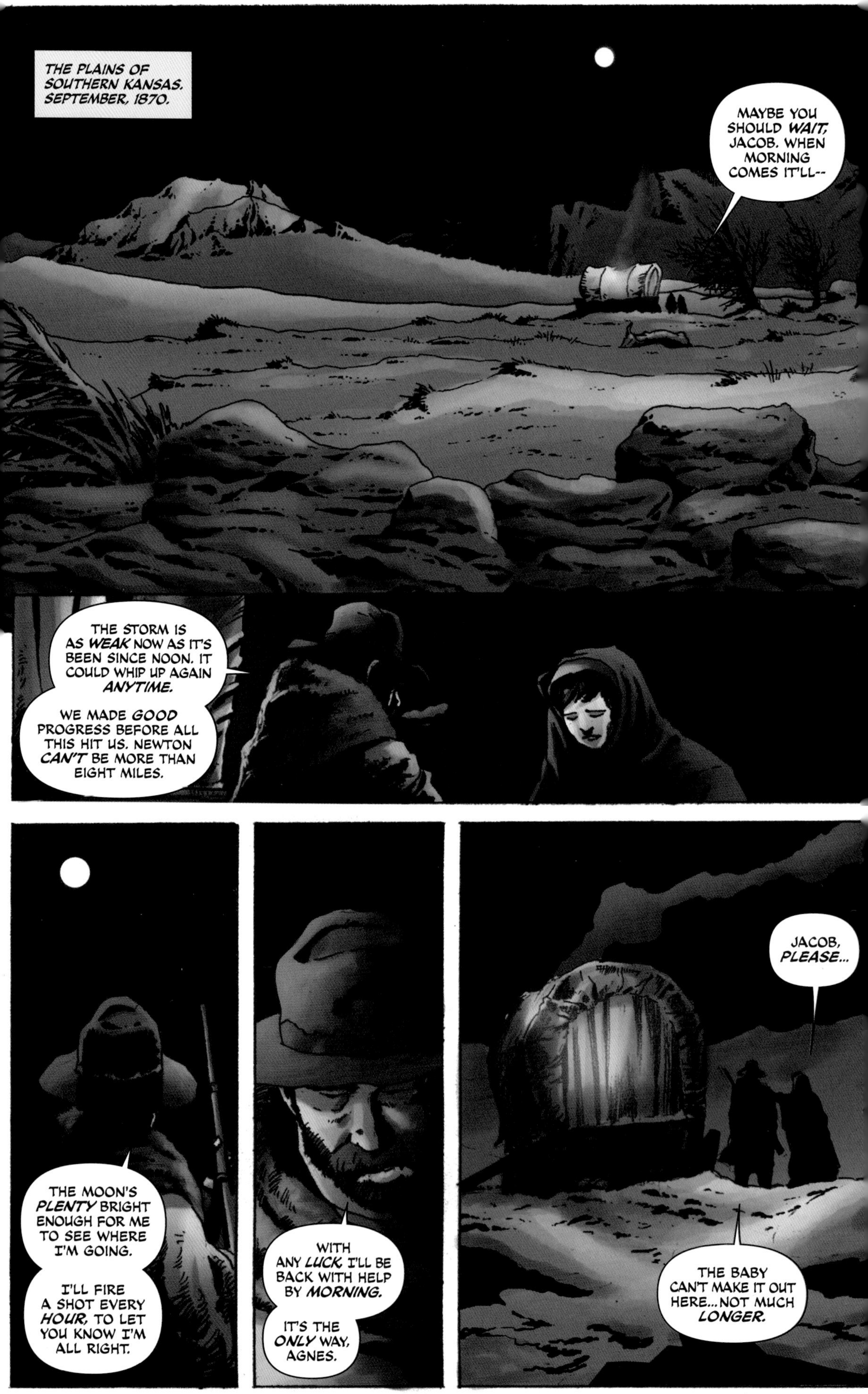

THE PLAINS OF SOUTHERN KANSAS. SEPTEMBER, 1870.
MAYBE YOU SHOULD WAIT, JACOB. WHEN MORNING COMES IT'LL--
THE STORM IS AS WEAK NOW AS IT'S BEEN SINCE NOON. IT COULD WHIP UP AGAIN ANYTIME.
WE MADE GOOD PROGRESS BEFORE ALL THIS HIT US. NEWTON CAN'T BE MORE THAN EIGHT MILES.
THE MOON'S PLENTY BRIGHT ENOUGH FOR ME TO SEE WHERE I'M GOING.
I'LL FIRE A SHOT EVERY HOUR, TO LET YOU KNOW I'M ALL RIGHT.
WITH ANY LUCK, I'LL BE BACK WITH HELP BY MORNING.
IT'S THE ONLY WAY, AGNES.
JACOB, PLEASE...
THE BABY CAN'T MAKE IT OUT HERE...NOT MUCH LONGER.

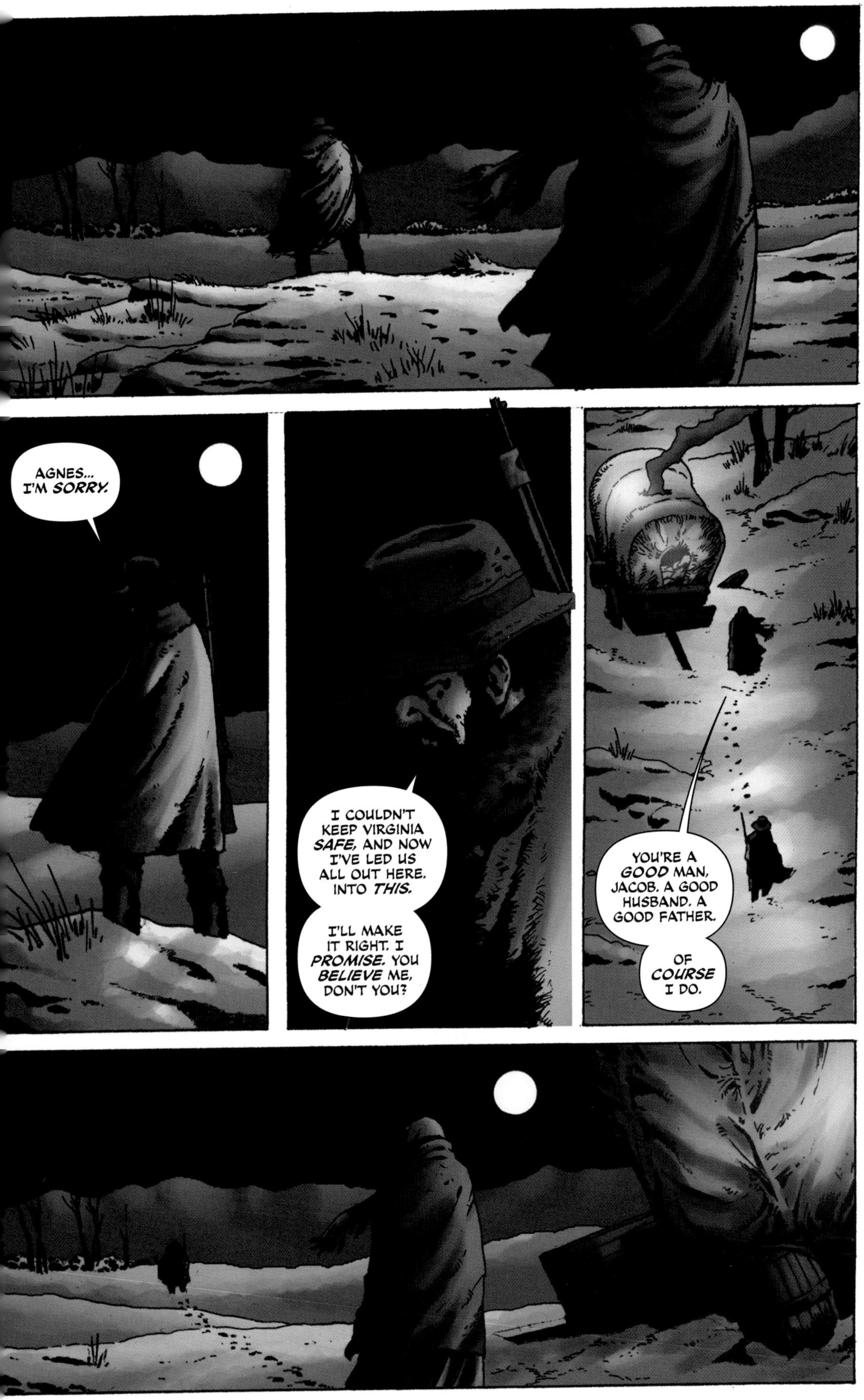

AGNES... I'M SORRY.
I COULDN'T KEEP VIRGINIA SAFE, AND NOW I'VE LED US ALL OUT HERE. INTO THIS.
I'LL MAKE IT RIGHT. I PROMISE. YOU BELIEVE ME, DON'T YOU?
YOU'RE A GOOD MAN, JACOB. A GOOD HUSBAND. A GOOD FATHER.
OF COURSE I DO.

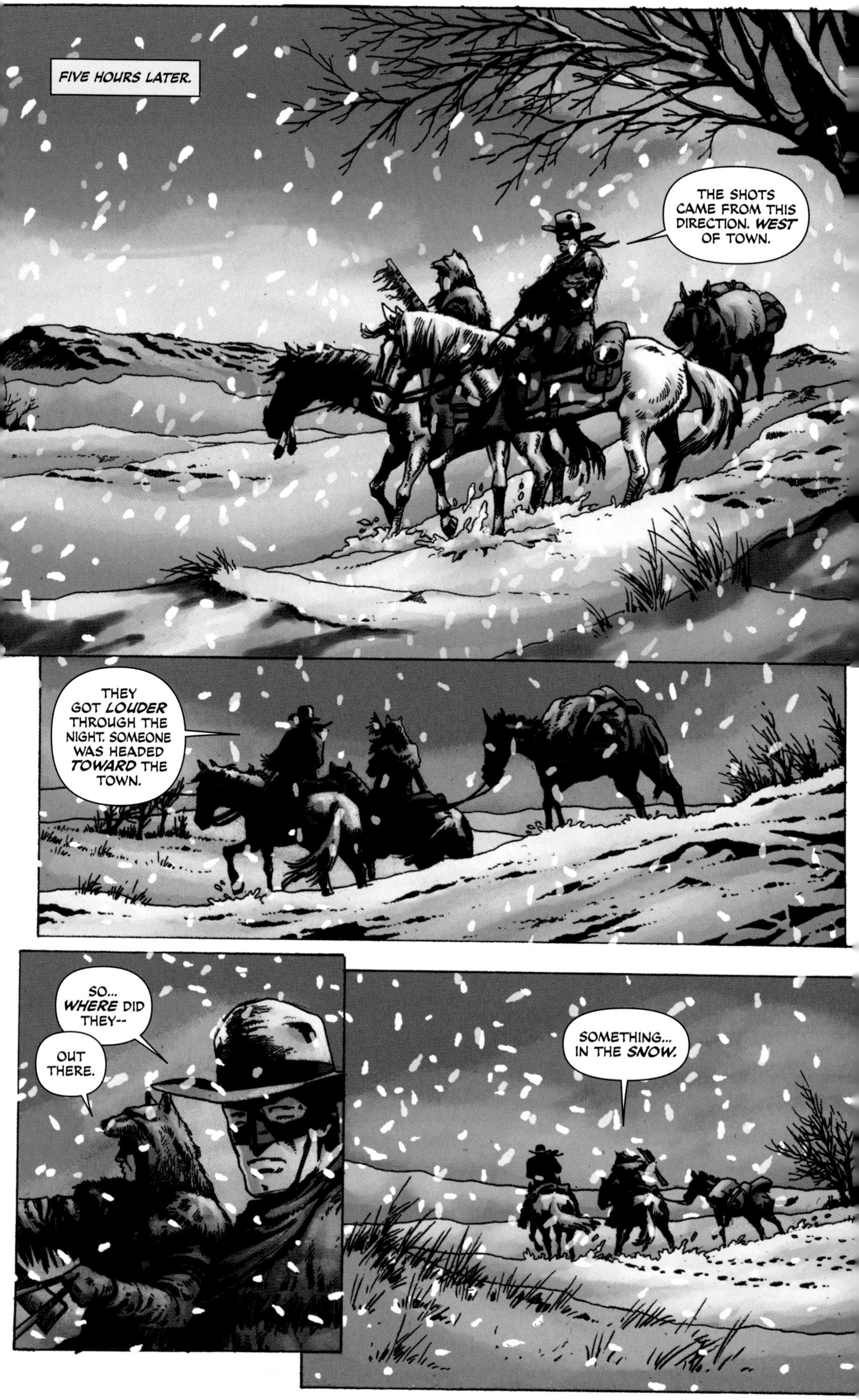
FIVE HOURS LATER.
THE SHOTS CAME FROM THIS DIRECTION. WEST OF TOWN.
THEY GOT LOUDER THROUGH THE NIGHT. SOMEONE WAS HEADED TOWARD THE TOWN.
SO... WHERE DID THEY--
OUT THERE.
SOMETHING... IN THE SNOW.

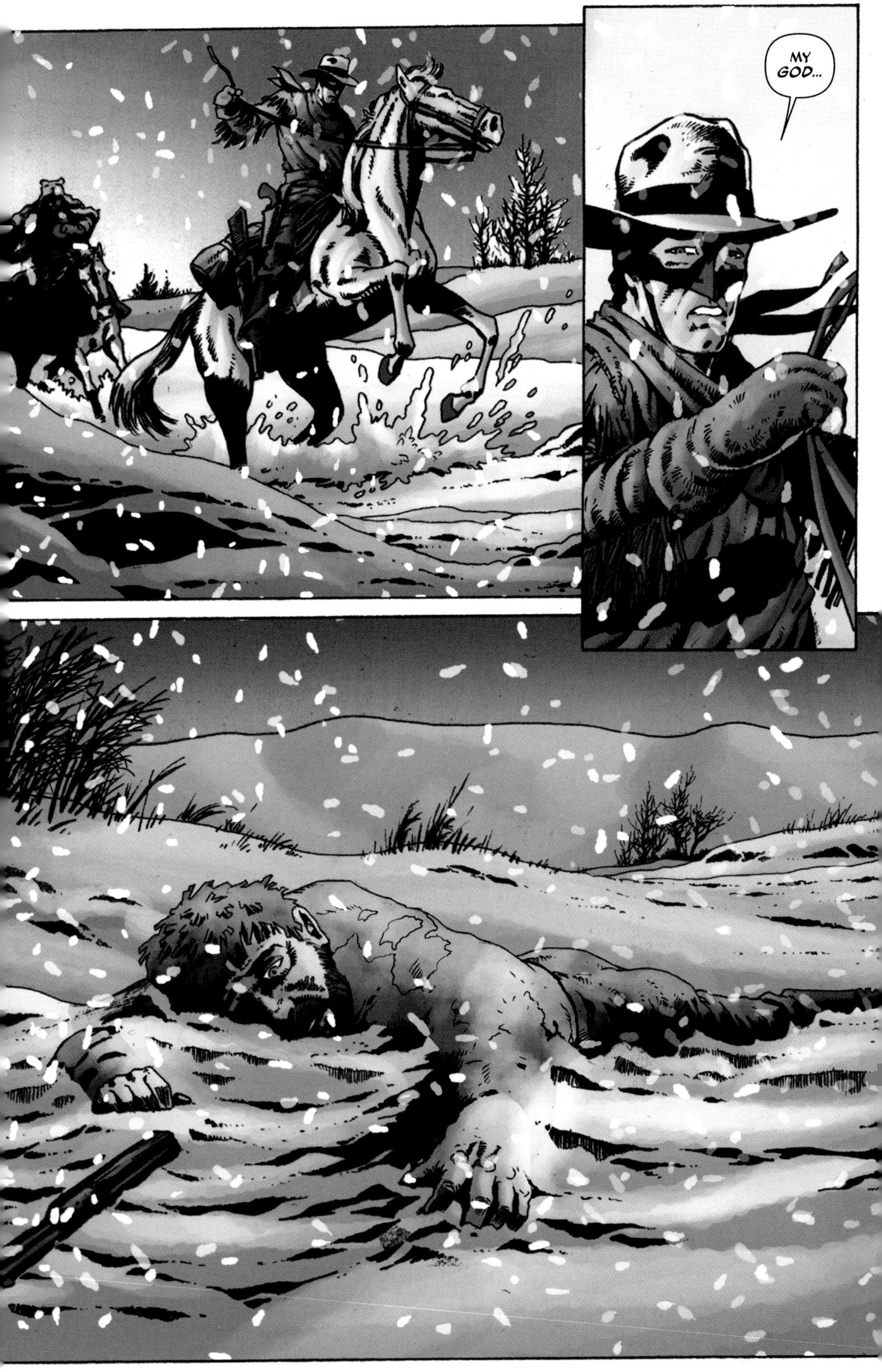
MY GOD...

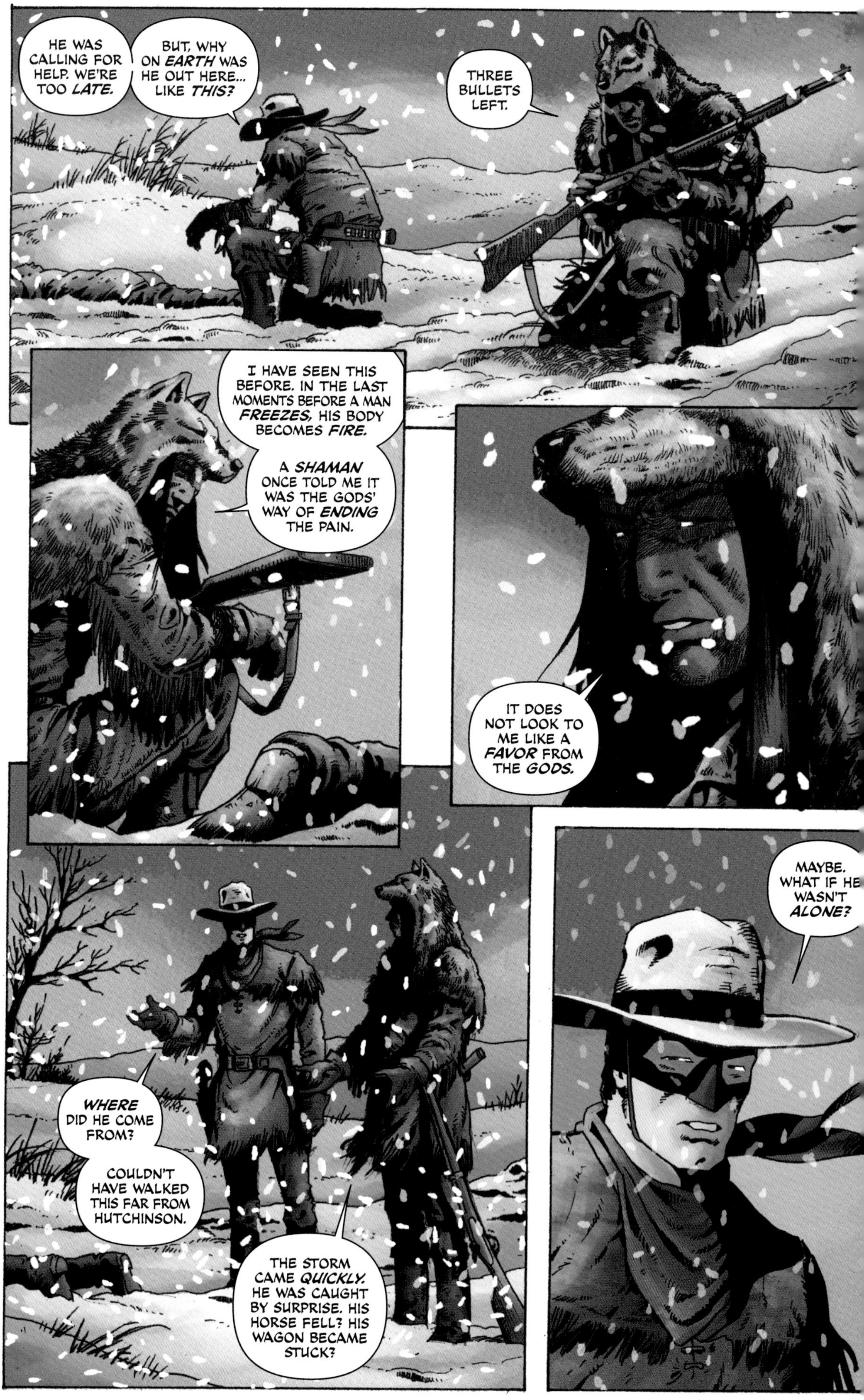

HE WAS CALLING FOR HELP. WE'RE TOO LATE.
BUT, WHY ON EARTH WAS HE OUT HERE... LIKE THIS?
THREE BULLETS LEFT.
I HAVE SEEN THIS BEFORE. IN THE LAST MOMENTS BEFORE A MAN FREEZES, HIS BODY BECOMES FIRE.
A SHAMAN ONCE TOLD ME IT WAS THE GODS' WAY OF ENDING THE PAIN.
IT DOES NOT LOOK TO ME LIKE A FAVOR FROM THE GODS.
WHERE DID HE COME FROM?
COULDN'T HAVE WALKED THIS FAR FROM HUTCHINSON.
THE STORM CAME QUICKLY. HE WAS CAUGHT BY SURPRISE. HIS HORSE FELL? HIS WAGON BECAME STUCK?
MAYBE. WHAT IF HE WASN'T ALONE?

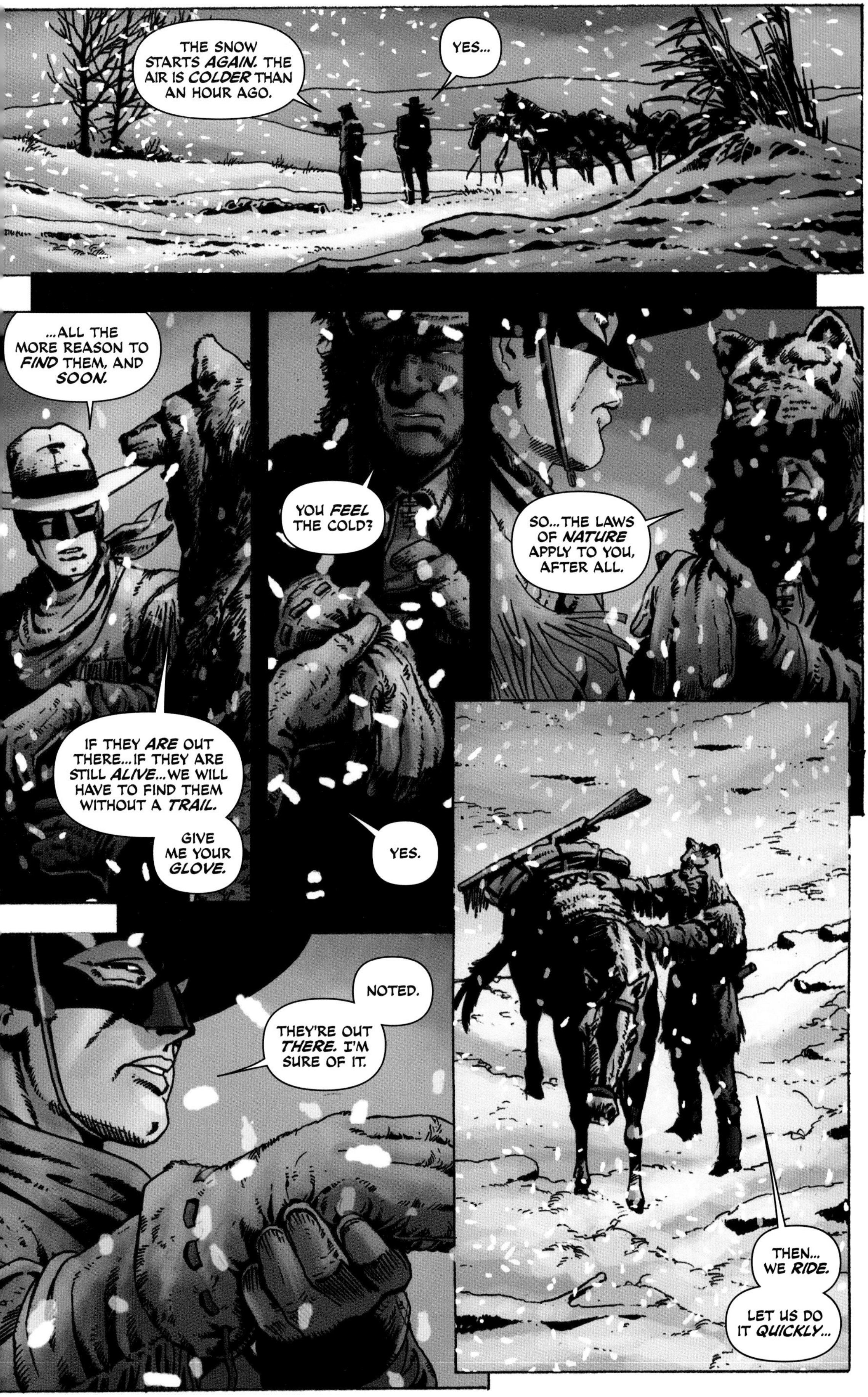
THE SNOW STARTS AGAIN. THE AIR IS COLDER THAN AN HOUR AGO.
YES...
...ALL THE MORE REASON TO FIND THEM, AND SOON.
IF THEY ARE OUT THERE...IF THEY ARE STILL ALIVE...WE WILL HAVE TO FIND THEM WITHOUT A TRAIL.
GIVE ME YOUR GLOVE.
YOU FEEL THE COLD?
YES.
SO...THE LAWS OF NATURE APPLY TO YOU, AFTER ALL.
NOTED.
THEY'RE OUT THERE. I'M SURE OF IT.
THEN... WE RIDE.
LET US DO IT QUICKLY...

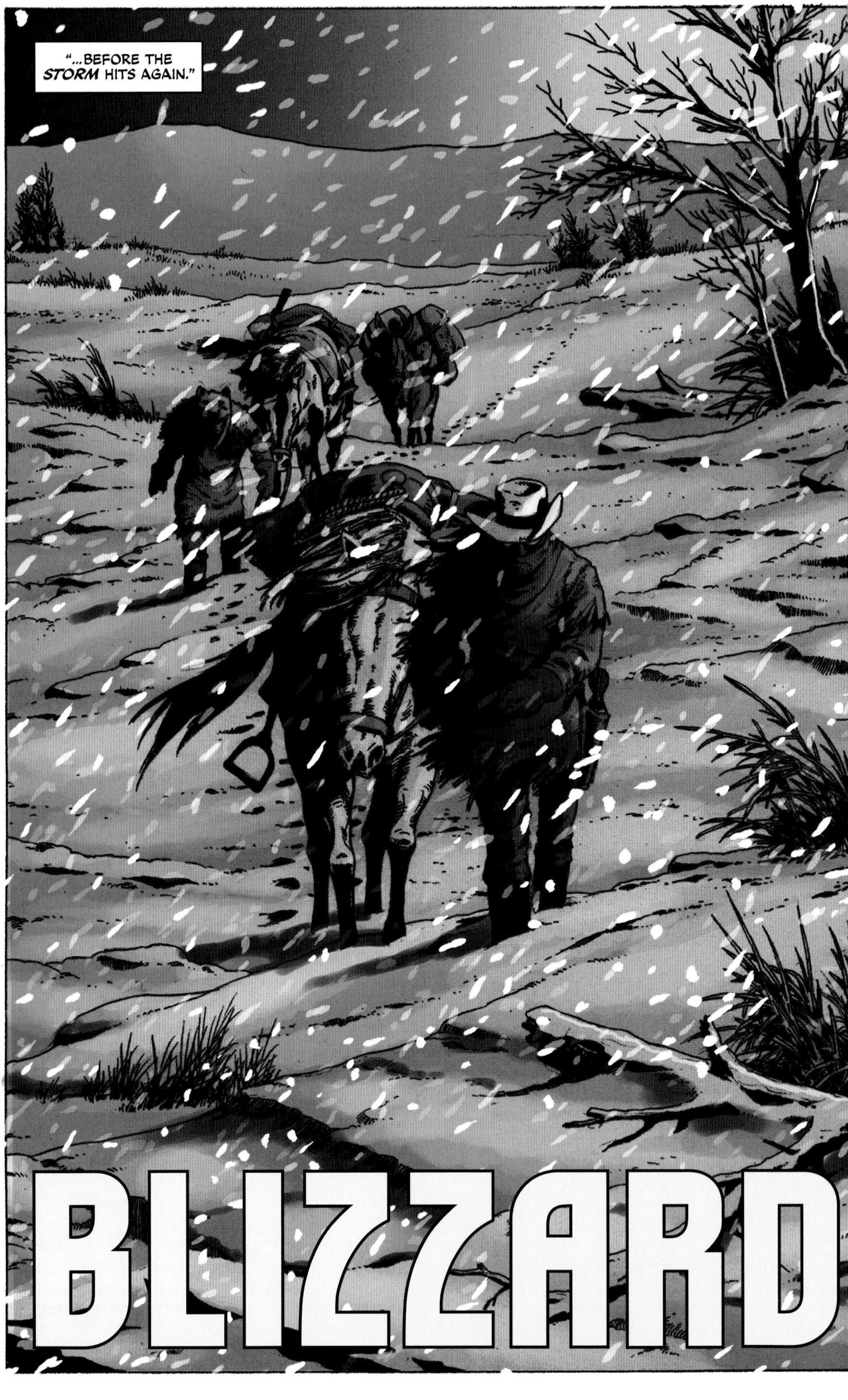
"...BEFORE THE STORM HITS AGAIN."
BLIZZARD

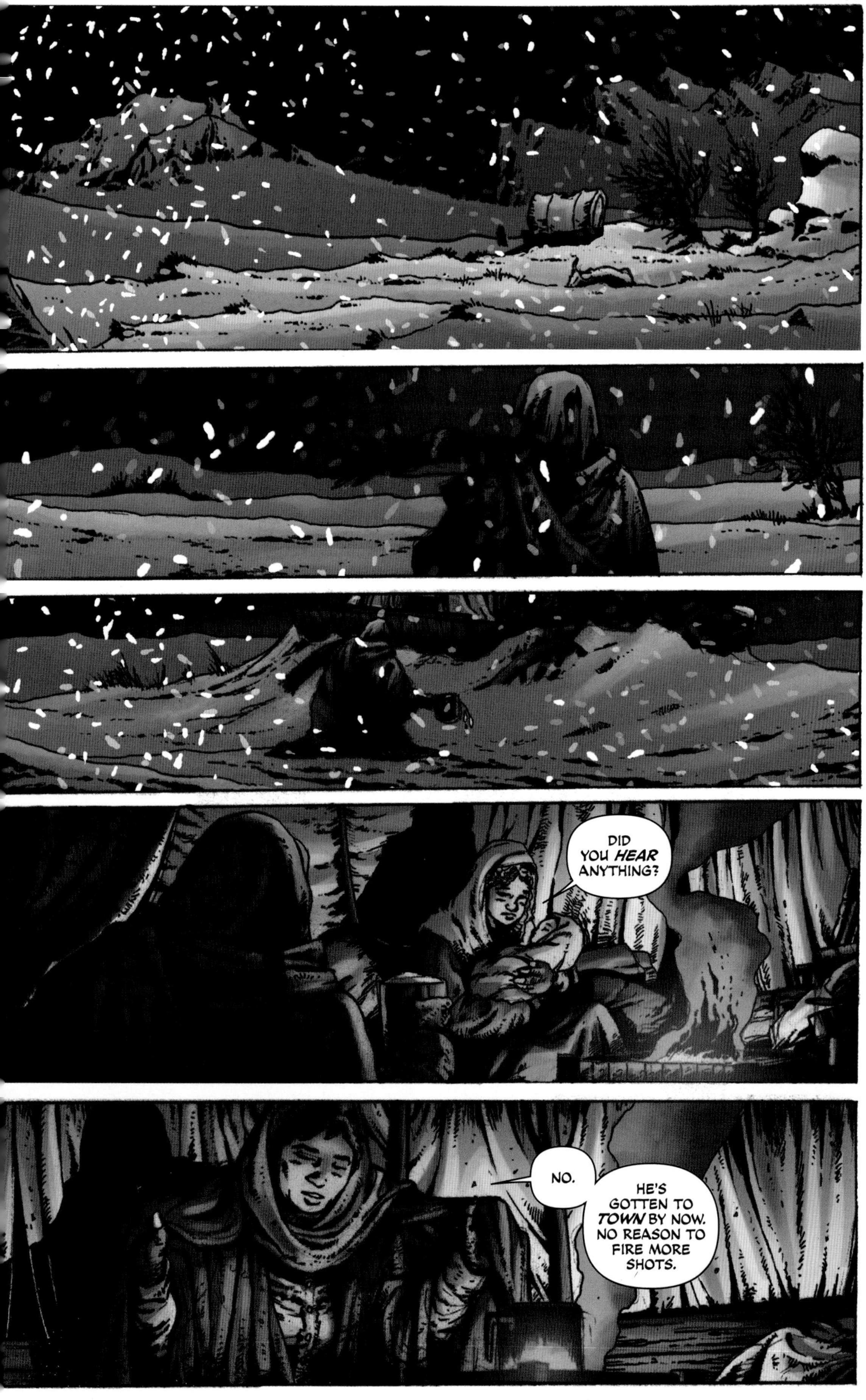
DID YOU *HEAR* ANYTHING?
NO.
HE'S GOTTEN TO *TOWN* BY NOW. NO REASON TO FIRE MORE SHOTS.

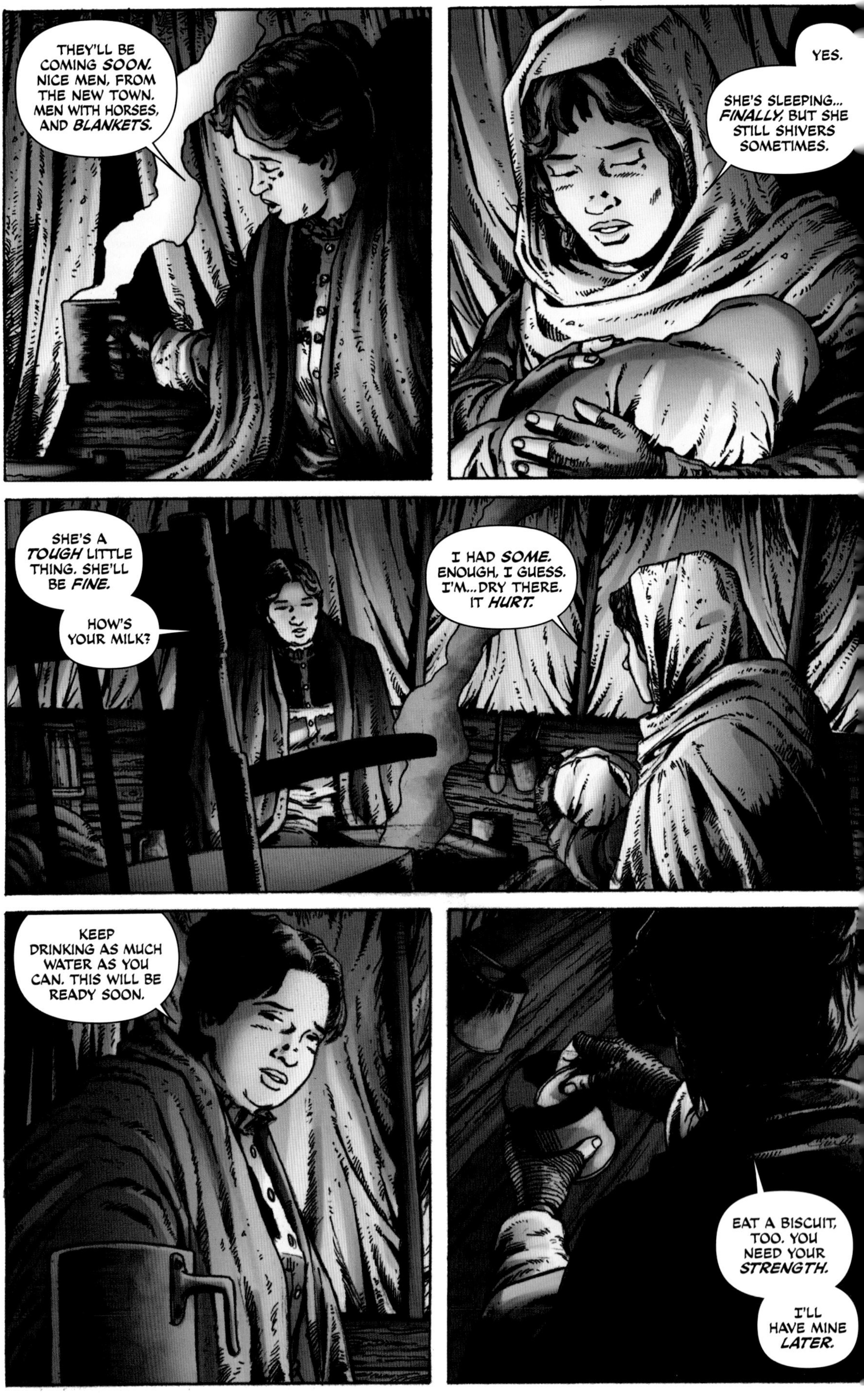
THEY'LL BE COMING SOON. NICE MEN, FROM THE NEW TOWN. MEN WITH HORSES, AND BLANKETS.
YES.
SHE'S SLEEPING... FINALLY, BUT SHE STILL SHIVERS SOMETIMES.
SHE'S A TOUGH LITTLE THING. SHE'LL BE FINE.
HOW'S YOUR MILK?
I HAD SOME. ENOUGH, I GUESS. I'M...DRY THERE. IT HURT.
KEEP DRINKING AS MUCH WATER AS YOU CAN. THIS WILL BE READY SOON.
EAT A BISCUIT, TOO. YOU NEED YOUR STRENGTH.
I'LL HAVE MINE LATER.

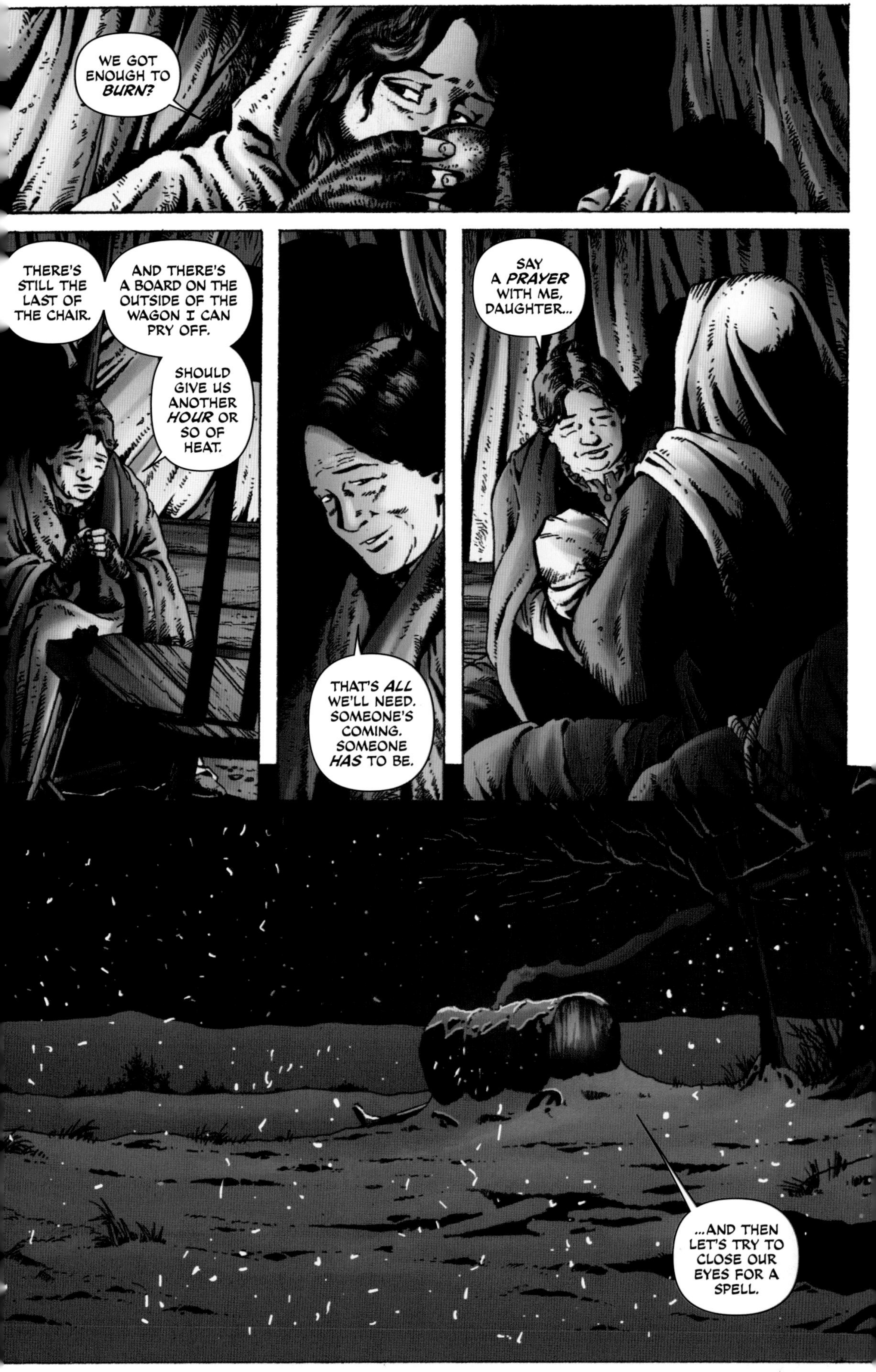
WE GOT ENOUGH TO BURN?
THERE'S STILL THE LAST OF THE CHAIR.
AND THERE'S A BOARD ON THE OUTSIDE OF THE WAGON I CAN PRY OFF.
SHOULD GIVE US ANOTHER HOUR OR SO OF HEAT.
THAT'S ALL WE'LL NEED. SOMEONE'S COMING. SOMEONE HAS TO BE.
SAY A PRAYER WITH ME, DAUGHTER...
...AND THEN LET'S TRY TO CLOSE OUR EYES FOR A SPELL.

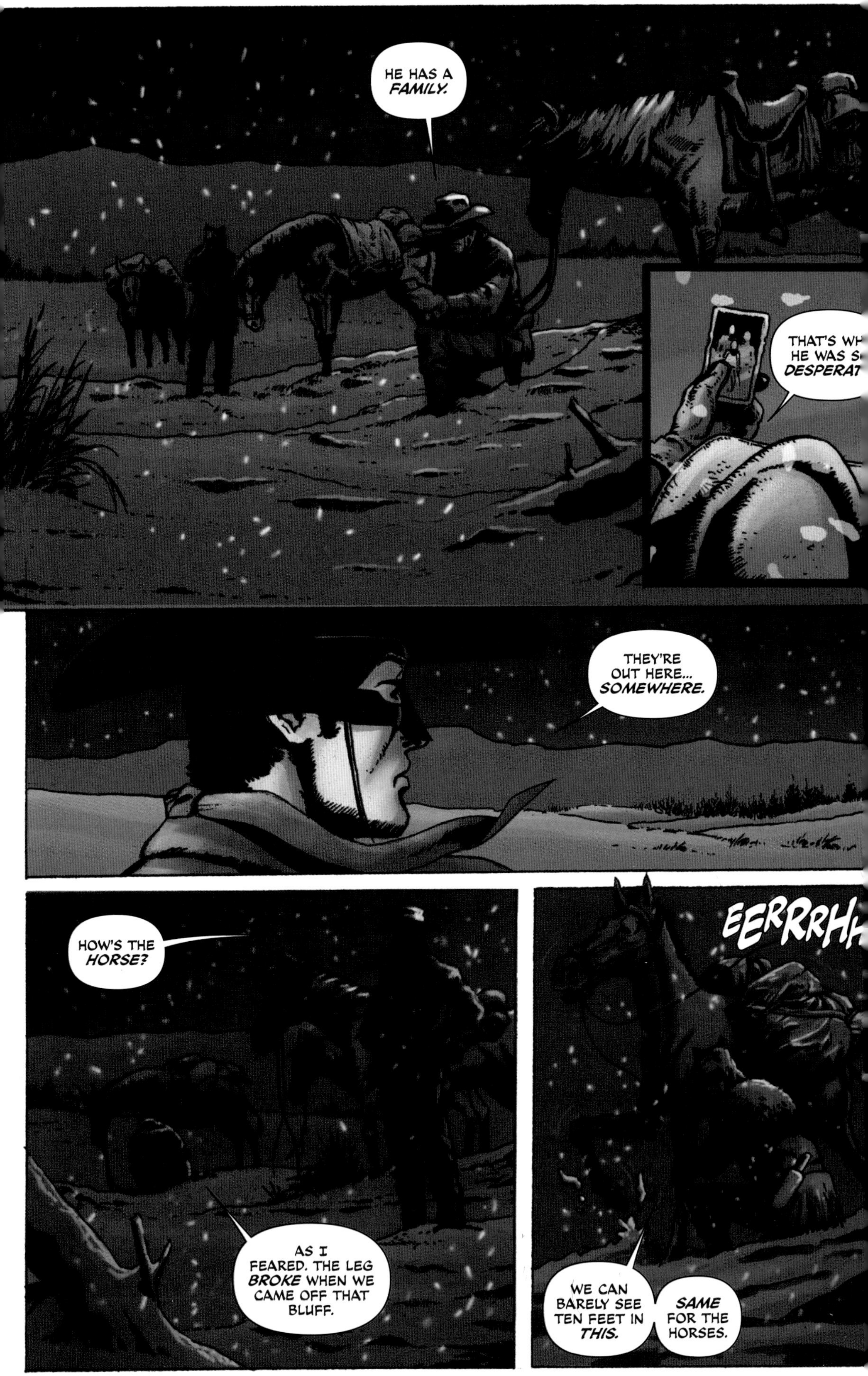
HE HAS A FAMILY.
THAT'S WH HE WAS S DESPERAT
THEY'RE OUT HERE... SOMEWHERE.
HOW'S THE HORSE?
AS I FEARED. THE LEG BROKE WHEN WE CAME OFF THAT BLUFF.
EERRRHH
WE CAN BARELY SEE TEN FEET IN THIS.
SAME FOR THE HORSES.

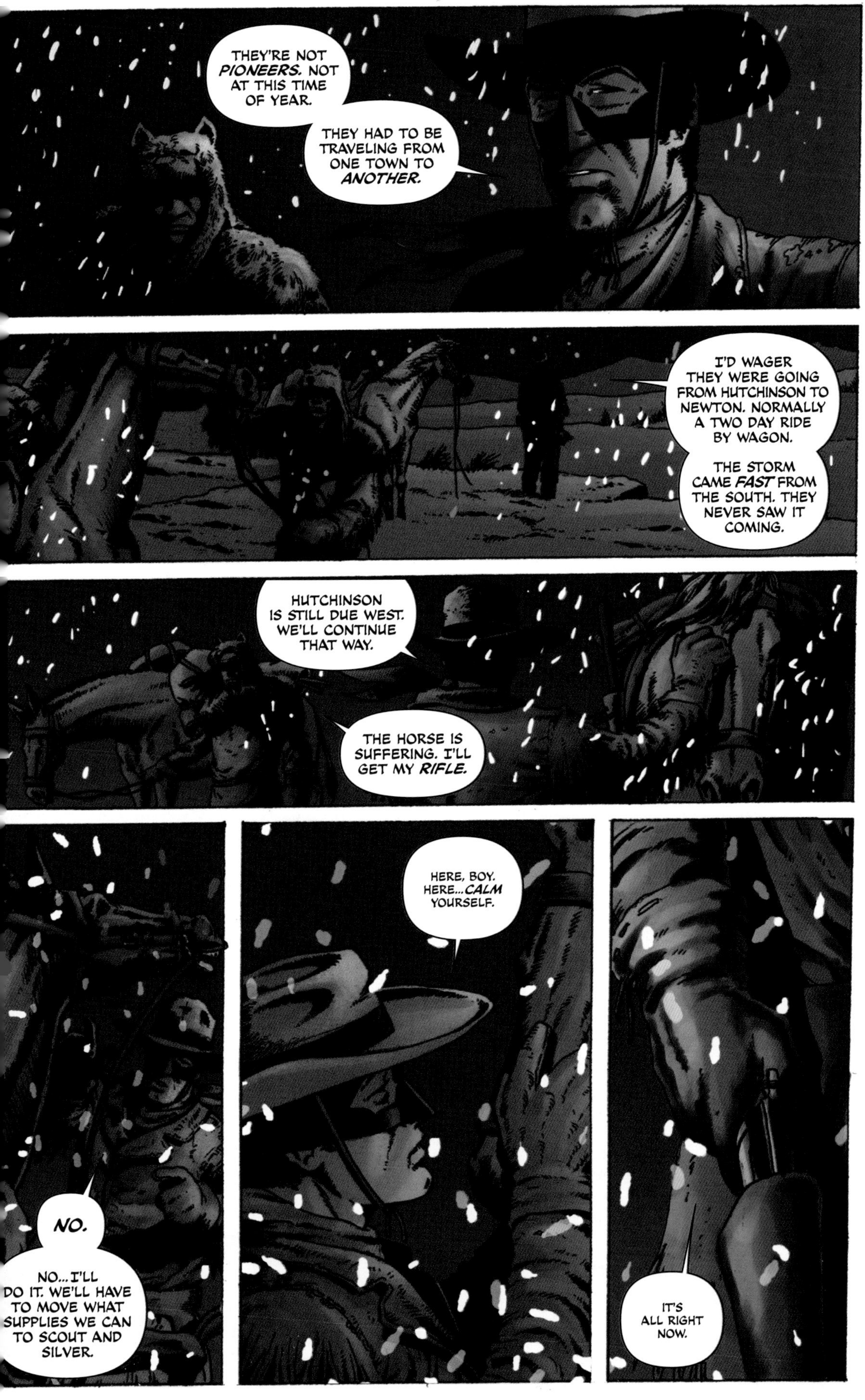
THEY'RE NOT *PIONEERS.* NOT AT THIS TIME OF YEAR.
THEY HAD TO BE TRAVELING FROM ONE TOWN TO *ANOTHER.*
I'D WAGER THEY WERE GOING FROM HUTCHINSON TO NEWTON. NORMALLY A TWO DAY RIDE BY WAGON.
THE STORM CAME *FAST* FROM THE SOUTH. THEY NEVER SAW IT COMING.
HUTCHINSON IS STILL DUE WEST. WE'LL CONTINUE THAT WAY.
THE HORSE IS SUFFERING. I'LL GET MY *RIFLE.*
NO.
NO... I'LL DO IT. WE'LL HAVE TO MOVE WHAT SUPPLIES WE CAN TO SCOUT AND SILVER.
HERE, BOY. HERE... *CALM* YOURSELF.
IT'S ALL RIGHT NOW.

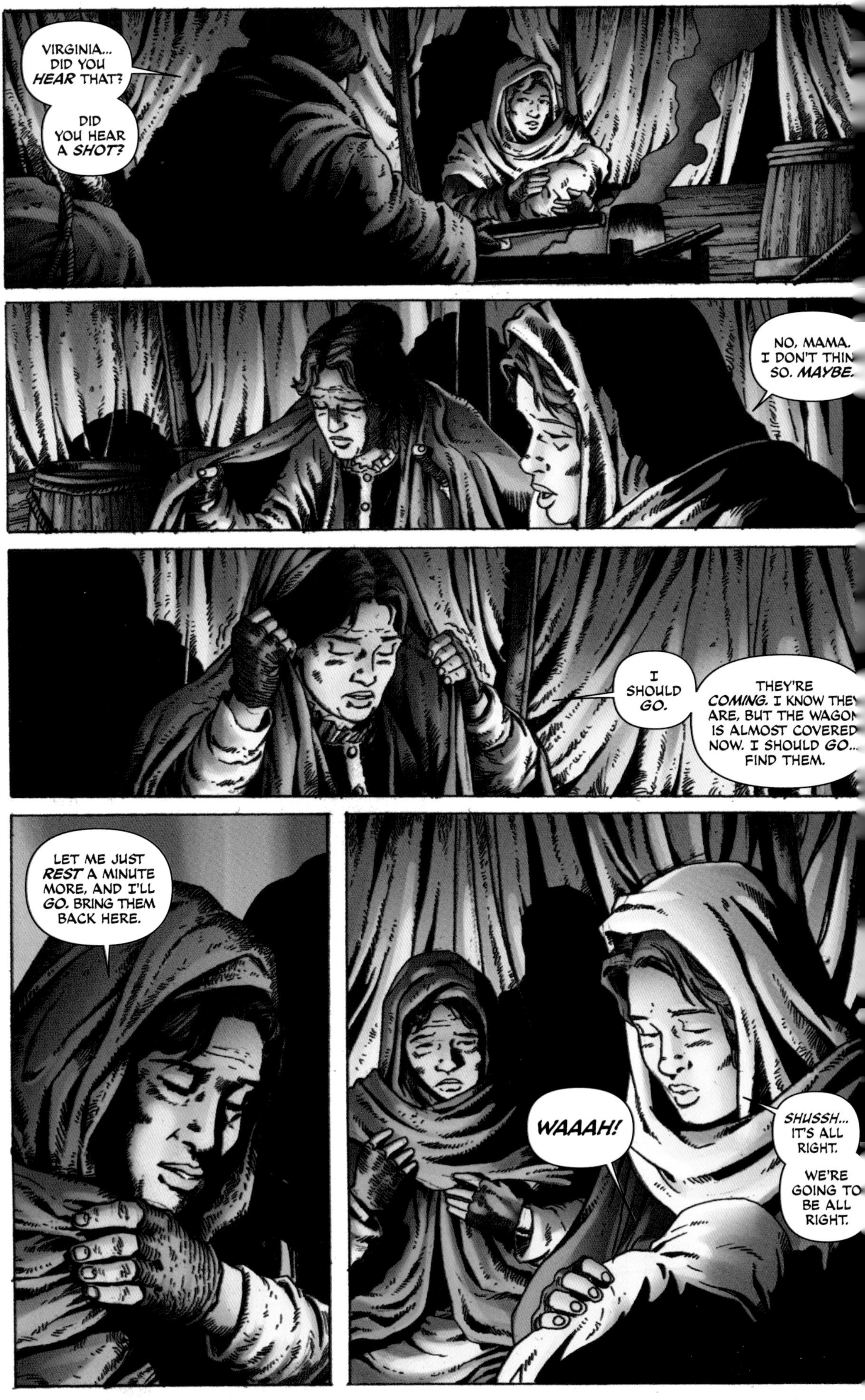
VIRGINIA... DID YOU HEAR THAT?
DID YOU HEAR A SHOT?
NO, MAMA. I DON'T THIN SO. MAYBE.
I SHOULD GO.
THEY'RE COMING. I KNOW THEY ARE, BUT THE WAGON IS ALMOST COVERED NOW. I SHOULD GO... FIND THEM.
LET ME JUST REST A MINUTE MORE, AND I'LL GO. BRING THEM BACK HERE.
WAAAH!
SHUSSH... IT'S ALL RIGHT.
WE'RE GOING TO BE ALL RIGHT.

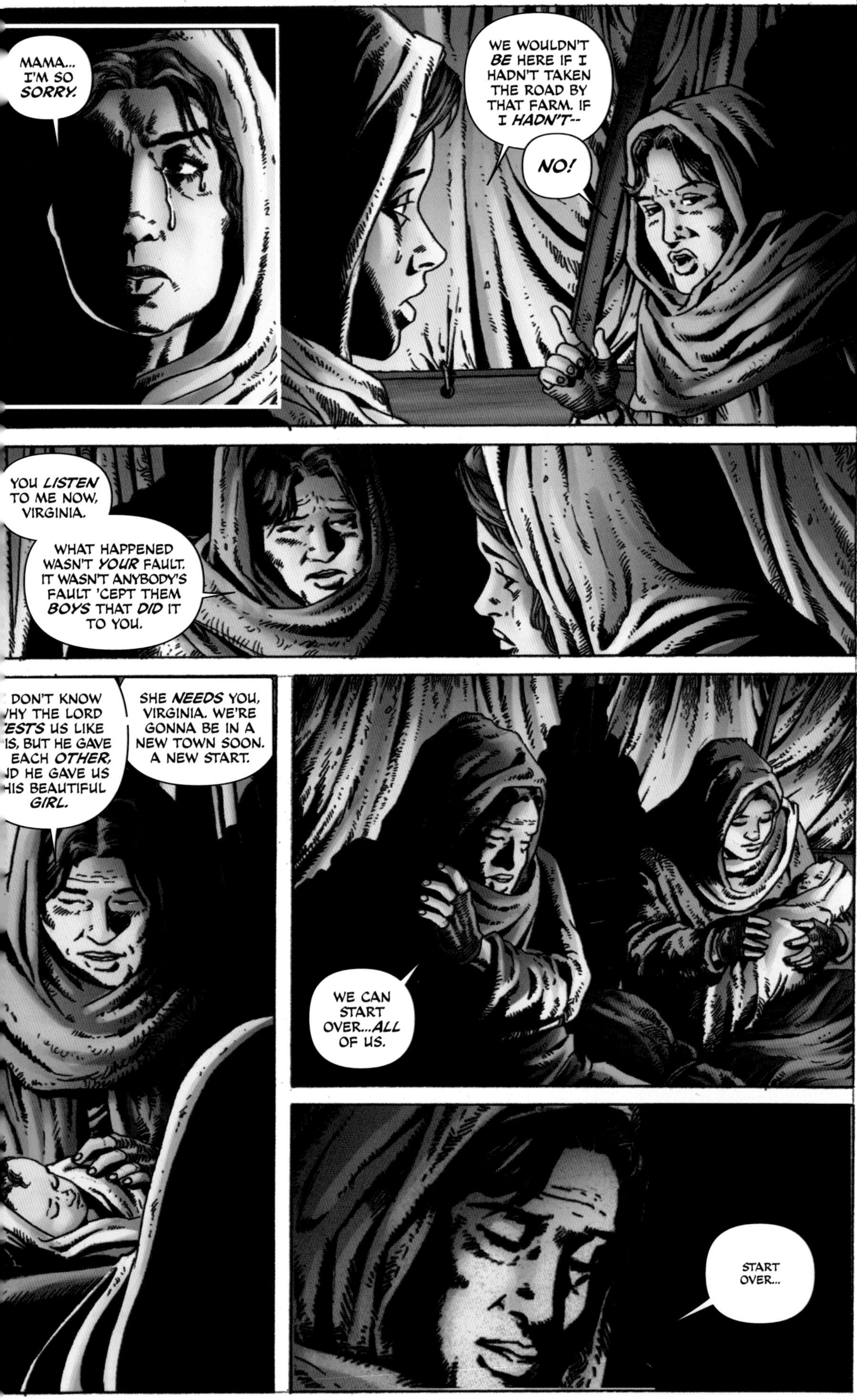
MAMA... I'M SO SORRY.
WE WOULDN'T BE HERE IF I HADN'T TAKEN THE ROAD BY THAT FARM. IF I HADN'T--
NO!
YOU LISTEN TO ME NOW, VIRGINIA.
WHAT HAPPENED WASN'T YOUR FAULT. IT WASN'T ANYBODY'S FAULT 'CEPT THEM BOYS THAT DID IT TO YOU.
DON'T KNOW HY THE LORD ESTS US LIKE IS, BUT HE GAVE EACH OTHER, ID HE GAVE US HIS BEAUTIFUL GIRL.
SHE NEEDS YOU, VIRGINIA. WE'RE GONNA BE IN A NEW TOWN SOON. A NEW START.
WE CAN START OVER...ALL OF US.
START OVER...

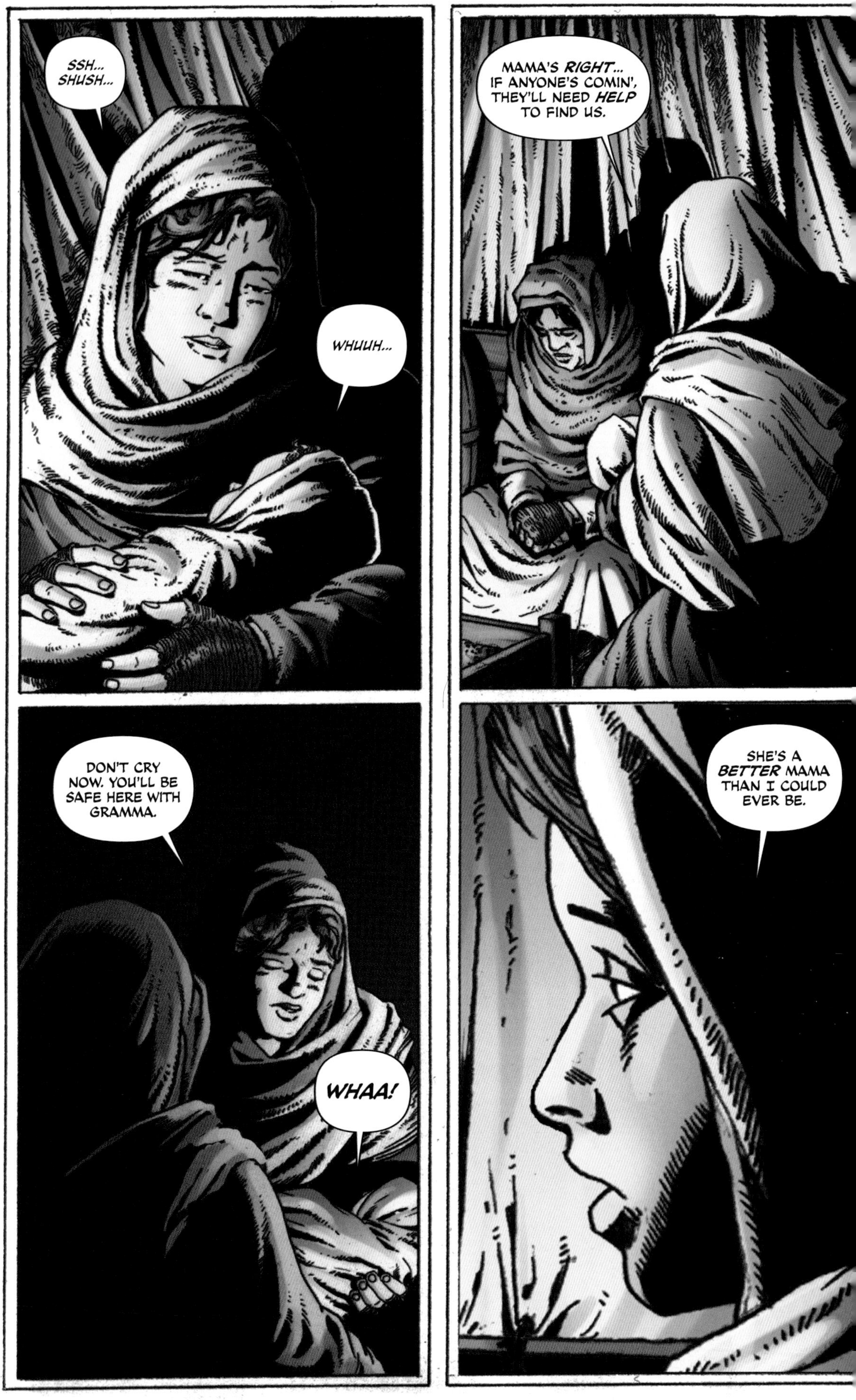
SSH... SHUSH...
WHUUH...
MAMA'S RIGHT... IF ANYONE'S COMIN', THEY'LL NEED HELP TO FIND US.
DON'T CRY NOW. YOU'LL BE SAFE HERE WITH GRAMMA.
WHAA!
SHE'S A BETTER MAMA THAN I COULD EVER BE.

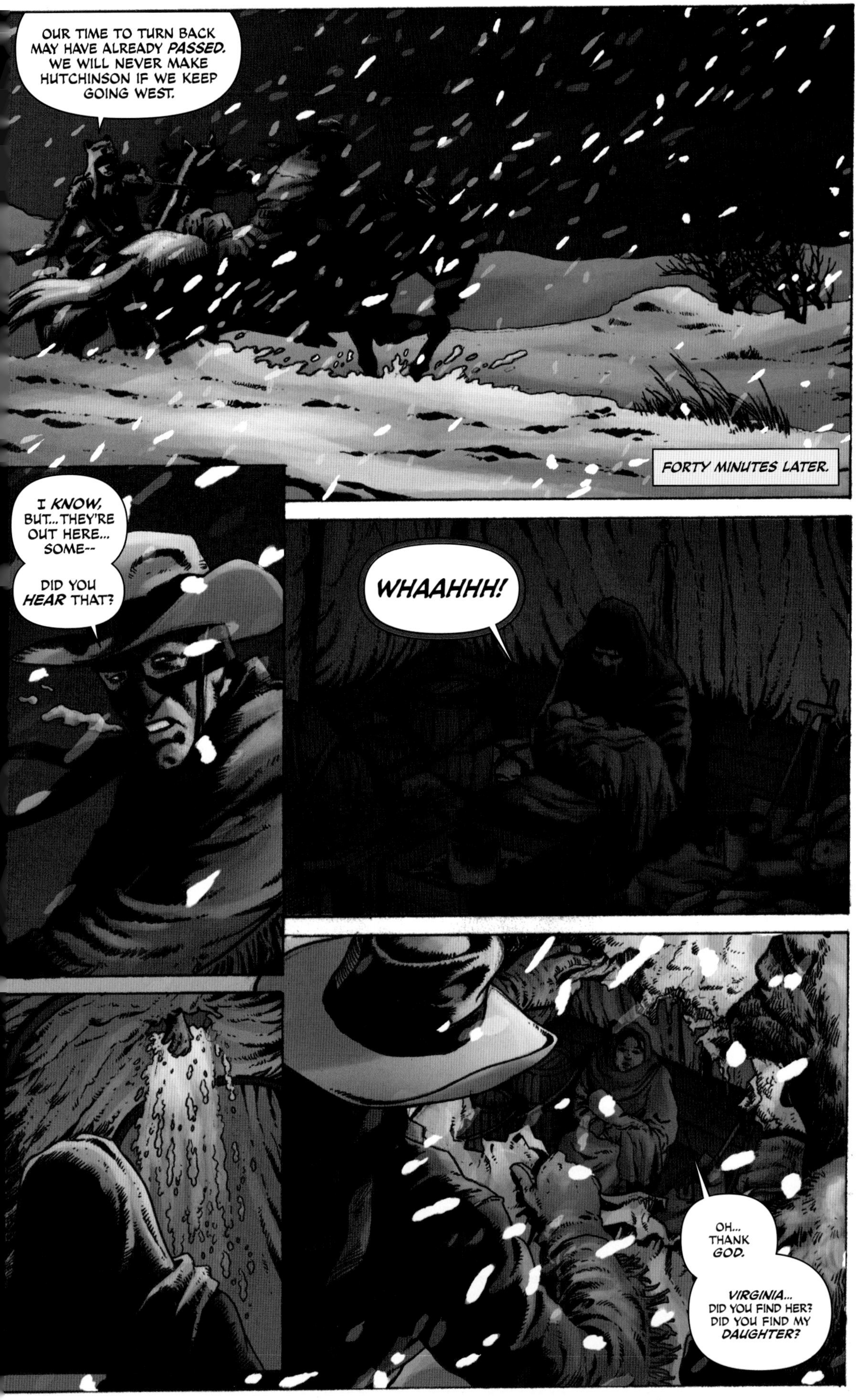
OUR TIME TO TURN BACK MAY HAVE ALREADY *PASSED.* WE WILL NEVER MAKE HUTCHINSON IF WE KEEP GOING WEST.
FORTY MINUTES LATER.
I *KNOW,* BUT... THEY'RE OUT HERE... SOME--
DID YOU *HEAR* THAT?
WHAAHHH!
OH... THANK *GOD.*
VIRGINIA... DID YOU FIND HER? DID YOU FIND MY *DAUGHTER?*

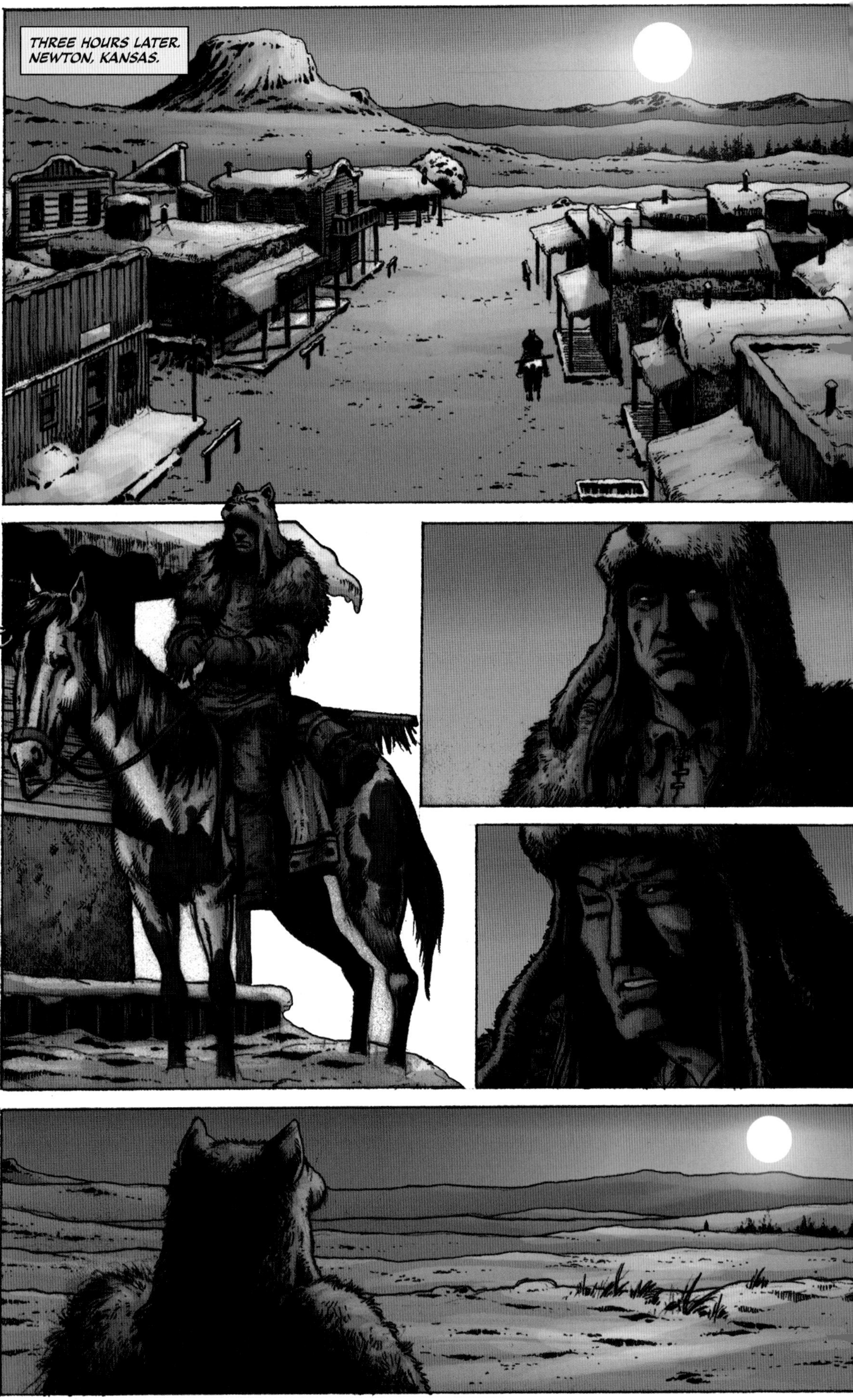
THREE HOURS LATER. NEWTON, KANSAS.

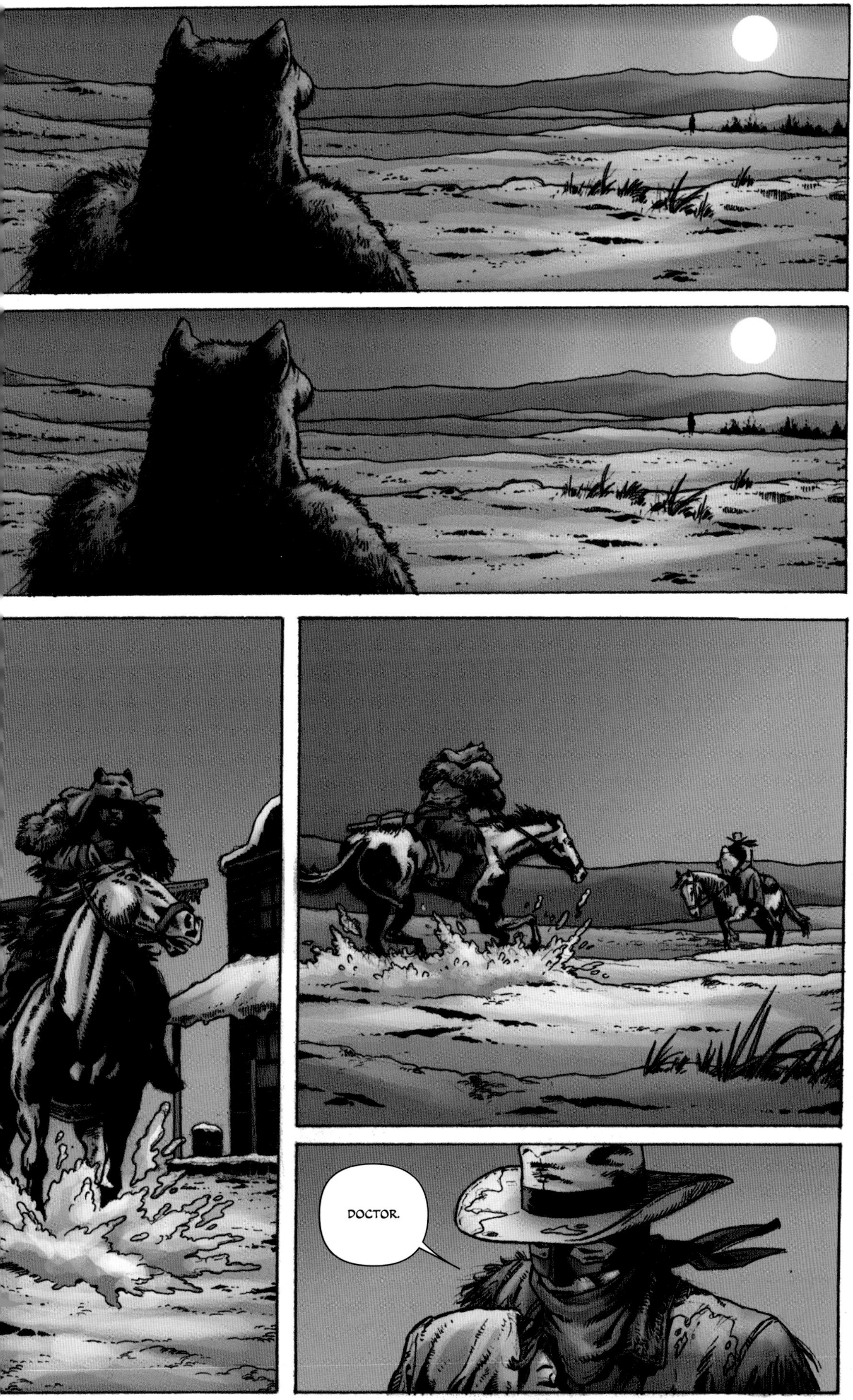
DOCTOR.

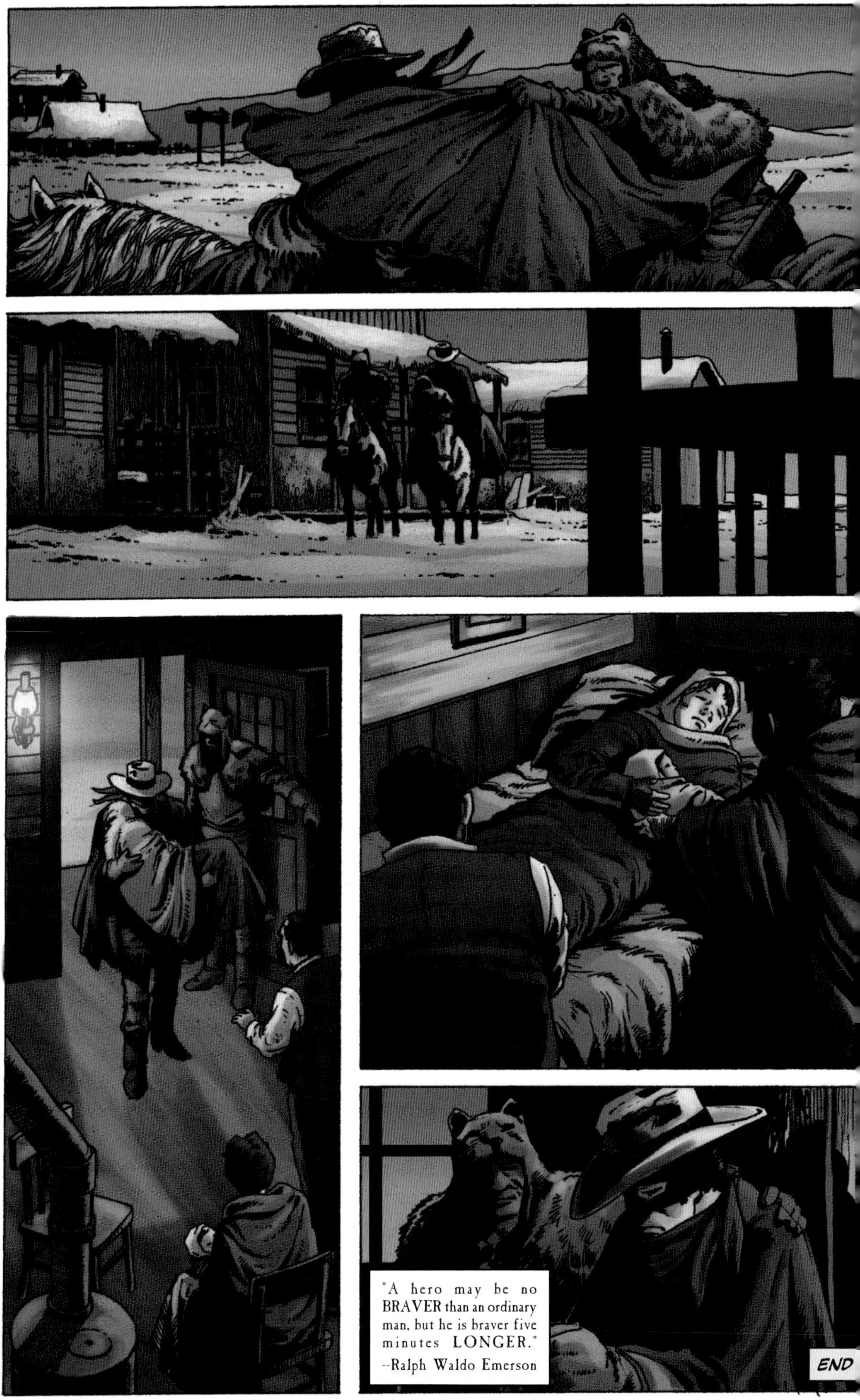
"A hero may be no BRAVER than an ordinary man, but he is braver five minutes LONGER."
--Ralph Waldo Emerson
END

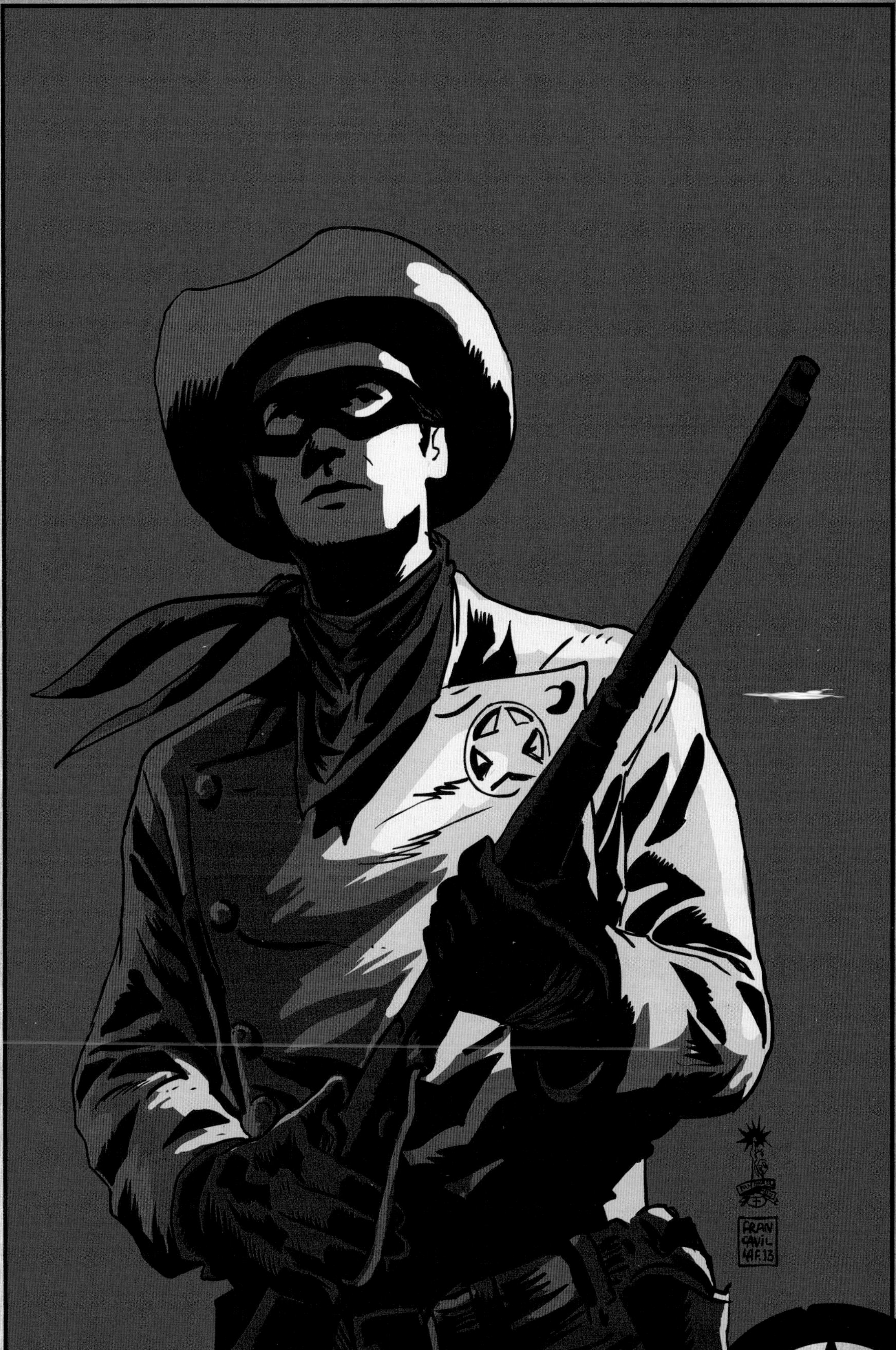

COVER BY **FRANCESCO FRANCAVILLA**

22

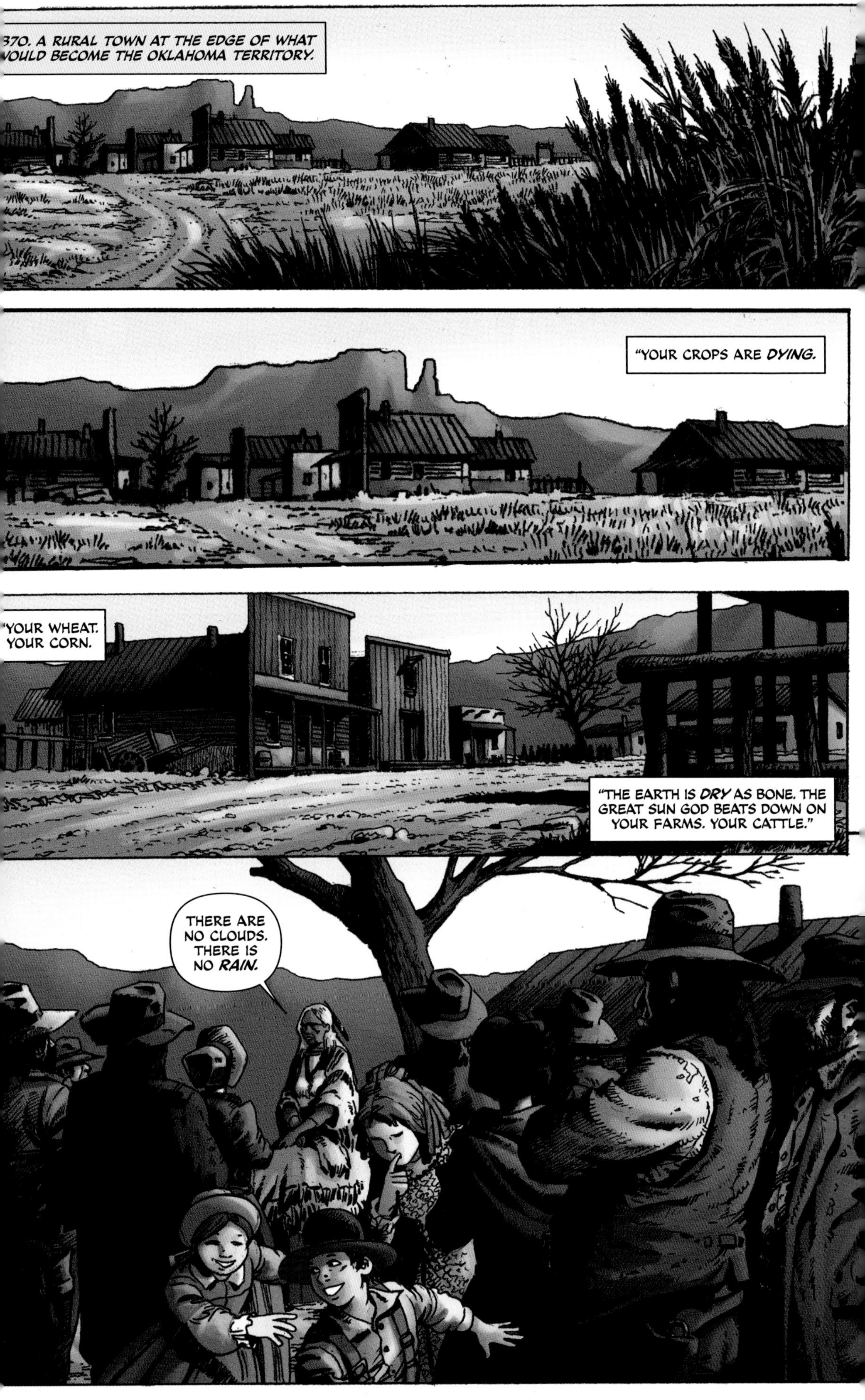

370. A RURAL TOWN AT THE EDGE OF WHAT
VOULD BECOME THE OKLAHOMA TERRITORY.
"YOUR CROPS ARE DYING.
"YOUR WHEAT. YOUR CORN.
"THE EARTH IS DRY AS BONE. THE GREAT SUN GOD BEATS DOWN ON YOUR FARMS. YOUR CATTLE."
THERE ARE NO CLOUDS. THERE IS NO RAIN.

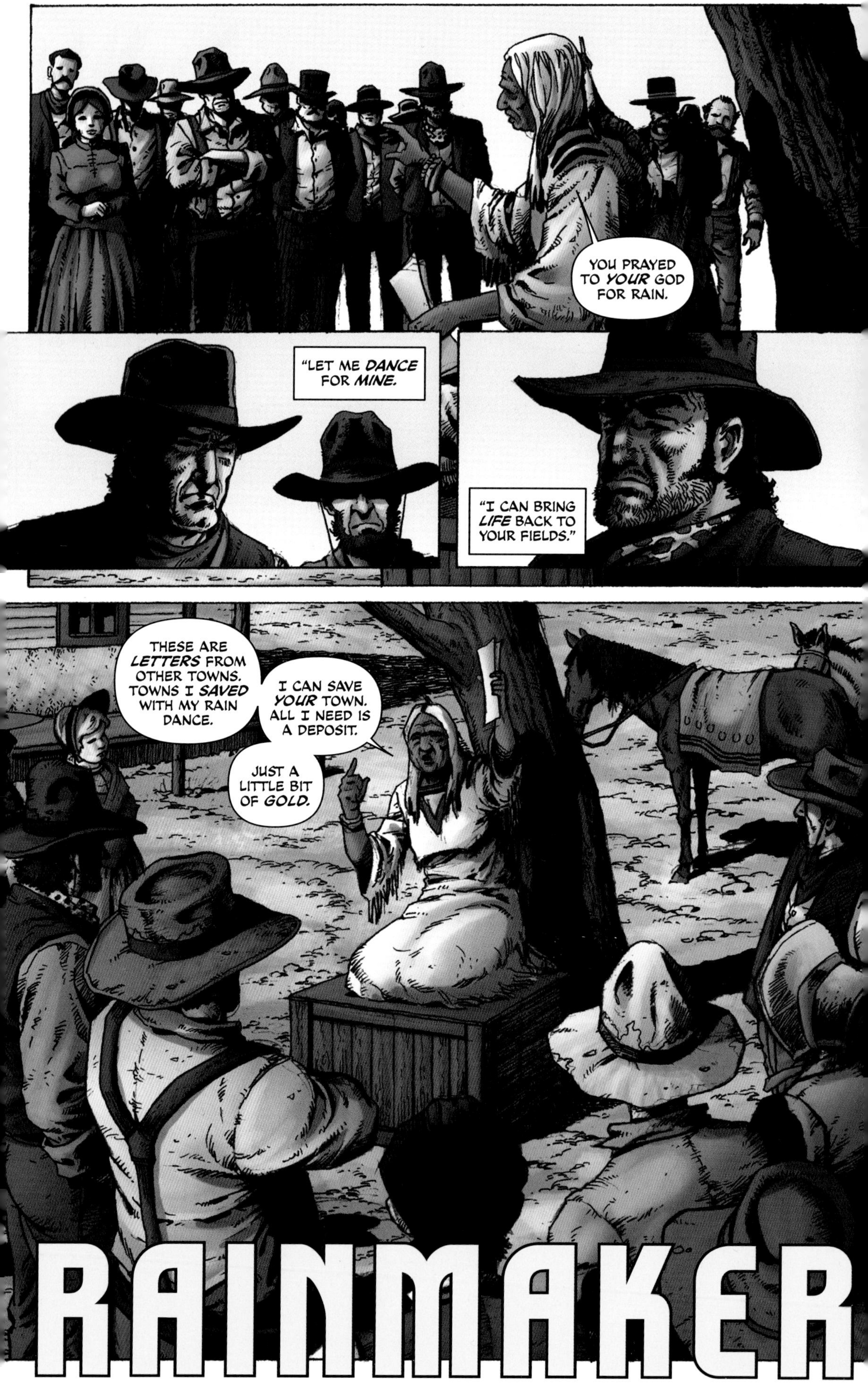
YOU PRAYED TO *YOUR* GOD FOR RAIN.
"LET ME *DANCE* FOR *MINE.*
"I CAN BRING *LIFE* BACK TO YOUR FIELDS."
THESE ARE *LETTERS* FROM OTHER TOWNS. TOWNS I *SAVED* WITH MY RAIN DANCE.
I CAN SAVE *YOUR* TOWN. ALL I NEED IS A DEPOSIT.
JUST A LITTLE BIT OF *GOLD.*
RAINMAKER

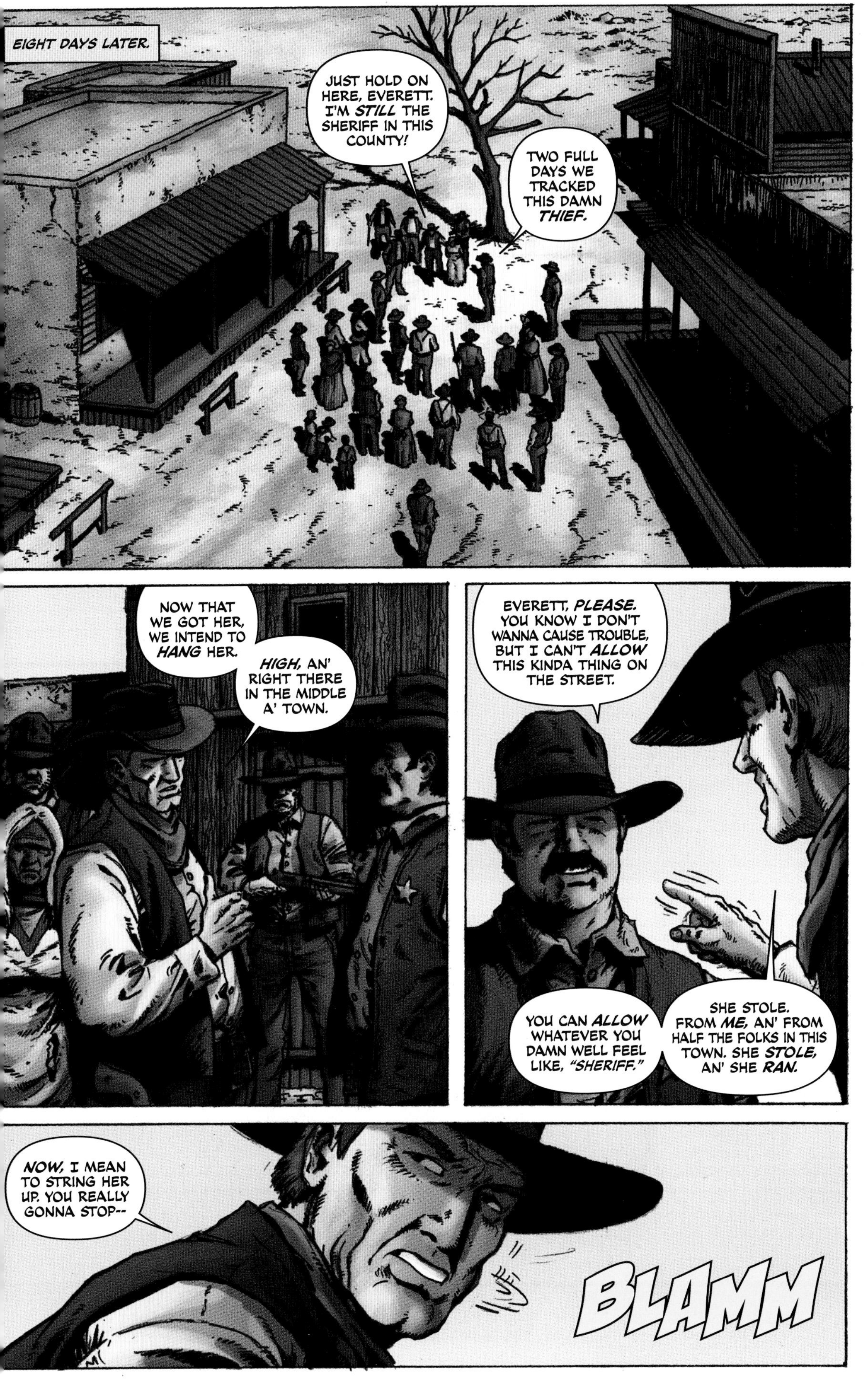
EIGHT DAYS LATER.
JUST HOLD ON HERE, EVERETT. I'M STILL THE SHERIFF IN THIS COUNTY!
TWO FULL DAYS WE TRACKED THIS DAMN THIEF.
NOW THAT WE GOT HER, WE INTEND TO HANG HER.
HIGH, AN' RIGHT THERE IN THE MIDDLE A' TOWN.
EVERETT, PLEASE. YOU KNOW I DON'T WANNA CAUSE TROUBLE, BUT I CAN'T ALLOW THIS KINDA THING ON THE STREET.
SHE STOLE. FROM ME, AN' FROM HALF THE FOLKS IN THIS TOWN. SHE STOLE, AN' SHE RAN.
YOU CAN ALLOW WHATEVER YOU DAMN WELL FEEL LIKE, "SHERIFF."
NOW, I MEAN TO STRING HER UP. YOU REALLY GONNA STOP--
BLAMM

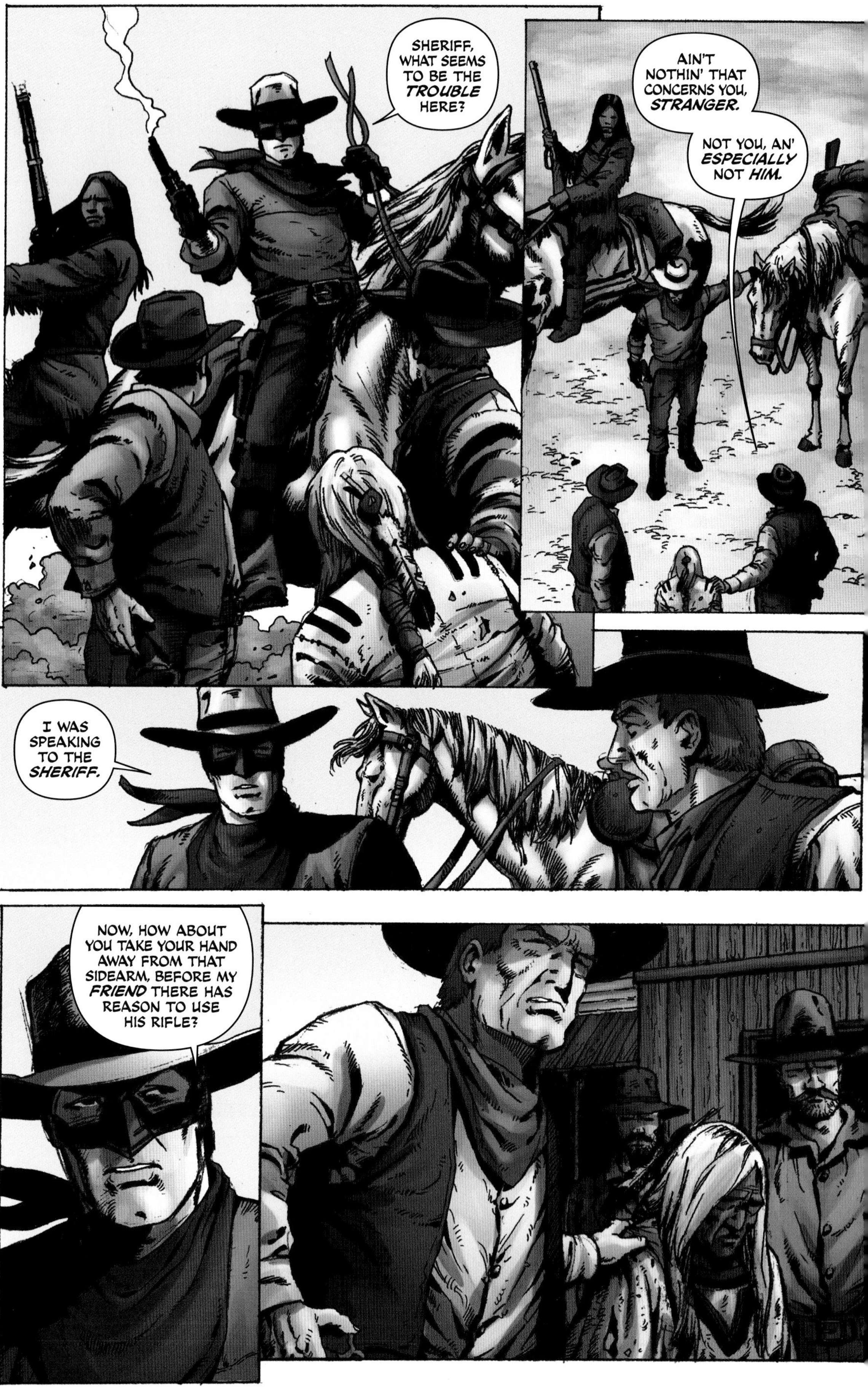

SHERIFF, WHAT SEEMS TO BE THE TROUBLE HERE?
AIN'T NOTHIN' THAT CONCERNS YOU, STRANGER.
NOT YOU, AN' ESPECIALLY NOT HIM.
I WAS SPEAKING TO THE SHERIFF.
NOW, HOW ABOUT YOU TAKE YOUR HAND AWAY FROM THAT SIDEARM, BEFORE MY FRIEND THERE HAS REASON TO USE HIS RIFLE?

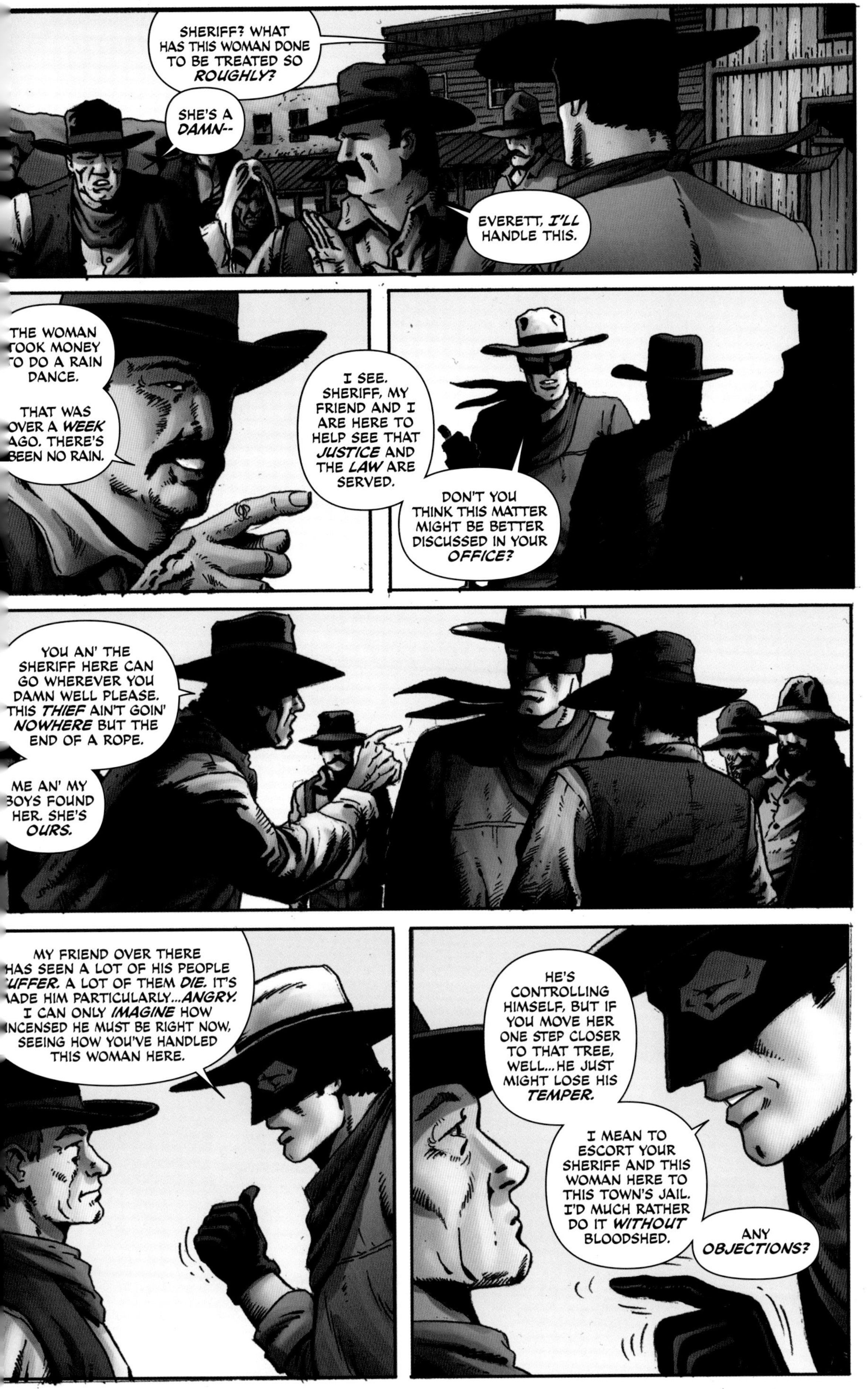

SHERIFF? WHAT HAS THIS WOMAN DONE TO BE TREATED SO *ROUGHLY?*
SHE'S A *DAMN--*
EVERETT, *I'LL* HANDLE THIS.
THE WOMAN TOOK MONEY TO DO A RAIN DANCE.
THAT WAS OVER A *WEEK* AGO. THERE'S BEEN NO RAIN.
I SEE. SHERIFF, MY FRIEND AND I ARE HERE TO HELP SEE THAT *JUSTICE* AND THE *LAW* ARE SERVED.
DON'T YOU THINK THIS MATTER MIGHT BE BETTER DISCUSSED IN YOUR *OFFICE?*
YOU AN' THE SHERIFF HERE CAN GO WHEREVER YOU DAMN WELL PLEASE. THIS *THIEF* AIN'T GOIN' *NOWHERE* BUT THE END OF A ROPE.
ME AN' MY BOYS FOUND HER. SHE'S *OURS.*
MY FRIEND OVER THERE HAS SEEN A LOT OF HIS PEOPLE SUFFER. A LOT OF THEM *DIE.* IT'S MADE HIM PARTICULARLY...*ANGRY.* I CAN ONLY *IMAGINE* HOW INCENSED HE MUST BE RIGHT NOW, SEEING HOW YOU'VE HANDLED THIS WOMAN HERE.
HE'S CONTROLLING HIMSELF, BUT IF YOU MOVE HER ONE STEP CLOSER TO THAT TREE, WELL...HE JUST MIGHT LOSE HIS *TEMPER.*
I MEAN TO ESCORT YOUR SHERIFF AND THIS WOMAN HERE TO THIS TOWN'S JAIL. I'D MUCH RATHER DO IT *WITHOUT* BLOODSHED.
ANY *OBJECTIONS?*

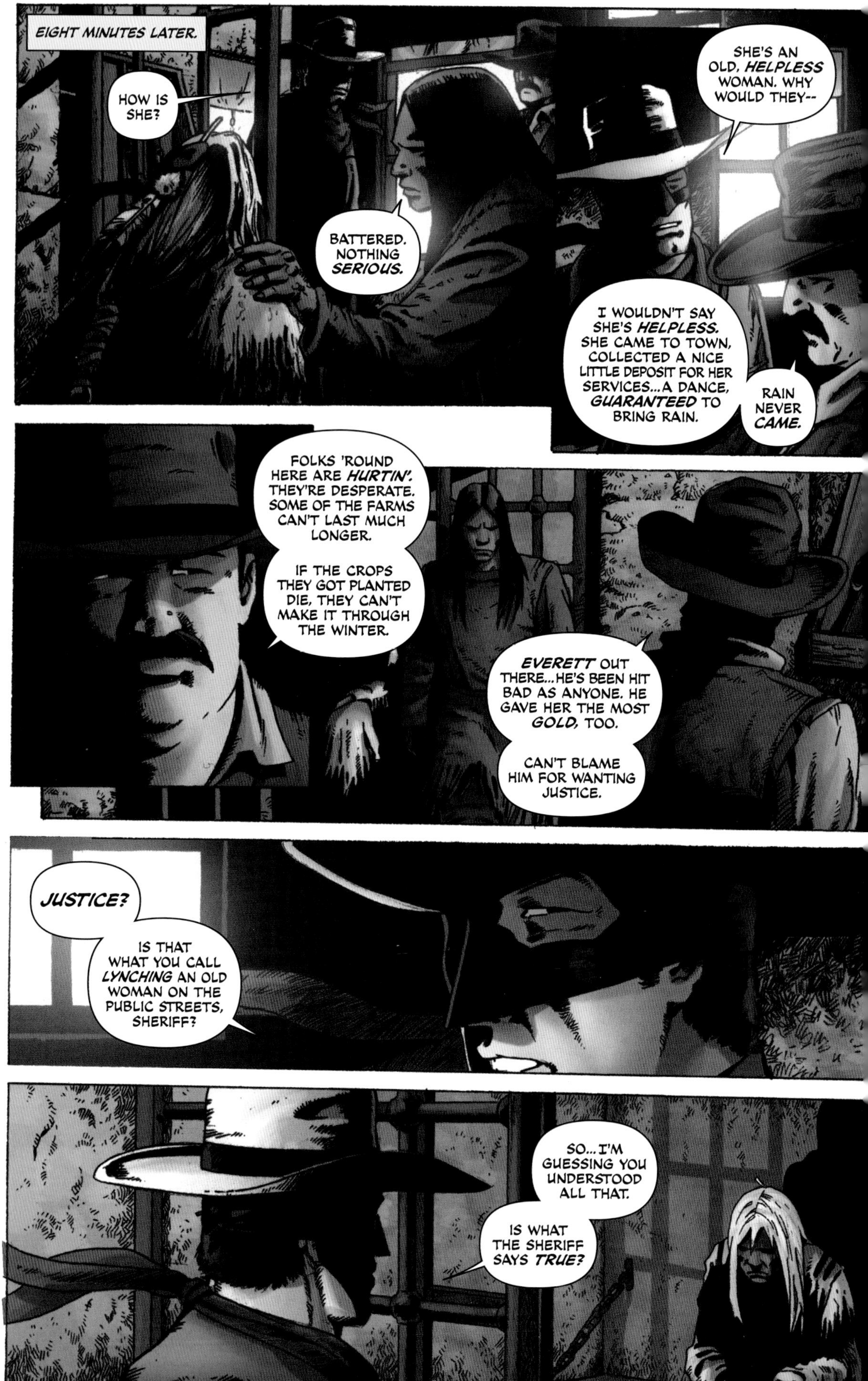
EIGHT MINUTES LATER.
HOW IS SHE?
BATTERED. NOTHING *SERIOUS.*
SHE'S AN OLD, *HELPLESS* WOMAN. WHY WOULD THEY--
I WOULDN'T SAY SHE'S *HELPLESS.* SHE CAME TO TOWN, COLLECTED A NICE LITTLE DEPOSIT FOR HER SERVICES...A DANCE, *GUARANTEED* TO BRING RAIN.
RAIN NEVER *CAME.*
FOLKS 'ROUND HERE ARE *HURTIN'.* THEY'RE DESPERATE. SOME OF THE FARMS CAN'T LAST MUCH LONGER.
IF THE CROPS THEY GOT PLANTED DIE, THEY CAN'T MAKE IT THROUGH THE WINTER.
EVERETT OUT THERE...HE'S BEEN HIT BAD AS ANYONE. HE GAVE HER THE MOST *GOLD,* TOO.
CAN'T BLAME HIM FOR WANTING JUSTICE.
JUSTICE?
IS THAT WHAT YOU CALL *LYNCHING* AN OLD WOMAN ON THE PUBLIC STREETS, SHERIFF?
SO... I'M GUESSING YOU UNDERSTOOD ALL THAT.
IS WHAT THE SHERIFF SAYS *TRUE?*

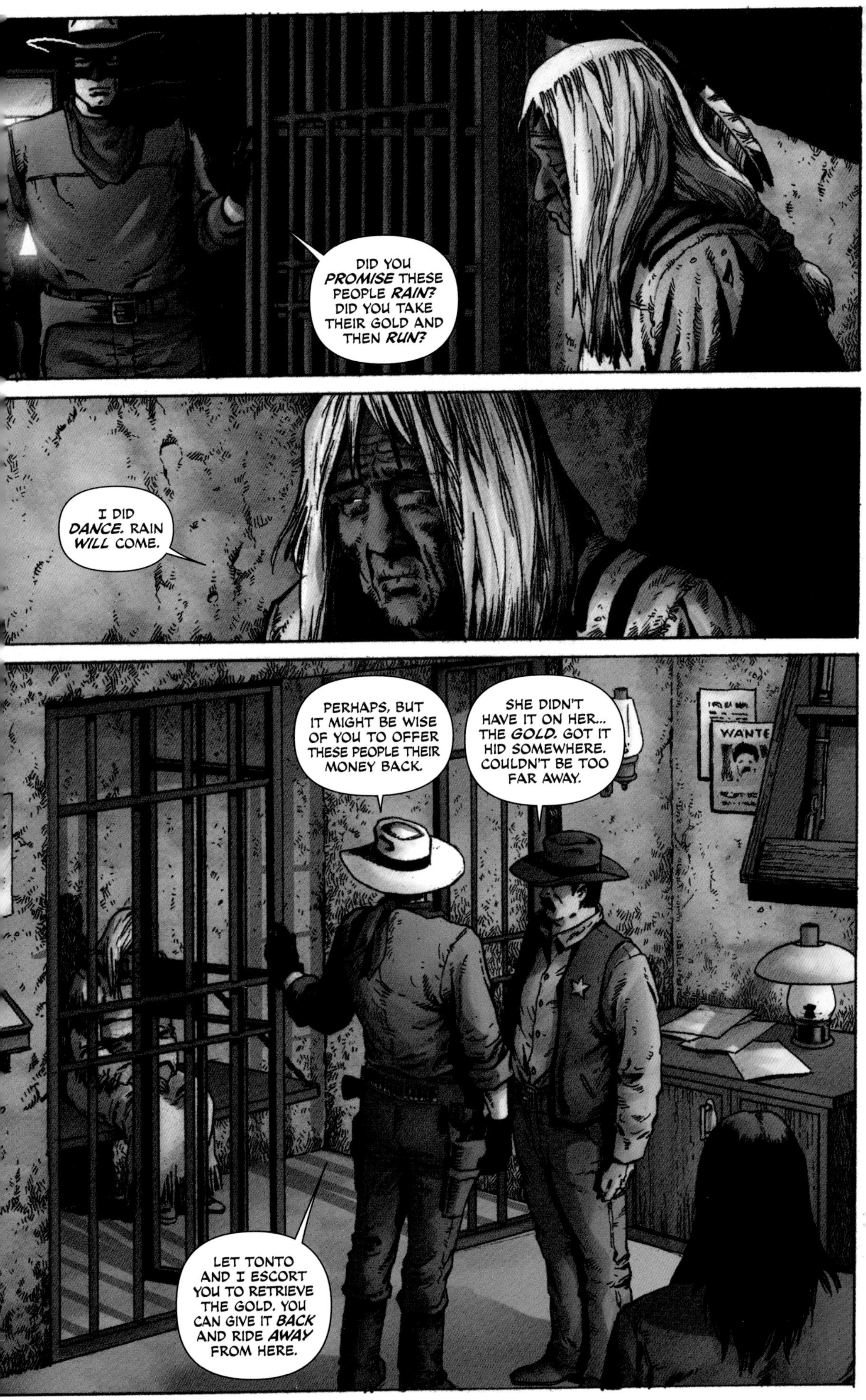
DID YOU PROMISE THESE PEOPLE RAIN? DID YOU TAKE THEIR GOLD AND THEN RUN?
I DID DANCE. RAIN WILL COME.
PERHAPS, BUT IT MIGHT BE WISE OF YOU TO OFFER THESE PEOPLE THEIR MONEY BACK.
SHE DIDN'T HAVE IT ON HER... THE GOLD. GOT IT HID SOMEWHERE. COULDN'T BE TOO FAR AWAY.
WANTE
LET TONTO AND I ESCORT YOU TO RETRIEVE THE GOLD. YOU CAN GIVE IT BACK AND RIDE AWAY FROM HERE.

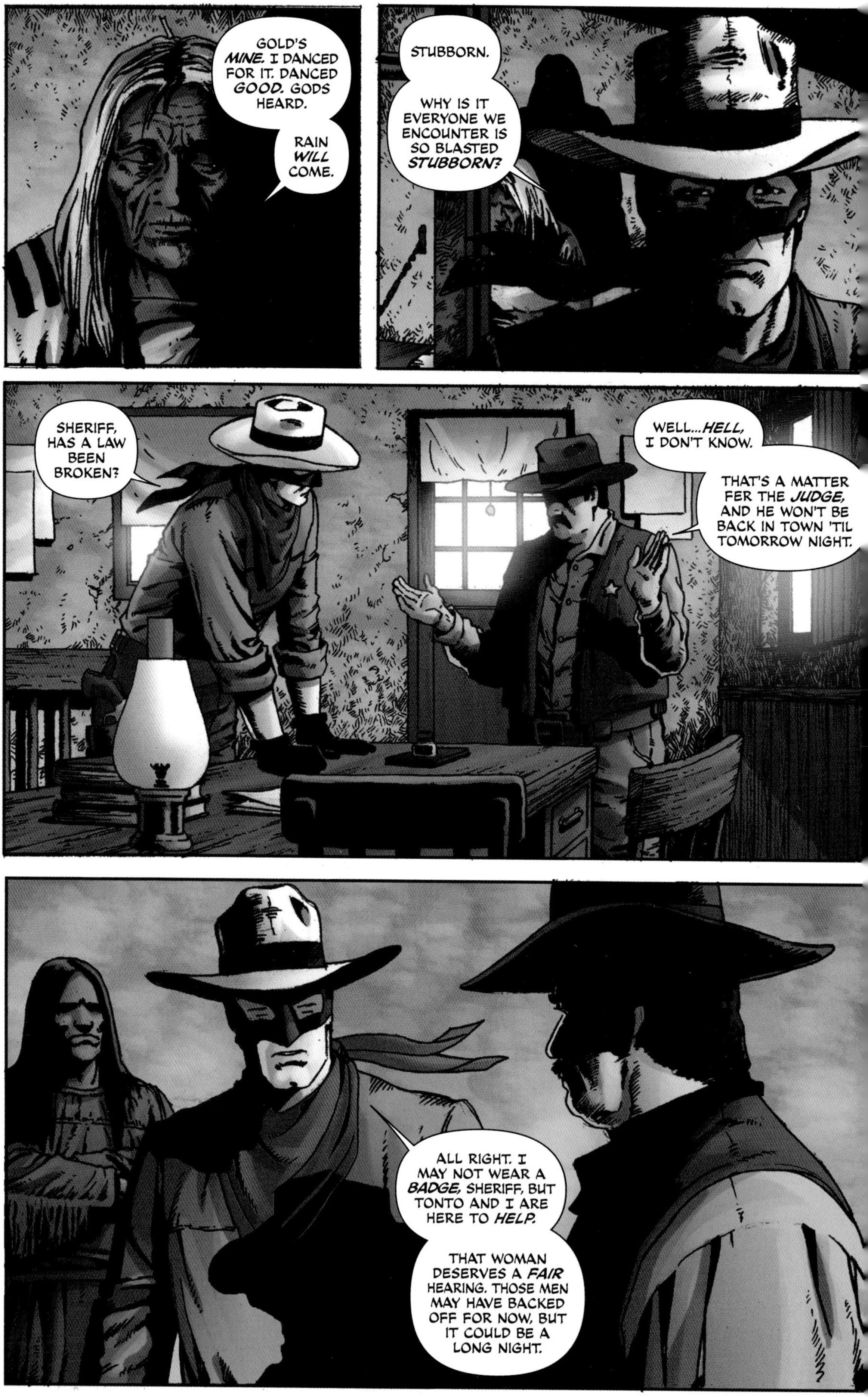
GOLD'S *MINE.* I DANCED FOR IT. DANCED *GOOD.* GODS HEARD.
RAIN *WILL* COME.
STUBBORN.
WHY IS IT EVERYONE WE ENCOUNTER IS SO BLASTED *STUBBORN?*
SHERIFF, HAS A LAW BEEN BROKEN?
WELL...*HELL,* I DON'T KNOW.
THAT'S A MATTER FER THE *JUDGE,* AND HE WON'T BE BACK IN TOWN 'TIL TOMORROW NIGHT.
ALL RIGHT. I MAY NOT WEAR A *BADGE,* SHERIFF, BUT TONTO AND I ARE HERE TO *HELP.*
THAT WOMAN DESERVES A *FAIR* HEARING. THOSE MEN MAY HAVE BACKED OFF FOR NOW, BUT IT COULD BE A LONG NIGHT.

DAMN WITCH PLAYIN' US FER *FOOLS* AND RUNNIN' OFF WITH OUR MONEY IS BAD ENOUGH.

NOW THIS MASKED MAN SHOWS UP, WITH HIS RED-FACED FRIEND.

YOU THINK THAT'S AN *ACCIDENT?*

WHAT'RE YOU SAYIN', EVERETT?

YOU GOT A DAMN *BRAIN* IN THAT HEAD OF YOURS, AIN'T YA?

THEY'RE ALL IN IT *TOGETHER!*

SHE COMES IN HERE, WAVIN' REFERENCES AROUND, PROMISIN' *RESULTS.*

DOES HER LITTLE *JIG* AND OFF SHE GOES. AN' IF SHE GETS CAUGHT, HER FRIENDS COME RIGHT ALONG AND PULL HER RIGHT OUTTA THE *NOOSE.*

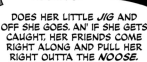

YOU THINK THEY'LL BE 'ROUND IN THE MORNING? NOT DAMN *LIKELY* THEY WON'T!

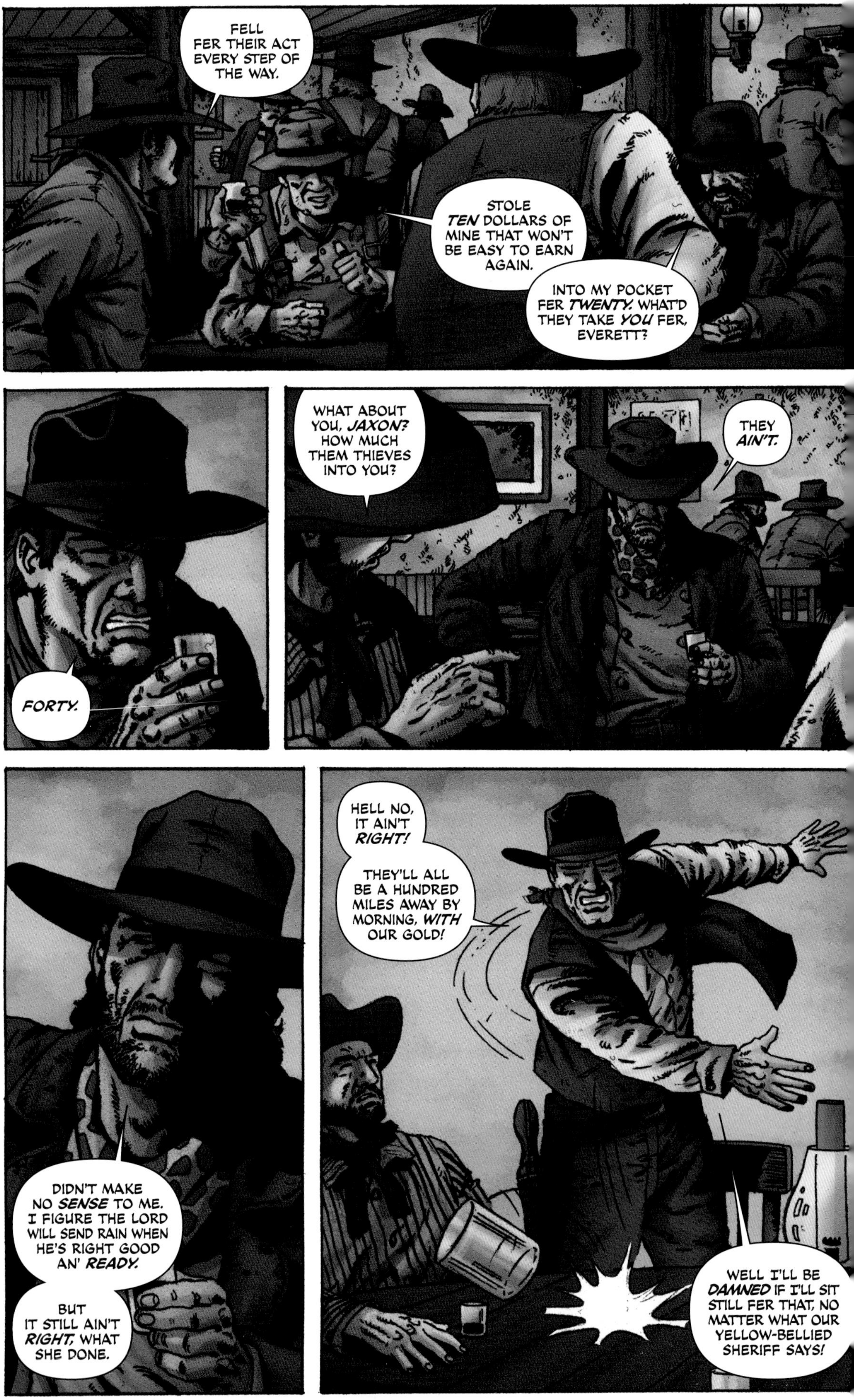
FELL FER THEIR ACT EVERY STEP OF THE WAY.
STOLE TEN DOLLARS OF MINE THAT WON'T BE EASY TO EARN AGAIN.
INTO MY POCKET FER TWENTY. WHAT'D THEY TAKE YOU FER, EVERETT?
FORTY.
WHAT ABOUT YOU, JAXON? HOW MUCH THEM THIEVES INTO YOU?
THEY AIN'T.
DIDN'T MAKE NO SENSE TO ME. I FIGURE THE LORD WILL SEND RAIN WHEN HE'S RIGHT GOOD AN' READY.
BUT IT STILL AIN'T RIGHT, WHAT SHE DONE.
HELL NO, IT AIN'T RIGHT!
THEY'LL ALL BE A HUNDRED MILES AWAY BY MORNING, WITH OUR GOLD!
WELL I'LL BE DAMNED IF I'LL SIT STILL FER THAT, NO MATTER WHAT OUR YELLOW-BELLIED SHERIFF SAYS!

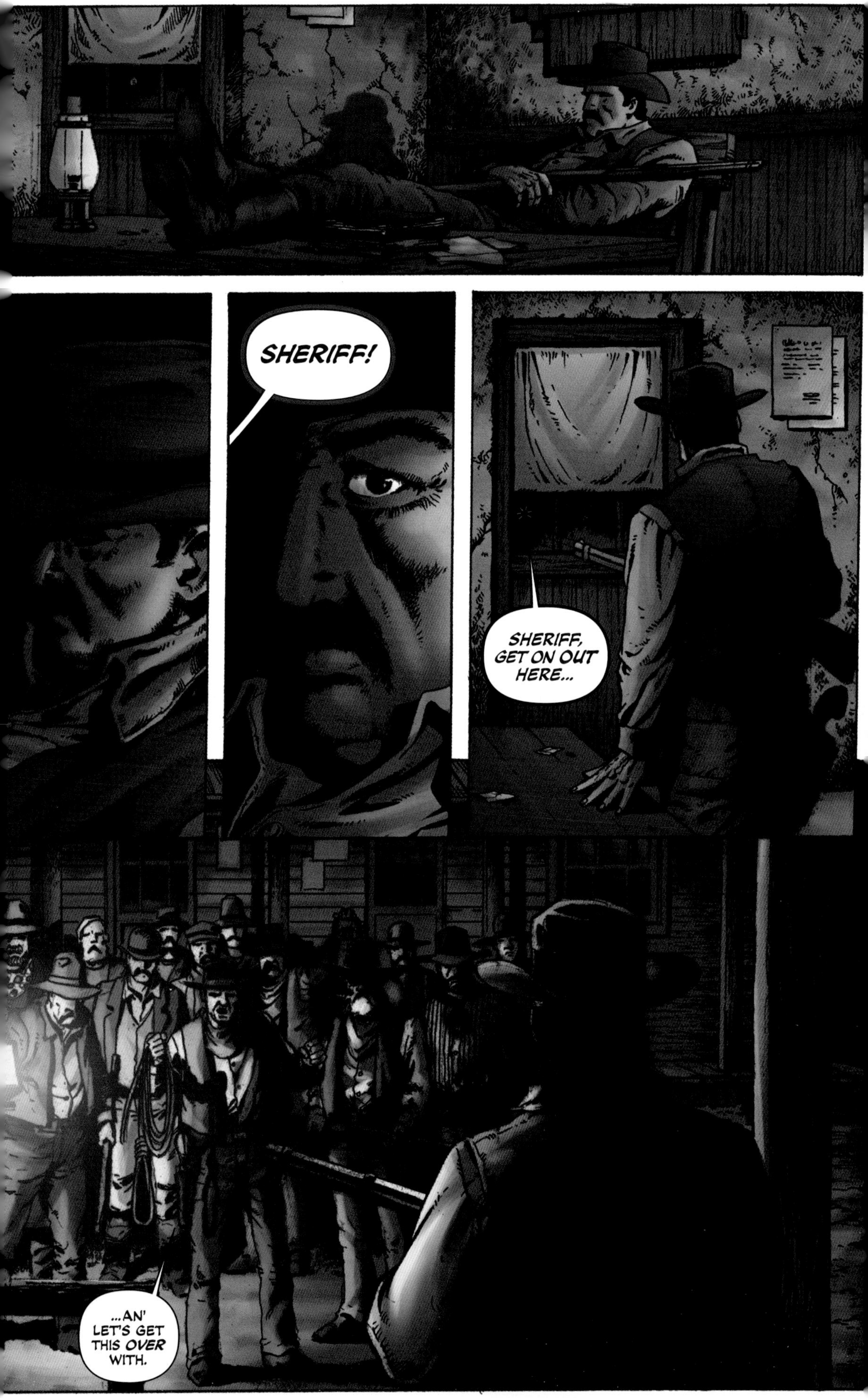
SHERIFF!
SHERIFF, GET ON OUT HERE...
...AN' LET'S GET THIS *OVER* WITH.

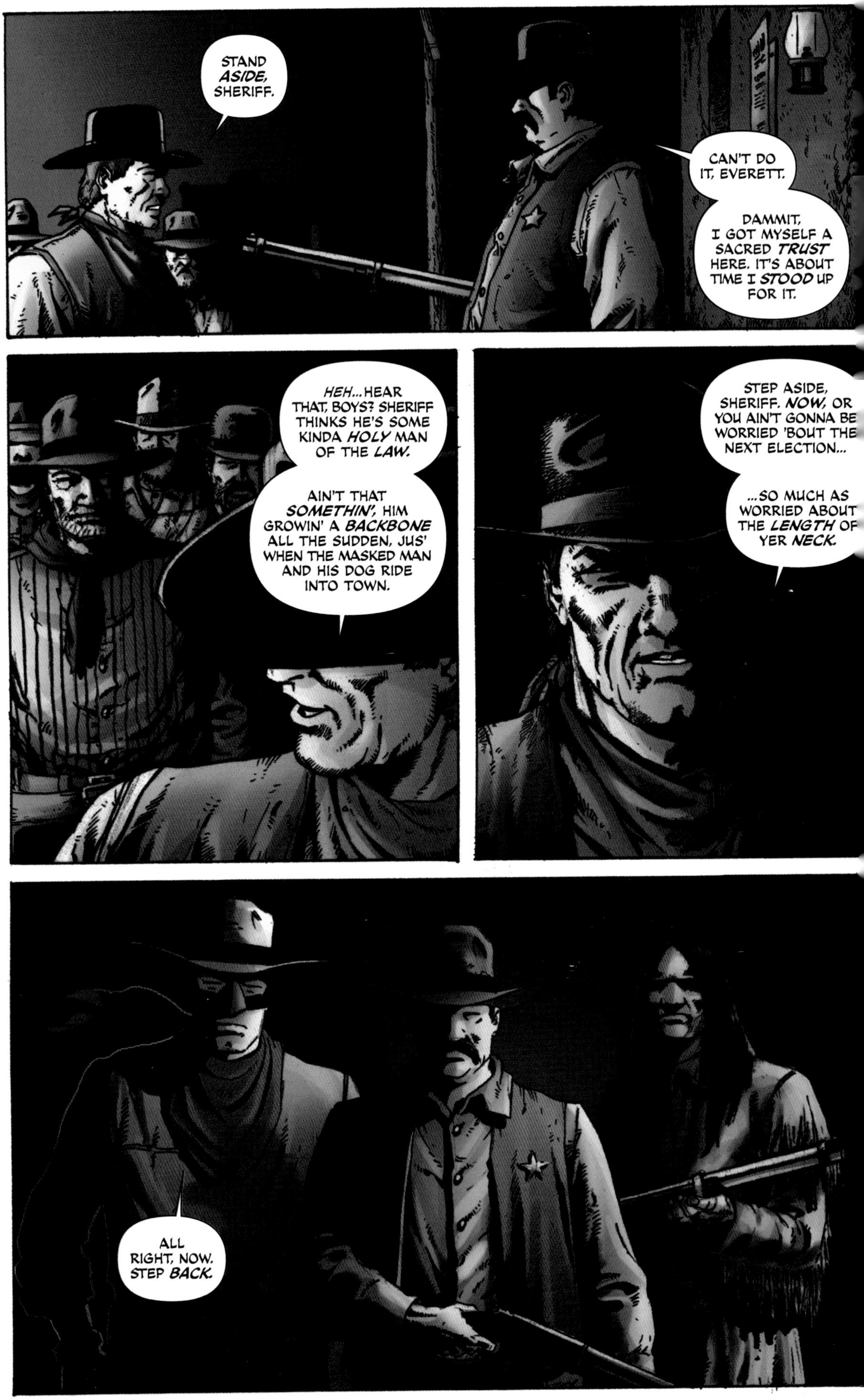
STAND ASIDE, SHERIFF.
CAN'T DO IT, EVERETT.
DAMMIT, I GOT MYSELF A SACRED TRUST HERE. IT'S ABOUT TIME I STOOD UP FOR IT.
HEH... HEAR THAT, BOYS? SHERIFF THINKS HE'S SOME KINDA HOLY MAN OF THE LAW.
AIN'T THAT SOMETHIN', HIM GROWIN' A BACKBONE ALL THE SUDDEN, JUS' WHEN THE MASKED MAN AND HIS DOG RIDE INTO TOWN.
STEP ASIDE, SHERIFF. NOW, OR YOU AIN'T GONNA BE WORRIED 'BOUT THE NEXT ELECTION...
...SO MUCH AS WORRIED ABOUT THE LENGTH OF YER NECK.
ALL RIGHT, NOW. STEP BACK.

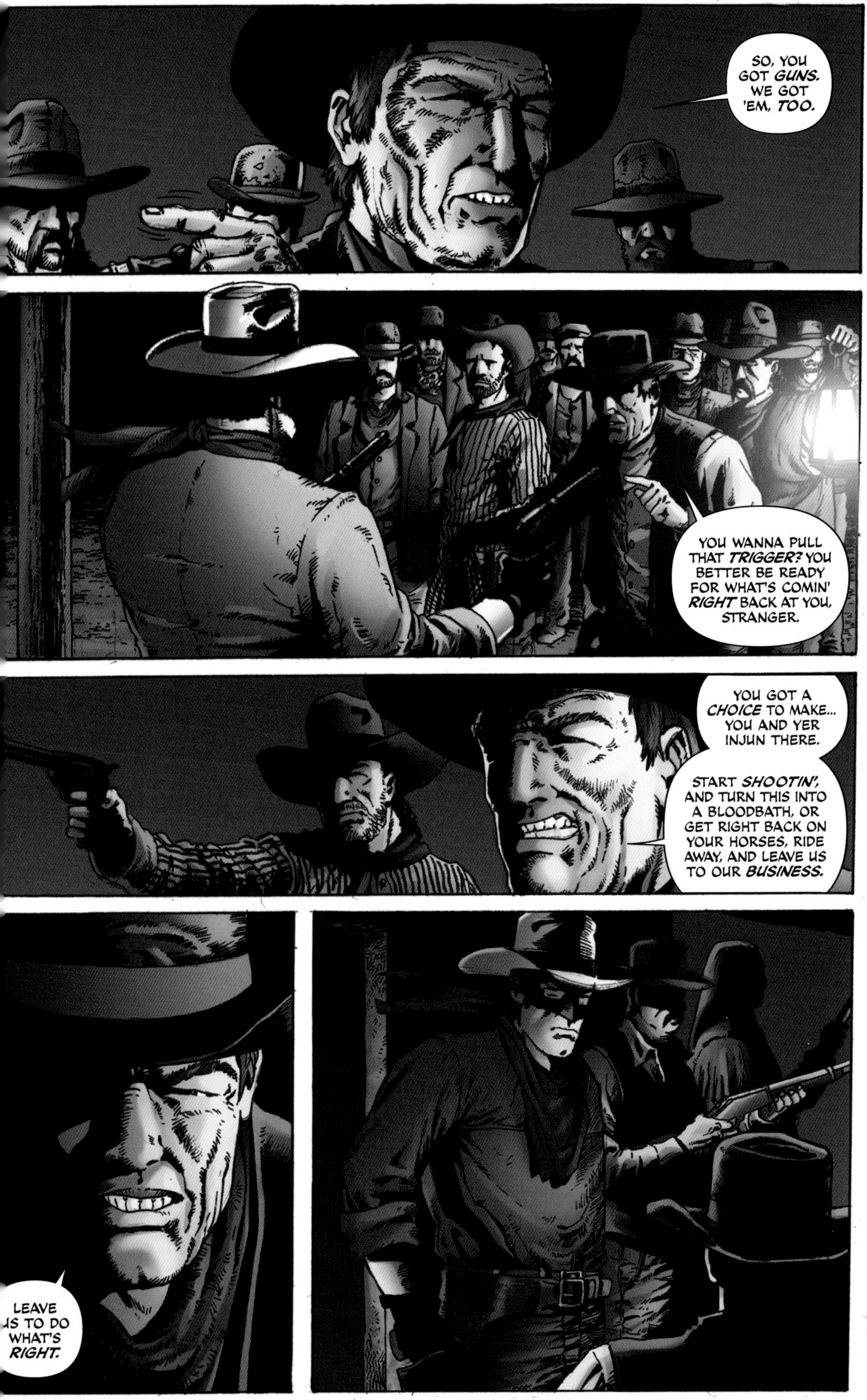
SO, YOU GOT *GUNS.* WE GOT 'EM, *TOO.*
YOU WANNA PULL THAT *TRIGGER?* YOU BETTER BE READY FOR WHAT'S COMIN' *RIGHT* BACK AT YOU, STRANGER.
YOU GOT A *CHOICE* TO MAKE... YOU AND YER INJUN THERE.
START *SHOOTIN',* AND TURN THIS INTO A BLOODBATH, OR GET RIGHT BACK ON YOUR HORSES, RIDE AWAY, AND LEAVE US TO OUR *BUSINESS.*
LEAVE US TO DO WHAT'S *RIGHT.*

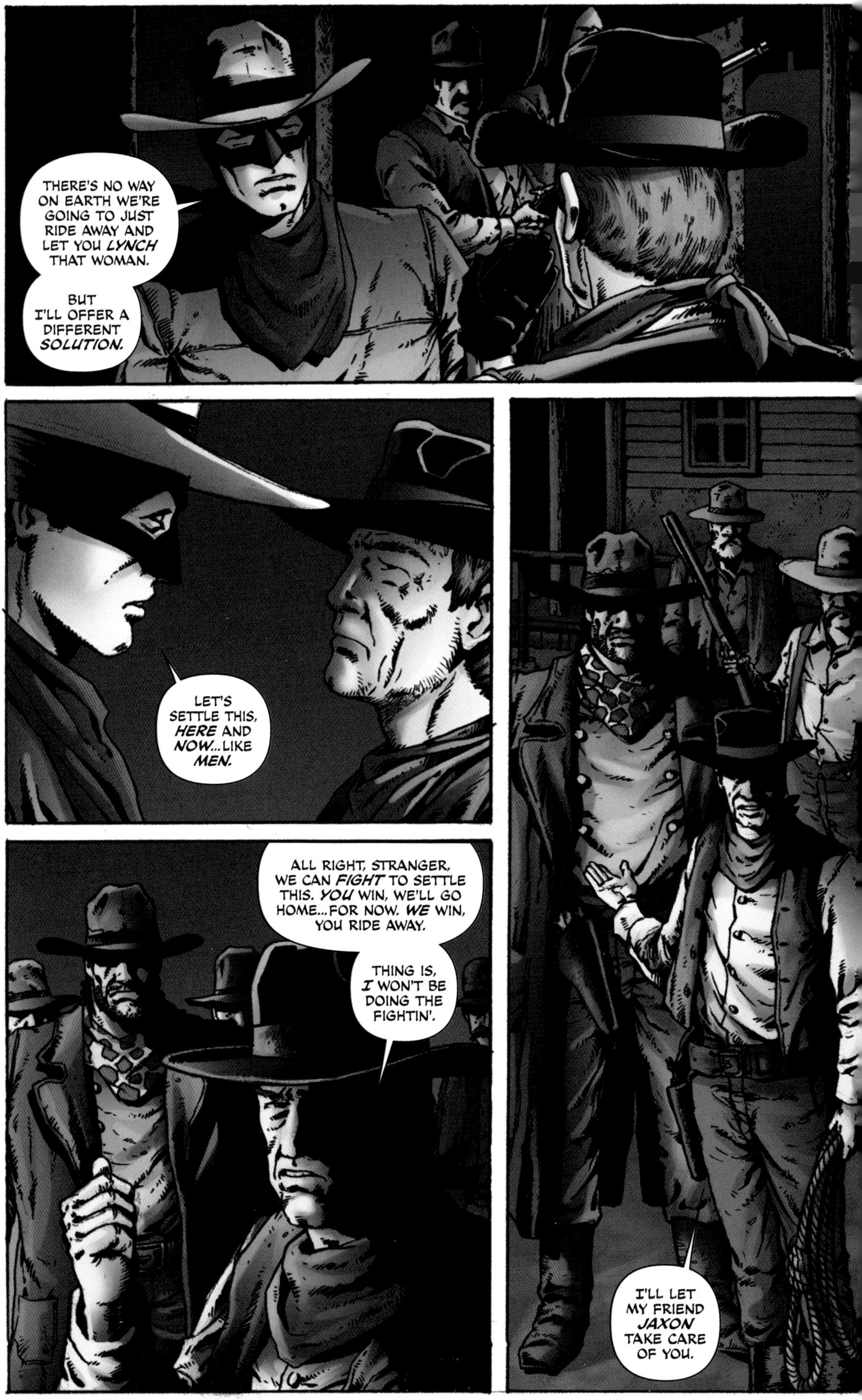
THERE'S NO WAY ON EARTH WE'RE GOING TO JUST RIDE AWAY AND LET YOU *LYNCH* THAT WOMAN.
BUT I'LL OFFER A DIFFERENT *SOLUTION.*
LET'S SETTLE THIS, ***HERE*** AND ***NOW***...LIKE ***MEN.***
ALL RIGHT, STRANGER, WE CAN *FIGHT* TO SETTLE THIS. *YOU* WIN, WE'LL GO HOME...FOR NOW. *WE* WIN, YOU RIDE AWAY.
THING IS, *I* WON'T BE DOING THE FIGHTIN'.
I'LL LET MY FRIEND *JAXON* TAKE CARE OF YOU.

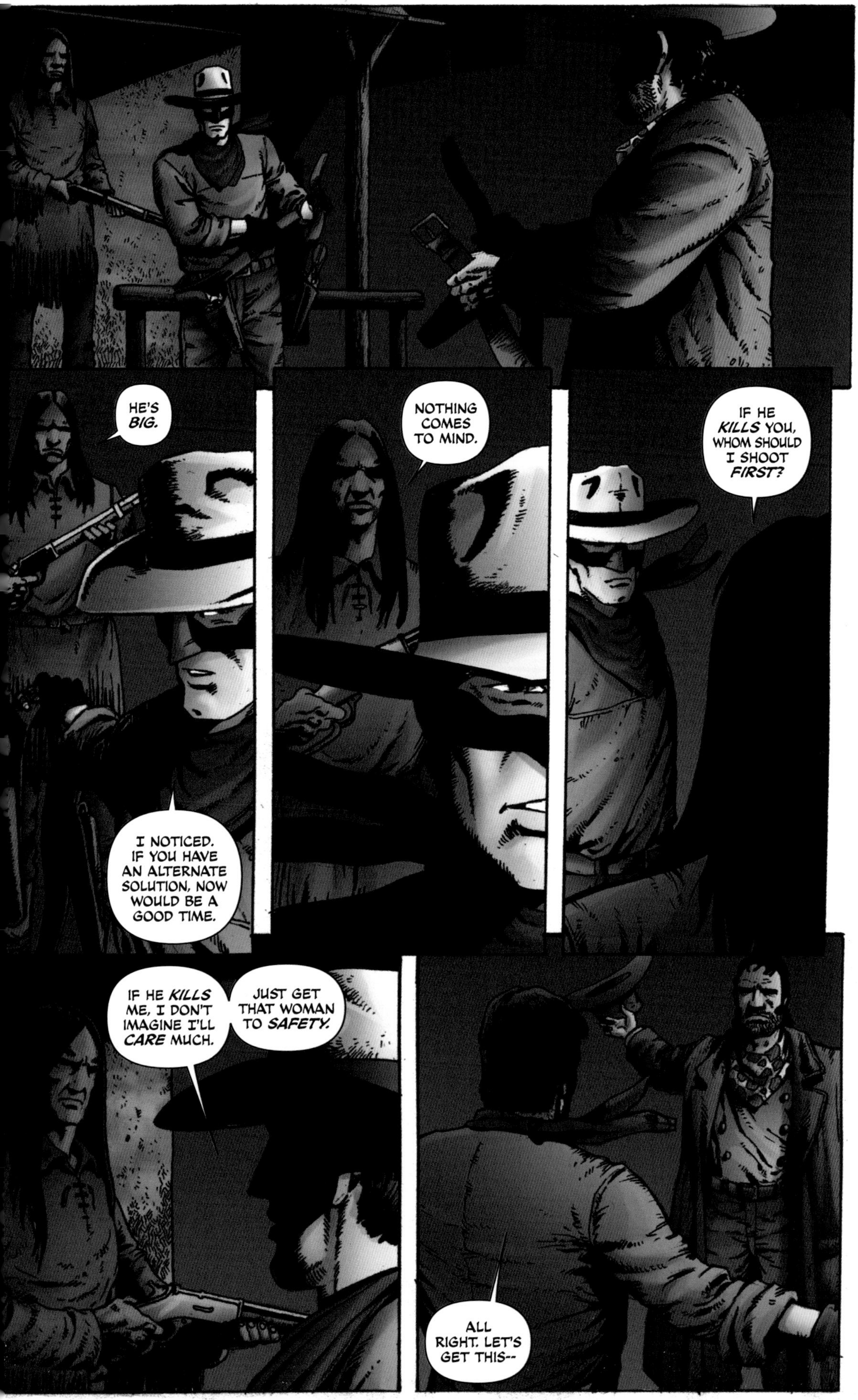
HE'S BIG.
I NOTICED. IF YOU HAVE AN ALTERNATE SOLUTION, NOW WOULD BE A GOOD TIME.
NOTHING COMES TO MIND.
IF HE KILLS YOU, WHOM SHOULD I SHOOT FIRST?
IF HE KILLS ME, I DON'T IMAGINE I'LL CARE MUCH.
JUST GET THAT WOMAN TO SAFETY.
ALL RIGHT. LET'S GET THIS--

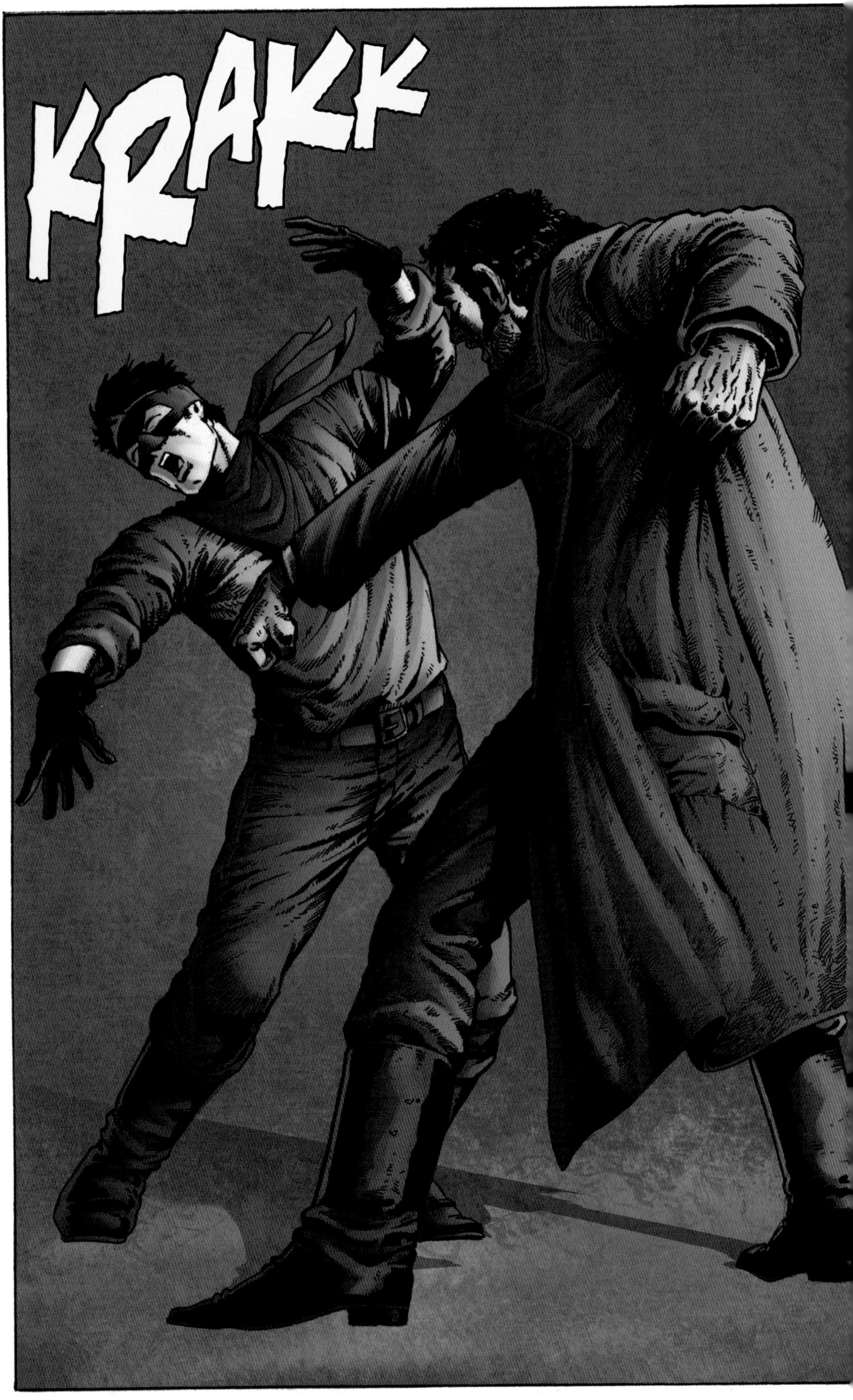
KRAKK

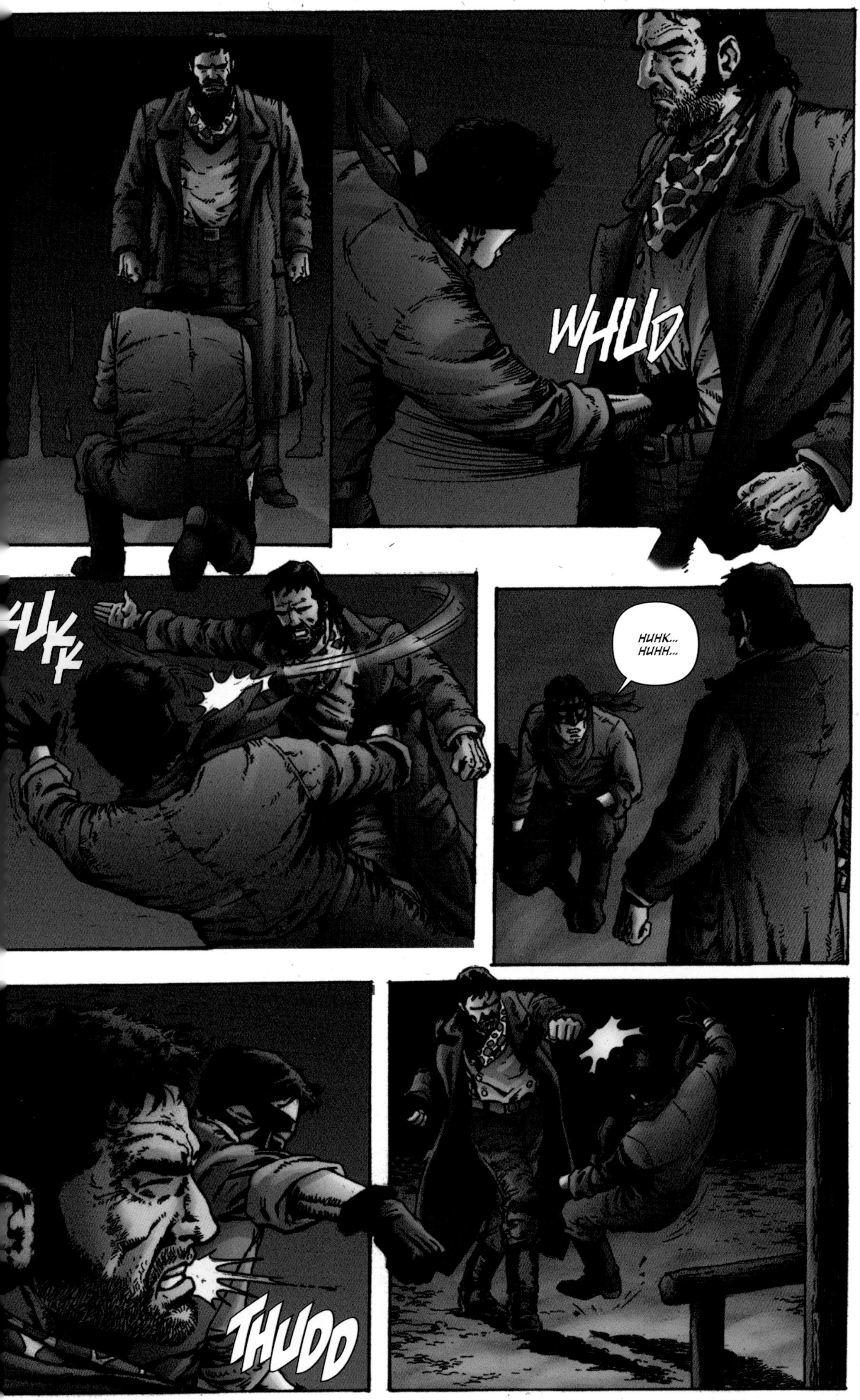
WHUD
ZUKK
HUHK...
HUHH...
THUDD

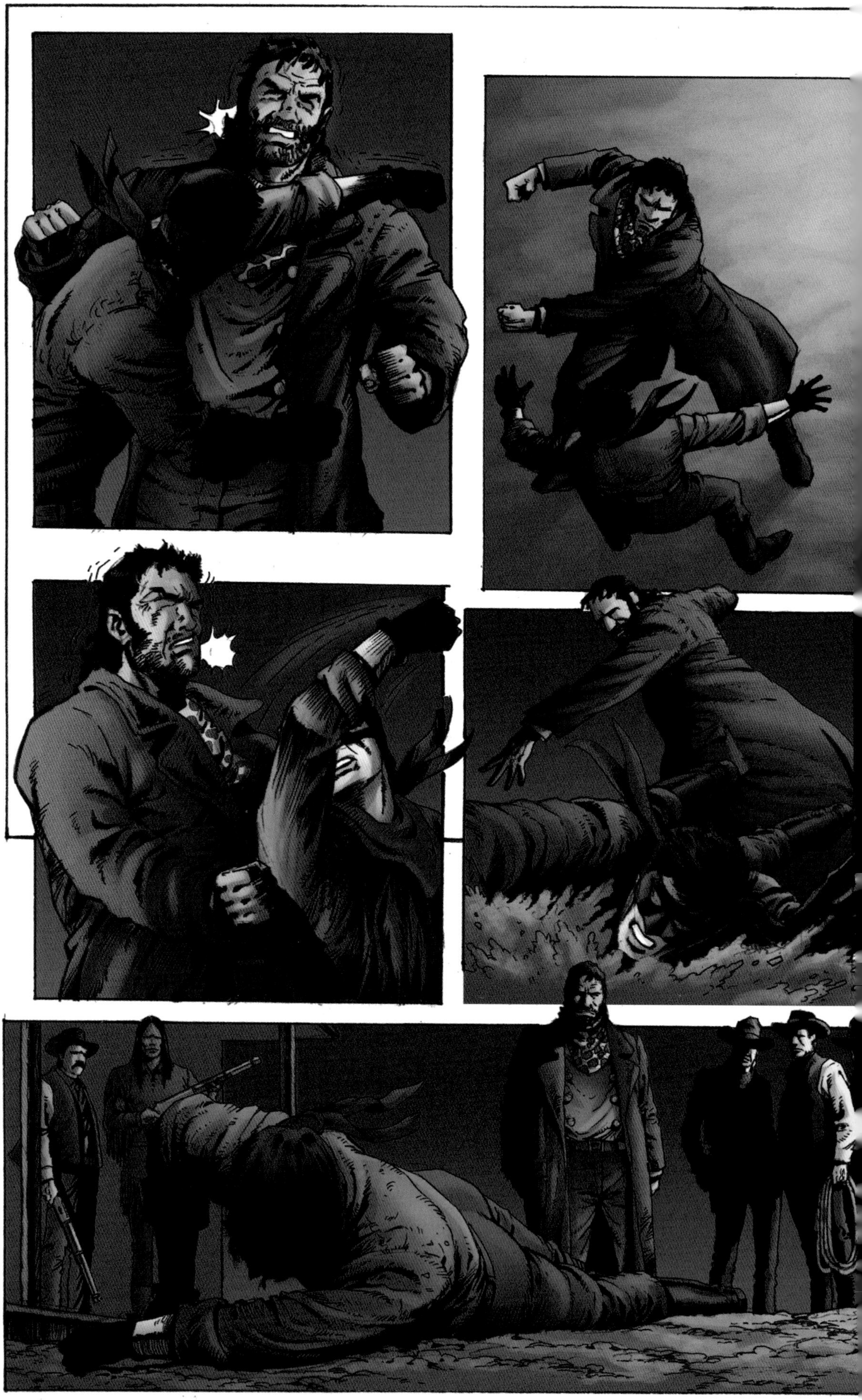

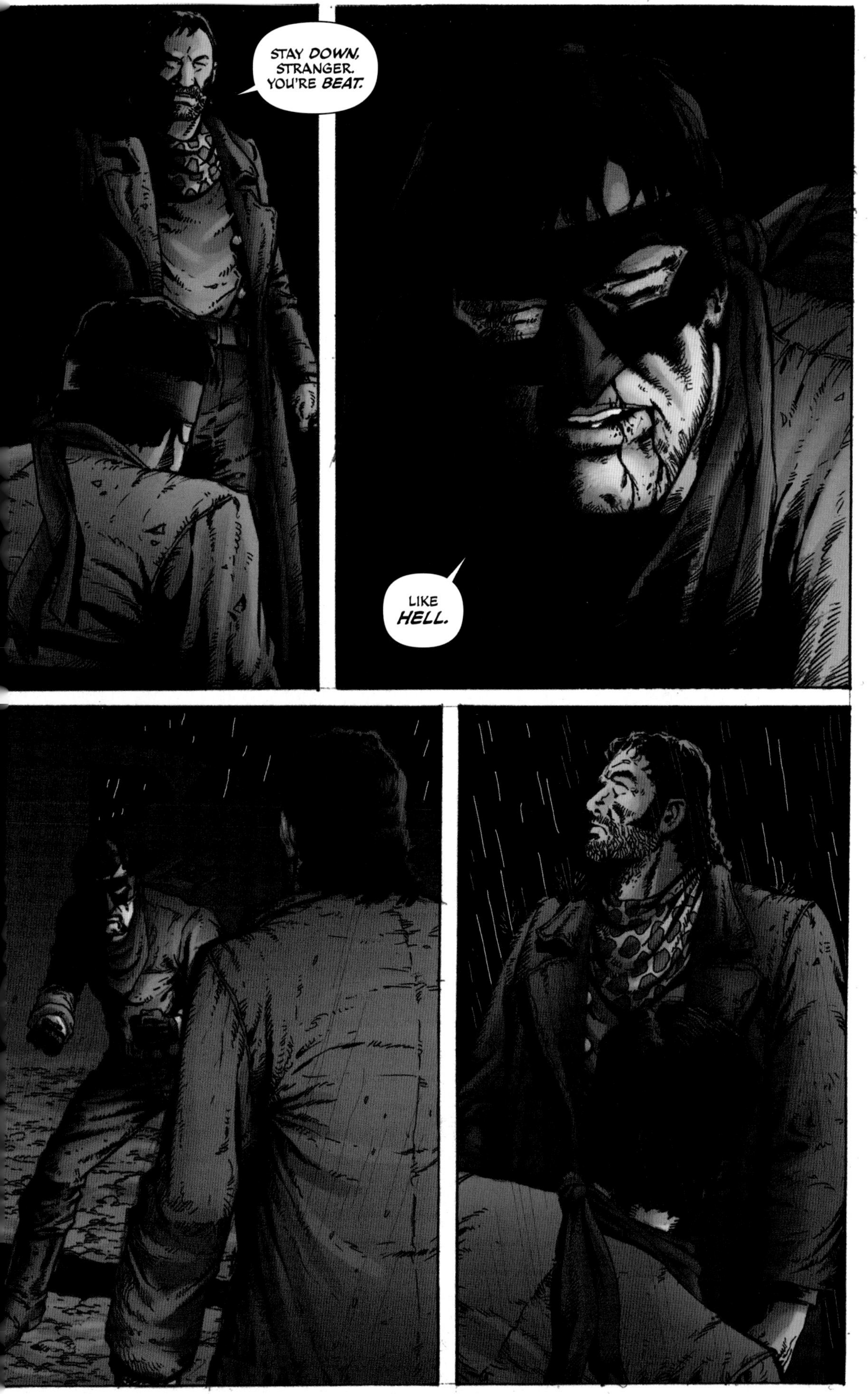
STAY *DOWN,* STRANGER. YOU'RE *BEAT.*
LIKE *HELL.*

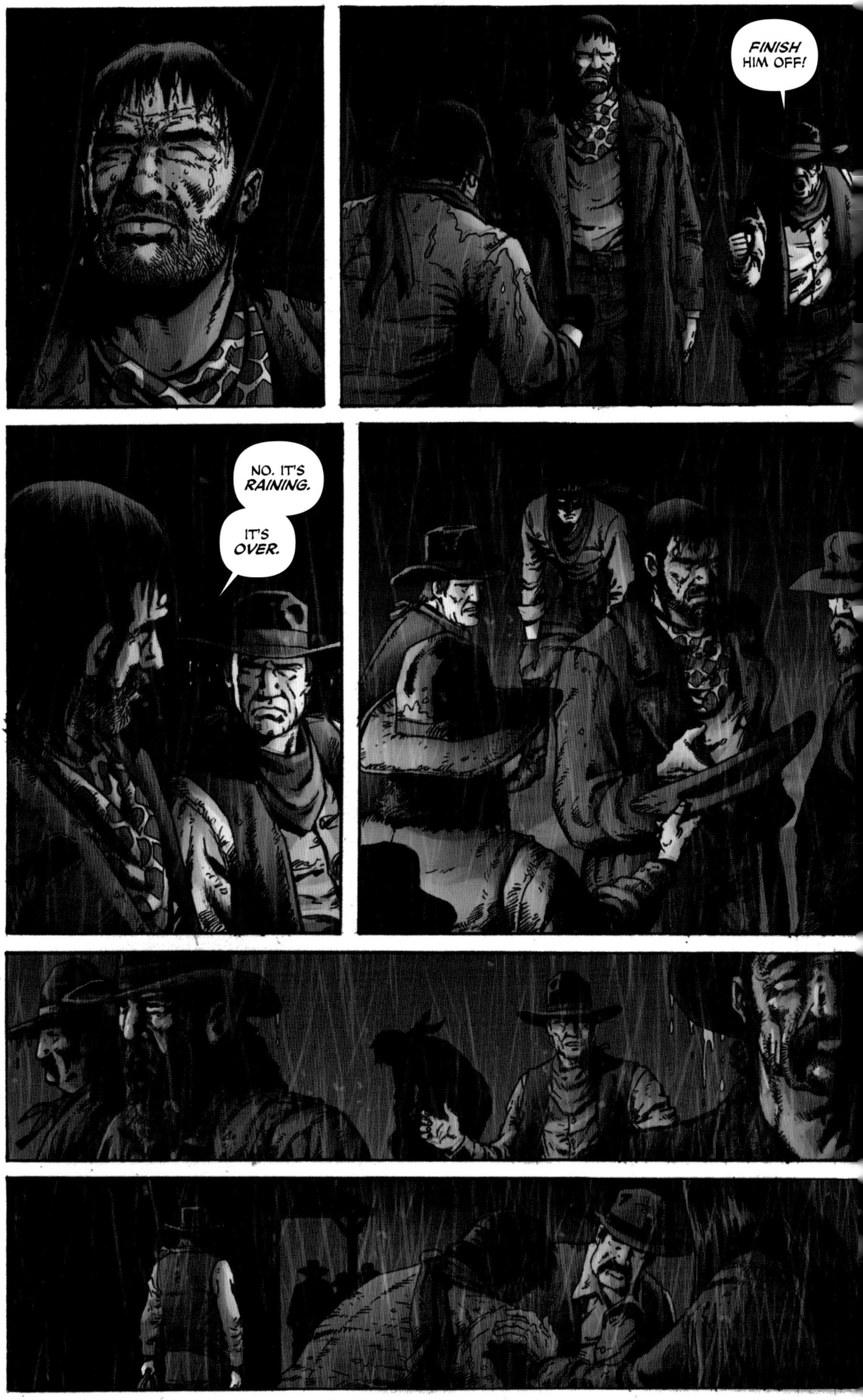
FINISH HIM OFF!
NO. IT'S RAINING.
IT'S OVER.

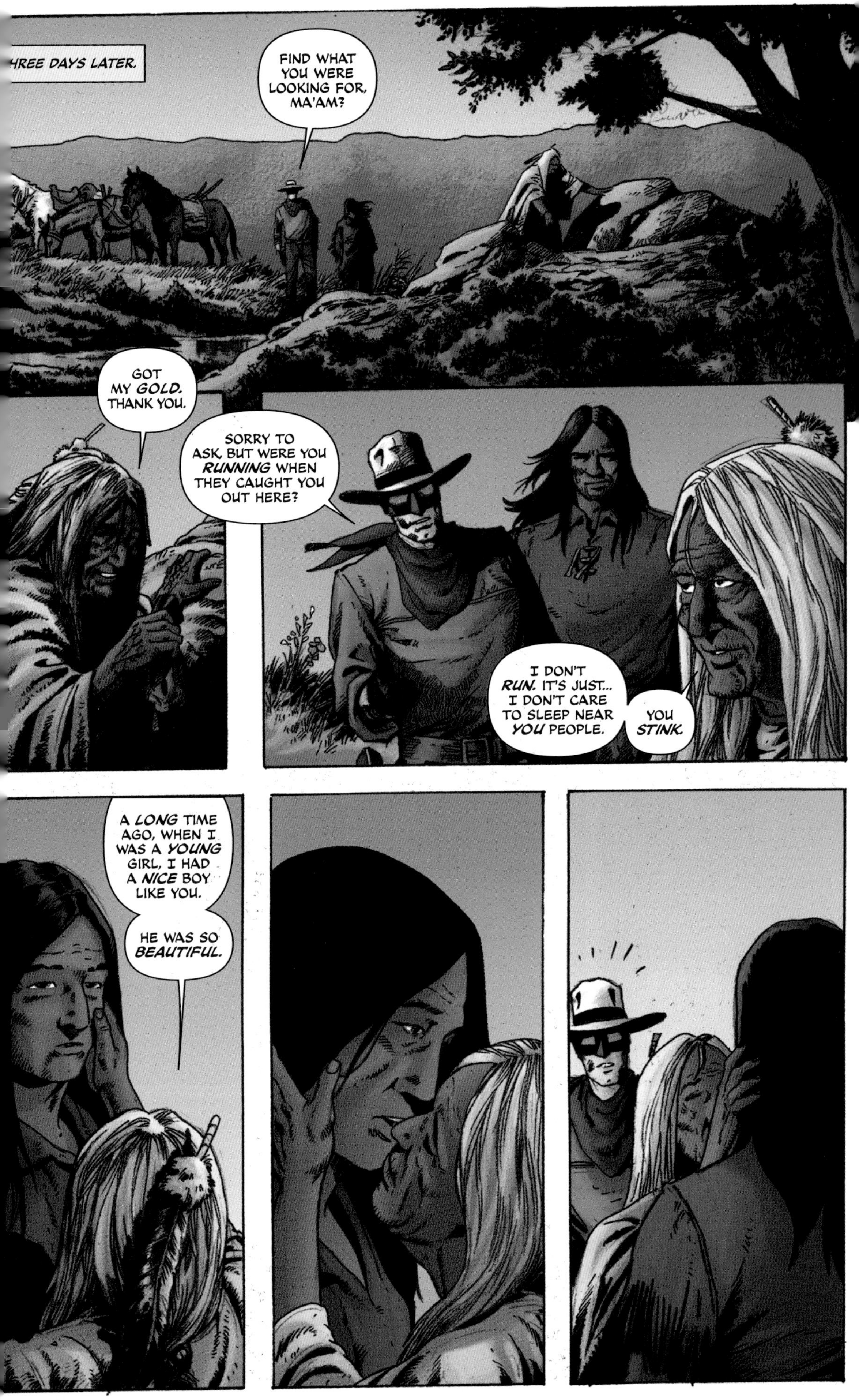

HREE DAYS LATER.
FIND WHAT YOU WERE LOOKING FOR, MA'AM?
GOT MY GOLD. THANK YOU.
SORRY TO ASK, BUT WERE YOU RUNNING WHEN THEY CAUGHT YOU OUT HERE?
I DON'T RUN. IT'S JUST... I DON'T CARE TO SLEEP NEAR YOU PEOPLE.
YOU STINK.
A LONG TIME AGO, WHEN I WAS A YOUNG GIRL, I HAD A NICE BOY LIKE YOU.
HE WAS SO BEAUTIFUL.

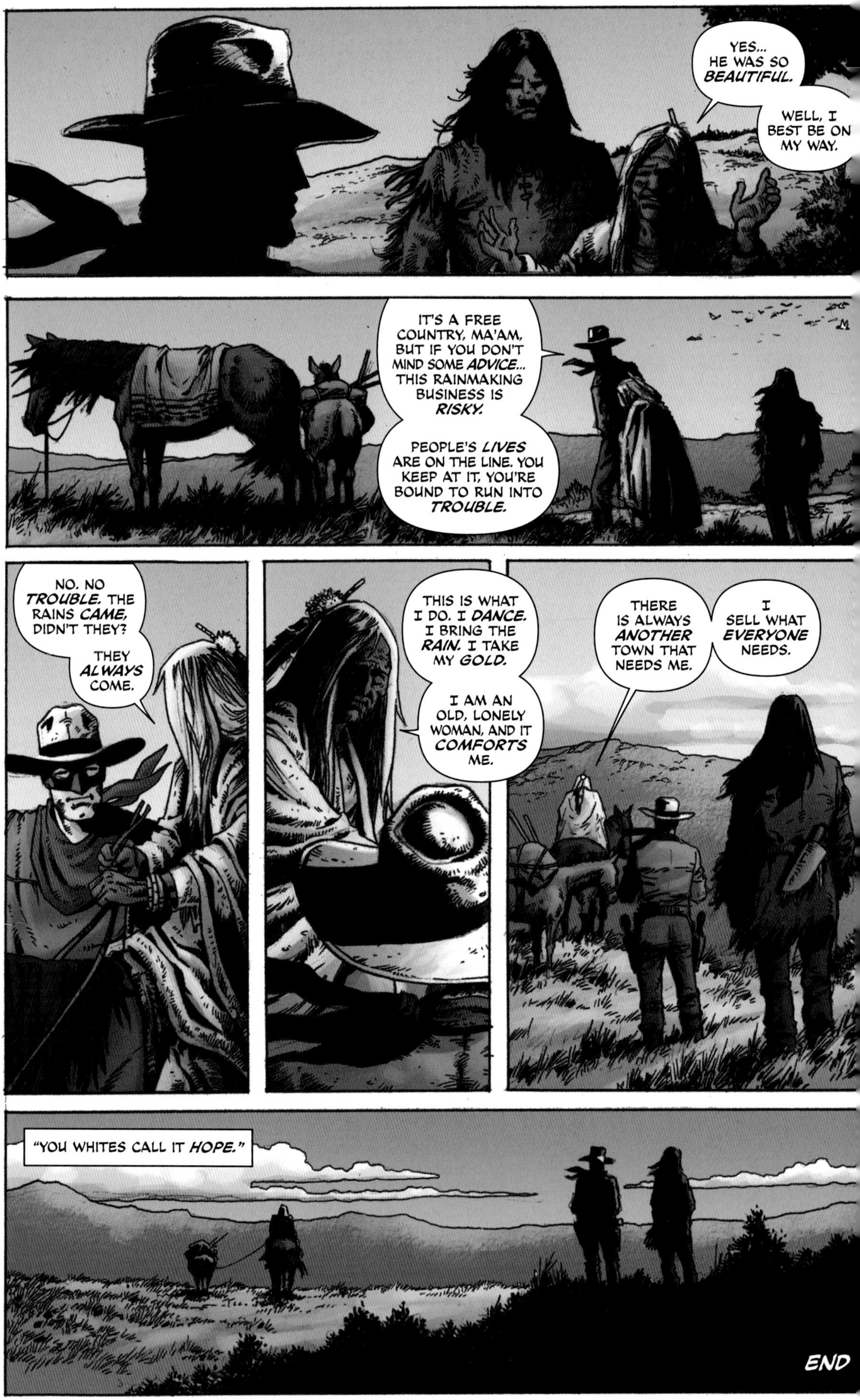
YES... HE WAS SO BEAUTIFUL.
WELL, I BEST BE ON MY WAY.
IT'S A FREE COUNTRY, MA'AM, BUT IF YOU DON'T MIND SOME ADVICE... THIS RAINMAKING BUSINESS IS RISKY.
PEOPLE'S LIVES ARE ON THE LINE. YOU KEEP AT IT, YOU'RE BOUND TO RUN INTO TROUBLE.
NO. NO TROUBLE. THE RAINS CAME, DIDN'T THEY?
THEY ALWAYS COME.
THIS IS WHAT I DO. I DANCE. I BRING THE RAIN. I TAKE MY GOLD.
I AM AN OLD, LONELY WOMAN, AND IT COMFORTS ME.
THERE IS ALWAYS ANOTHER TOWN THAT NEEDS ME.
I SELL WHAT EVERYONE NEEDS.
"YOU WHITES CALL IT HOPE."
END

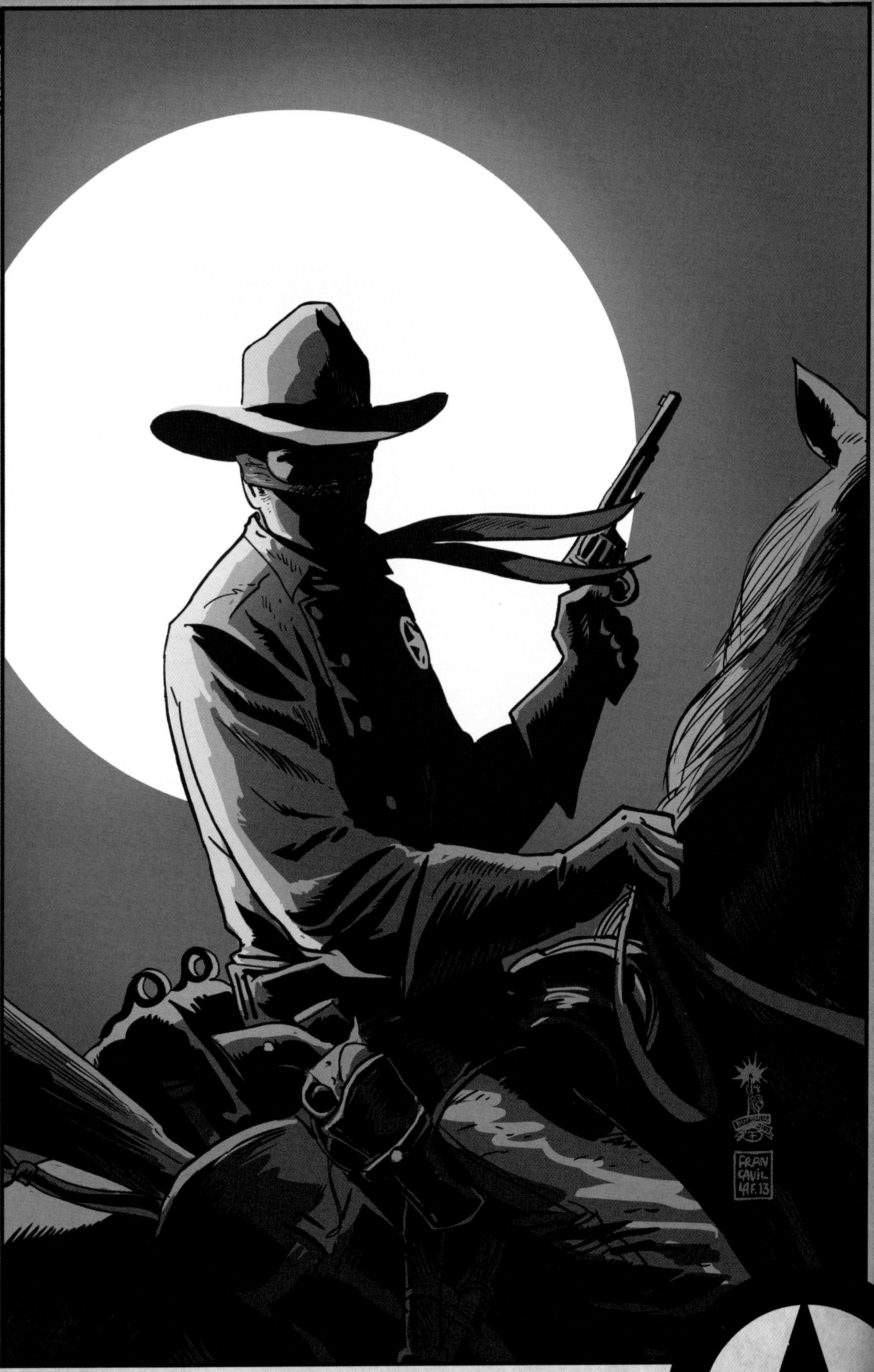

COVER BY **FRANCESCO FRANCAVILLA**

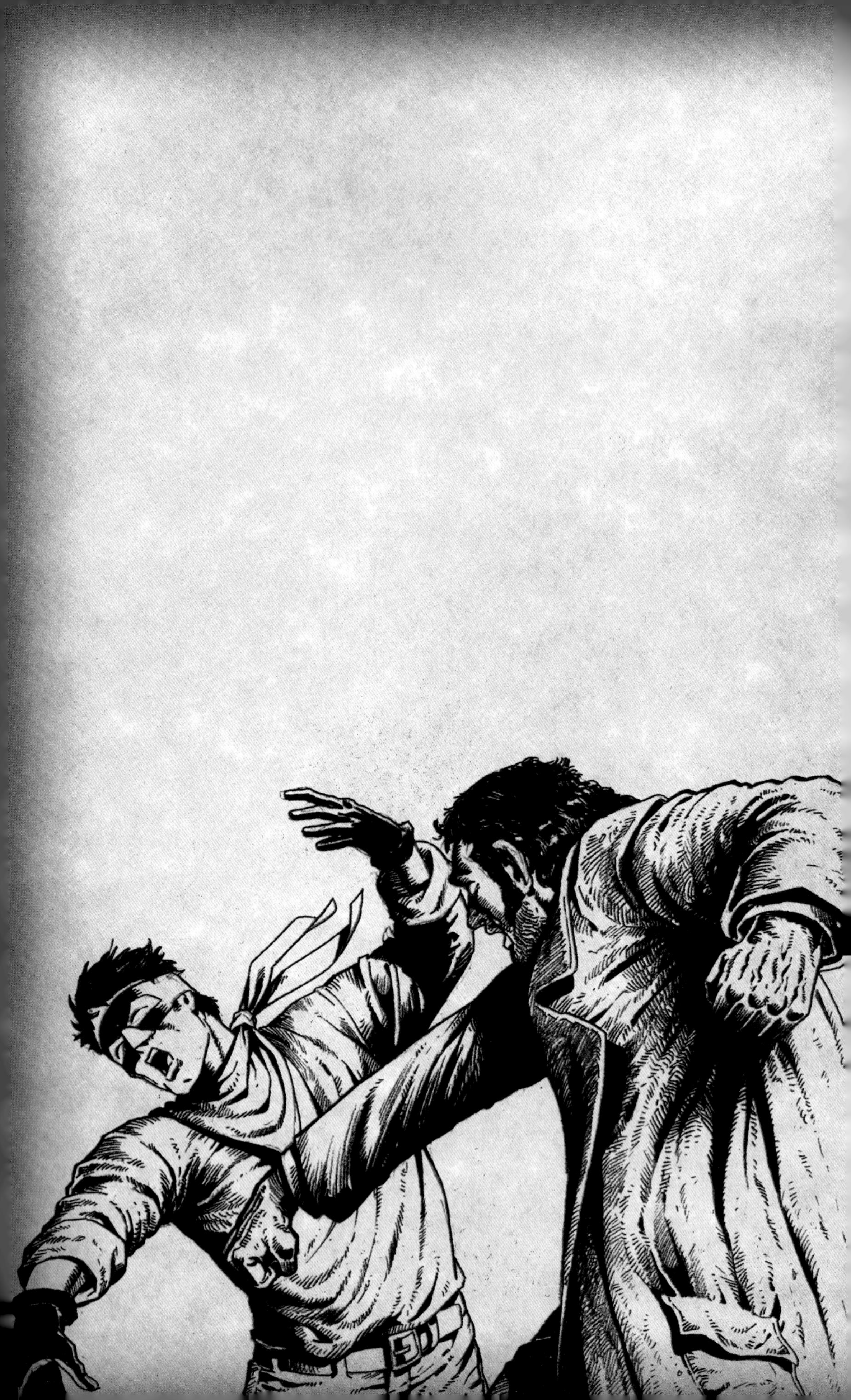

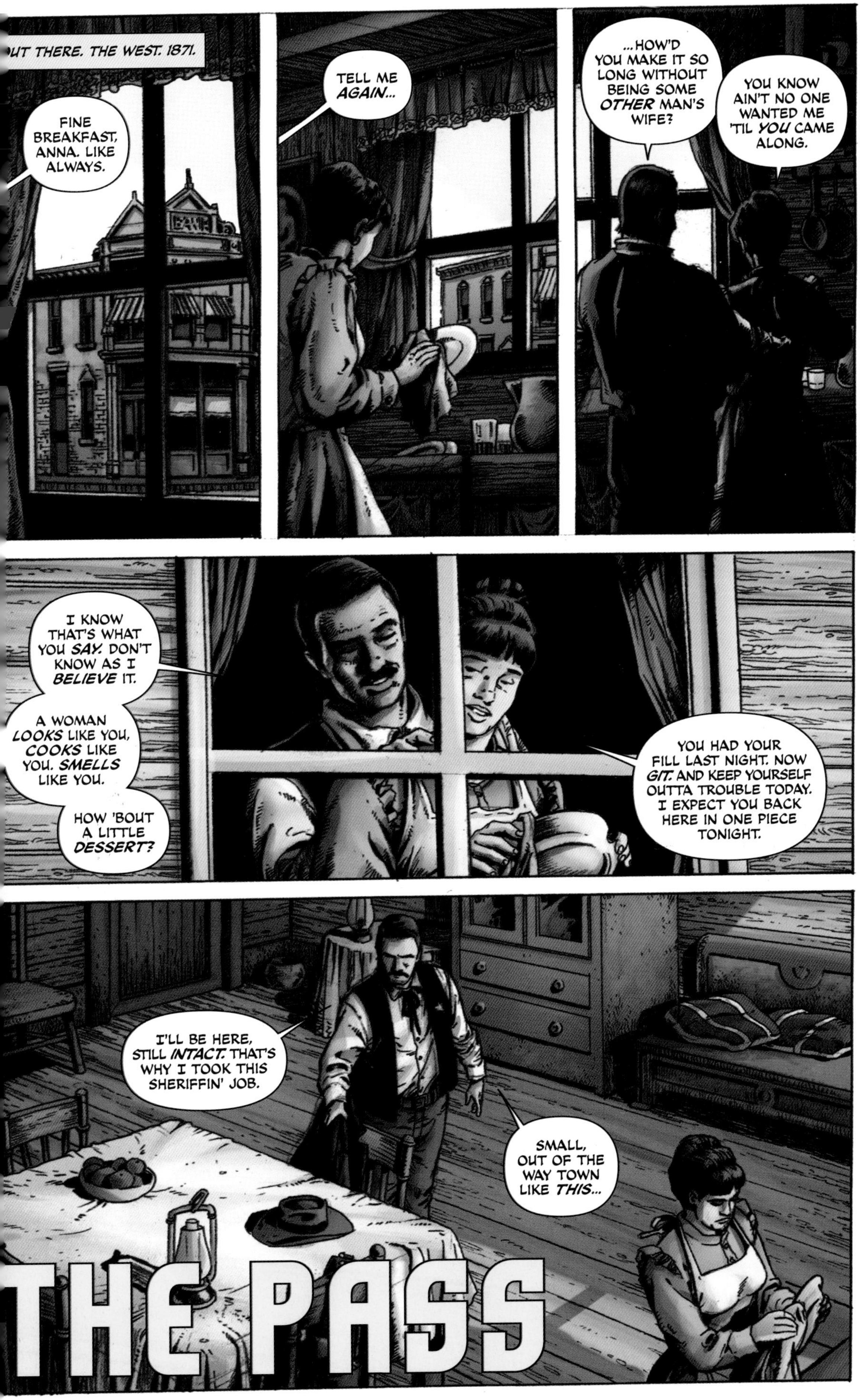

OUT THERE. THE WEST. 1871.
FINE BREAKFAST, ANNA. LIKE ALWAYS.
TELL ME AGAIN...
...HOW'D YOU MAKE IT SO LONG WITHOUT BEING SOME OTHER MAN'S WIFE?
YOU KNOW AIN'T NO ONE WANTED ME 'TIL YOU CAME ALONG.
I KNOW THAT'S WHAT YOU SAY. DON'T KNOW AS I BELIEVE IT.
A WOMAN LOOKS LIKE YOU, COOKS LIKE YOU. SMELLS LIKE YOU.
HOW 'BOUT A LITTLE DESSERT?
YOU HAD YOUR FILL LAST NIGHT. NOW GIT. AND KEEP YOURSELF OUTTA TROUBLE TODAY. I EXPECT YOU BACK HERE IN ONE PIECE TONIGHT.
I'LL BE HERE, STILL INTACT. THAT'S WHY I TOOK THIS SHERIFFIN' JOB.
SMALL, OUT OF THE WAY TOWN LIKE THIS...
THE PASS

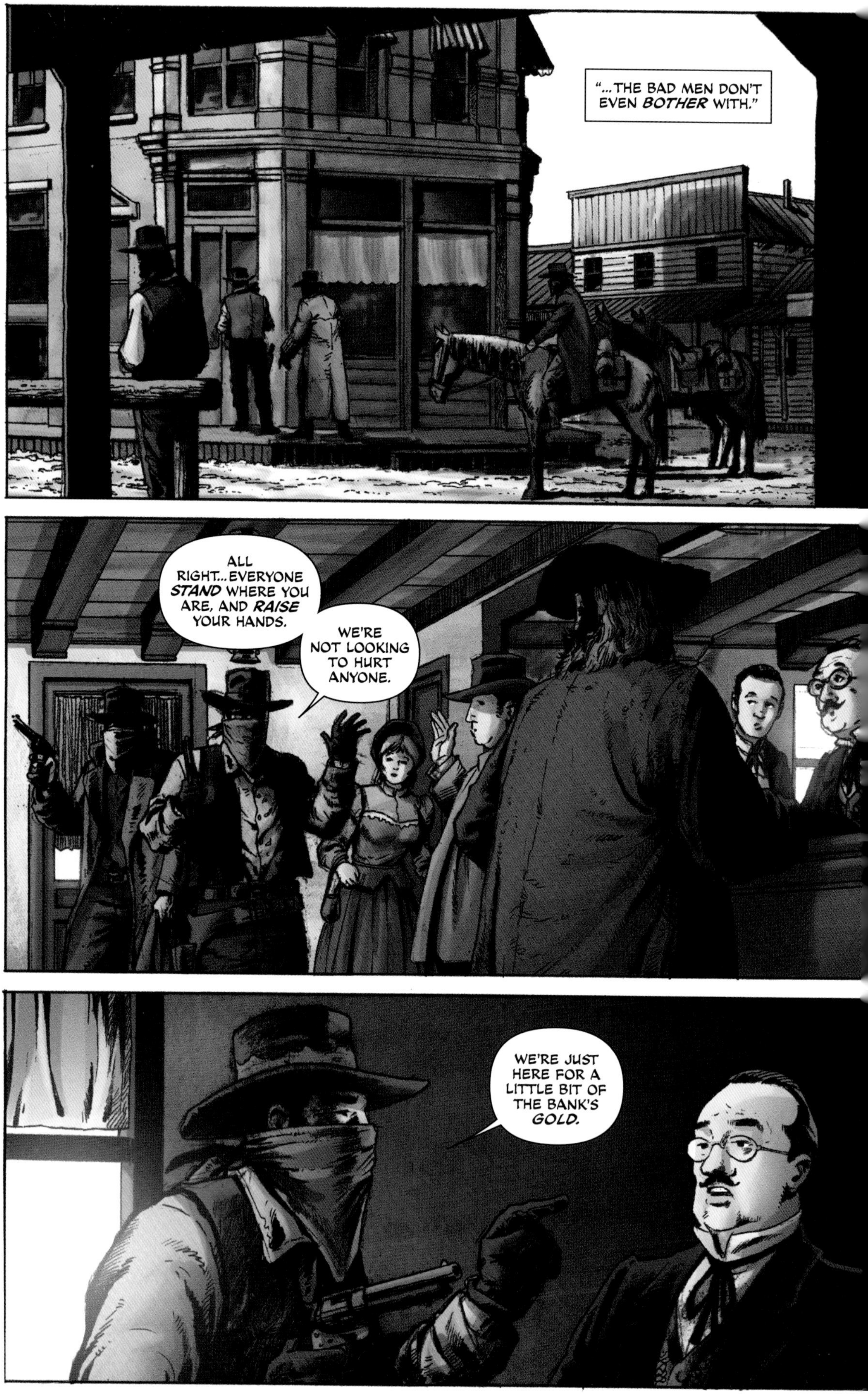
"...THE BAD MEN DON'T EVEN *BOTHER* WITH."
ALL RIGHT...EVERYONE *STAND* WHERE YOU ARE, AND *RAISE* YOUR HANDS.
WE'RE NOT LOOKING TO HURT ANYONE.
WE'RE JUST HERE FOR A LITTLE BIT OF THE BANK'S *GOLD.*

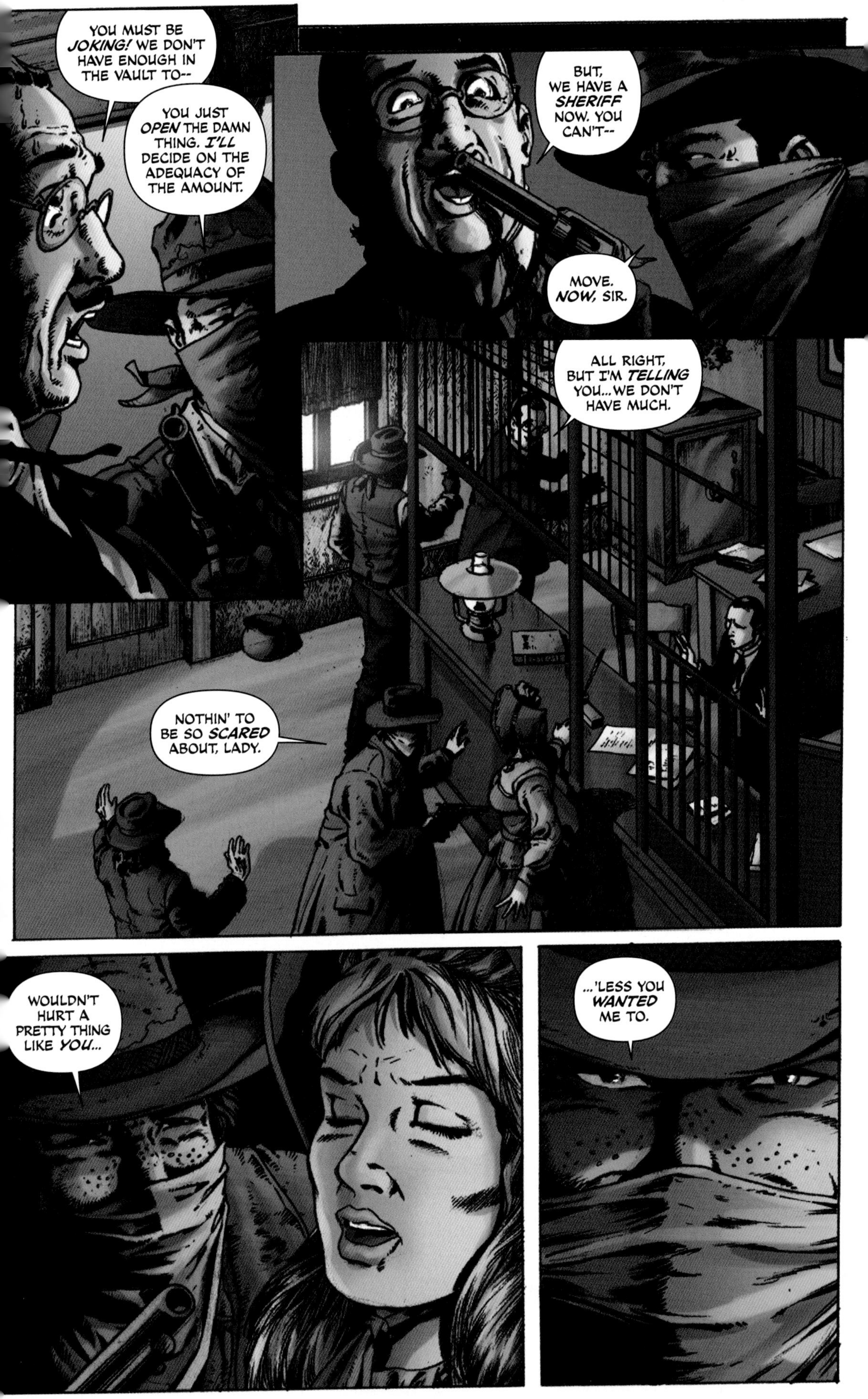

YOU MUST BE *JOKING!* WE DON'T HAVE ENOUGH IN THE VAULT TO--
YOU JUST *OPEN* THE DAMN THING. *I'LL* DECIDE ON THE ADEQUACY OF THE AMOUNT.
BUT, WE HAVE A *SHERIFF* NOW. YOU CAN'T--
MOVE. *NOW,* SIR.
ALL RIGHT, BUT I'M *TELLING* YOU...WE DON'T HAVE MUCH.
NOTHIN' TO BE SO *SCARED* ABOUT, LADY.
WOULDN'T HURT A PRETTY THING LIKE *YOU*...
...'LESS YOU *WANTED* ME TO.

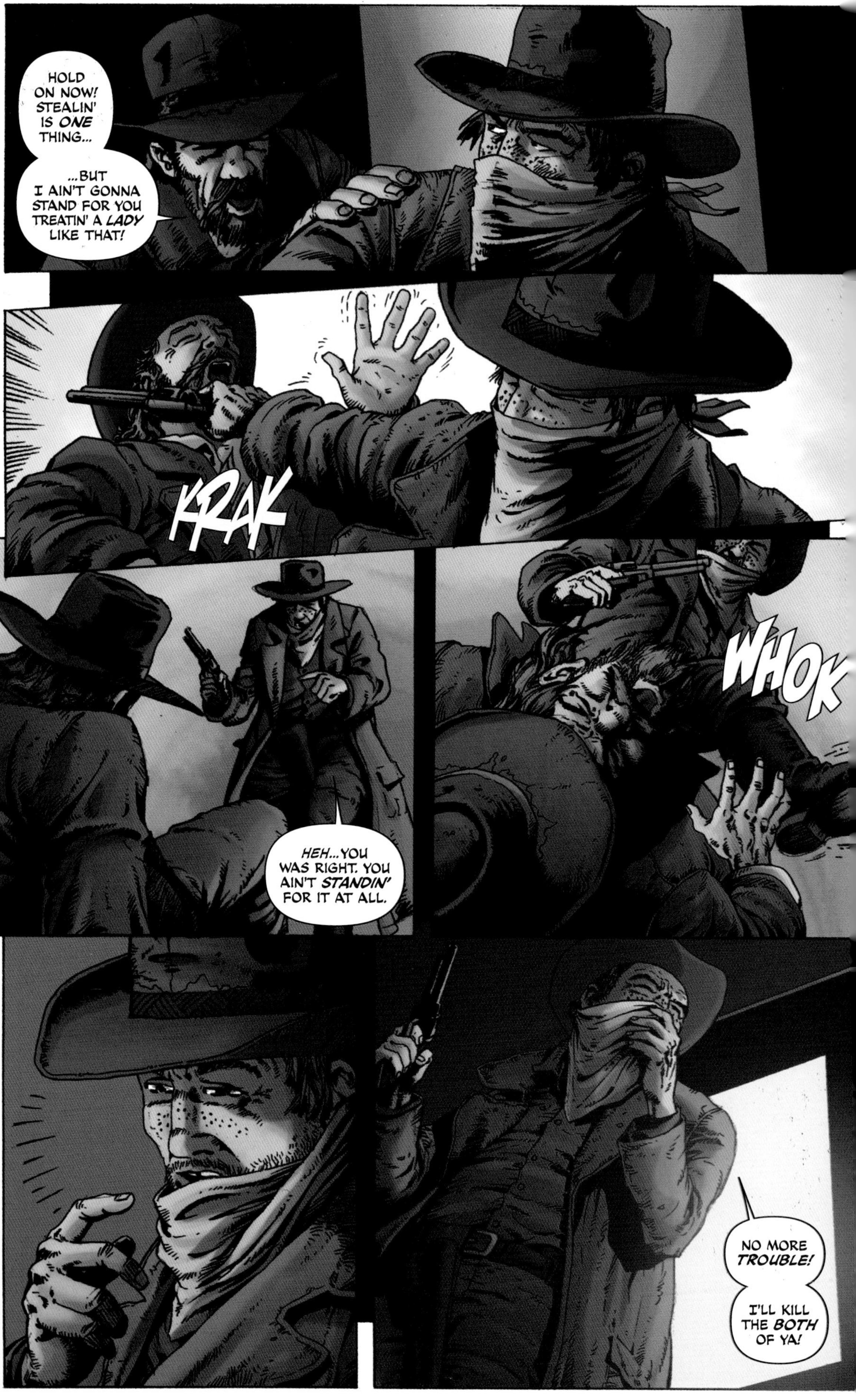
HOLD ON NOW! STEALIN' IS ONE THING...
...BUT I AIN'T GONNA STAND FOR YOU TREATIN' A LADY LIKE THAT!
KRAK
WHOK
HEH...YOU WAS RIGHT. YOU AIN'T STANDIN' FOR IT AT ALL.
NO MORE TROUBLE!
I'LL KILL THE BOTH OF YA!

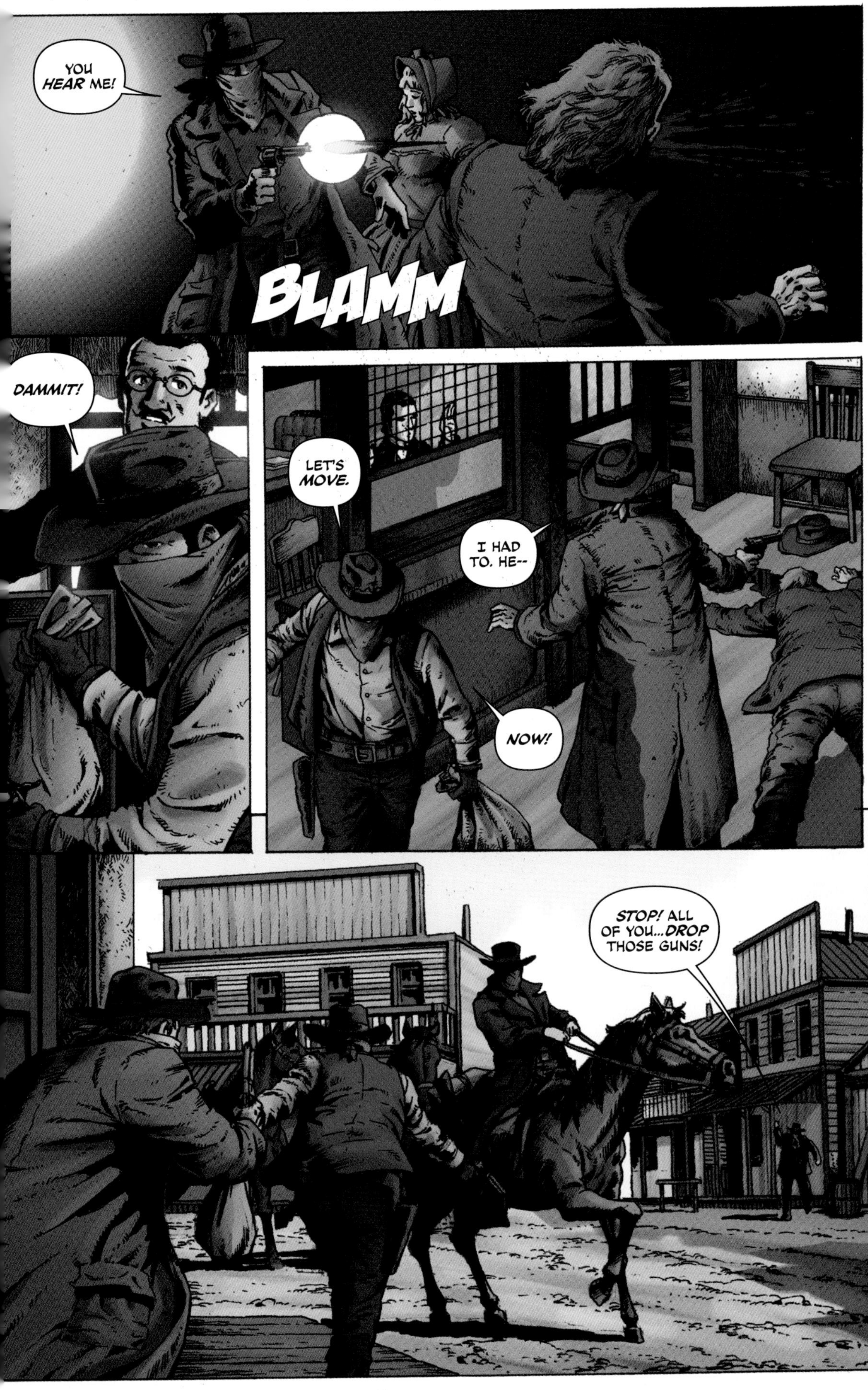

YOU HEAR ME!
BLAMM
DAMMIT!
LET'S MOVE.
I HAD TO. HE--
NOW!
STOP! ALL OF YOU...DROP THOSE GUNS!

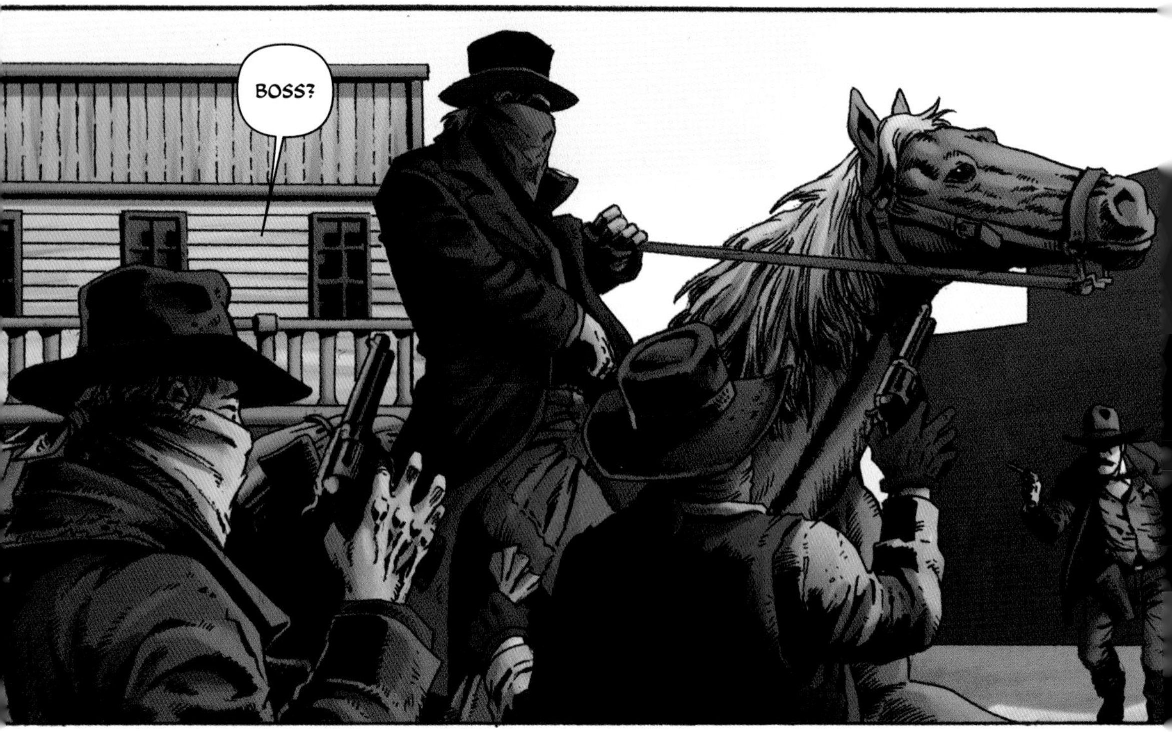
BOSS?

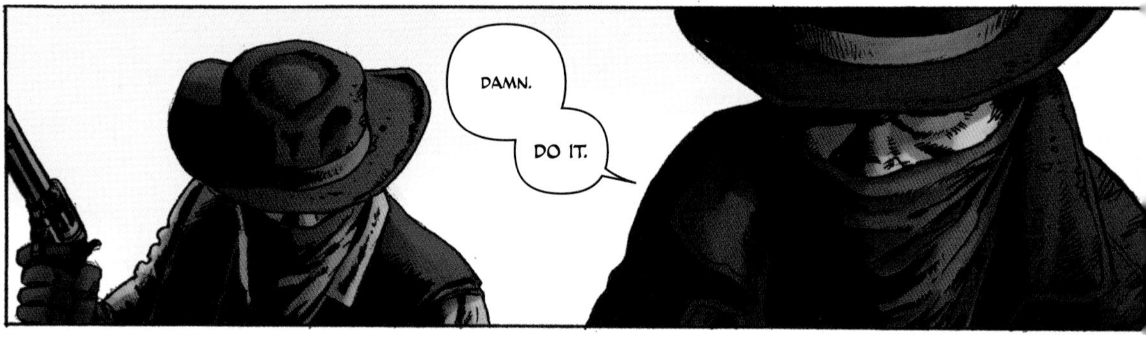
DAMN.
DO IT.

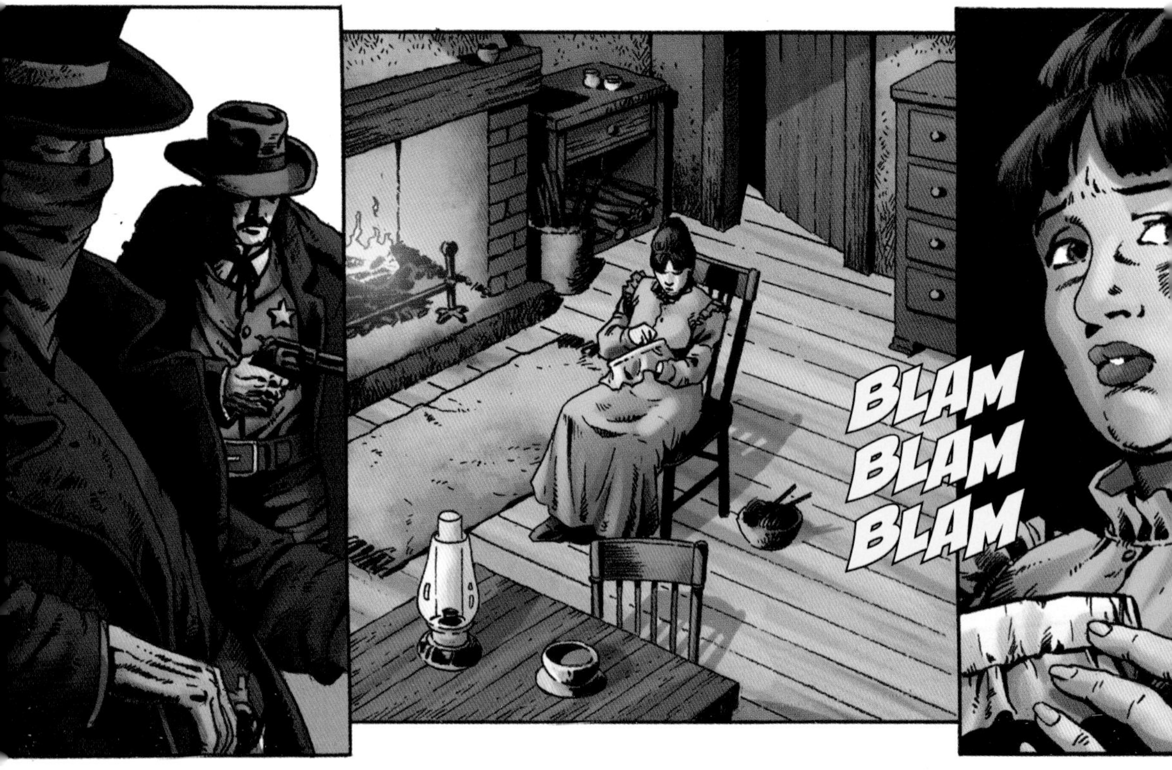
BLAM
BLAM
BLAM

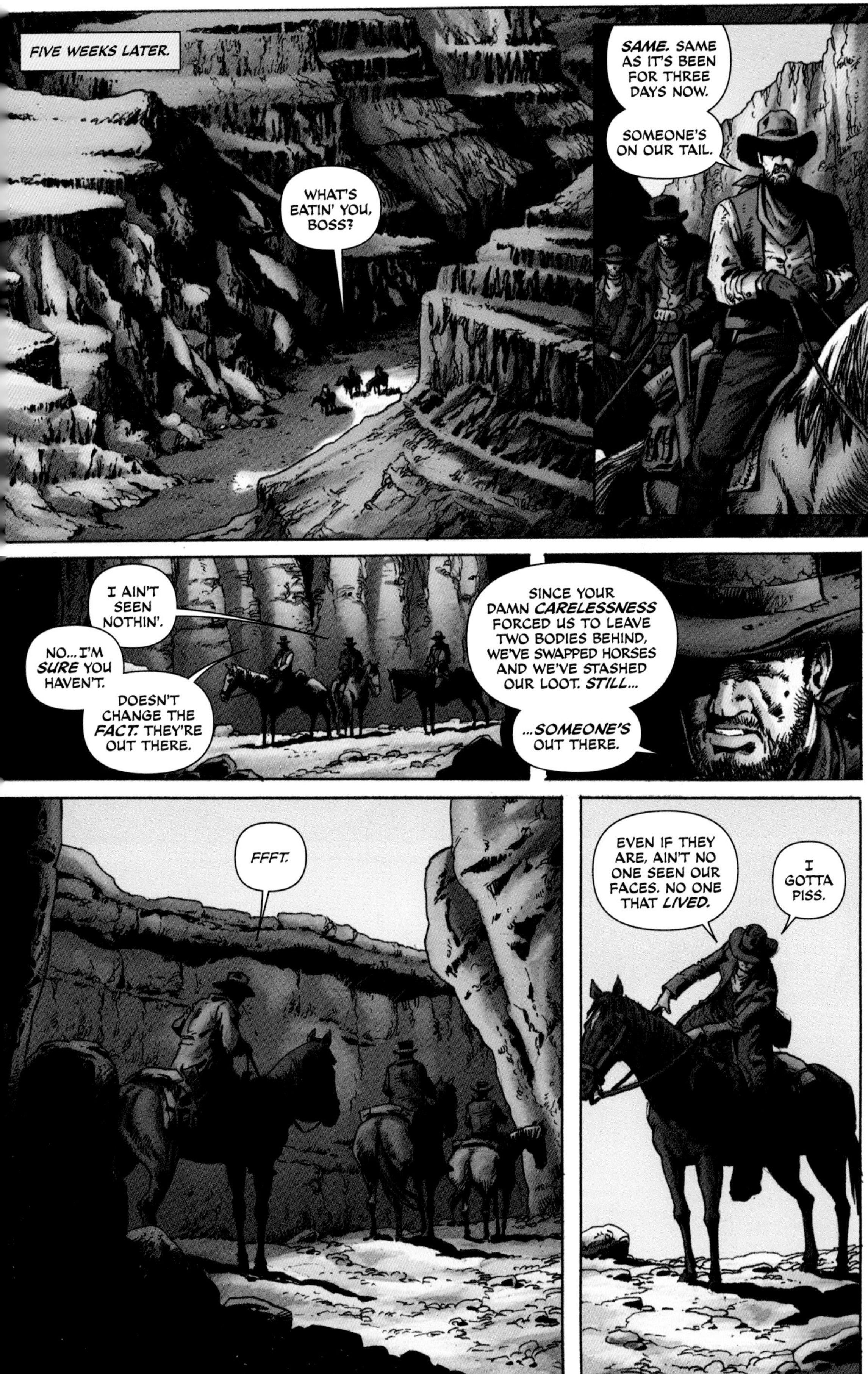
FIVE WEEKS LATER.
WHAT'S EATIN' YOU, BOSS?
SAME. SAME AS IT'S BEEN FOR THREE DAYS NOW.
SOMEONE'S ON OUR TAIL.
I AIN'T SEEN NOTHIN'.
NO... I'M SURE YOU HAVEN'T.
DOESN'T CHANGE THE FACT. THEY'RE OUT THERE.
SINCE YOUR DAMN CARELESSNESS FORCED US TO LEAVE TWO BODIES BEHIND, WE'VE SWAPPED HORSES AND WE'VE STASHED OUR LOOT. STILL...
...SOMEONE'S OUT THERE.
FFFT.
EVEN IF THEY ARE, AIN'T NO ONE SEEN OUR FACES. NO ONE THAT LIVED.
I GOTTA PISS.

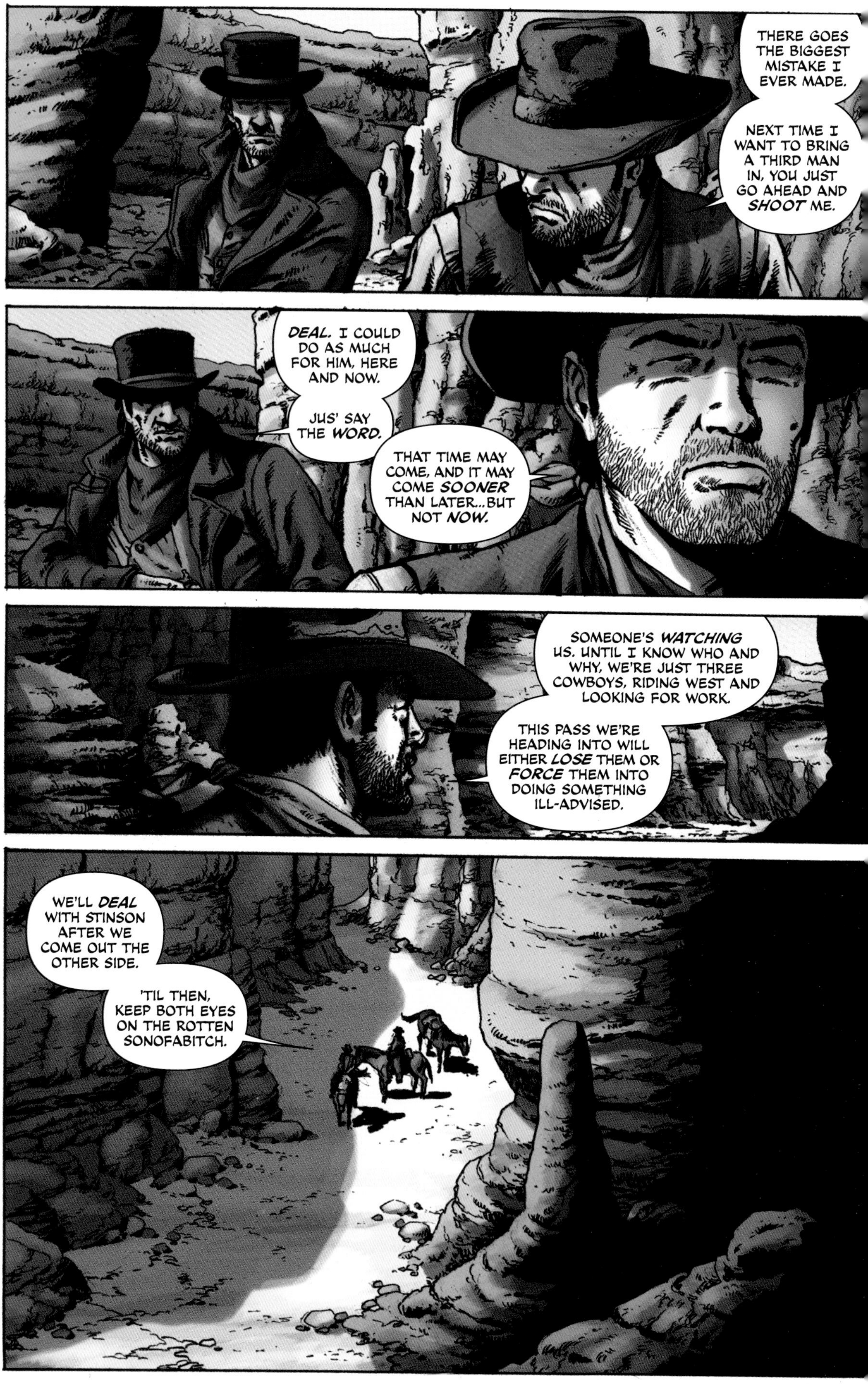
THERE GOES THE BIGGEST MISTAKE I EVER MADE.
NEXT TIME I WANT TO BRING A THIRD MAN IN, YOU JUST GO AHEAD AND *SHOOT* ME.
DEAL. I COULD DO AS MUCH FOR HIM, HERE AND NOW.
JUS' SAY THE *WORD.*
THAT TIME MAY COME, AND IT MAY COME *SOONER* THAN LATER...BUT NOT *NOW.*
SOMEONE'S *WATCHING* US. UNTIL I KNOW WHO AND WHY, WE'RE JUST THREE COWBOYS, RIDING WEST AND LOOKING FOR WORK.
THIS PASS WE'RE HEADING INTO WILL EITHER *LOSE* THEM OR *FORCE* THEM INTO DOING SOMETHING ILL-ADVISED.
WE'LL *DEAL* WITH STINSON AFTER WE COME OUT THE OTHER SIDE.
'TIL THEN, KEEP BOTH EYES ON THE ROTTEN SONOFABITCH.

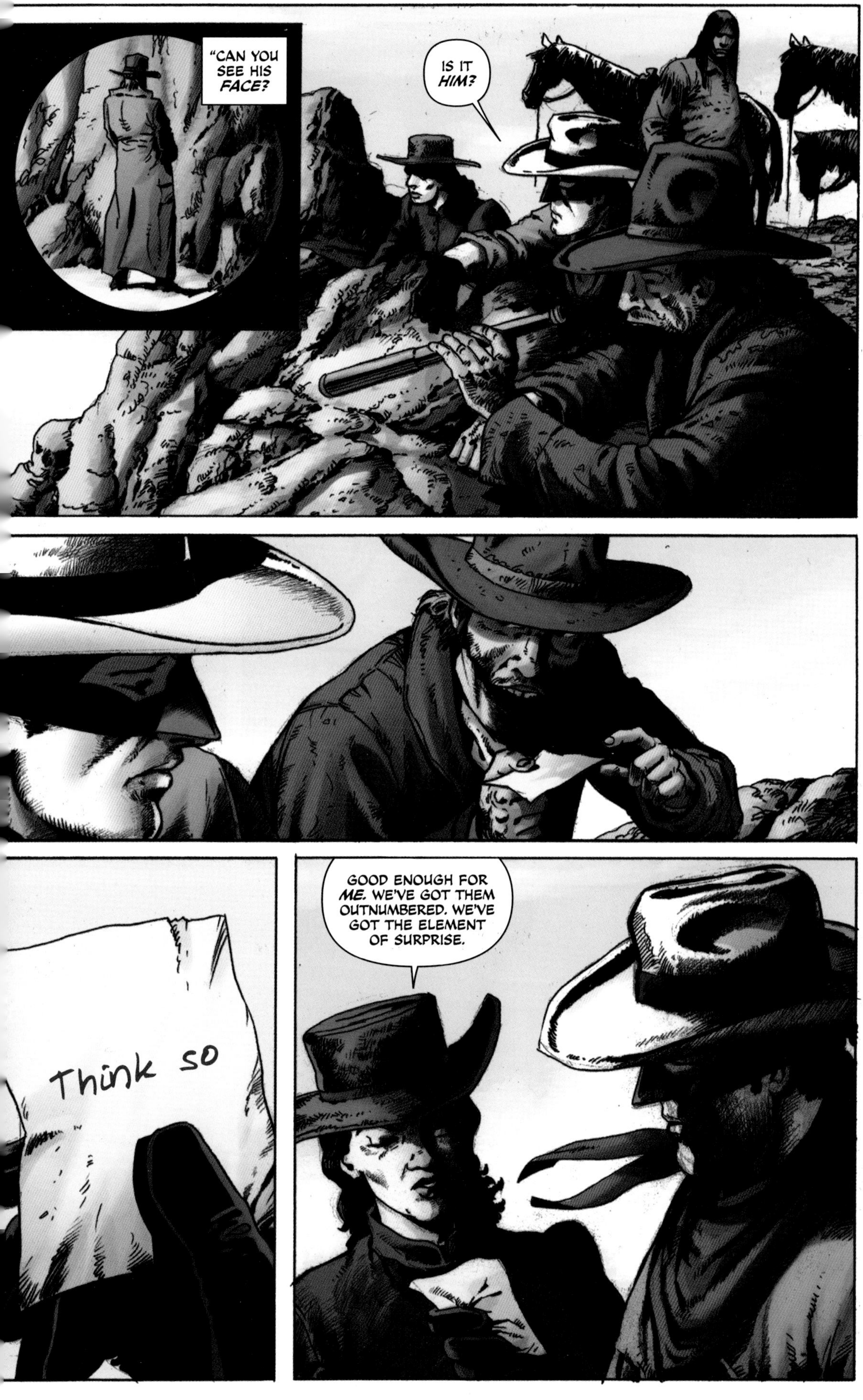

"CAN YOU SEE HIS *FACE?*
IS IT *HIM?*
Think so
GOOD ENOUGH FOR *ME.* WE'VE GOT THEM OUTNUMBERED. WE'VE GOT THE ELEMENT OF SURPRISE.

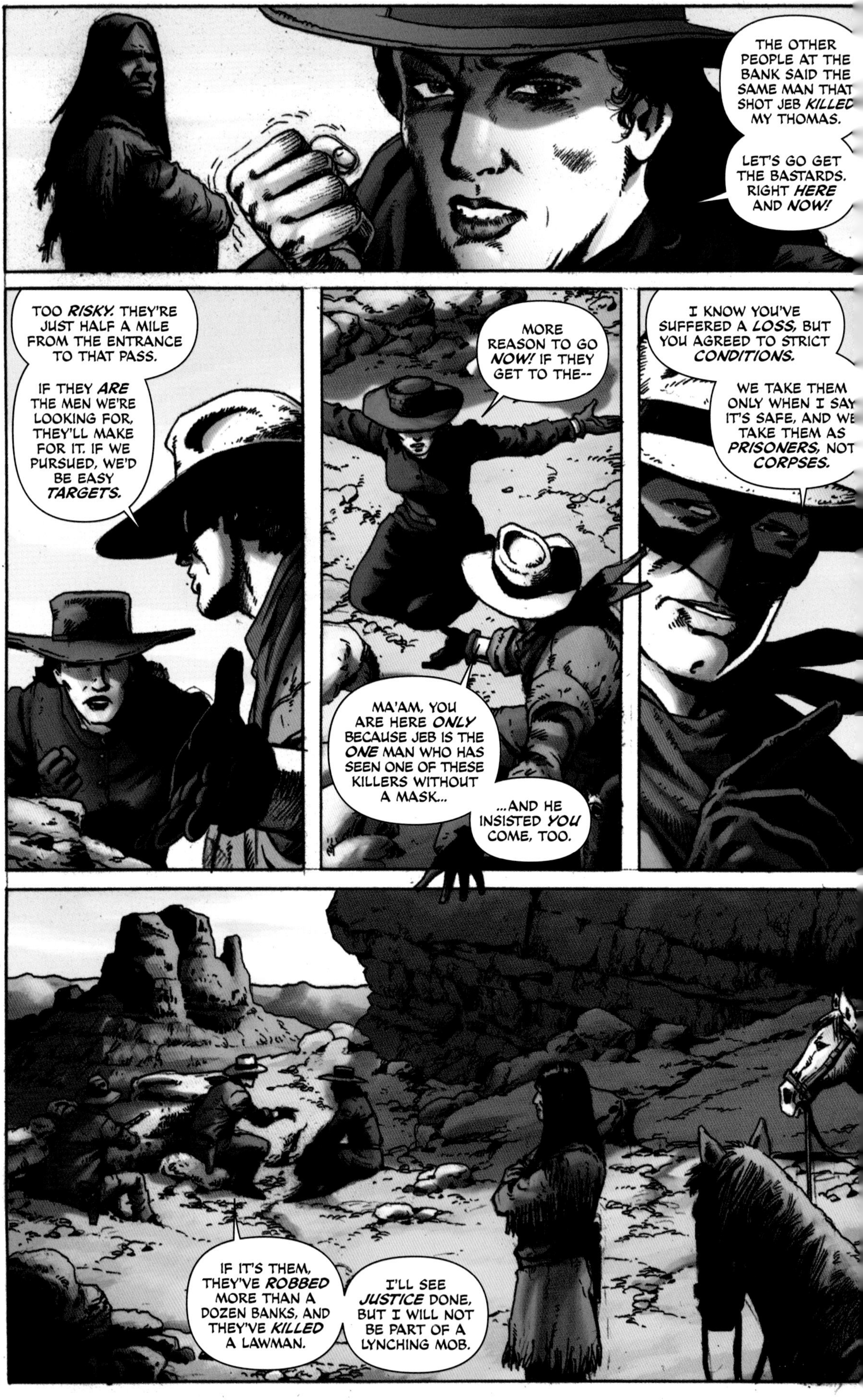
THE OTHER PEOPLE AT THE BANK SAID THE SAME MAN THAT SHOT JEB *KILLED* MY THOMAS.
LET'S GO GET THE BASTARDS. RIGHT *HERE* AND *NOW!*
TOO *RISKY.* THEY'RE JUST HALF A MILE FROM THE ENTRANCE TO THAT PASS.
IF THEY *ARE* THE MEN WE'RE LOOKING FOR, THEY'LL MAKE FOR IT. IF WE PURSUED, WE'D BE EASY *TARGETS.*
MORE REASON TO GO *NOW!* IF THEY GET TO THE--
MA'AM, YOU ARE HERE *ONLY* BECAUSE JEB IS THE *ONE* MAN WHO HAS SEEN ONE OF THESE KILLERS WITHOUT A MASK...
...AND HE INSISTED *YOU* COME, TOO.
I KNOW YOU'VE SUFFERED A *LOSS,* BUT YOU AGREED TO STRICT *CONDITIONS.*
WE TAKE THEM ONLY WHEN I SAY IT'S SAFE, AND WE TAKE THEM AS *PRISONERS,* NOT *CORPSES.*
IF IT'S THEM, THEY'VE *ROBBED* MORE THAN A DOZEN BANKS, AND THEY'VE *KILLED* A LAWMAN.
I'LL SEE *JUSTICE* DONE, BUT I WILL NOT BE PART OF A LYNCHING MOB.

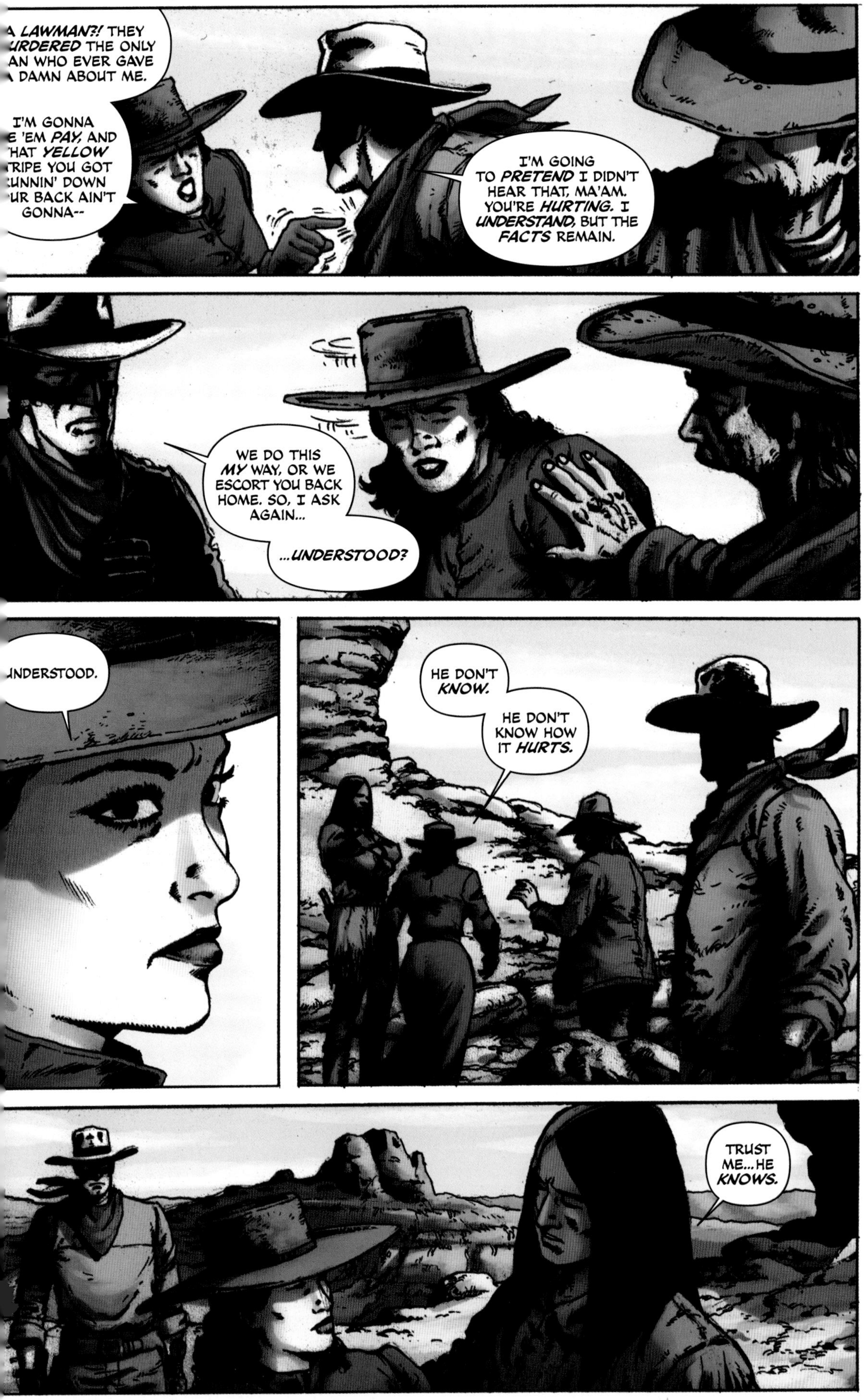
A LAWMAN?! THEY URDERED THE ONLY AN WHO EVER GAVE A DAMN ABOUT ME.
I'M GONNA E 'EM PAY, AND THAT YELLOW TRIPE YOU GOT UNNIN' DOWN UR BACK AIN'T GONNA--
I'M GOING TO PRETEND I DIDN'T HEAR THAT, MA'AM. YOU'RE HURTING. I UNDERSTAND, BUT THE FACTS REMAIN.
WE DO THIS MY WAY, OR WE ESCORT YOU BACK HOME. SO, I ASK AGAIN...
...UNDERSTOOD?
NDERSTOOD.
HE DON'T KNOW.
HE DON'T KNOW HOW IT HURTS.
TRUST ME...HE KNOWS.

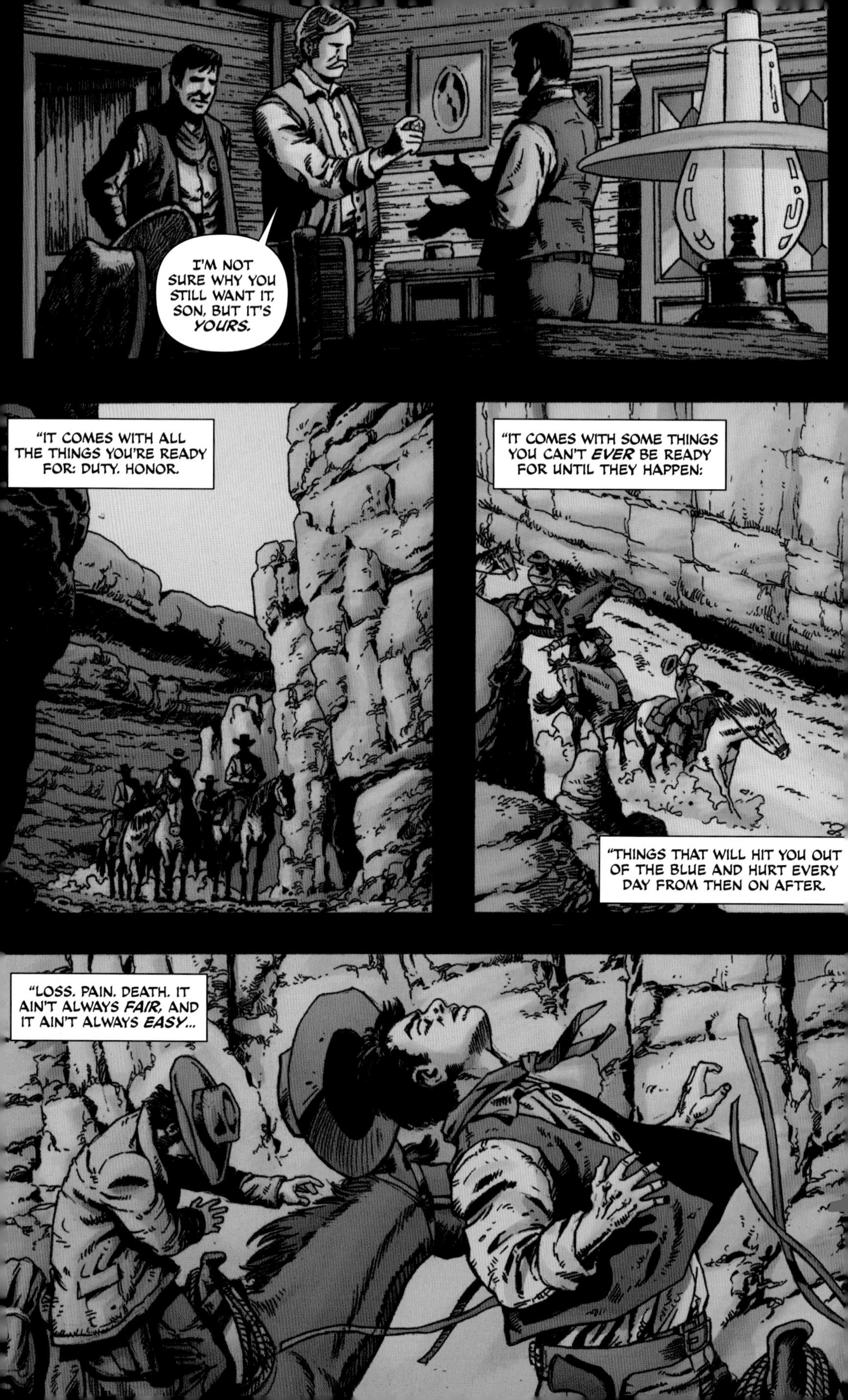
I'M NOT SURE WHY YOU STILL WANT IT, SON, BUT IT'S YOURS.
"IT COMES WITH ALL THE THINGS YOU'RE READY FOR: DUTY. HONOR.
"IT COMES WITH SOME THINGS YOU CAN'T EVER BE READY FOR UNTIL THEY HAPPEN:
"THINGS THAT WILL HIT YOU OUT OF THE BLUE AND HURT EVERY DAY FROM THEN ON AFTER.
"LOSS. PAIN. DEATH. IT AIN'T ALWAYS FAIR, AND IT AIN'T ALWAYS EASY...

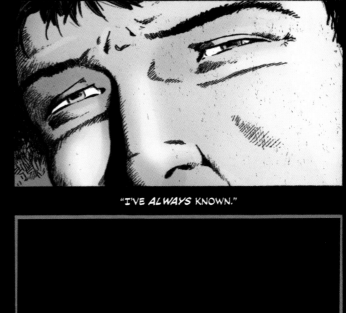

"...BUT I *KNOW* YOU CAN TAKE IT, SON.

"I'VE *ALWAYS* KNOWN."

HUH...?

EVENIN', JEB.

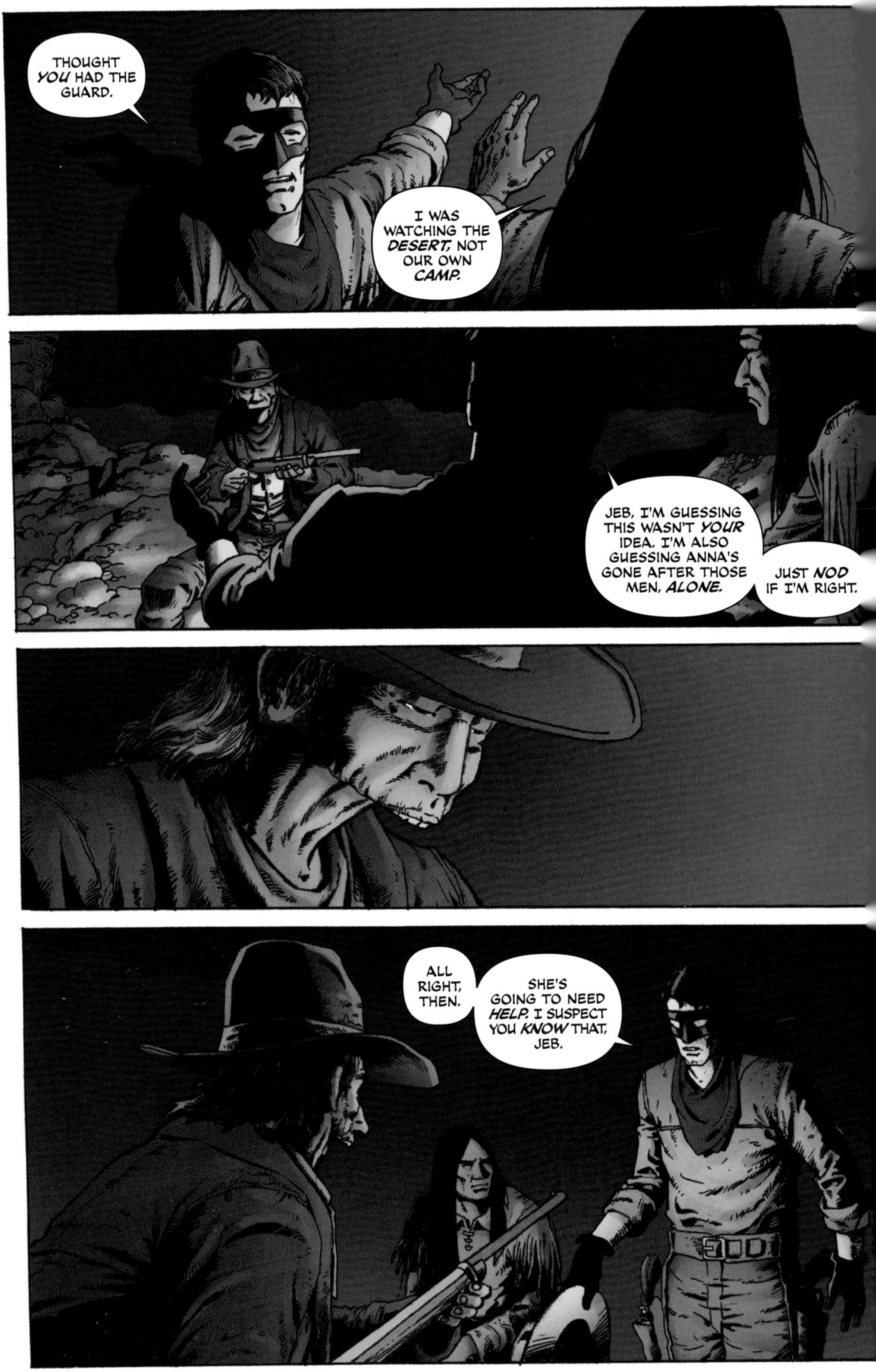
THOUGHT YOU HAD THE GUARD.
I WAS WATCHING THE DESERT, NOT OUR OWN CAMP.
JEB, I'M GUESSING THIS WASN'T YOUR IDEA. I'M ALSO GUESSING ANNA'S GONE AFTER THOSE MEN, ALONE.
JUST NOD IF I'M RIGHT.
ALL RIGHT, THEN.
SHE'S GOING TO NEED HELP. I SUSPECT YOU KNOW THAT, JEB.

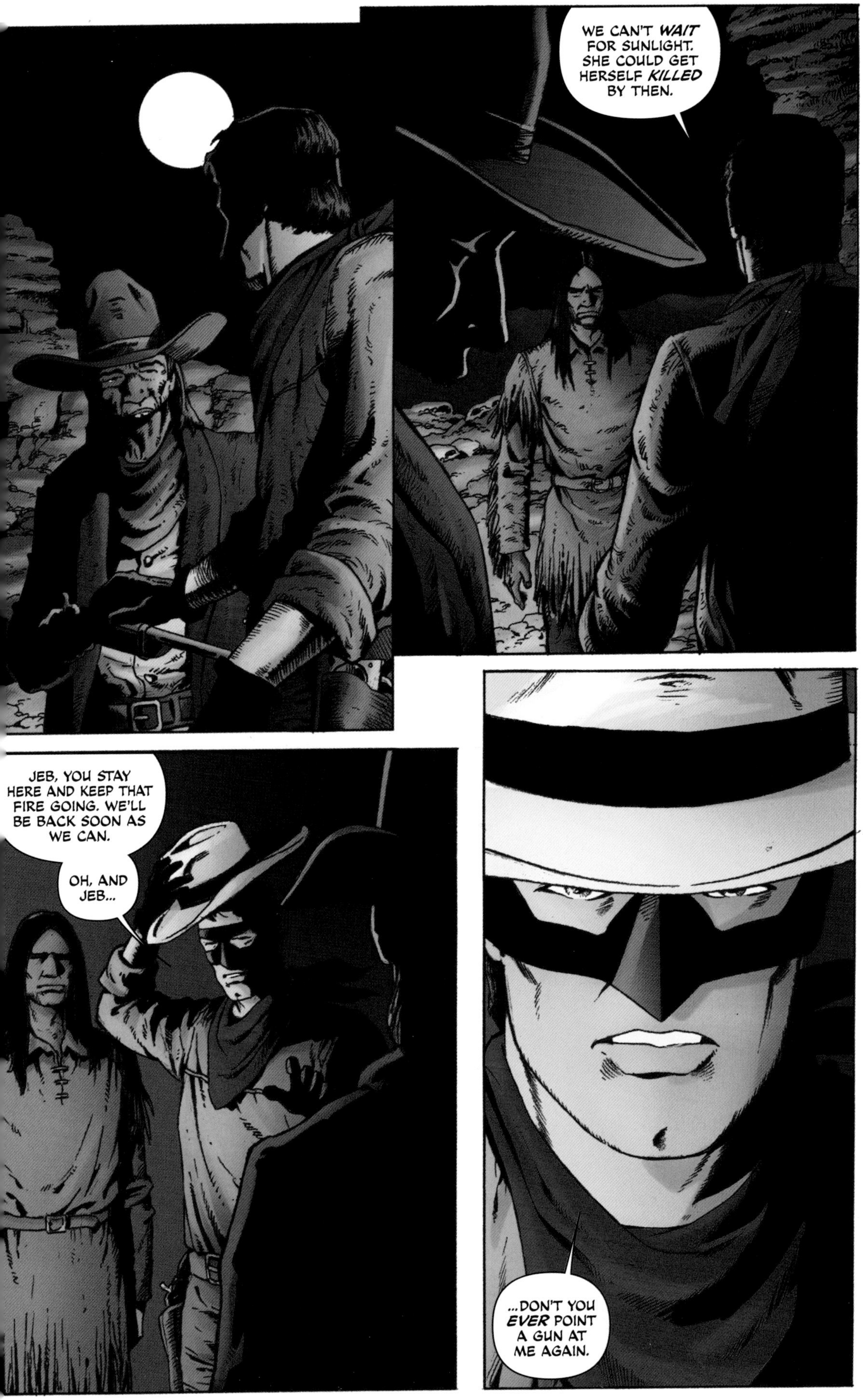

WE CAN'T *WAIT* FOR SUNLIGHT. SHE COULD GET HERSELF *KILLED* BY THEN.
JEB, YOU STAY HERE AND KEEP THAT FIRE GOING. WE'LL BE BACK SOON AS WE CAN.
OH, AND JEB...
...DON'T YOU *EVER* POINT A GUN AT ME AGAIN.

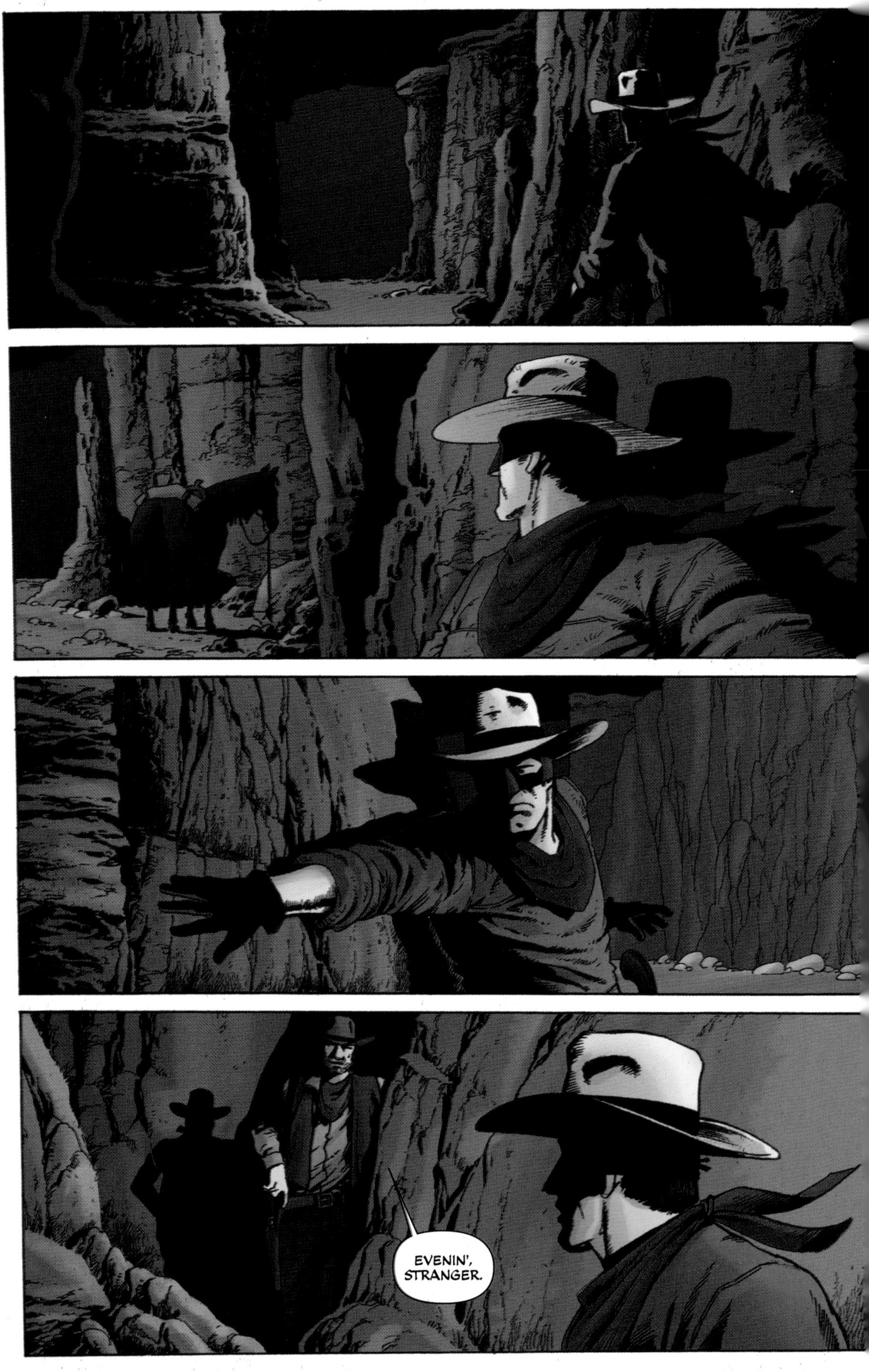
EVENIN', STRANGER.

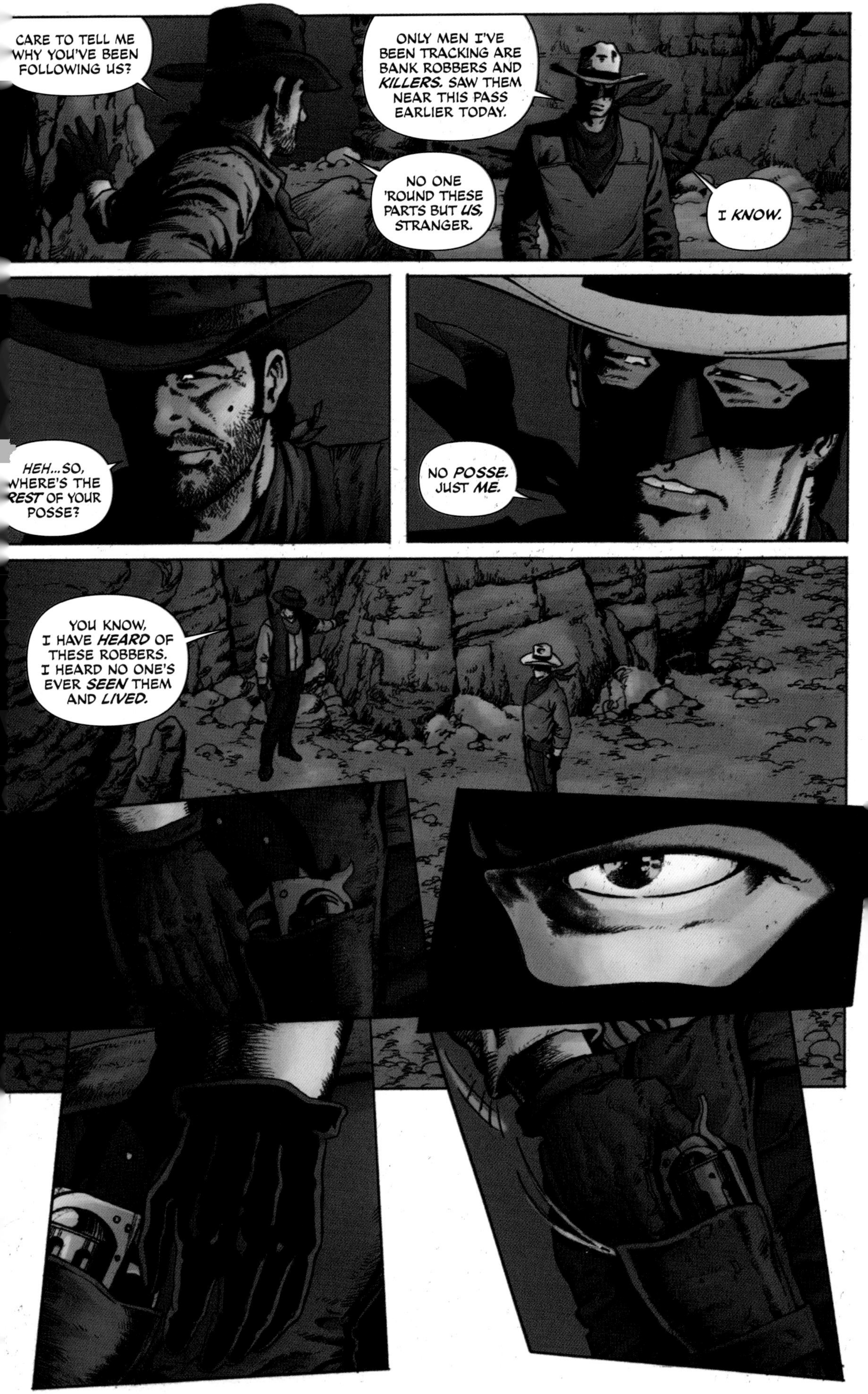
CARE TO TELL ME WHY YOU'VE BEEN FOLLOWING US?
ONLY MEN I'VE BEEN TRACKING ARE BANK ROBBERS AND KILLERS. SAW THEM NEAR THIS PASS EARLIER TODAY.
NO ONE 'ROUND THESE PARTS BUT US, STRANGER.
I KNOW.
HEH...SO, WHERE'S THE REST OF YOUR POSSE?
NO POSSE. JUST ME.
YOU KNOW, I HAVE HEARD OF THESE ROBBERS. I HEARD NO ONE'S EVER SEEN THEM AND LIVED.

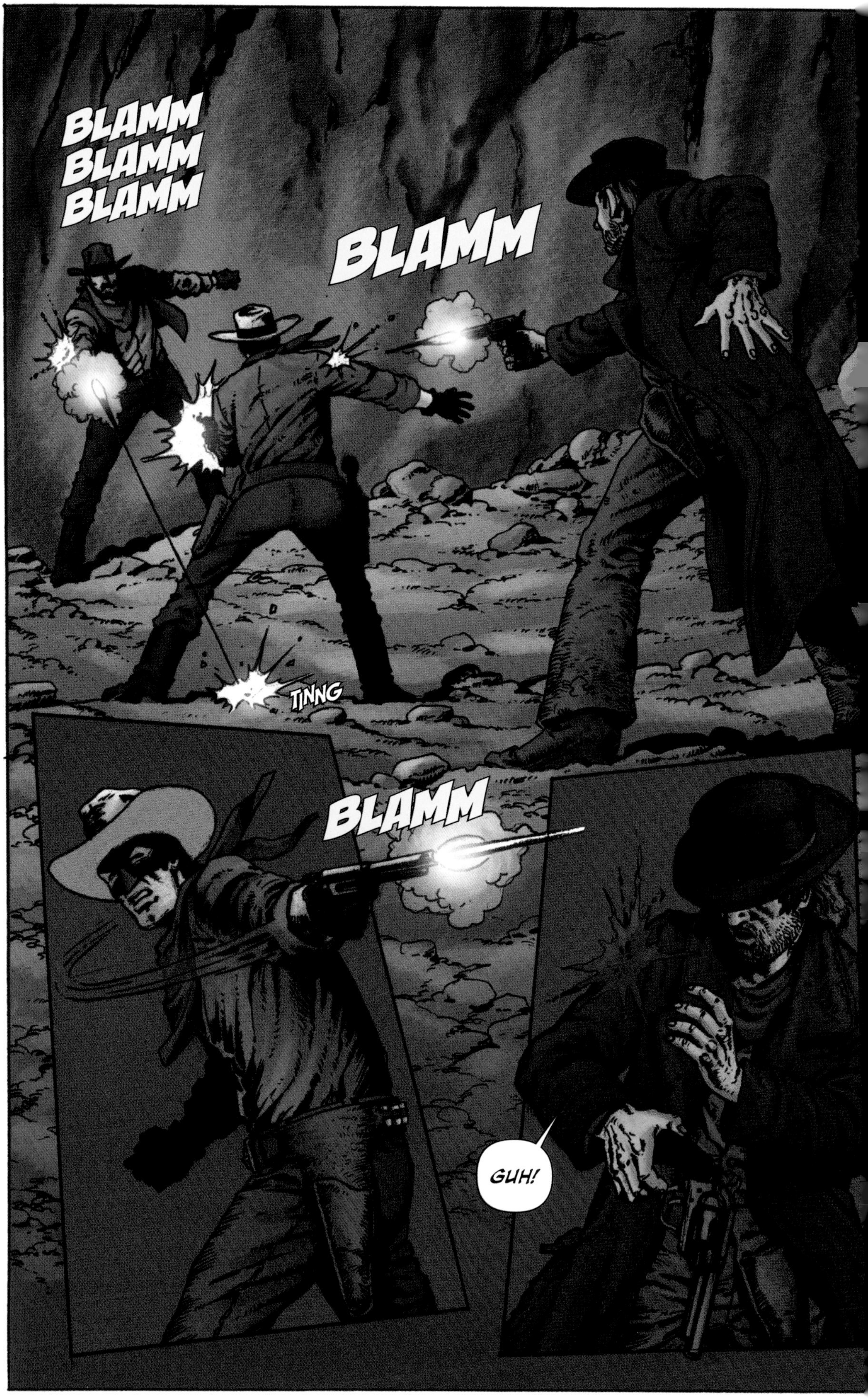
BLAMM
BLAMM
BLAMM
BLAMM
TINNG
BLAMM
GUH!

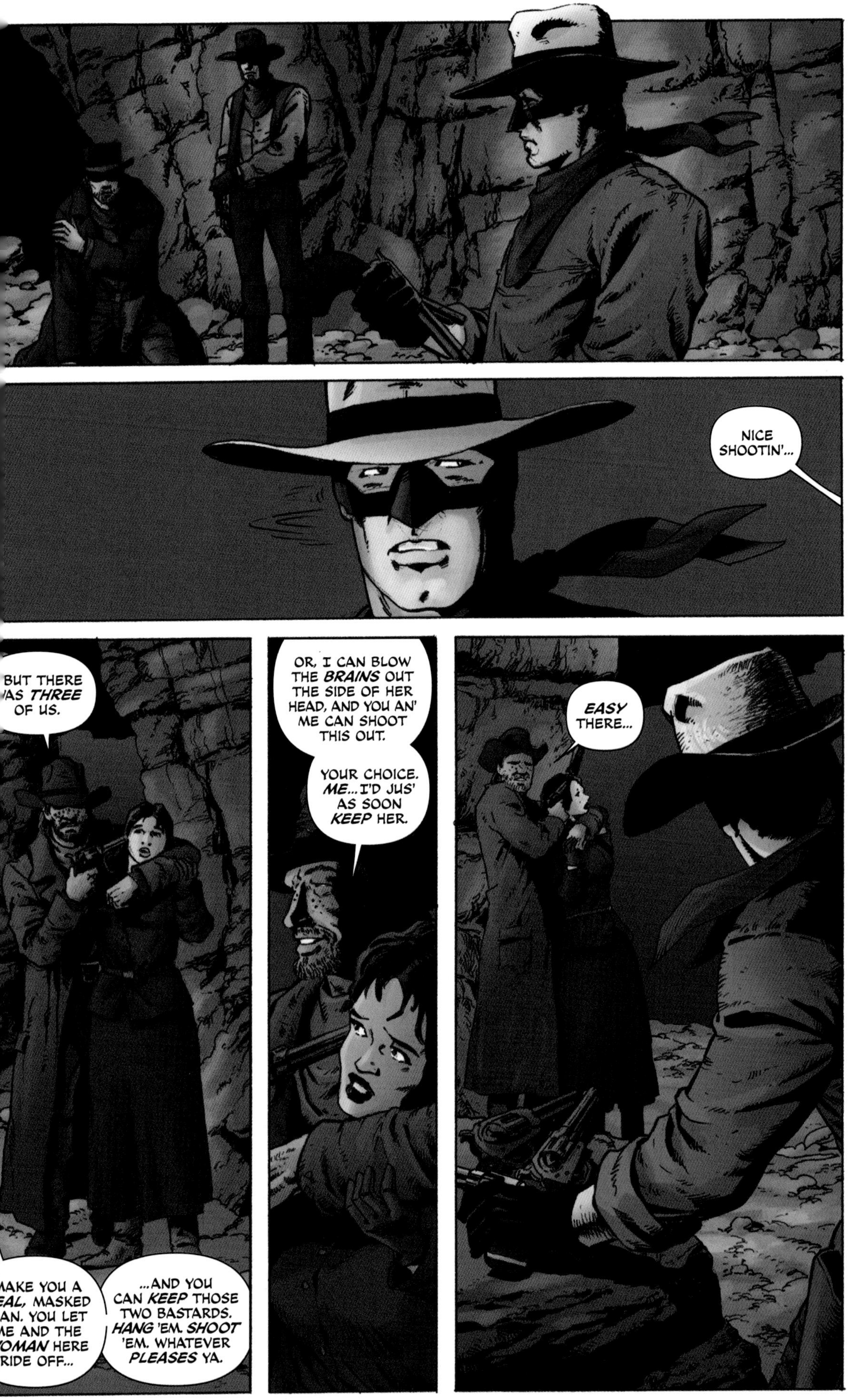
NICE SHOOTIN'...
BUT THERE AS THREE OF US.
OR, I CAN BLOW THE BRAINS OUT THE SIDE OF HER HEAD, AND YOU AN' ME CAN SHOOT THIS OUT.
YOUR CHOICE. ME...I'D JUS' AS SOON KEEP HER.
EASY THERE...
MAKE YOU A EAL, MASKED AN. YOU LET ME AND THE OMAN HERE RIDE OFF...
...AND YOU CAN KEEP THOSE TWO BASTARDS. HANG 'EM. SHOOT 'EM. WHATEVER PLEASES YA.

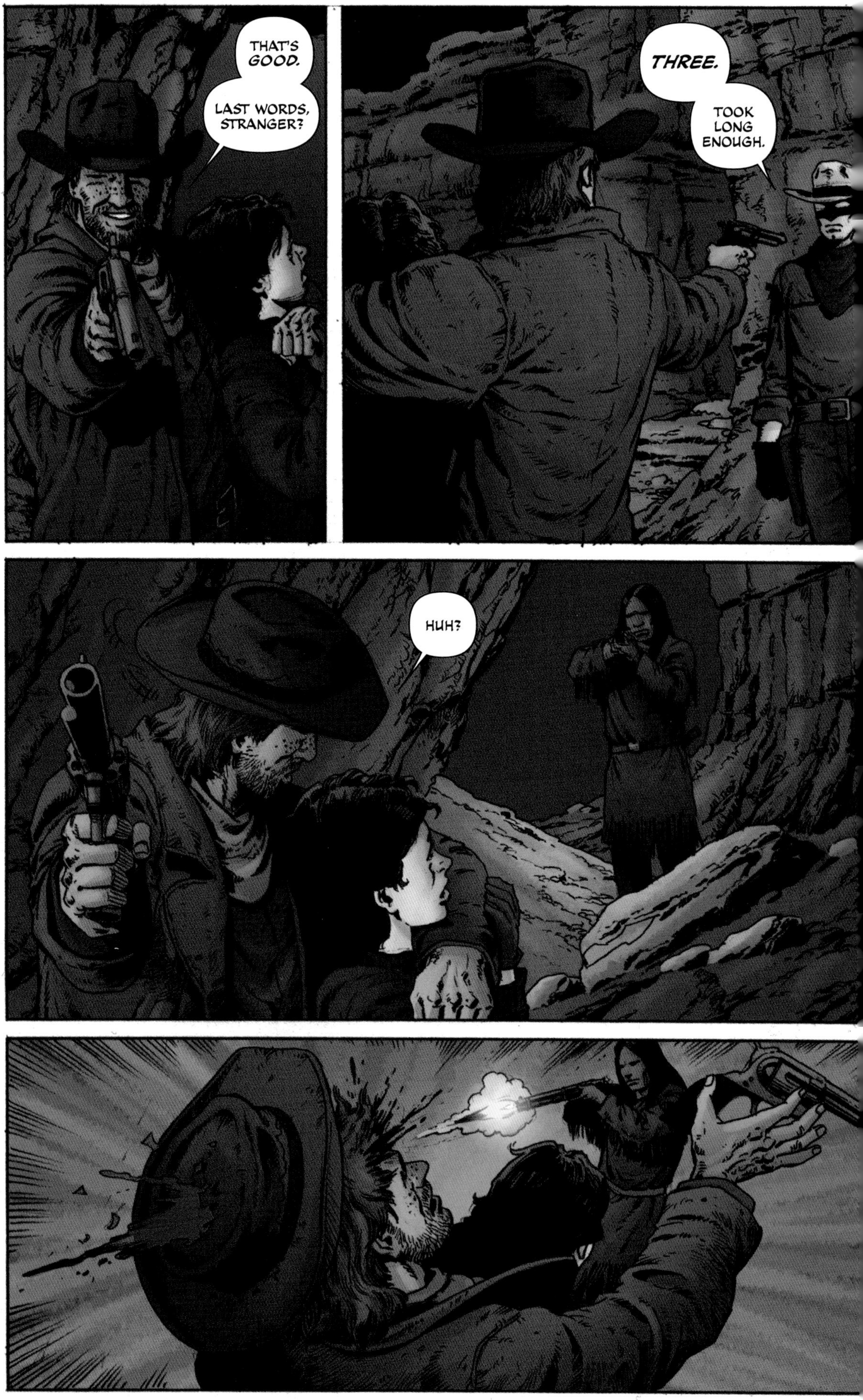

THAT'S *GOOD.*
LAST WORDS, STRANGER?
THREE.
TOOK LONG ENOUGH.
HUH?

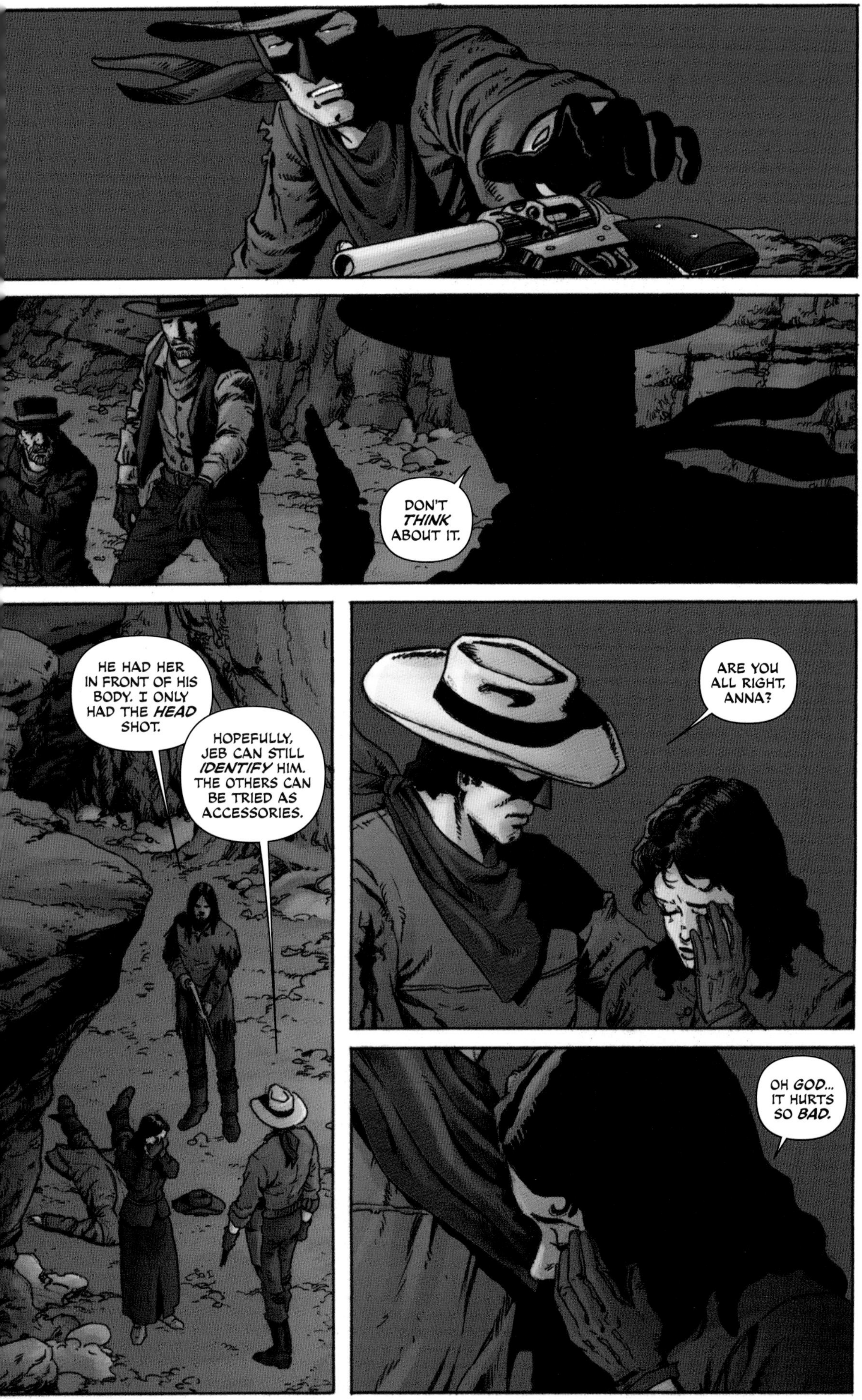
DON'T *THINK* ABOUT IT.
HE HAD HER IN FRONT OF HIS BODY. I ONLY HAD THE *HEAD* SHOT.
HOPEFULLY, JEB CAN STILL *IDENTIFY* HIM. THE OTHERS CAN BE TRIED AS ACCESSORIES.
ARE YOU ALL RIGHT, ANNA?
OH *GOD*... IT HURTS SO *BAD.*

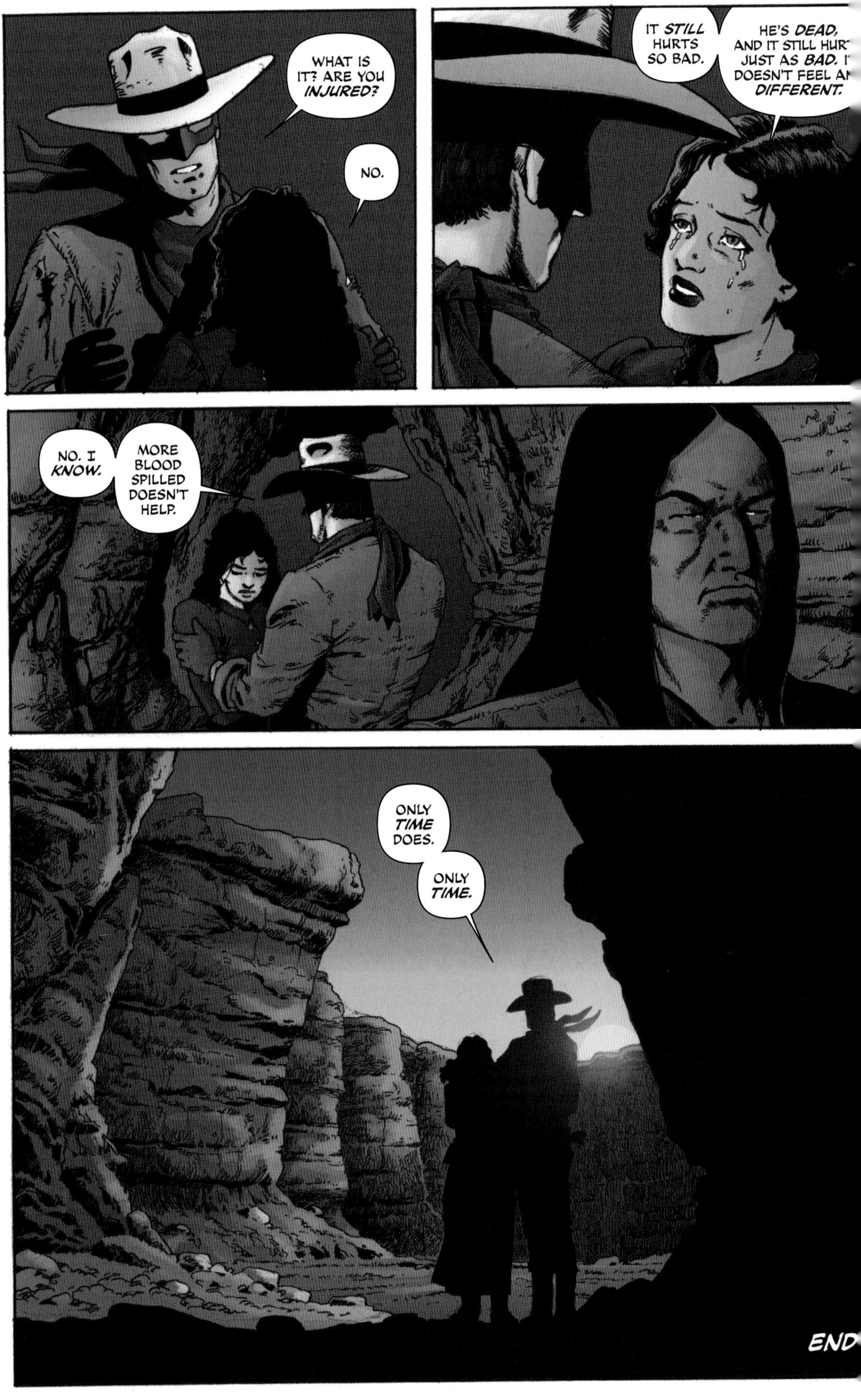

WHAT IS IT? ARE YOU *INJURED?*
NO.
IT *STILL* HURTS SO BAD.
HE'S *DEAD,* AND IT STILL HUR JUST AS *BAD.* I DOESN'T FEEL A *DIFFERENT.*
NO. I *KNOW.*
MORE BLOOD SPILLED DOESN'T HELP.
ONLY *TIME* DOES.
ONLY *TIME.*
END

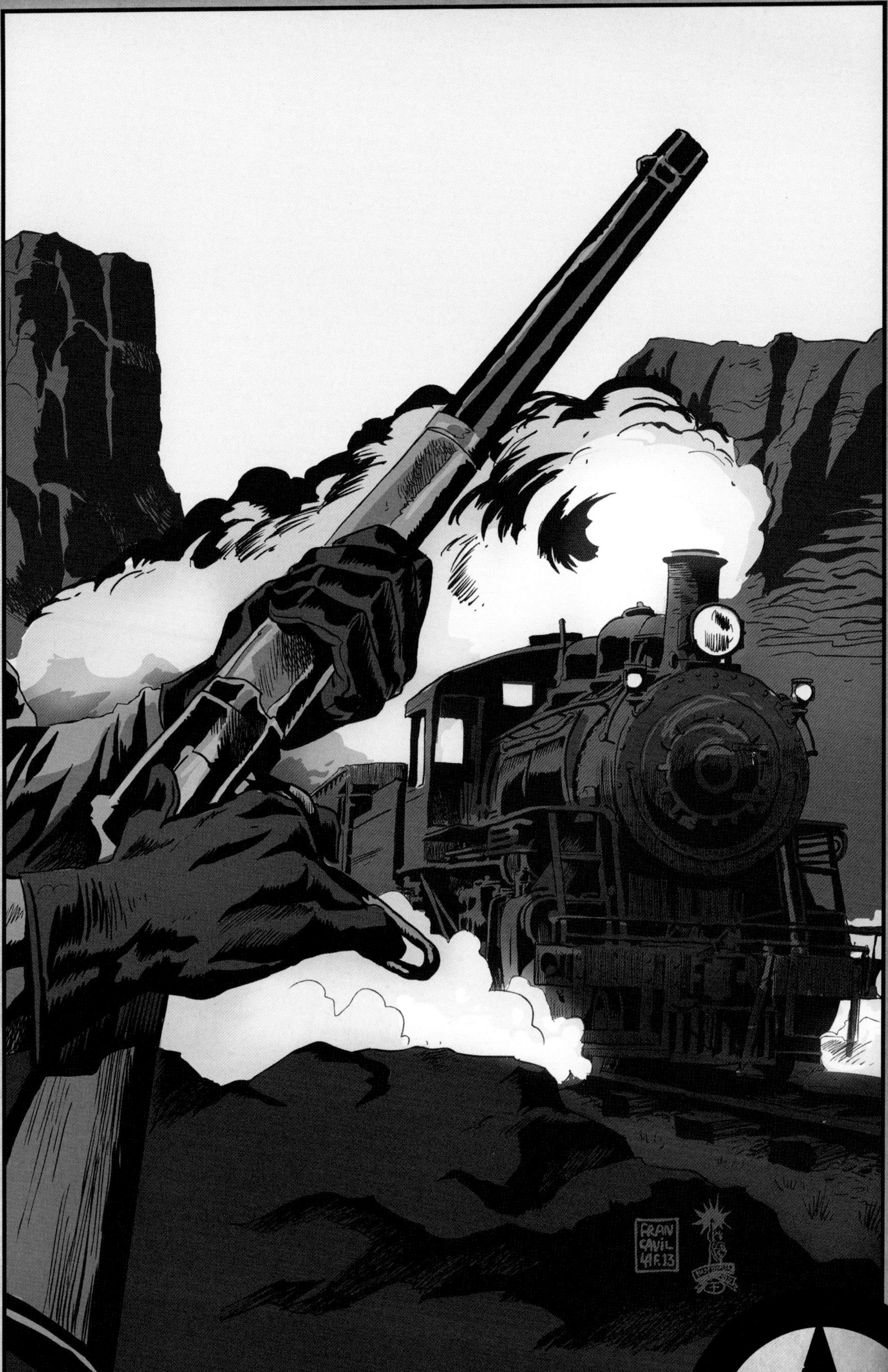
FRAN
CAVIL
LA F. 13

COVER BY **FRANCESCO FRANCAVILLA**

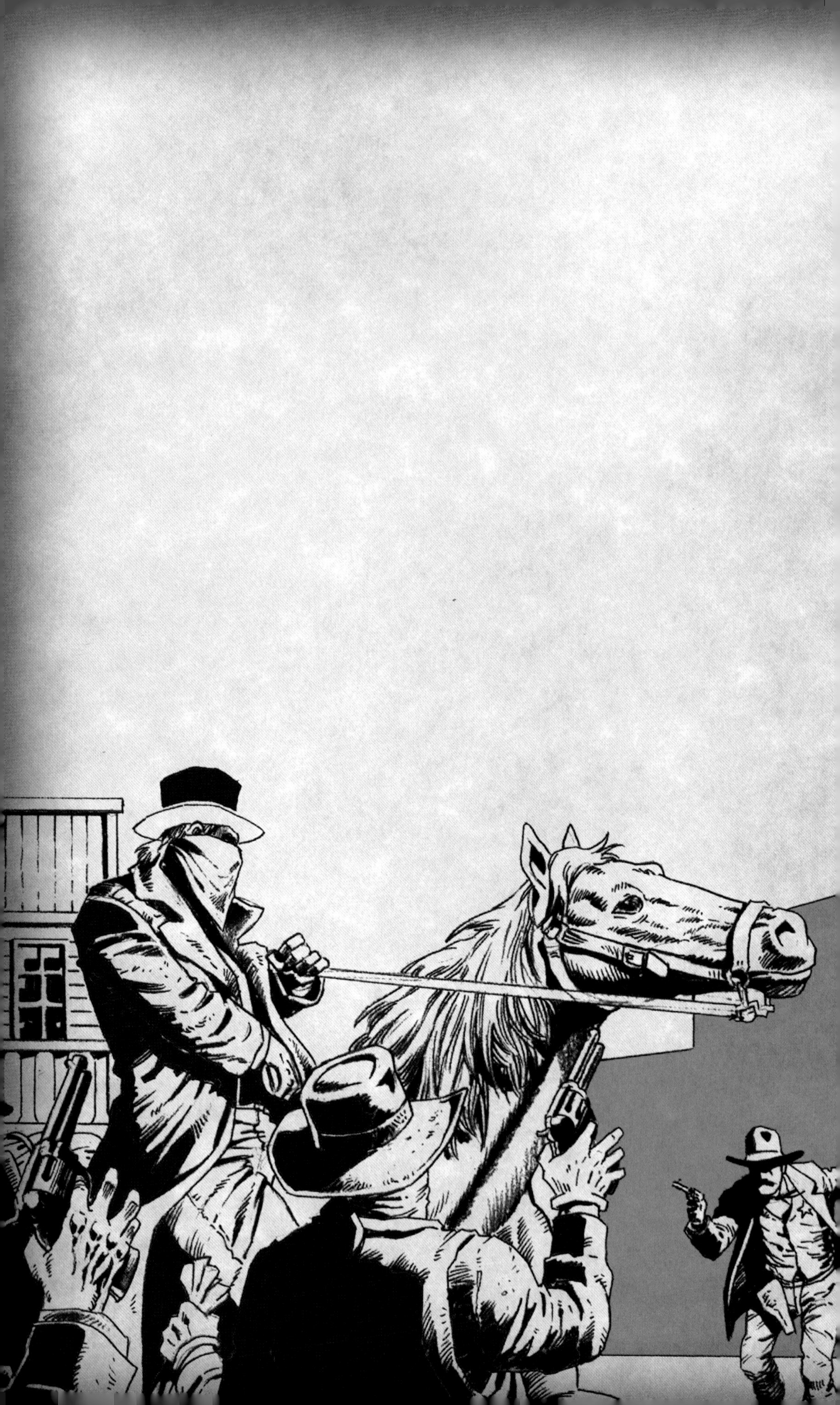

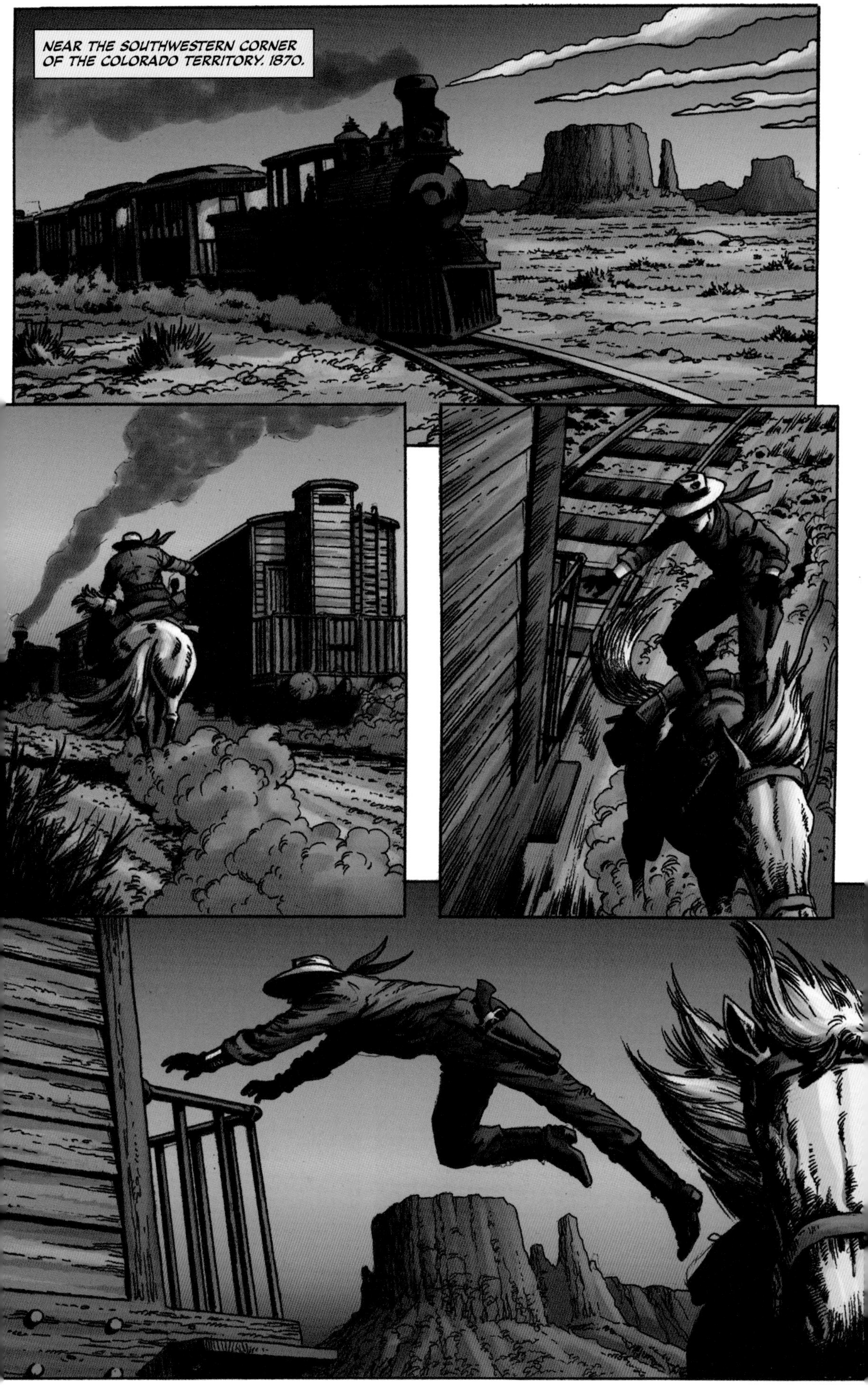
NEAR THE SOUTHWESTERN CORNER
OF THE COLORADO TERRITORY. 1870.

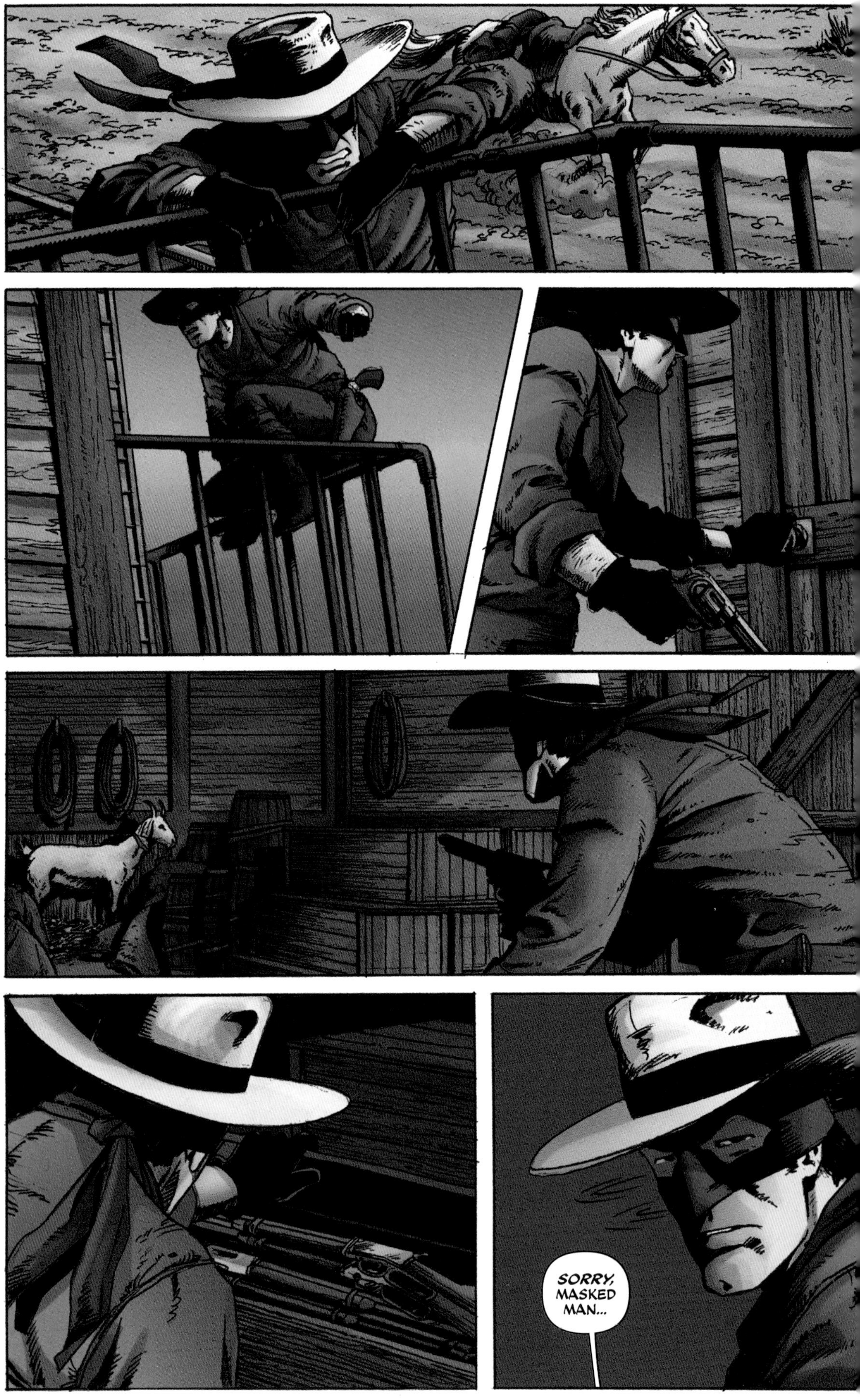
SORRY, MASKED MAN...

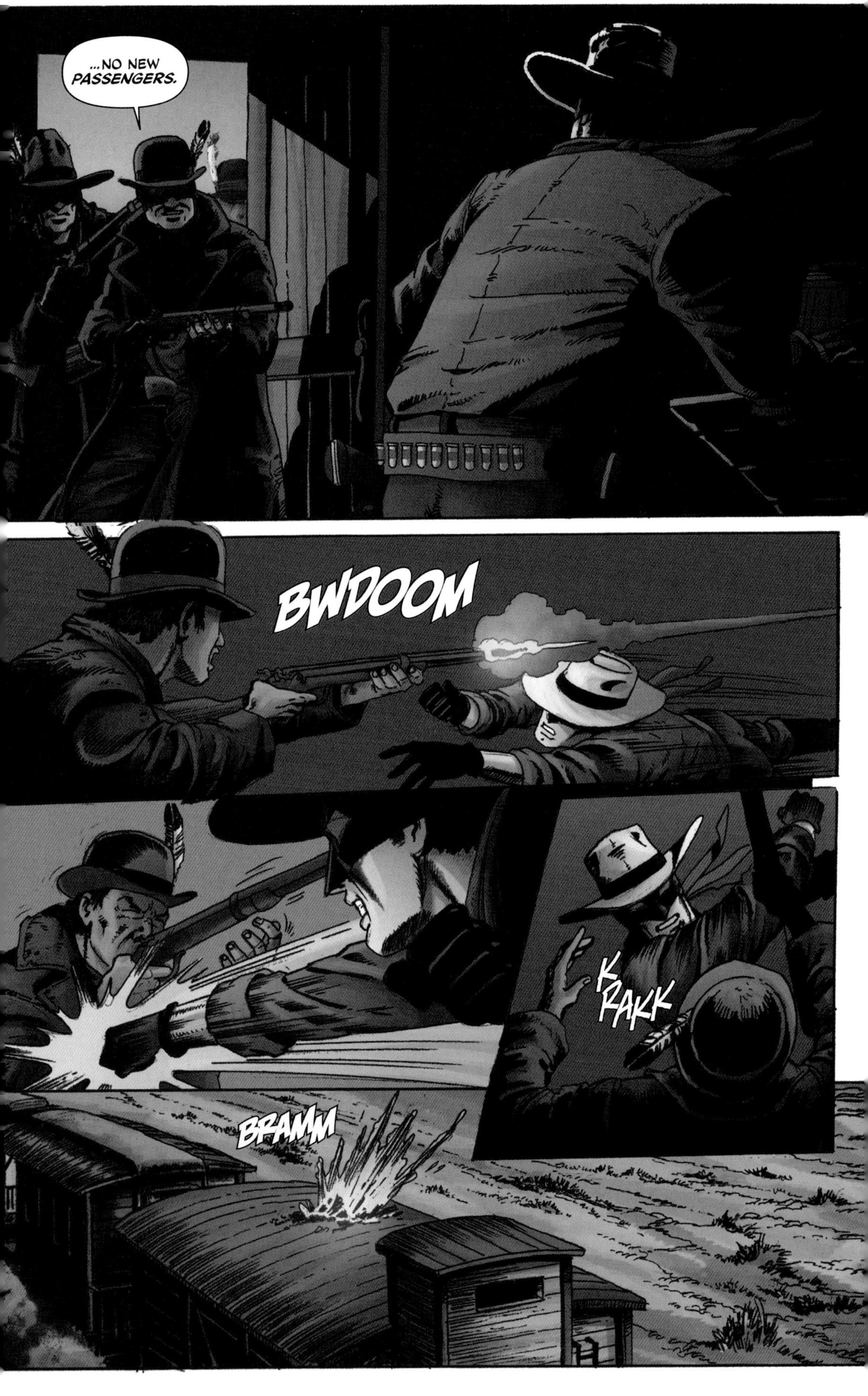
...NO NEW
PASSENGERS.
BWDOOM
KRAKK
BRAMM

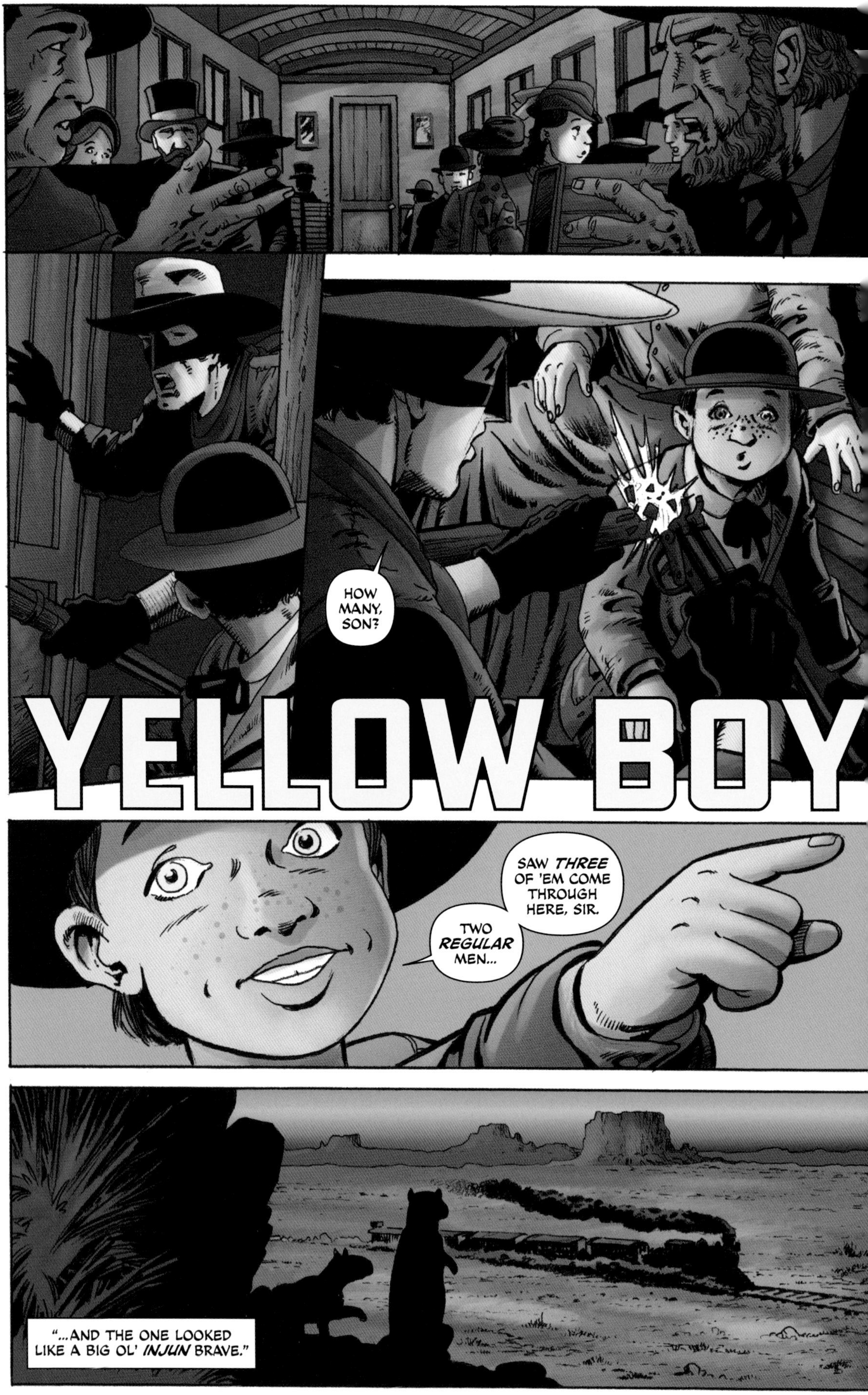
HOW MANY, SON?
YELLOW BOY
SAW *THREE* OF 'EM COME THROUGH HERE, SIR.
TWO *REGULAR* MEN...
"...AND THE ONE LOOKED LIKE A BIG OL' *INJUN* BRAVE."

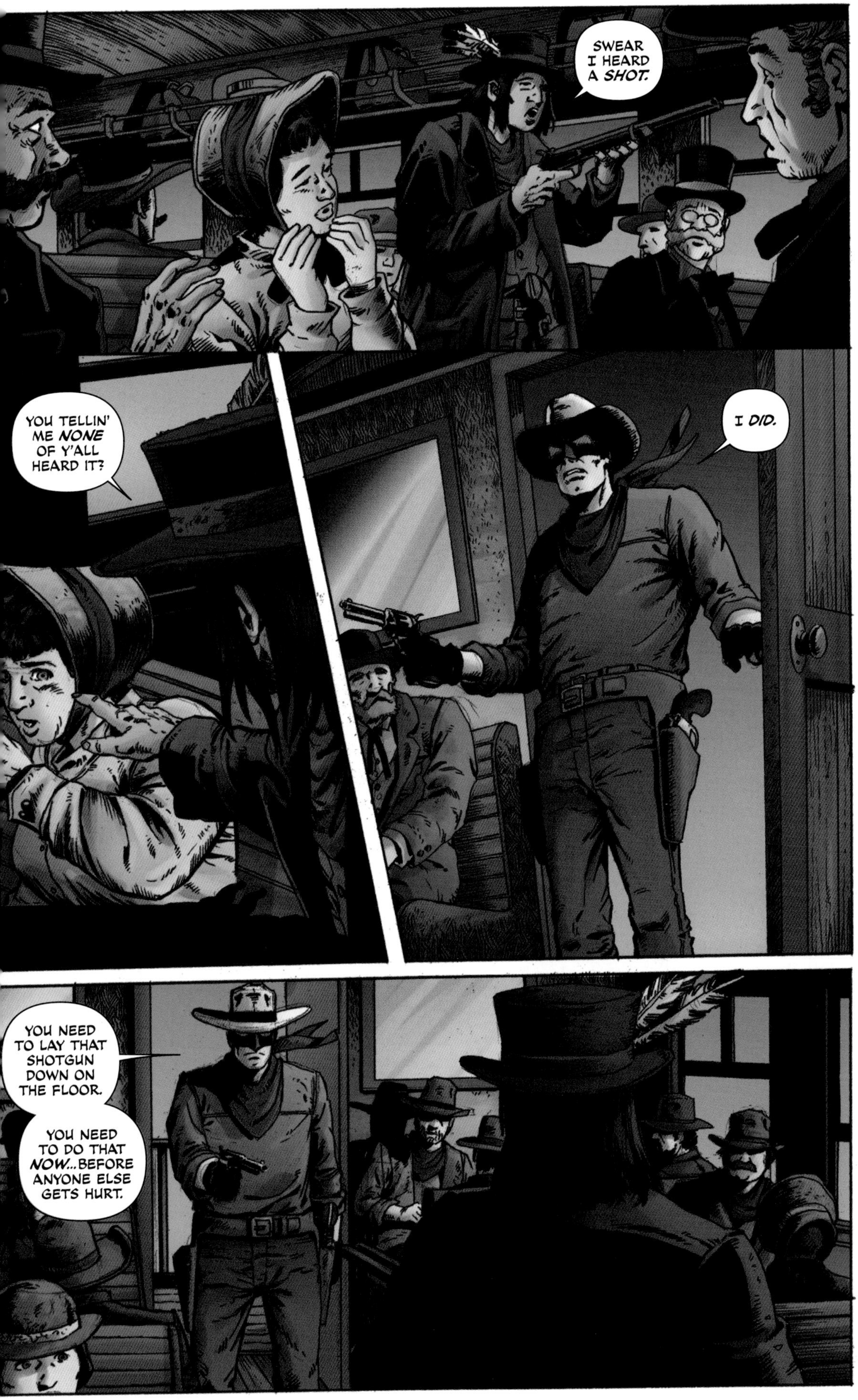
SWEAR I HEARD A *SHOT.*
YOU TELLIN' ME *NONE* OF Y'ALL HEARD IT?
I *DID.*
YOU NEED TO LAY THAT SHOTGUN DOWN ON THE FLOOR.
YOU NEED TO DO THAT *NOW*...BEFORE ANYONE ELSE GETS HURT.

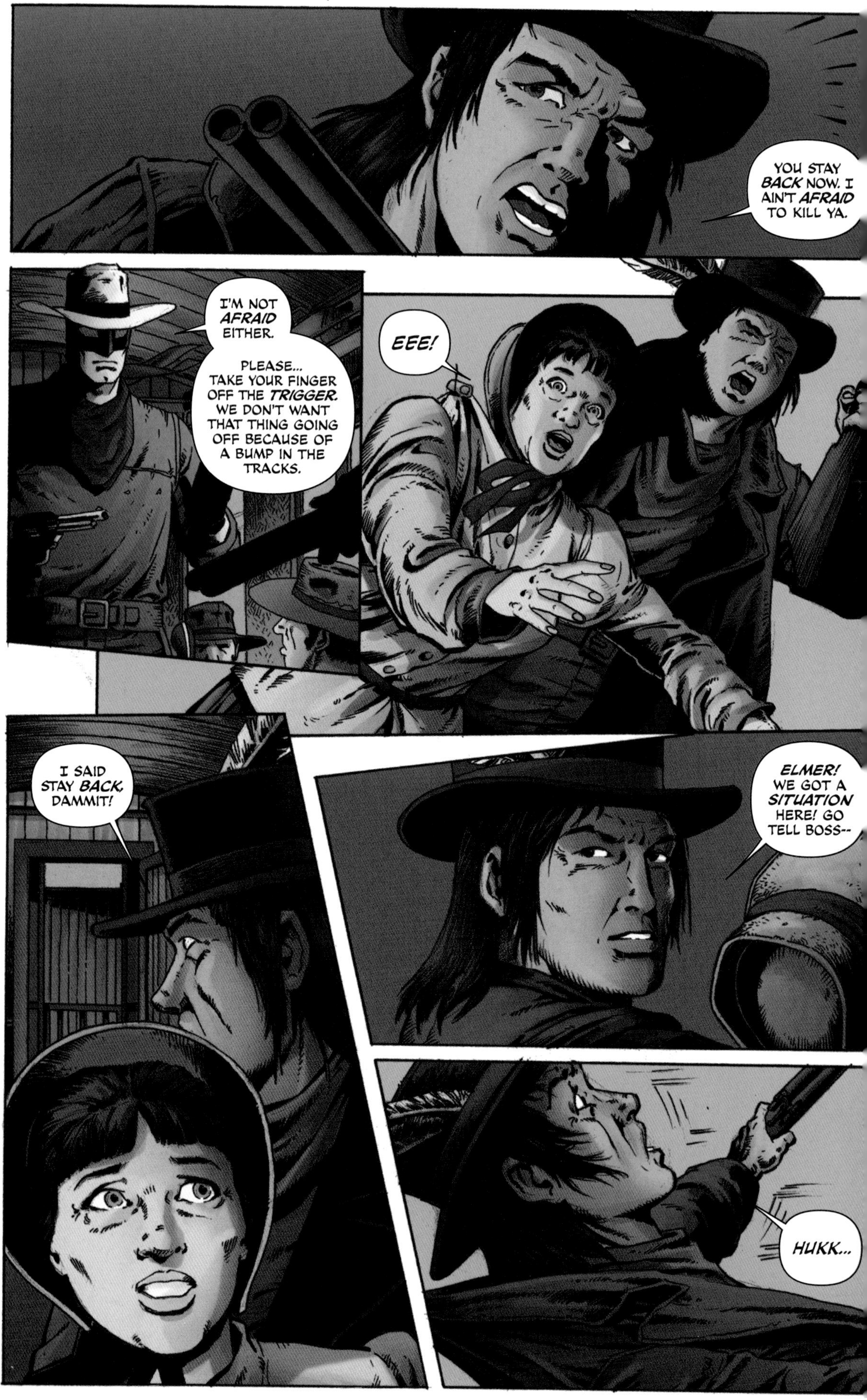
YOU STAY *BACK* NOW. I AIN'T *AFRAID* TO KILL YA.
I'M NOT *AFRAID* EITHER.
PLEASE... TAKE YOUR FINGER OFF THE *TRIGGER.* WE DON'T WANT THAT THING GOING OFF BECAUSE OF A BUMP IN THE TRACKS.
EEE!
I SAID STAY *BACK,* DAMMIT!
ELMER! WE GOT A *SITUATION* HERE! GO TELL BOSS--
HUKK...

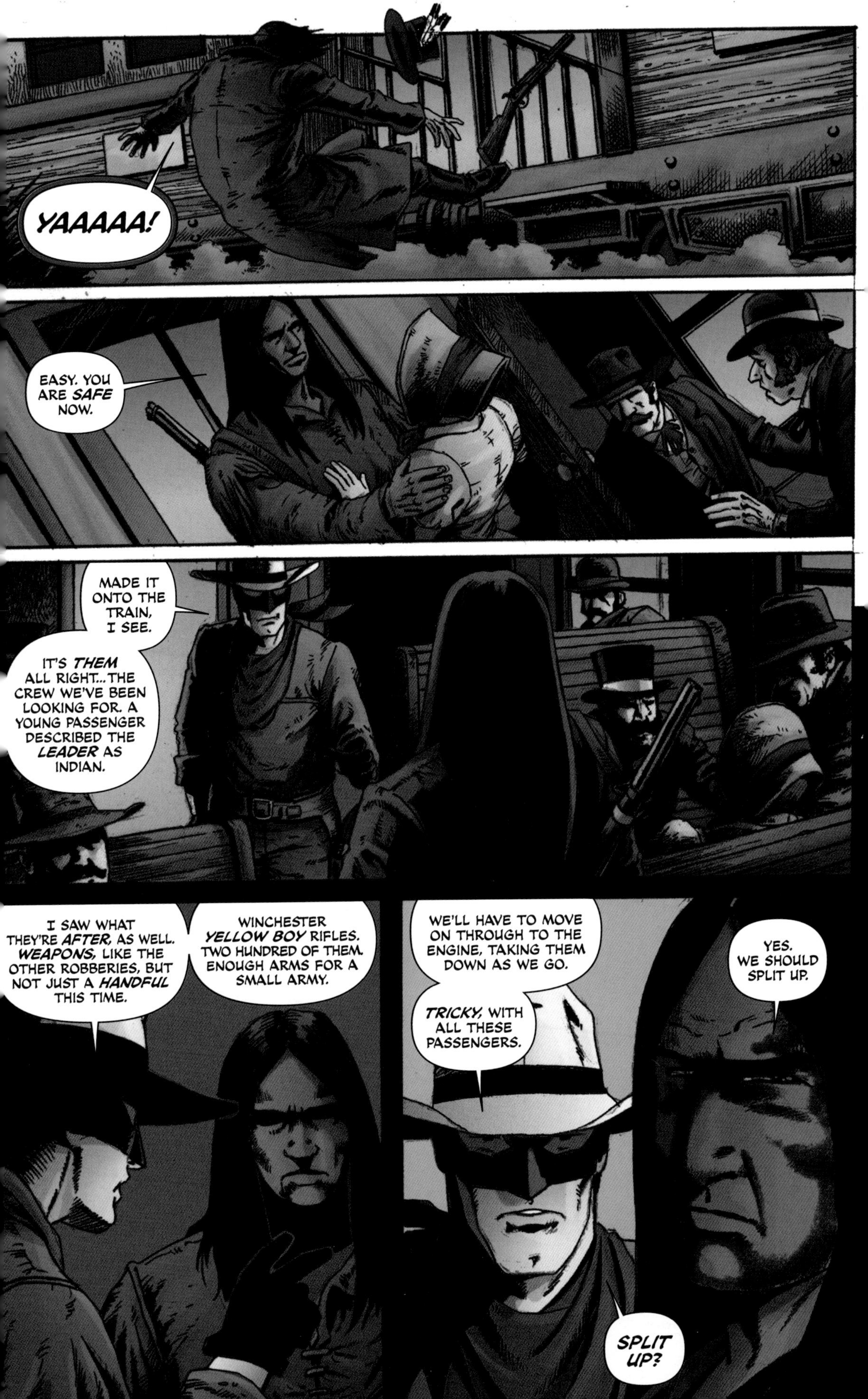
YAAAAA!
EASY. YOU ARE SAFE NOW.
MADE IT ONTO THE TRAIN, I SEE.
IT'S THEM ALL RIGHT... THE CREW WE'VE BEEN LOOKING FOR. A YOUNG PASSENGER DESCRIBED THE LEADER AS INDIAN.
I SAW WHAT THEY'RE AFTER, AS WELL. WEAPONS, LIKE THE OTHER ROBBERIES, BUT NOT JUST A HANDFUL THIS TIME.
WINCHESTER YELLOW BOY RIFLES. TWO HUNDRED OF THEM. ENOUGH ARMS FOR A SMALL ARMY.
WE'LL HAVE TO MOVE ON THROUGH TO THE ENGINE, TAKING THEM DOWN AS WE GO.
TRICKY, WITH ALL THESE PASSENGERS.
YES. WE SHOULD SPLIT UP.
SPLIT UP?

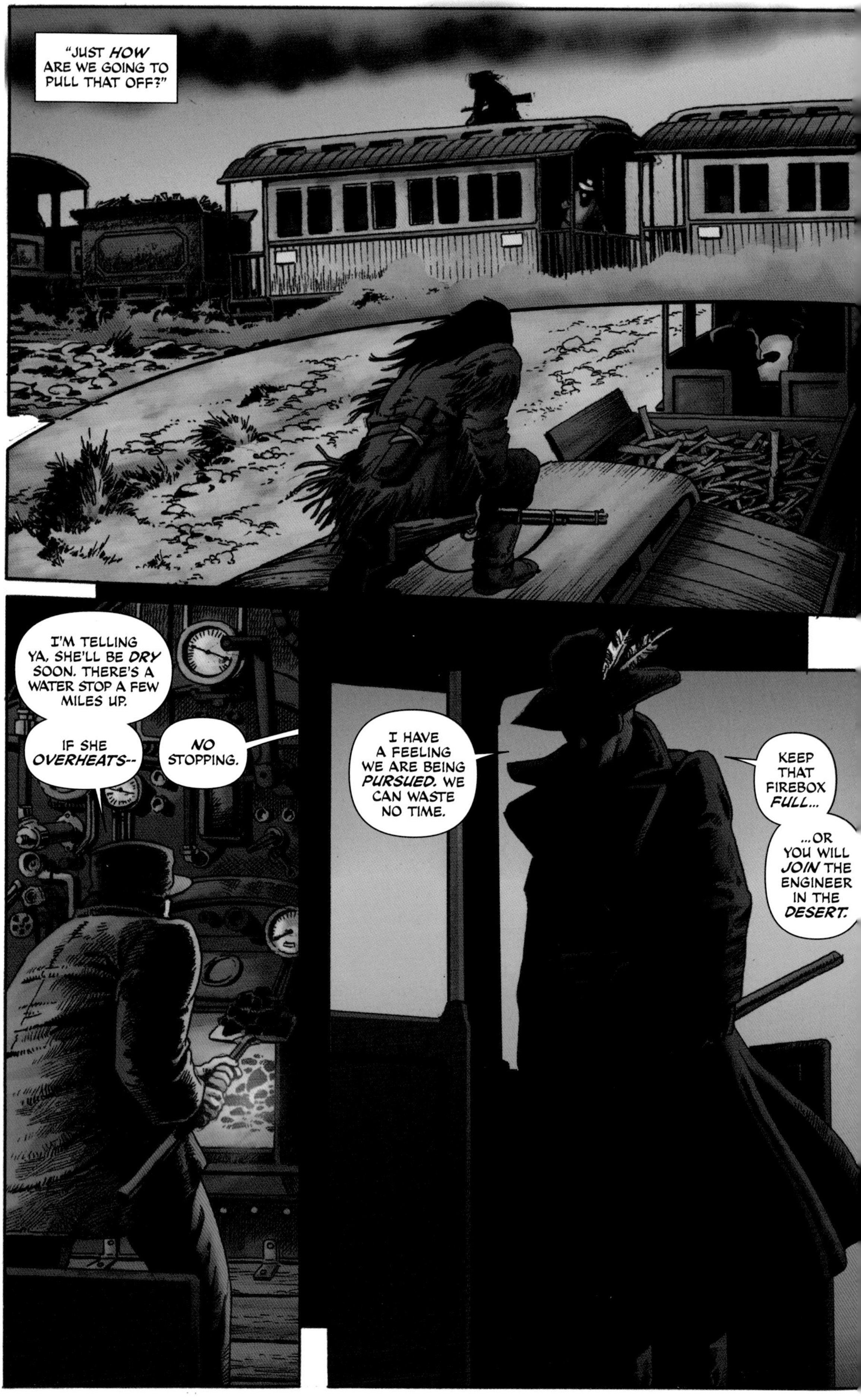

"JUST HOW ARE WE GOING TO PULL THAT OFF?"
I'M TELLING YA, SHE'LL BE DRY SOON. THERE'S A WATER STOP A FEW MILES UP.
IF SHE OVERHEATS--
NO STOPPING.
I HAVE A FEELING WE ARE BEING PURSUED. WE CAN WASTE NO TIME.
KEEP THAT FIREBOX FULL...
...OR YOU WILL JOIN THE ENGINEER IN THE DESERT.

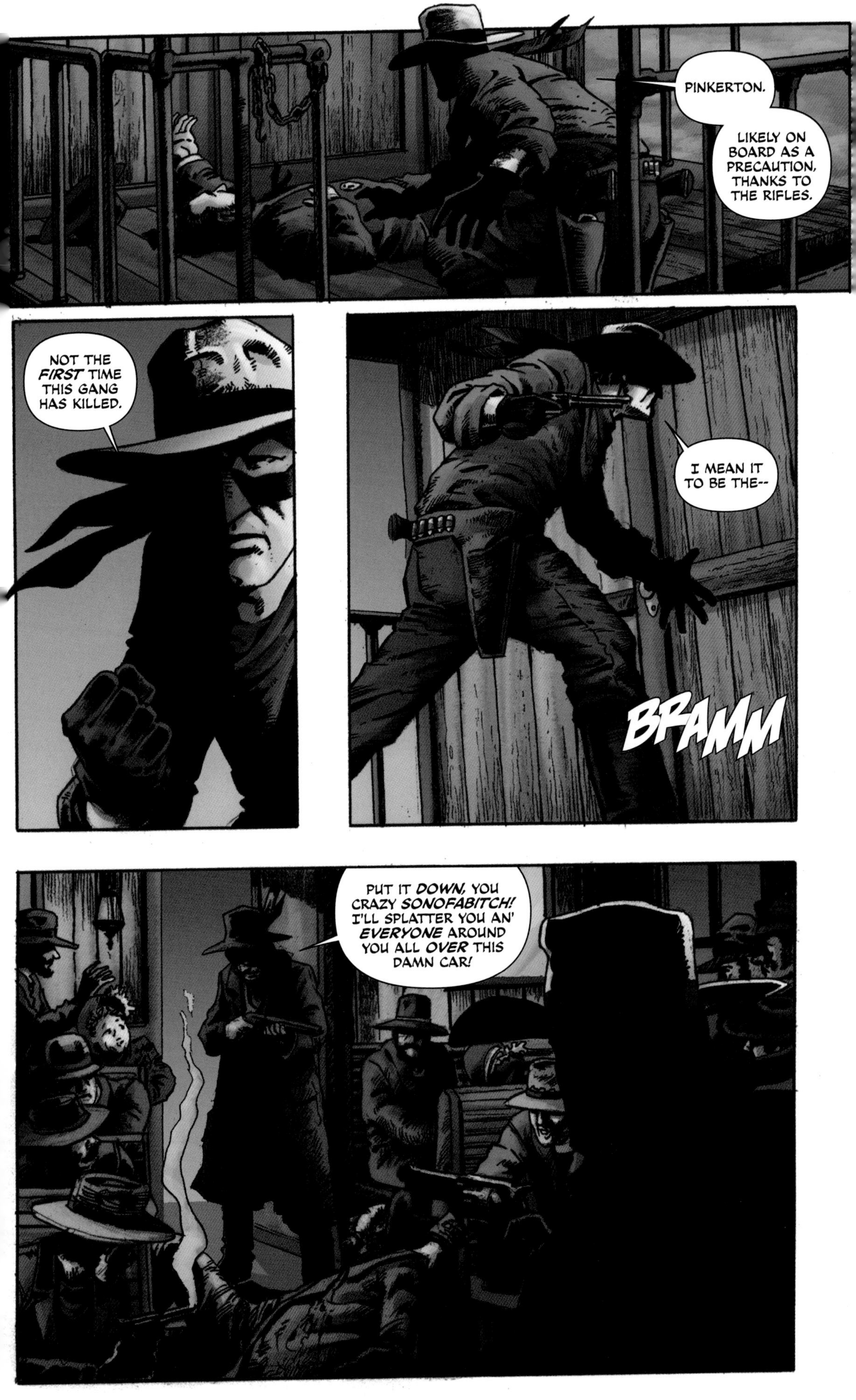
PINKERTON.
LIKELY ON BOARD AS A PRECAUTION, THANKS TO THE RIFLES.
NOT THE *FIRST* TIME THIS GANG HAS KILLED.
I MEAN IT TO BE THE--
BRAMM
PUT IT *DOWN*, YOU CRAZY *SONOFABITCH!* I'LL SPLATTER YOU AN' *EVERYONE* AROUND YOU ALL *OVER* THIS DAMN CAR!

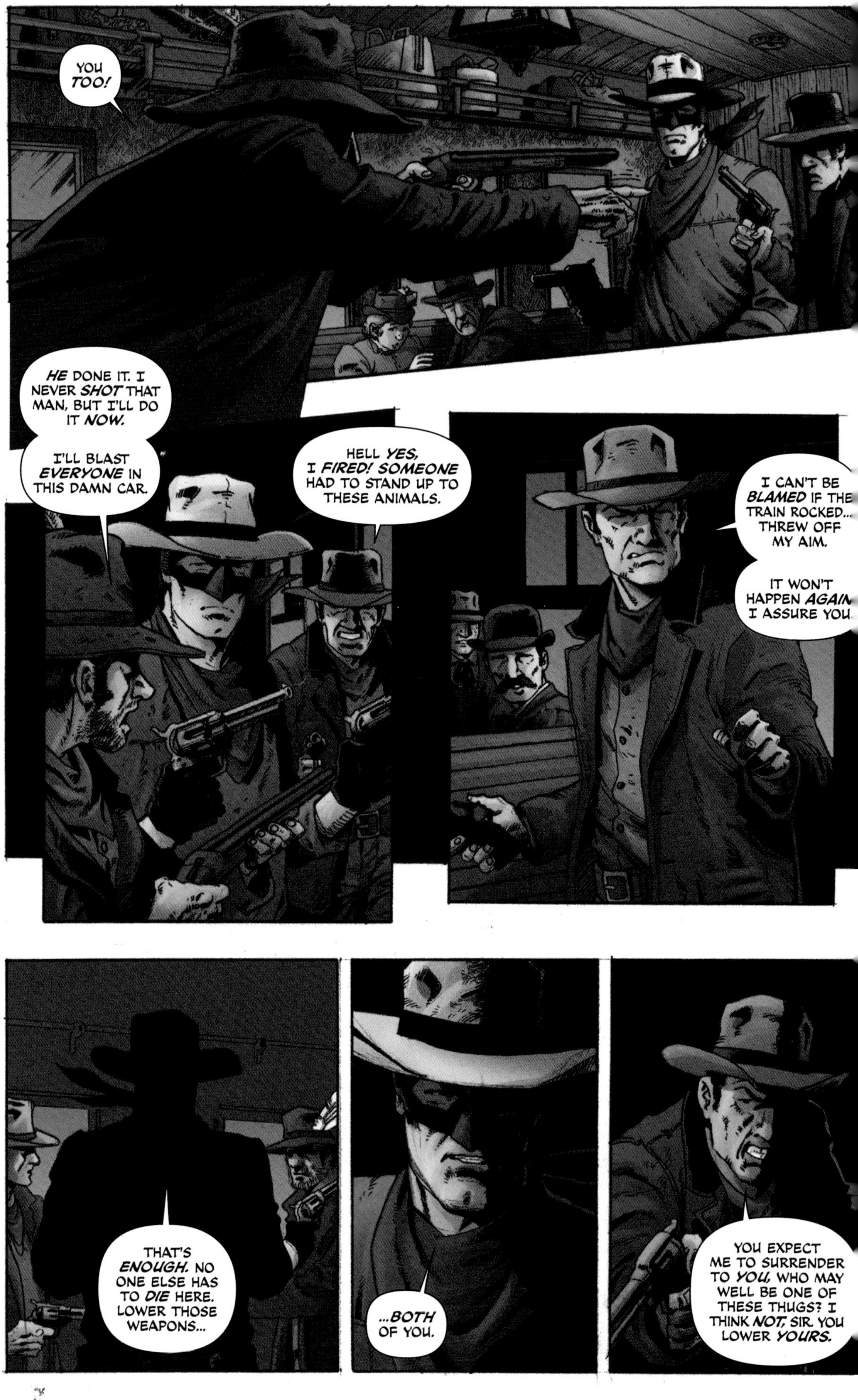
YOU TOO!
HE DONE IT. I NEVER SHOT THAT MAN, BUT I'LL DO IT NOW.
I'LL BLAST EVERYONE IN THIS DAMN CAR.
HELL YES, I FIRED! SOMEONE HAD TO STAND UP TO THESE ANIMALS.
I CAN'T BE BLAMED IF THE TRAIN ROCKED... THREW OFF MY AIM.
IT WON'T HAPPEN AGAIN, I ASSURE YOU.
THAT'S ENOUGH. NO ONE ELSE HAS TO DIE HERE. LOWER THOSE WEAPONS...
...BOTH OF YOU.
YOU EXPECT ME TO SURRENDER TO YOU, WHO MAY WELL BE ONE OF THESE THUGS? I THINK NOT, SIR. YOU LOWER YOURS.

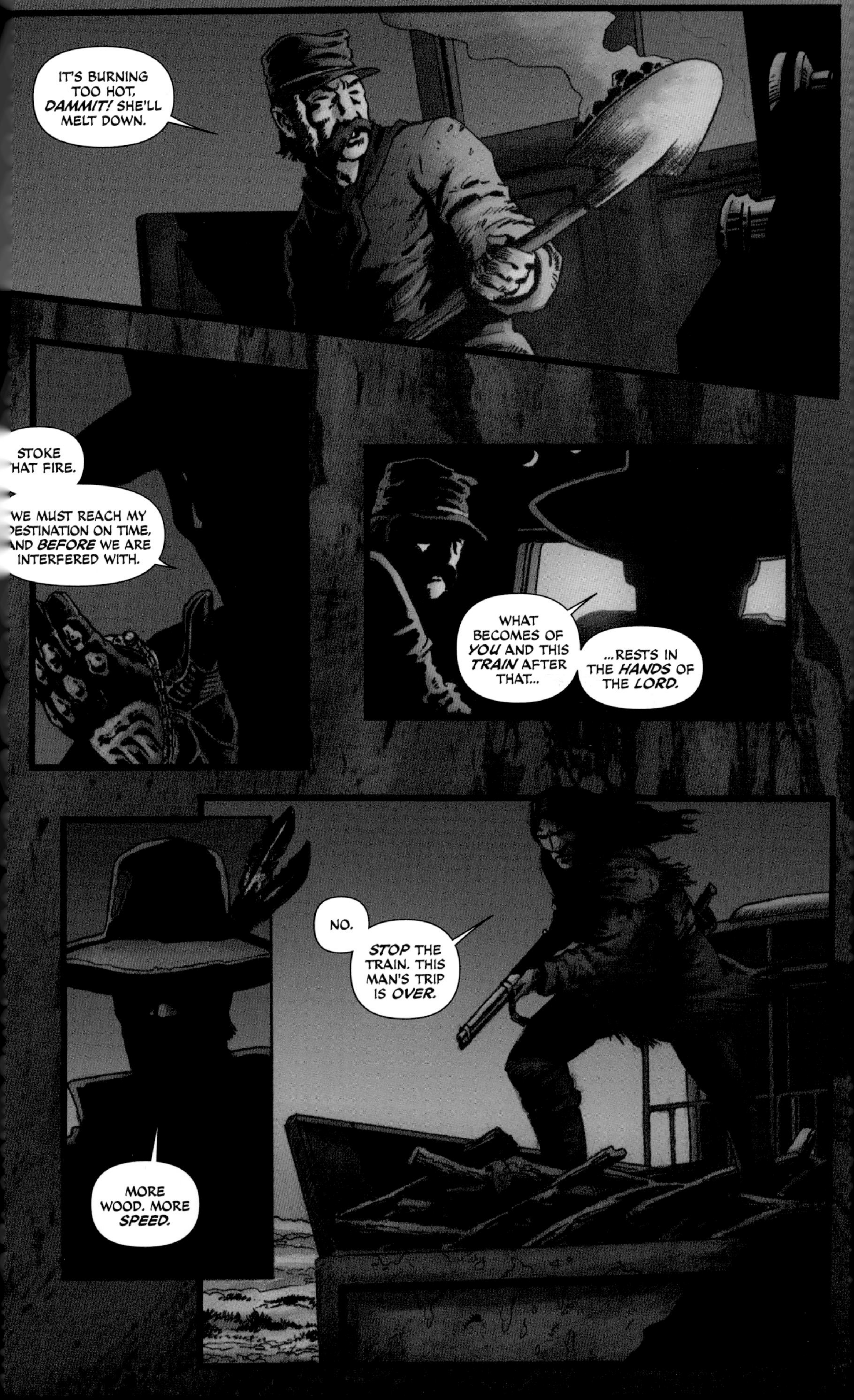
IT'S BURNING TOO HOT, *DAMMIT!* SHE'LL MELT DOWN.
STOKE THAT FIRE.
WE MUST REACH MY DESTINATION ON TIME, AND *BEFORE* WE ARE INTERFERED WITH.
WHAT BECOMES OF *YOU* AND THIS *TRAIN* AFTER THAT...
...RESTS IN THE *HANDS* OF THE *LORD.*
MORE WOOD. MORE *SPEED.*
NO.
STOP THE TRAIN. THIS MAN'S TRIP IS *OVER.*

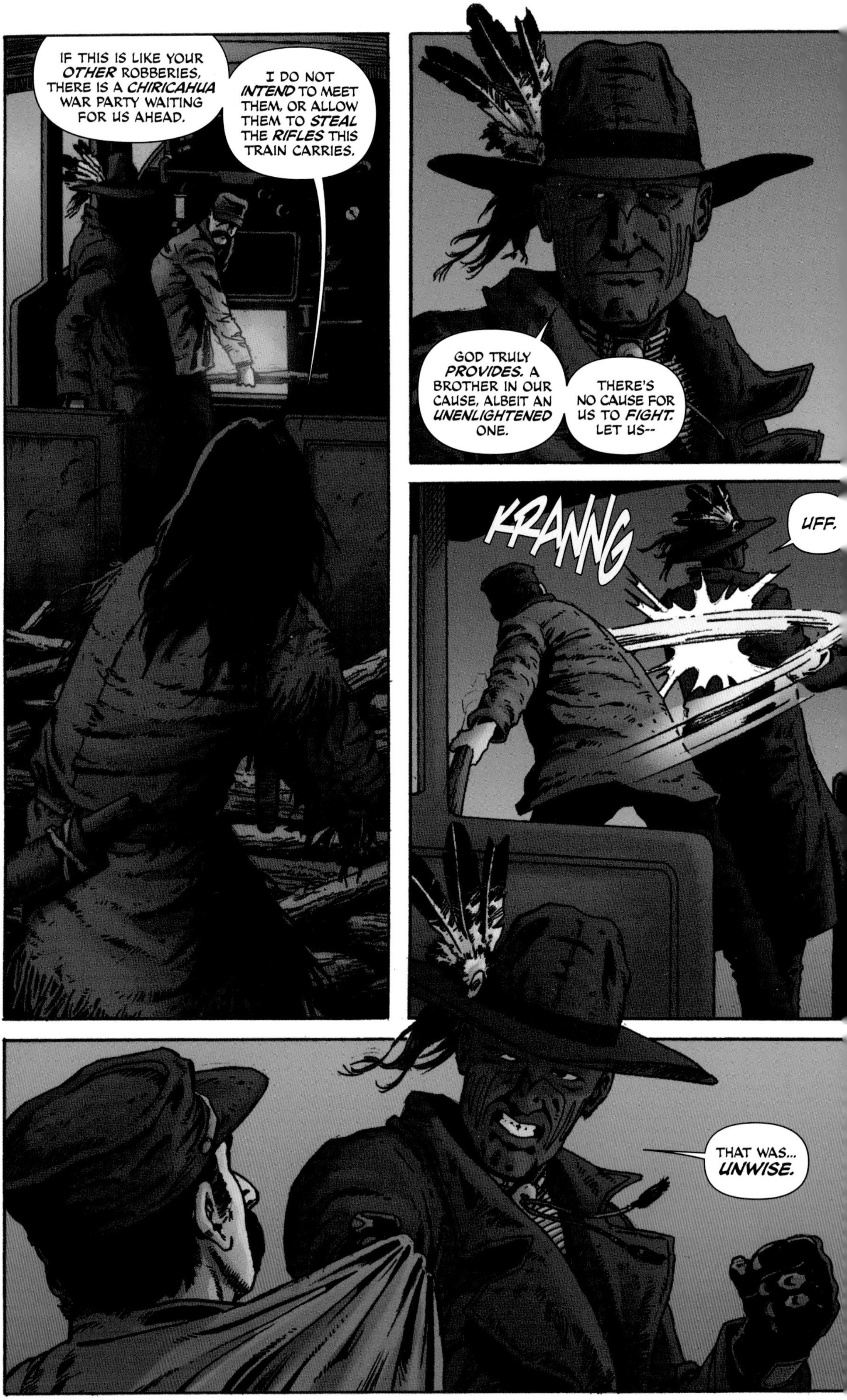
IF THIS IS LIKE YOUR OTHER ROBBERIES, THERE IS A CHIRICAHUA WAR PARTY WAITING FOR US AHEAD.
I DO NOT INTEND TO MEET THEM, OR ALLOW THEM TO STEAL THE RIFLES THIS TRAIN CARRIES.
GOD TRULY PROVIDES. A BROTHER IN OUR CAUSE, ALBEIT AN UNENLIGHTENED ONE.
THERE'S NO CAUSE FOR US TO FIGHT. LET US--
KRANNG
UFF.
THAT WAS... UNWISE.

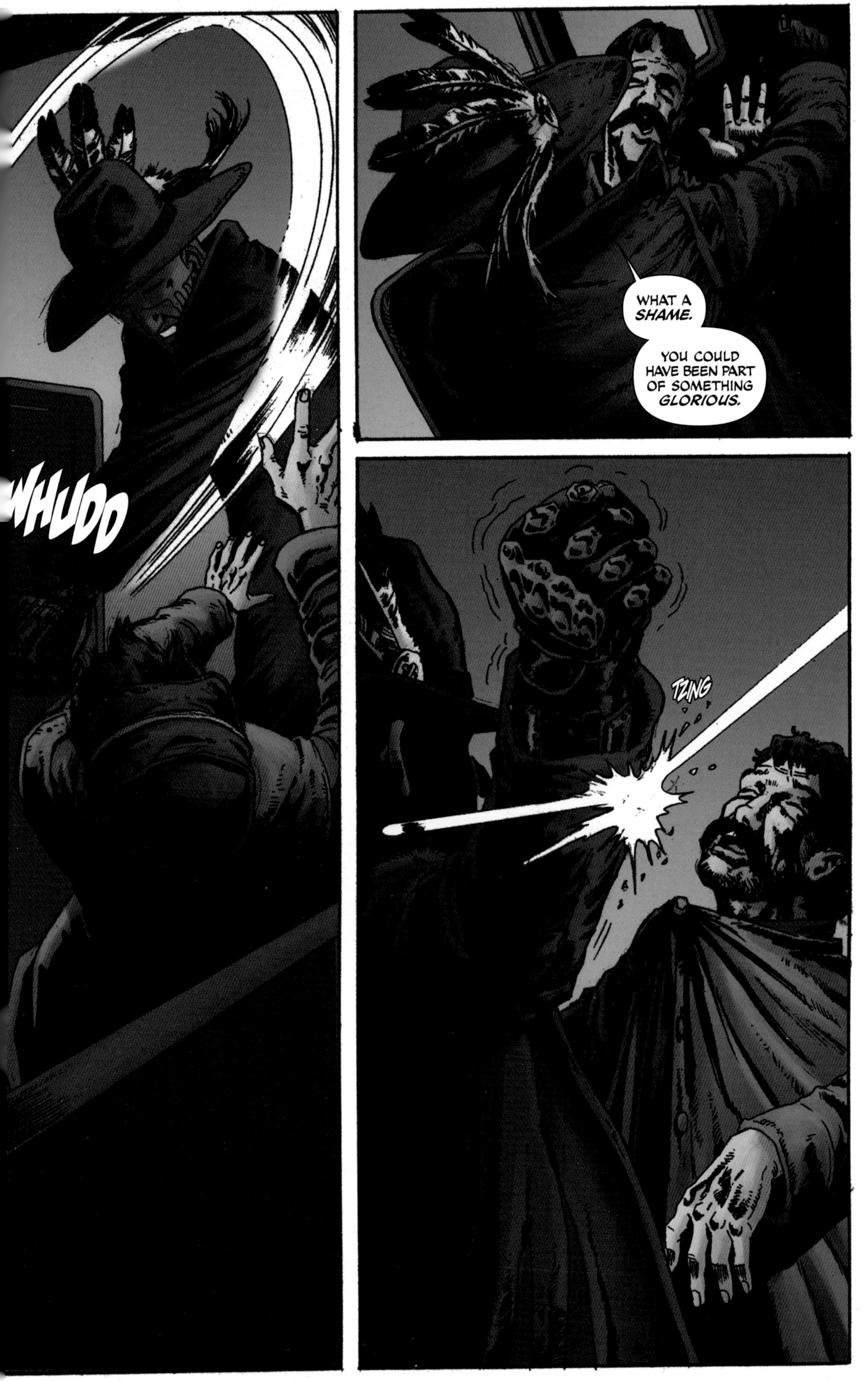
WHUDD
WHAT A SHAME.
YOU COULD HAVE BEEN PART OF SOMETHING GLORIOUS.
TZING

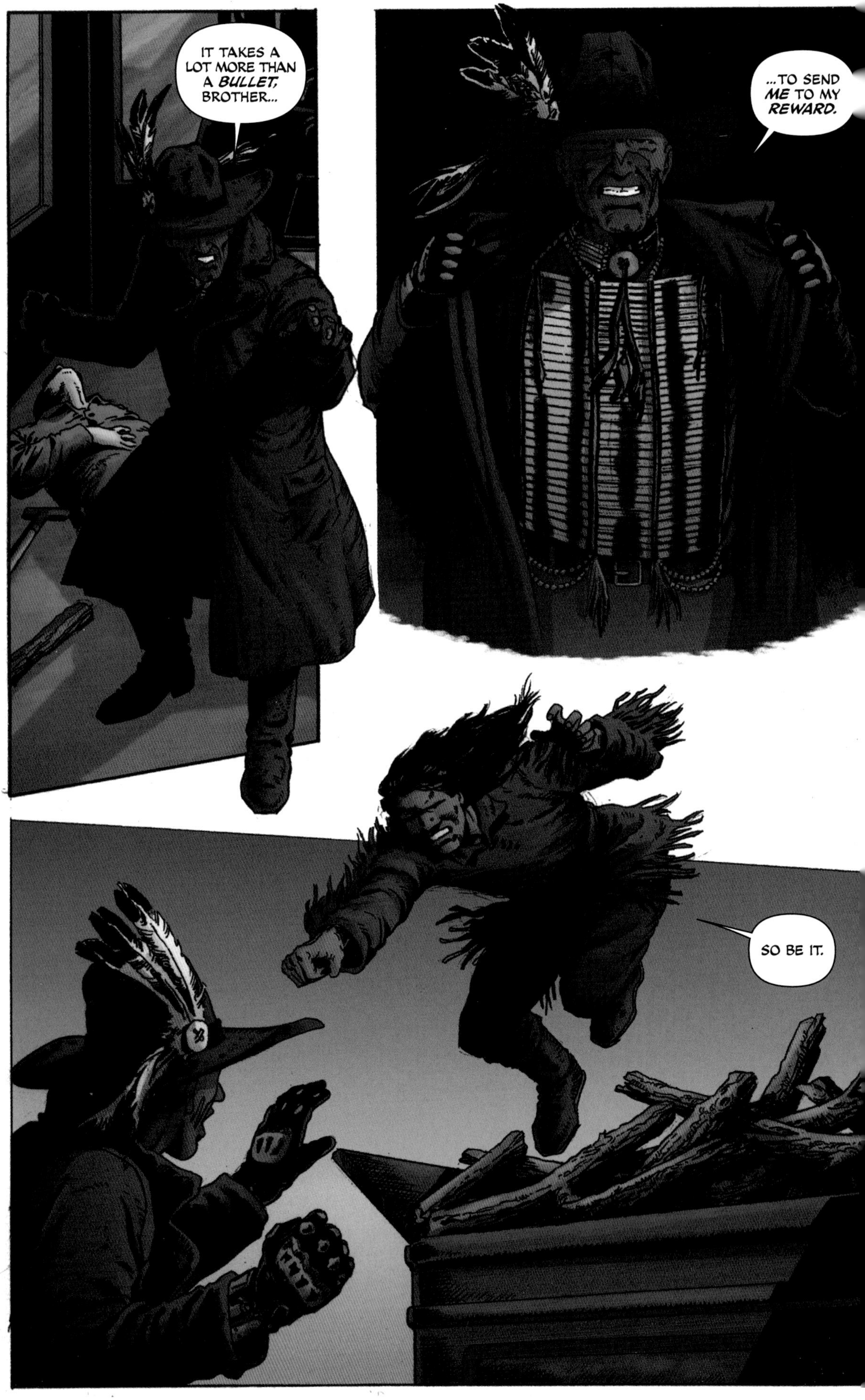
IT TAKES A LOT MORE THAN A *BULLET,* BROTHER...
...TO SEND *ME* TO MY *REWARD.*
SO BE IT.

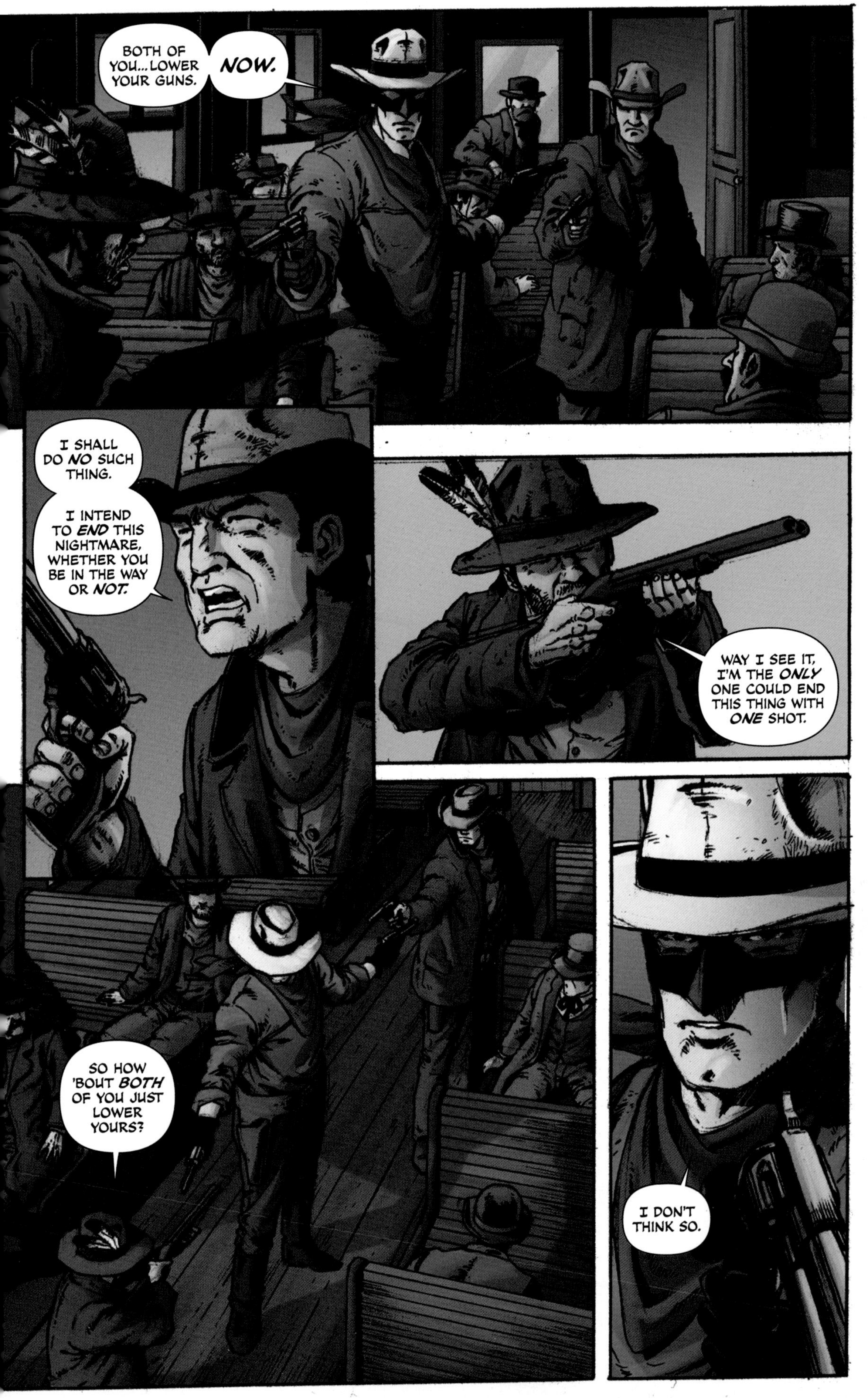
BOTH OF YOU...LOWER YOUR GUNS.
NOW.
I SHALL DO NO SUCH THING.
I INTEND TO END THIS NIGHTMARE, WHETHER YOU BE IN THE WAY OR NOT.
WAY I SEE IT, I'M THE ONLY ONE COULD END THIS THING WITH ONE SHOT.
SO HOW 'BOUT BOTH OF YOU JUST LOWER YOURS?
I DON'T THINK SO.

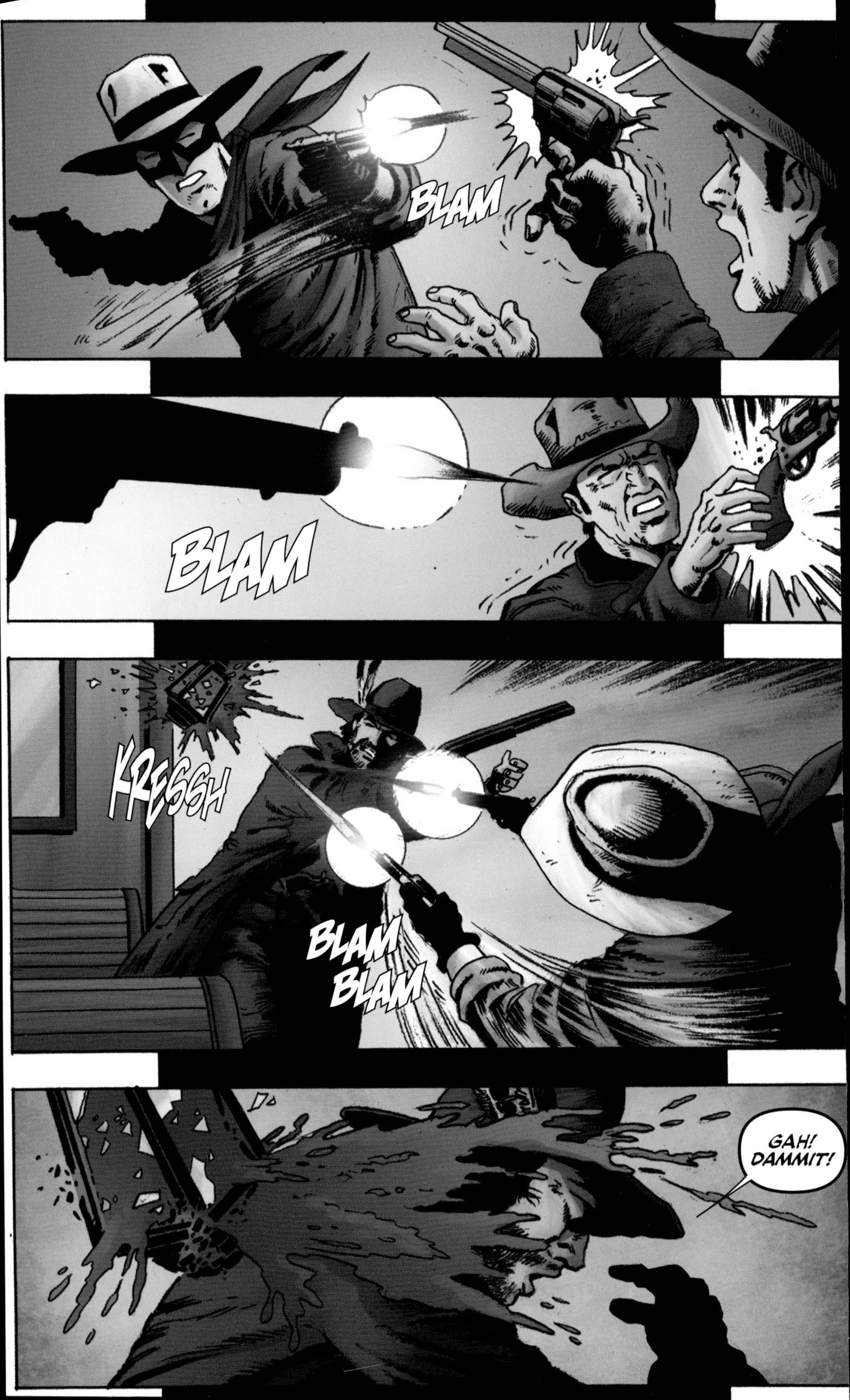
BLAM
BLAM
KRESSH
BLAM
BLAM
GAH! DAMMIT!

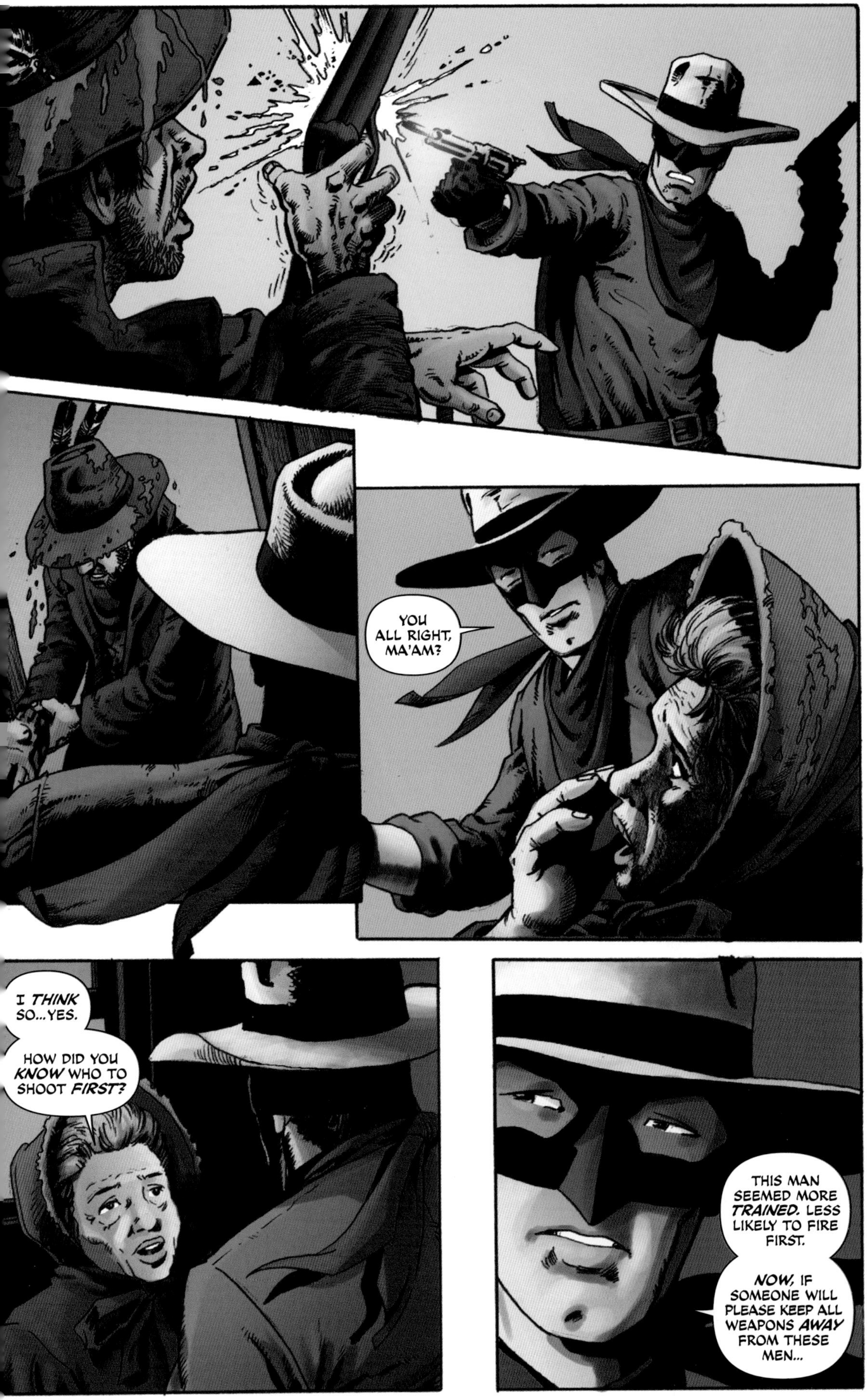

YOU ALL RIGHT, MA'AM?
I *THINK* SO...YES.
HOW DID YOU *KNOW* WHO TO SHOOT *FIRST?*
THIS MAN SEEMED MORE *TRAINED.* LESS LIKELY TO FIRE FIRST.
NOW, IF SOMEONE WILL PLEASE KEEP ALL WEAPONS *AWAY* FROM THESE MEN...

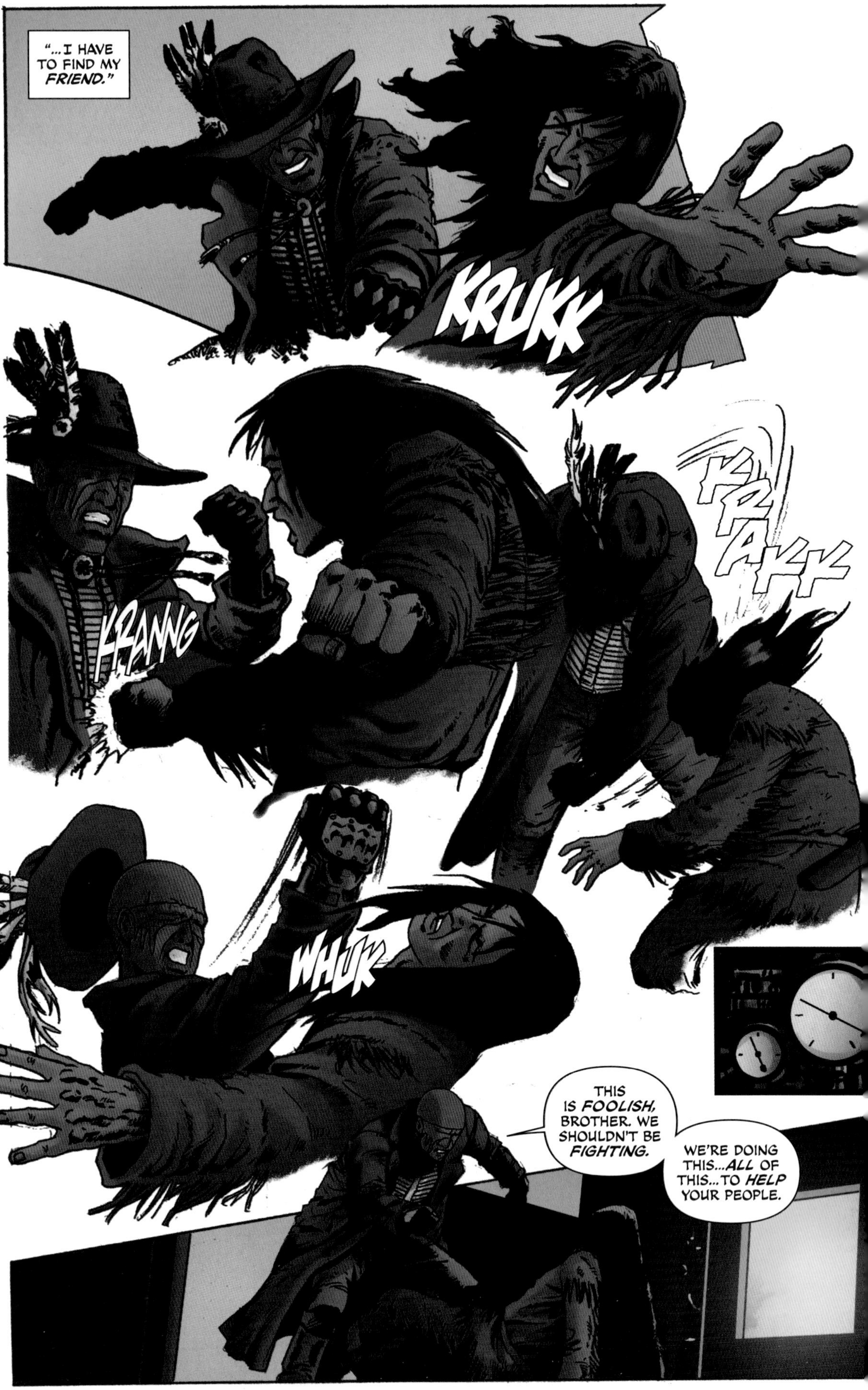
"...I HAVE TO FIND MY FRIEND."
KRUKK
KRANNG
KRAKK
WHUK
THIS IS FOOLISH, BROTHER. WE SHOULDN'T BE FIGHTING.
WE'RE DOING THIS...ALL OF THIS...TO HELP YOUR PEOPLE.

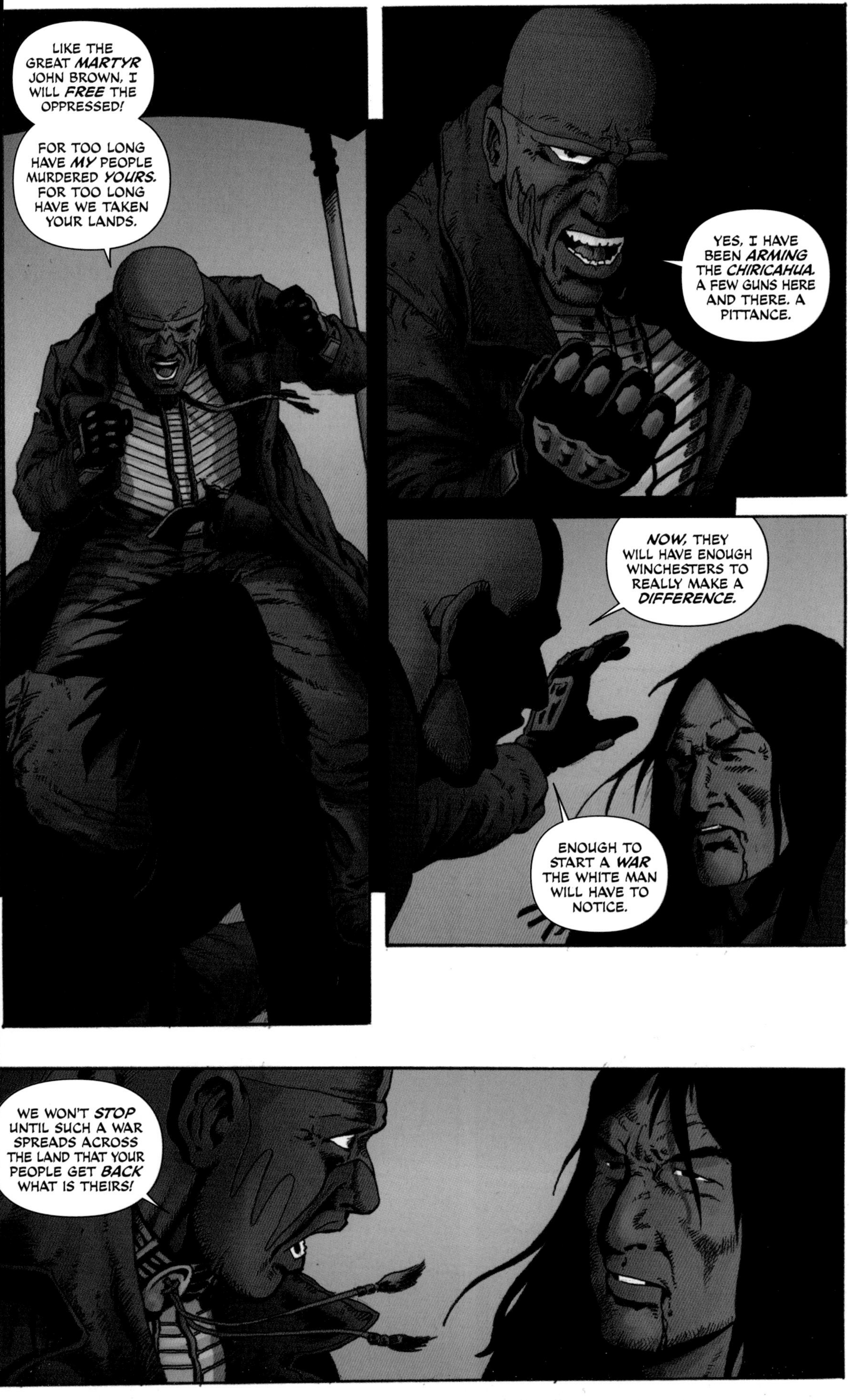
LIKE THE GREAT MARTYR JOHN BROWN, I WILL FREE THE OPPRESSED!
FOR TOO LONG HAVE MY PEOPLE MURDERED YOURS. FOR TOO LONG HAVE WE TAKEN YOUR LANDS.
YES, I HAVE BEEN ARMING THE CHIRICAHUA. A FEW GUNS HERE AND THERE. A PITTANCE.
NOW, THEY WILL HAVE ENOUGH WINCHESTERS TO REALLY MAKE A DIFFERENCE.
ENOUGH TO START A WAR THE WHITE MAN WILL HAVE TO NOTICE.
WE WON'T STOP UNTIL SUCH A WAR SPREADS ACROSS THE LAND THAT YOUR PEOPLE GET BACK WHAT IS THEIRS!

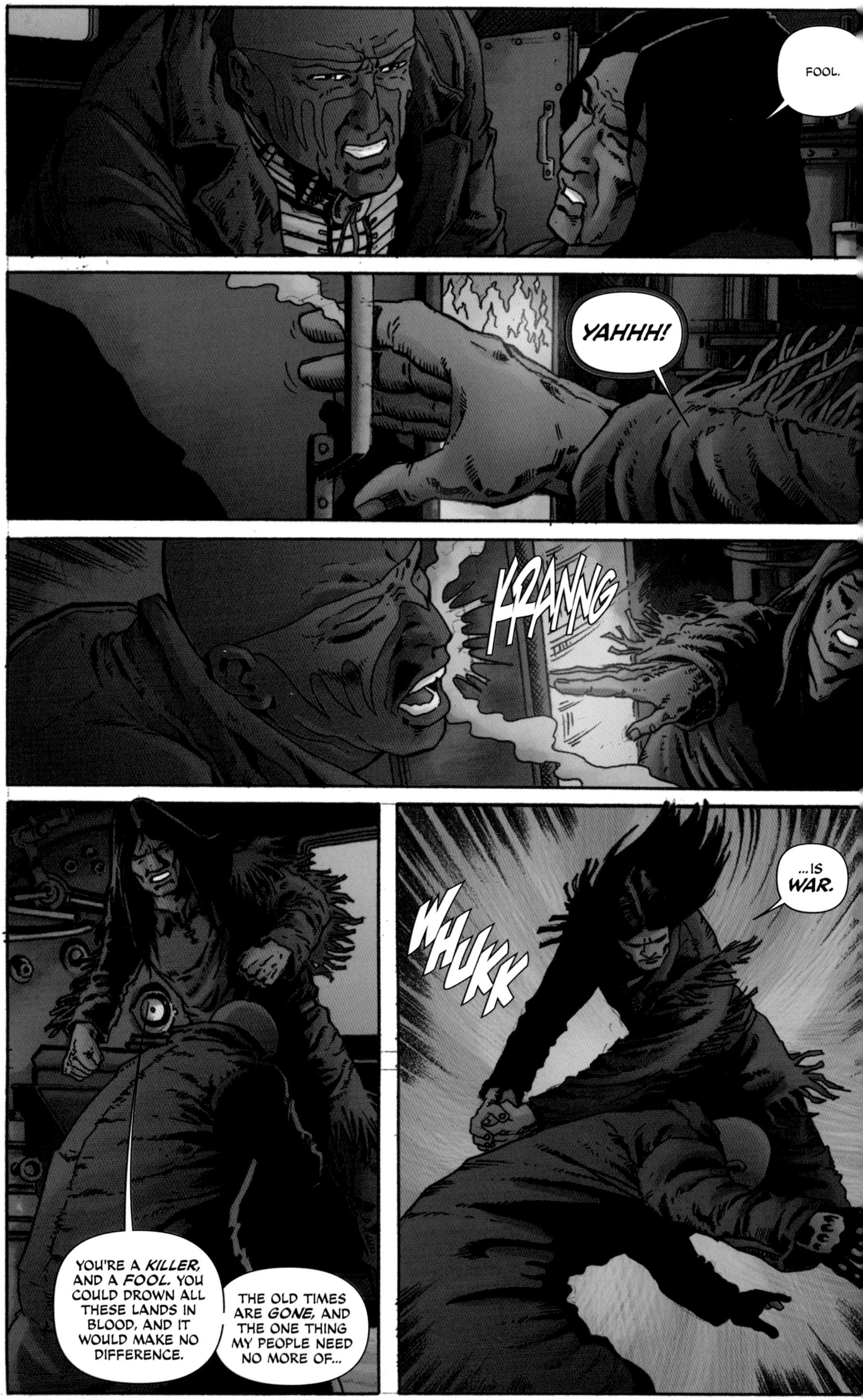
FOOL.
YAHHH!
KRANNG
YOU'RE A KILLER, AND A FOOL. YOU COULD DROWN ALL THESE LANDS IN BLOOD, AND IT WOULD MAKE NO DIFFERENCE.
THE OLD TIMES ARE GONE, AND THE ONE THING MY PEOPLE NEED NO MORE OF...
WHUKK
...IS WAR.

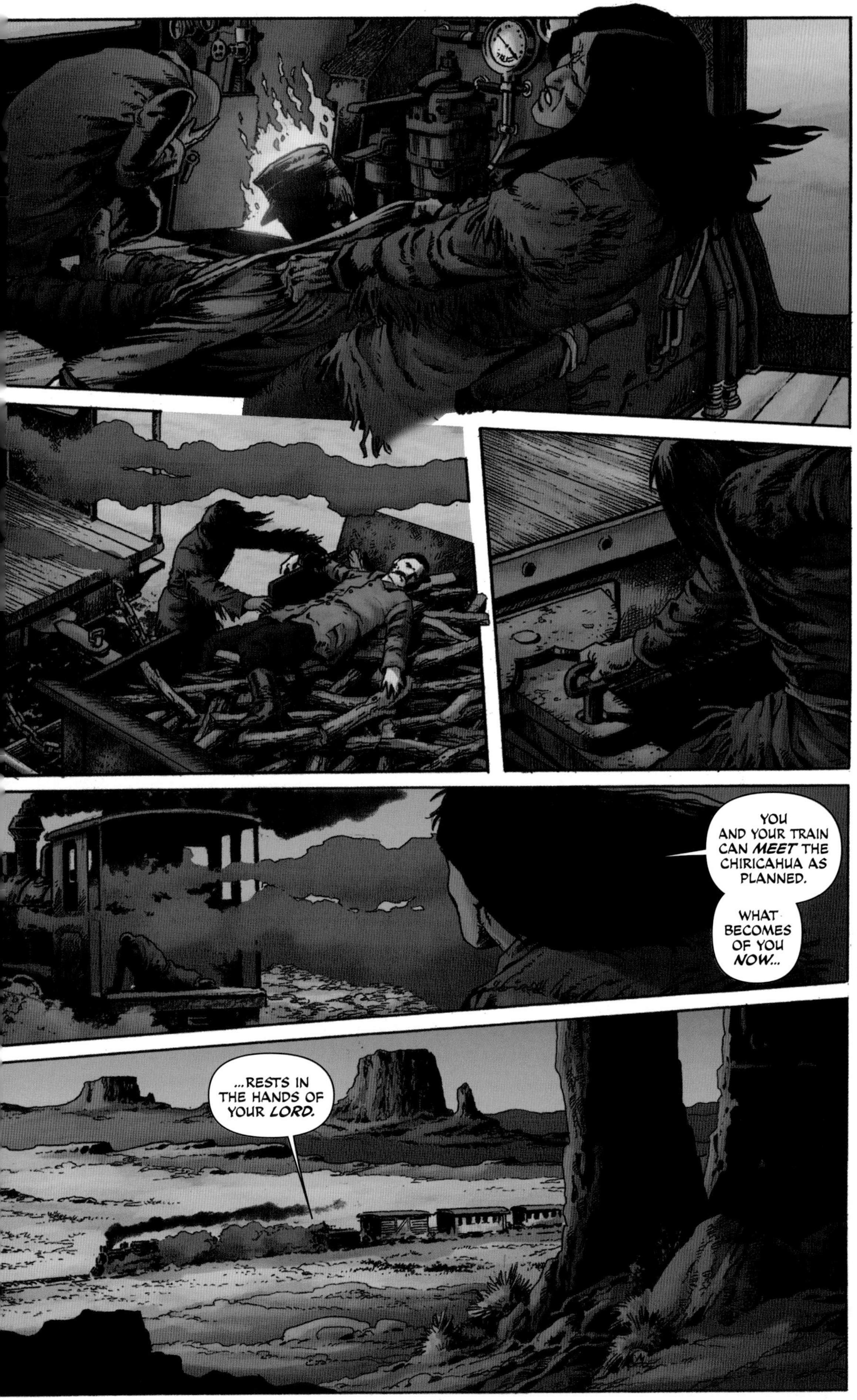
YOU AND YOUR TRAIN CAN MEET THE CHIRICAHUA AS PLANNED.
WHAT BECOMES OF YOU NOW...
...RESTS IN THE HANDS OF YOUR LORD.

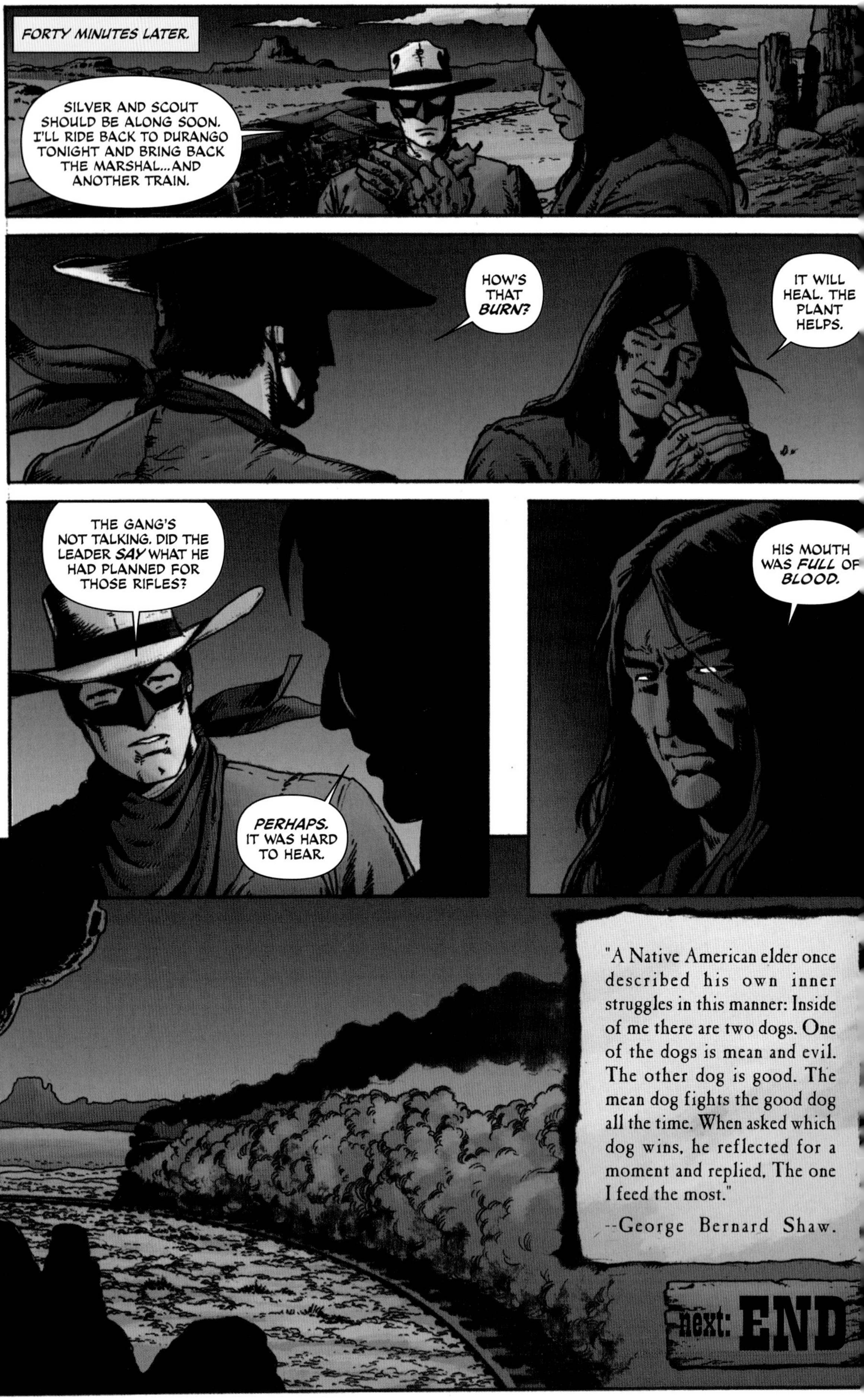
FORTY MINUTES LATER.
SILVER AND SCOUT SHOULD BE ALONG SOON. I'LL RIDE BACK TO DURANGO TONIGHT AND BRING BACK THE MARSHAL...AND ANOTHER TRAIN.
HOW'S THAT BURN?
IT WILL HEAL. THE PLANT HELPS.
THE GANG'S NOT TALKING. DID THE LEADER SAY WHAT HE HAD PLANNED FOR THOSE RIFLES?
PERHAPS. IT WAS HARD TO HEAR.
HIS MOUTH WAS FULL OF BLOOD.
"A Native American elder once described his own inner struggles in this manner: Inside of me there are two dogs. One of the dogs is mean and evil. The other dog is good. The mean dog fights the good dog all the time. When asked which dog wins, he reflected for a moment and replied, The one I feed the most."
--George Bernard Shaw.
next: END

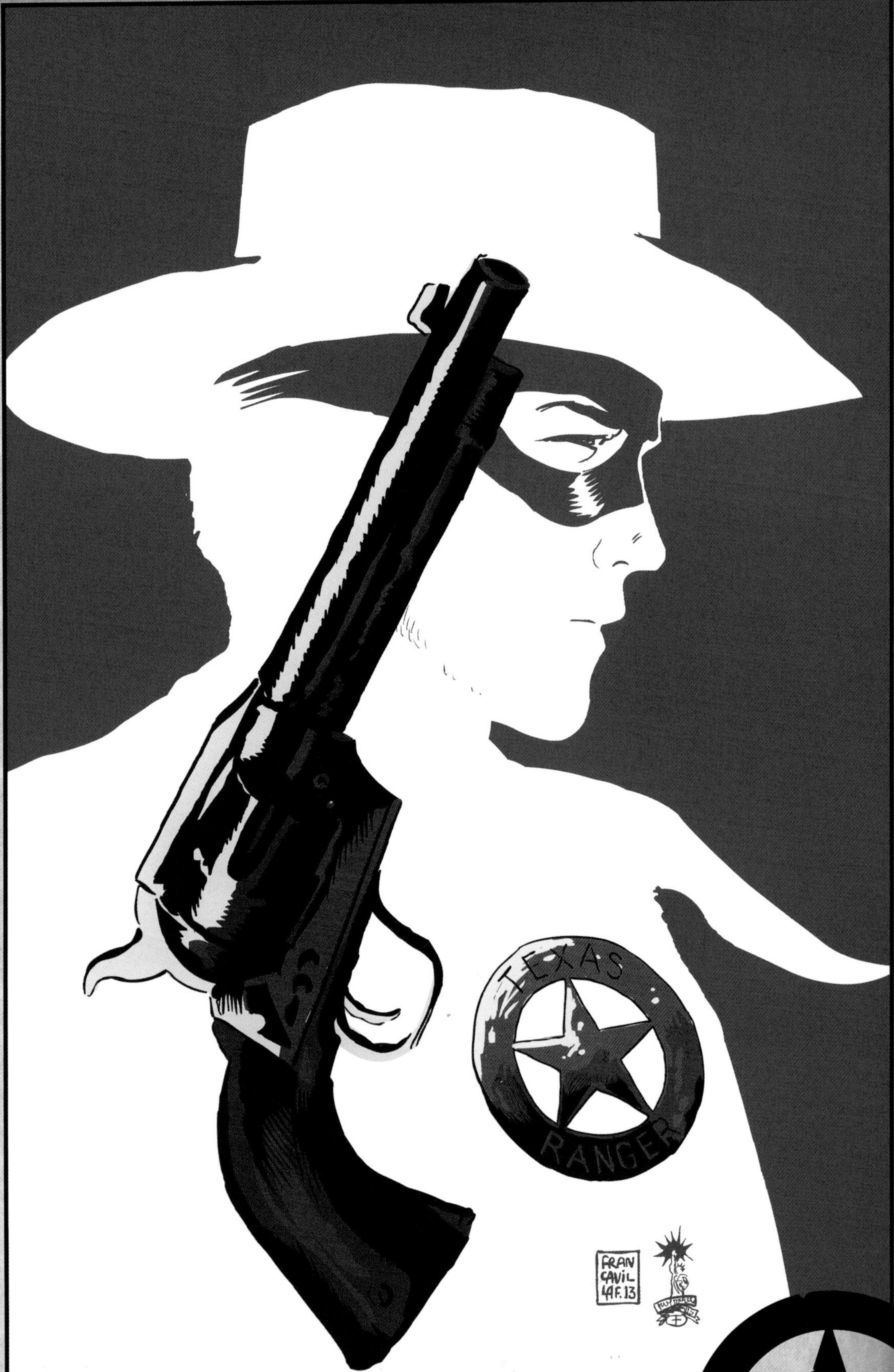
TEXAS
RANGER

25

COVER BY **FRANCESCO FRANCAVILLA**

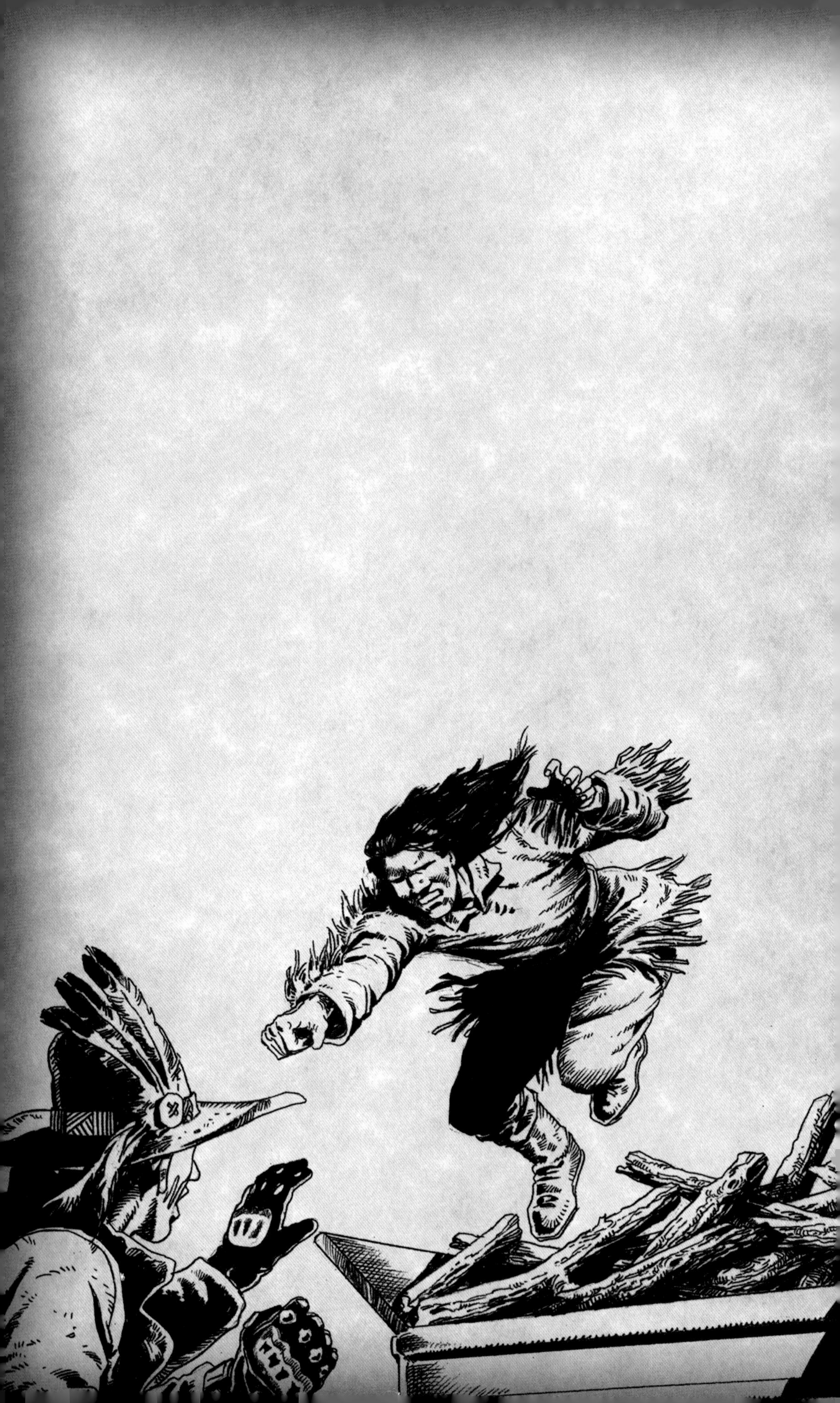

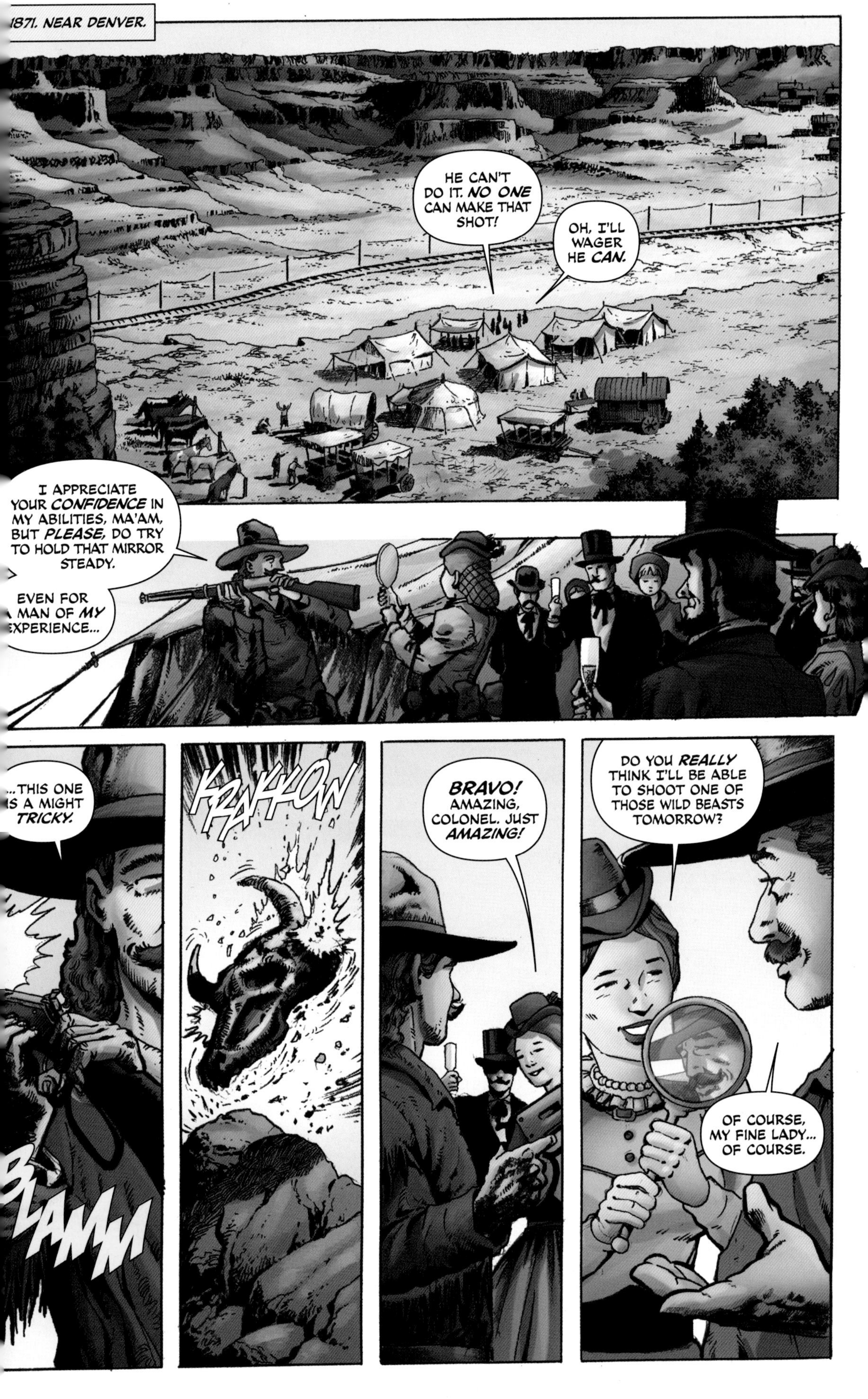
1871. NEAR DENVER.
HE CAN'T DO IT. NO ONE CAN MAKE THAT SHOT!
OH, I'LL WAGER HE CAN.
I APPRECIATE YOUR CONFIDENCE IN MY ABILITIES, MA'AM, BUT PLEASE, DO TRY TO HOLD THAT MIRROR STEADY.
EVEN FOR A MAN OF MY EXPERIENCE...
...THIS ONE IS A MIGHT TRICKY.
BLAMM
KRAKKOW
BRAVO! AMAZING, COLONEL. JUST AMAZING!
DO YOU REALLY THINK I'LL BE ABLE TO SHOOT ONE OF THOSE WILD BEASTS TOMORROW?
OF COURSE, MY FINE LADY... OF COURSE.

COLONEL JACKSON MASTERS GUARANTEES *THREE* THINGS TO ALL HIS CUSTOMERS:

THE *FINEST* OUT-OF-DOORS ACCOMMODATIONS, AN *ENDLESS* SUPPLY OF EUROPE'S FINEST CHAMPAGNE...

...AND A CHANCE FOR *EVERY* PAYING CUSTOMER TO SHOOT A REAL, LIVE *BUFFALO*.

COME AND SEE **COLONEL MASTERS AUTHENTIC WILD WEST SAFARI**

OH, I CAN SCARCELY *WAIT!*

NOW, FORGIVE ME... I HAVE PREPARATIONS TO MAKE. ENJOY THE REST OF THE EVENING, MY FRIENDS.

YOU TRACKED THE HERD?

YES, SIR. WHAT'S LEFT OF 'EM IS STILL NEAR THE TRACKS. NEAR 'NUFF, ANYWAY.

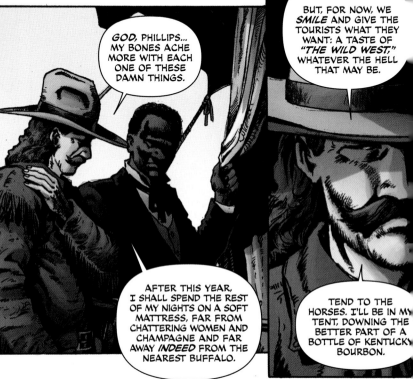

GOD, PHILLIPS... MY BONES ACHE MORE WITH EACH ONE OF THESE DAMN THINGS.

BUT, FOR NOW, WE *SMILE* AND GIVE THE TOURISTS WHAT THEY WANT: A TASTE OF *"THE WILD WEST,"* WHATEVER THE HELL THAT MAY BE.

AFTER THIS YEAR, I SHALL SPEND THE REST OF MY NIGHTS ON A SOFT MATTRESS, FAR FROM CHATTERING WOMEN AND CHAMPAGNE AND FAR AWAY *INDEED* FROM THE NEAREST BUFFALO.

TEND TO THE HORSES. I'LL BE IN MY TENT, DOWNING THE BETTER PART OF A BOTTLE OF KENTUCKY BOURBON.

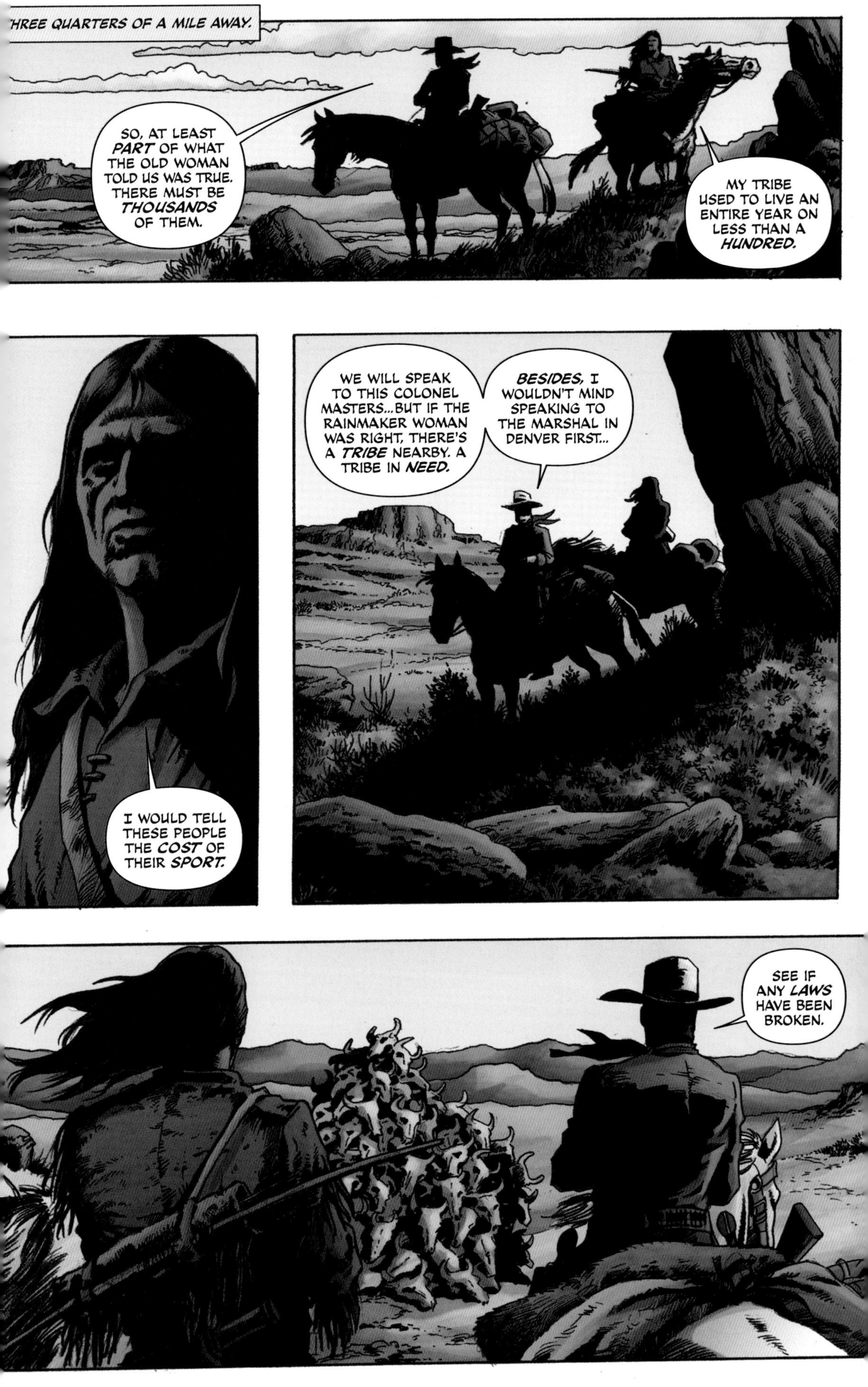
THREE QUARTERS OF A MILE AWAY.
SO, AT LEAST PART OF WHAT THE OLD WOMAN TOLD US WAS TRUE. THERE MUST BE THOUSANDS OF THEM.
MY TRIBE USED TO LIVE AN ENTIRE YEAR ON LESS THAN A HUNDRED.
I WOULD TELL THESE PEOPLE THE COST OF THEIR SPORT.
WE WILL SPEAK TO THIS COLONEL MASTERS...BUT IF THE RAINMAKER WOMAN WAS RIGHT, THERE'S A TRIBE NEARBY. A TRIBE IN NEED.
BESIDES, I WOULDN'T MIND SPEAKING TO THE MARSHAL IN DENVER FIRST...
SEE IF ANY LAWS HAVE BEEN BROKEN.

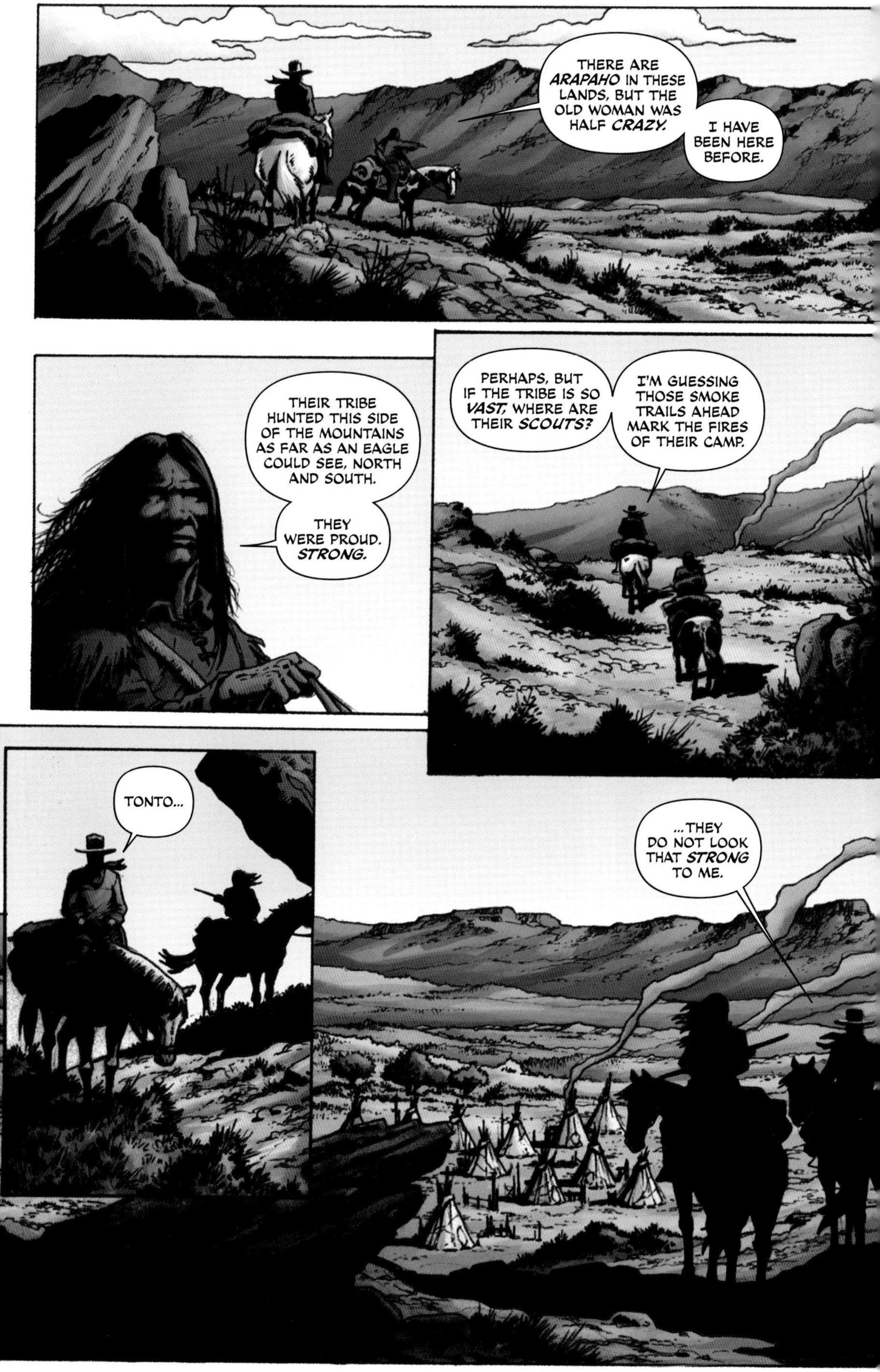
THERE ARE ARAPAHO IN THESE LANDS, BUT THE OLD WOMAN WAS HALF CRAZY.
I HAVE BEEN HERE BEFORE.
THEIR TRIBE HUNTED THIS SIDE OF THE MOUNTAINS AS FAR AS AN EAGLE COULD SEE, NORTH AND SOUTH.
THEY WERE PROUD. STRONG.
PERHAPS, BUT IF THE TRIBE IS SO VAST, WHERE ARE THEIR SCOUTS?
I'M GUESSING THOSE SMOKE TRAILS AHEAD MARK THE FIRES OF THEIR CAMP.
TONTO...
...THEY DO NOT LOOK THAT STRONG TO ME.

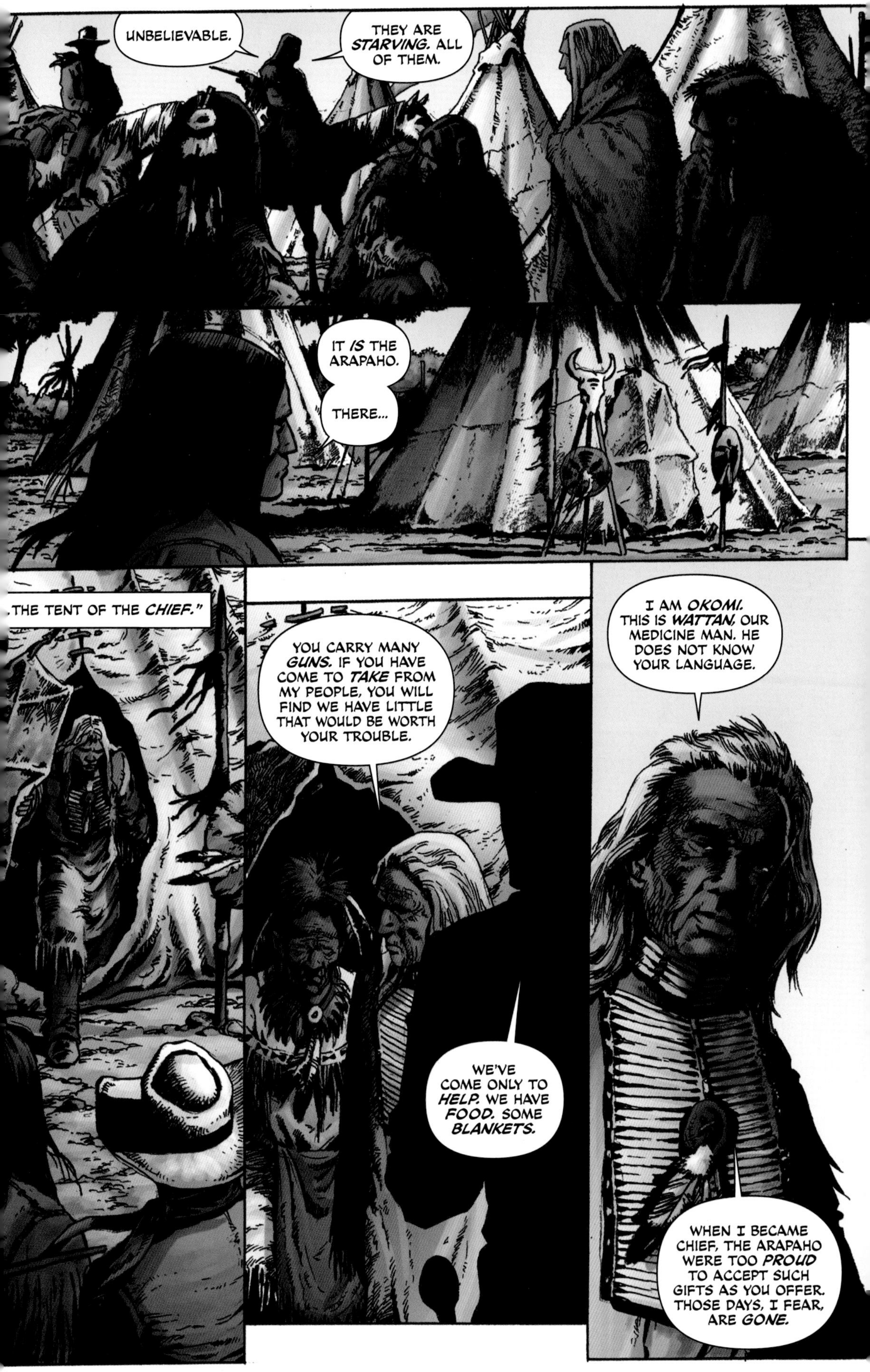

UNBELIEVABLE.
THEY ARE *STARVING.* ALL OF THEM.
IT *IS* THE ARAPAHO.
THERE...
..THE TENT OF THE *CHIEF.*"
YOU CARRY MANY *GUNS.* IF YOU HAVE COME TO *TAKE* FROM MY PEOPLE, YOU WILL FIND WE HAVE LITTLE THAT WOULD BE WORTH YOUR TROUBLE.
WE'VE COME ONLY TO *HELP.* WE HAVE *FOOD.* SOME *BLANKETS.*
I AM *OKOMI.* THIS IS *WATTAN,* OUR MEDICINE MAN. HE DOES NOT KNOW YOUR LANGUAGE.
WHEN I BECAME CHIEF, THE ARAPAHO WERE TOO *PROUD* TO ACCEPT SUCH GIFTS AS YOU OFFER. THOSE DAYS, I FEAR, ARE *GONE.*

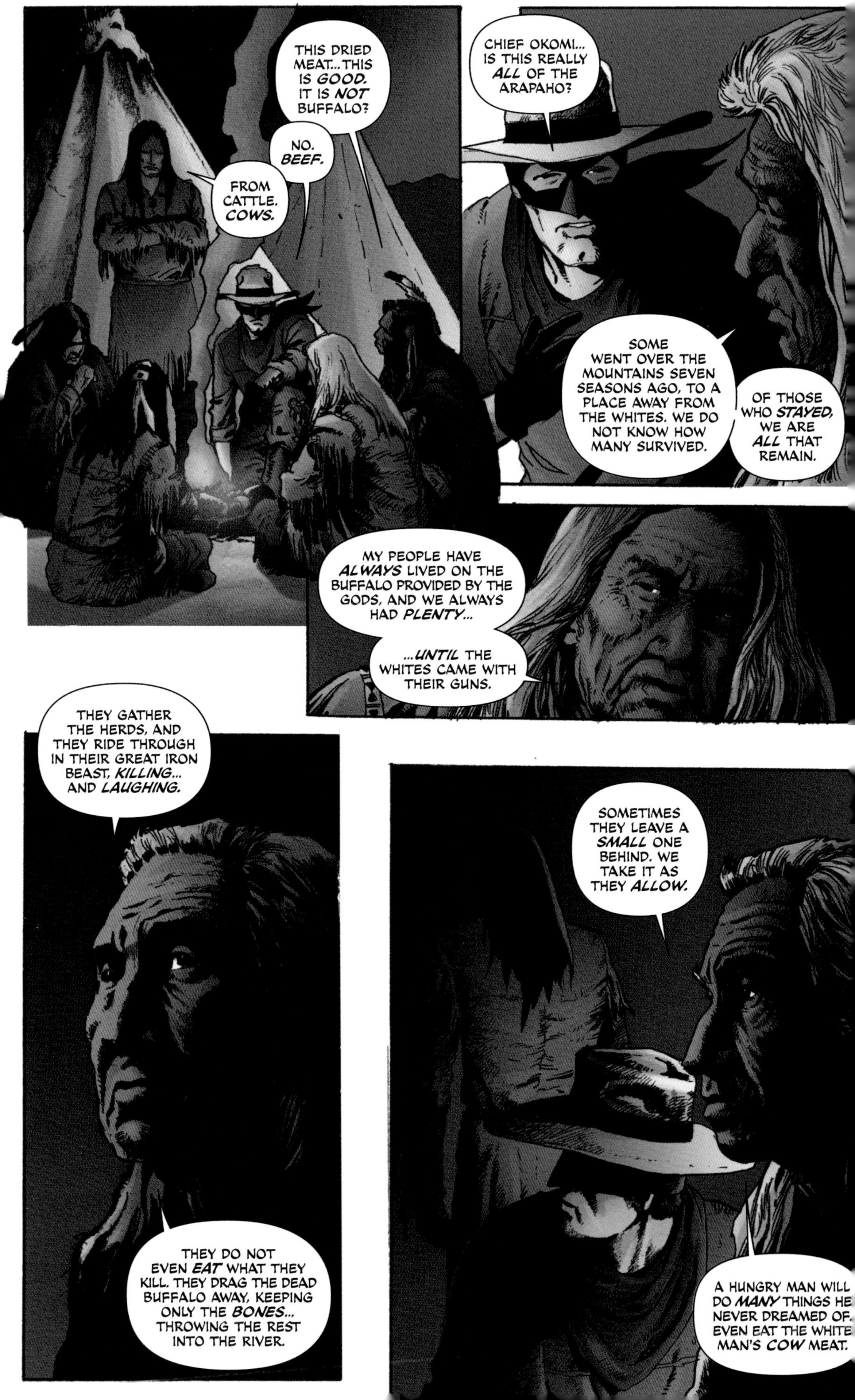
THIS DRIED MEAT...THIS IS GOOD. IT IS NOT BUFFALO?
NO. BEEF.
FROM CATTLE. COWS.
CHIEF OKOMI... IS THIS REALLY ALL OF THE ARAPAHO?
SOME WENT OVER THE MOUNTAINS SEVEN SEASONS AGO, TO A PLACE AWAY FROM THE WHITES. WE DO NOT KNOW HOW MANY SURVIVED.
OF THOSE WHO STAYED, WE ARE ALL THAT REMAIN.
MY PEOPLE HAVE ALWAYS LIVED ON THE BUFFALO PROVIDED BY THE GODS, AND WE ALWAYS HAD PLENTY...
...UNTIL THE WHITES CAME WITH THEIR GUNS.
THEY GATHER THE HERDS, AND THEY RIDE THROUGH IN THEIR GREAT IRON BEAST, KILLING... AND LAUGHING.
THEY DO NOT EVEN EAT WHAT THEY KILL. THEY DRAG THE DEAD BUFFALO AWAY, KEEPING ONLY THE BONES... THROWING THE REST INTO THE RIVER.
SOMETIMES THEY LEAVE A SMALL ONE BEHIND. WE TAKE IT AS THEY ALLOW.
A HUNGRY MAN WILL DO MANY THINGS HE NEVER DREAMED OF. EVEN EAT THE WHITE MAN'S COW MEAT.

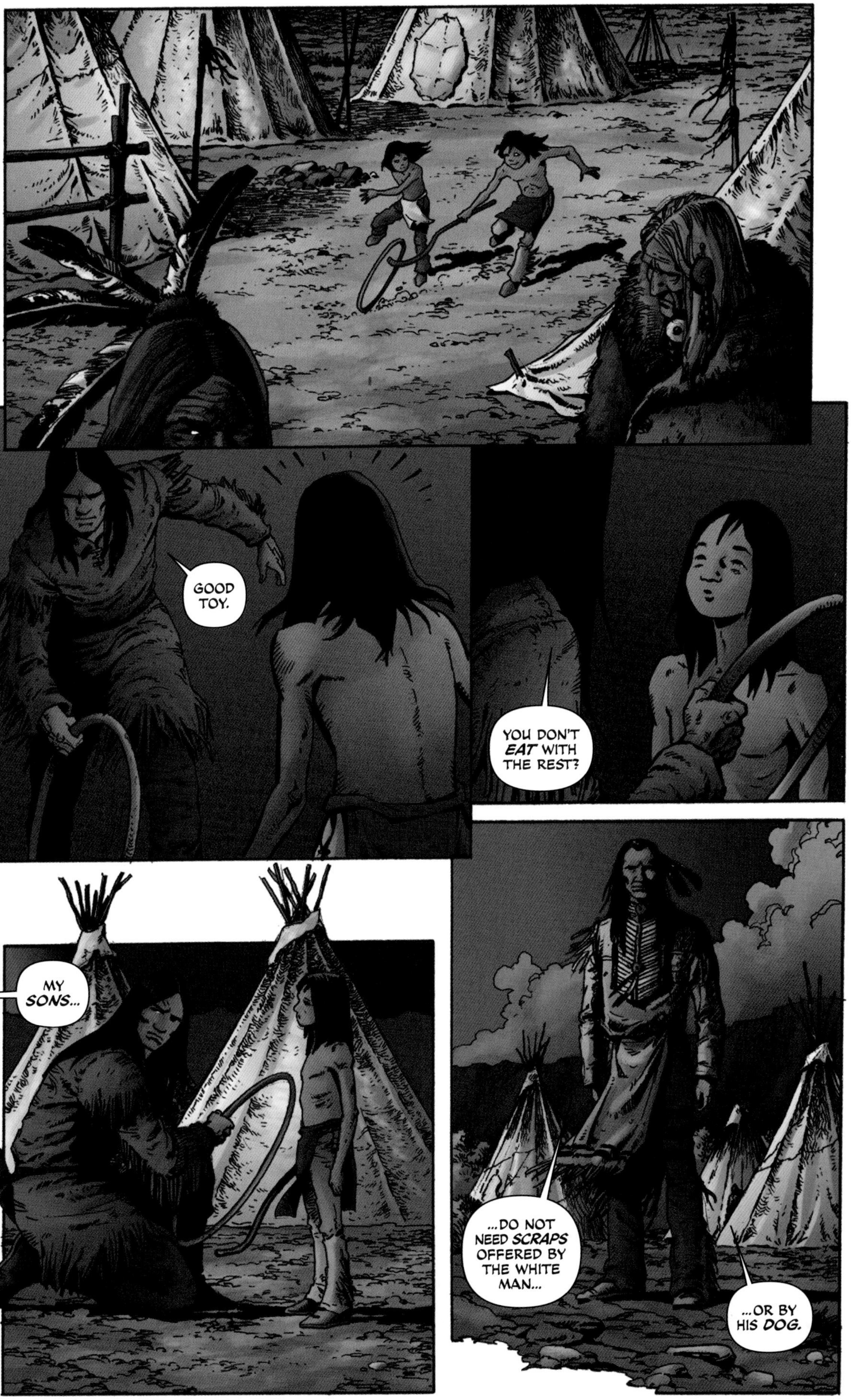
GOOD TOY.
YOU DON'T EAT WITH THE REST?
MY SONS...
...DO NOT NEED SCRAPS OFFERED BY THE WHITE MAN...
...OR BY HIS DOG.

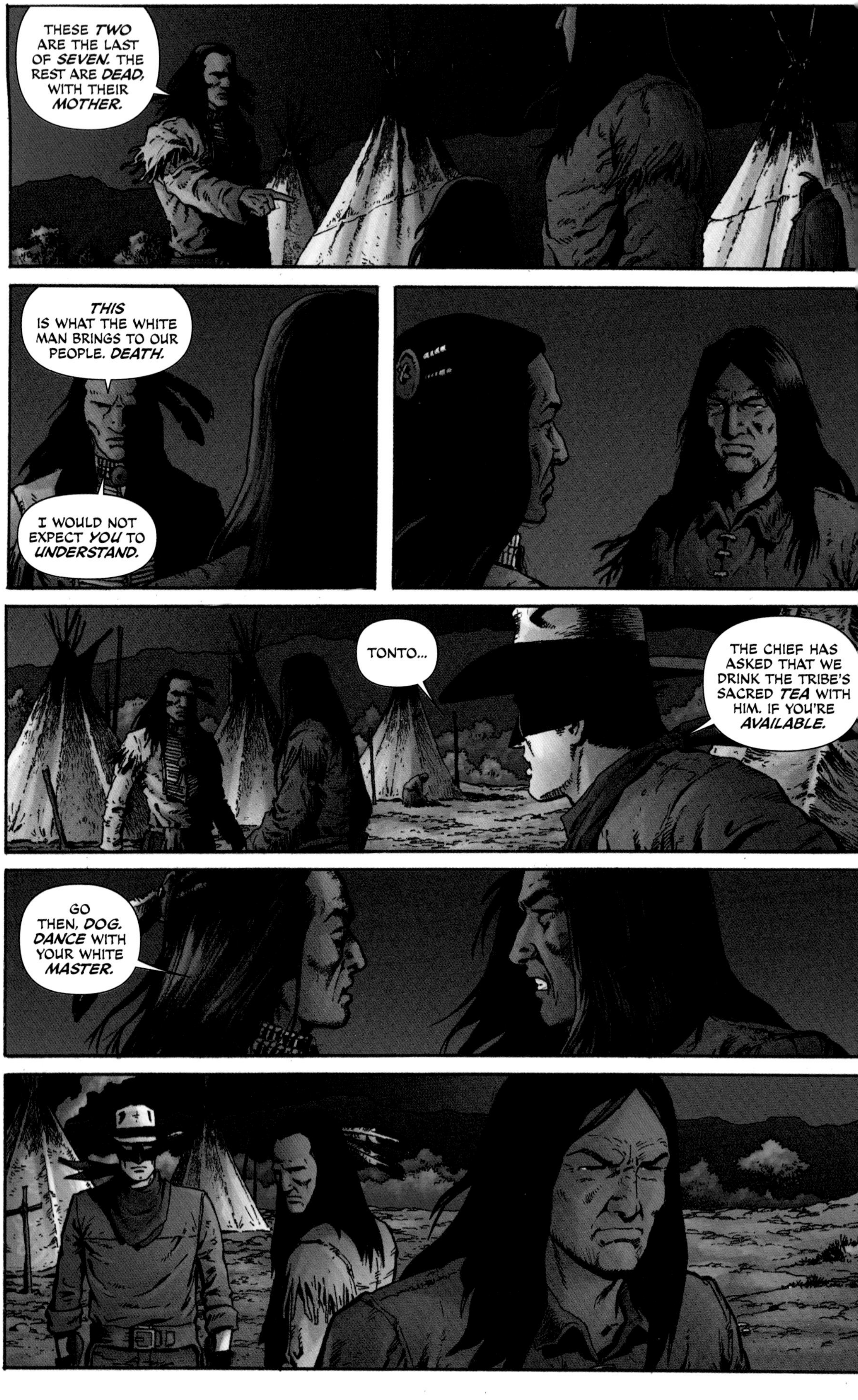
THESE TWO ARE THE LAST OF SEVEN. THE REST ARE DEAD, WITH THEIR MOTHER.
THIS IS WHAT THE WHITE MAN BRINGS TO OUR PEOPLE. DEATH.
I WOULD NOT EXPECT YOU TO UNDERSTAND.
TONTO...
THE CHIEF HAS ASKED THAT WE DRINK THE TRIBE'S SACRED TEA WITH HIM. IF YOU'RE AVAILABLE.
GO THEN, DOG. DANCE WITH YOUR WHITE MASTER.

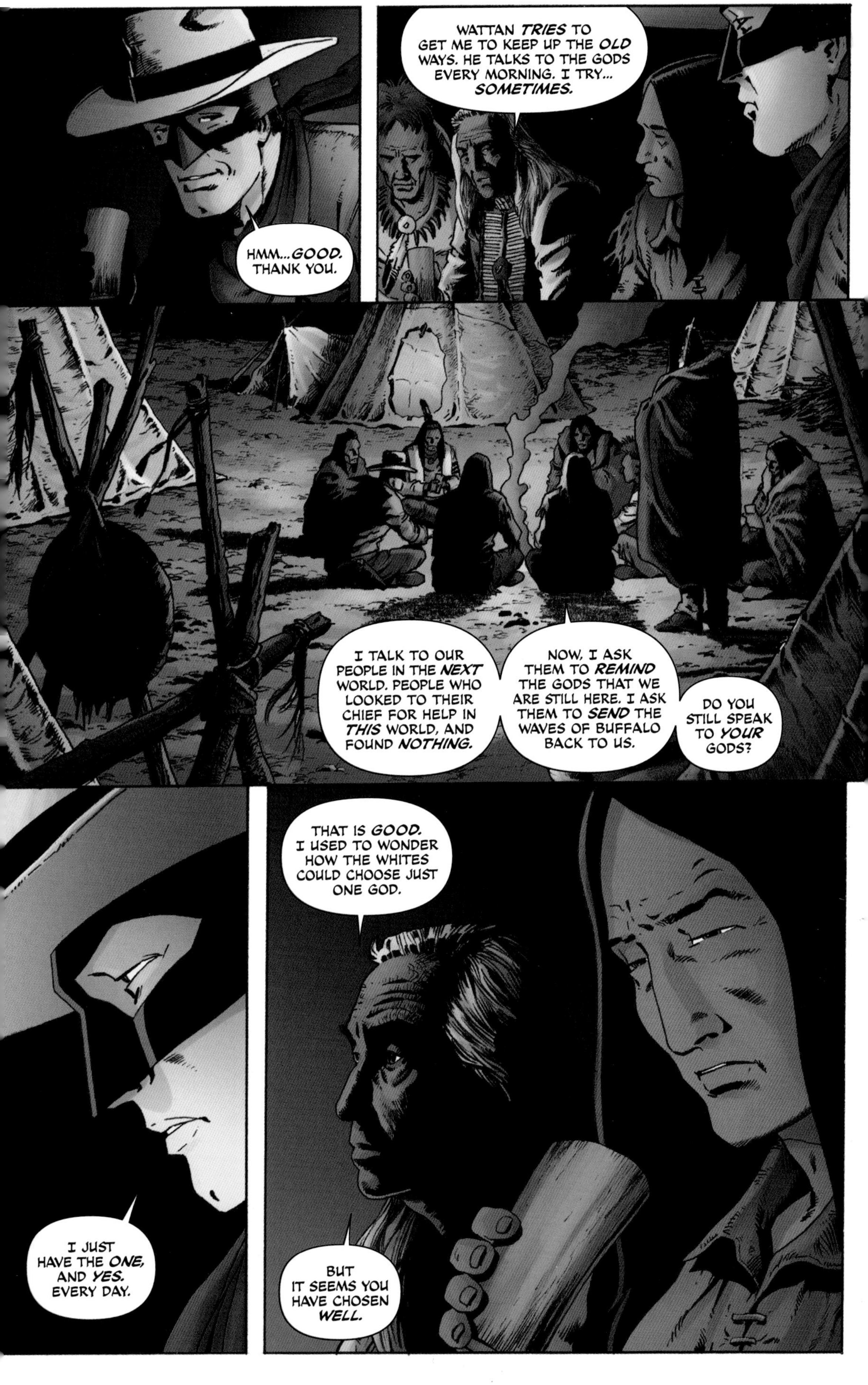
HMM...GOOD. THANK YOU.
WATTAN TRIES TO GET ME TO KEEP UP THE OLD WAYS. HE TALKS TO THE GODS EVERY MORNING. I TRY... SOMETIMES.
I TALK TO OUR PEOPLE IN THE NEXT WORLD. PEOPLE WHO LOOKED TO THEIR CHIEF FOR HELP IN THIS WORLD, AND FOUND NOTHING.
NOW, I ASK THEM TO REMIND THE GODS THAT WE ARE STILL HERE. I ASK THEM TO SEND THE WAVES OF BUFFALO BACK TO US.
DO YOU STILL SPEAK TO YOUR GODS?
I JUST HAVE THE ONE, AND YES. EVERY DAY.
THAT IS GOOD. I USED TO WONDER HOW THE WHITES COULD CHOOSE JUST ONE GOD.
BUT IT SEEMS YOU HAVE CHOSEN WELL.

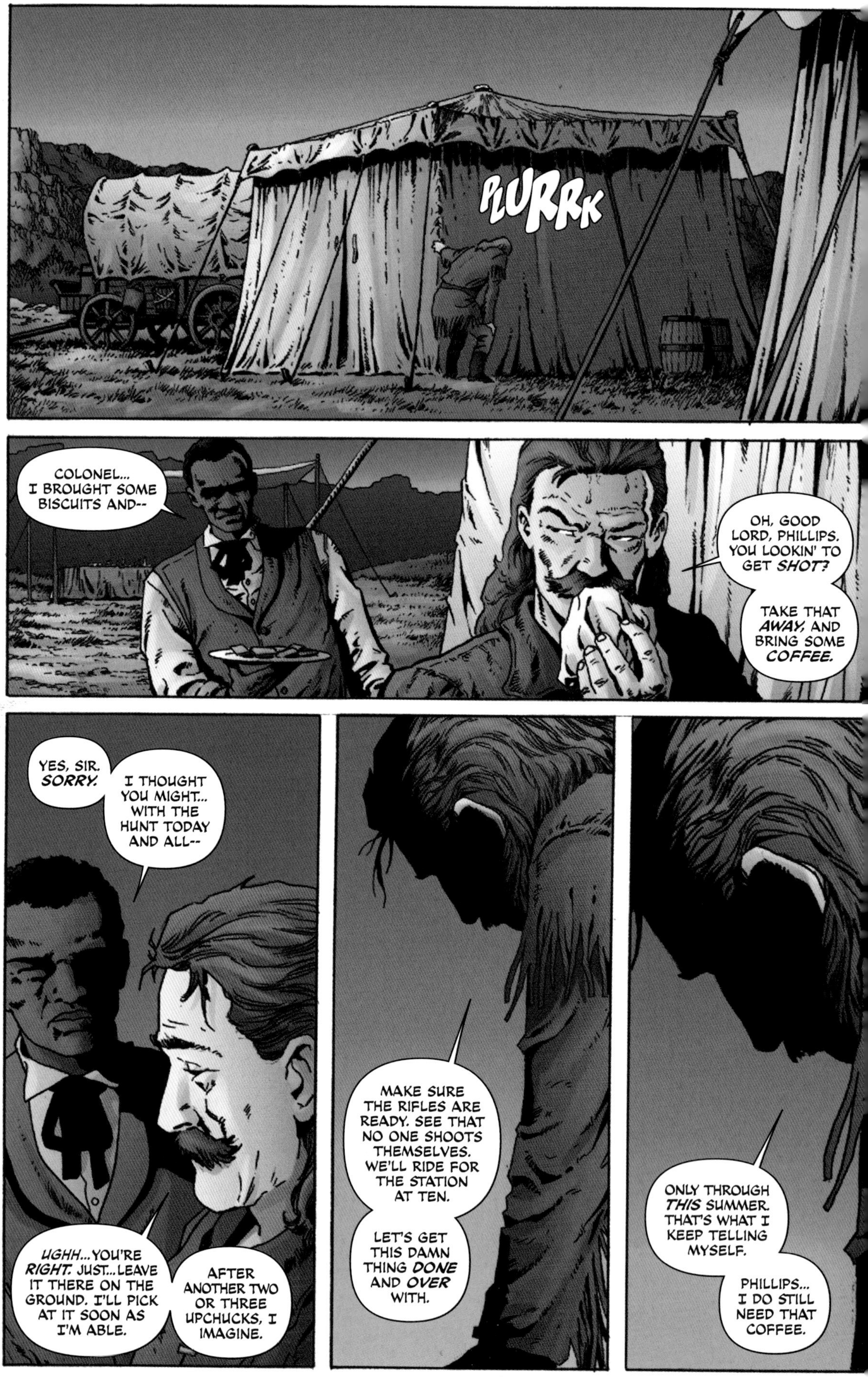
PLURRRK
COLONEL... I BROUGHT SOME BISCUITS AND--
OH, GOOD LORD, PHILLIPS. YOU LOOKIN' TO GET SHOT?
TAKE THAT AWAY, AND BRING SOME COFFEE.
YES, SIR. SORRY.
I THOUGHT YOU MIGHT... WITH THE HUNT TODAY AND ALL--
UGHH... YOU'RE RIGHT. JUST... LEAVE IT THERE ON THE GROUND. I'LL PICK AT IT SOON AS I'M ABLE.
AFTER ANOTHER TWO OR THREE UPCHUCKS, I IMAGINE.
MAKE SURE THE RIFLES ARE READY. SEE THAT NO ONE SHOOTS THEMSELVES. WE'LL RIDE FOR THE STATION AT TEN.
LET'S GET THIS DAMN THING DONE AND OVER WITH.
ONLY THROUGH THIS SUMMER. THAT'S WHAT I KEEP TELLING MYSELF.
PHILLIPS... I DO STILL NEED THAT COFFEE.

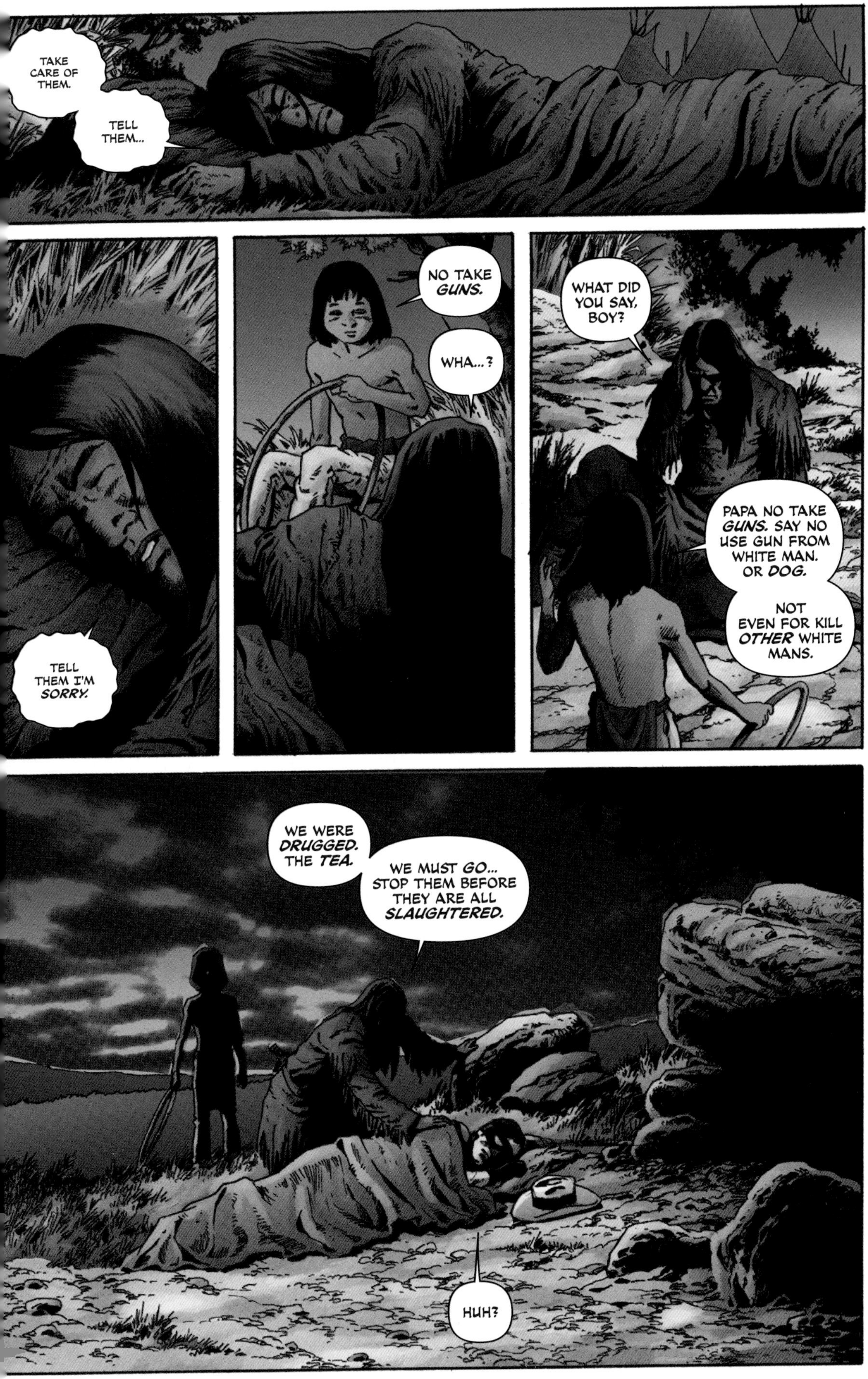
TAKE CARE OF THEM.
TELL THEM...
TELL THEM I'M *SORRY.*
NO TAKE *GUNS.*
WHA...?
WHAT DID YOU SAY, BOY?
PAPA NO TAKE *GUNS.* SAY NO USE GUN FROM WHITE MAN. OR *DOG.*
NOT EVEN FOR KILL *OTHER* WHITE MANS.
WE WERE *DRUGGED.* THE *TEA.*
WE MUST *GO*... STOP THEM BEFORE THEY ARE ALL *SLAUGHTERED.*
HUH?

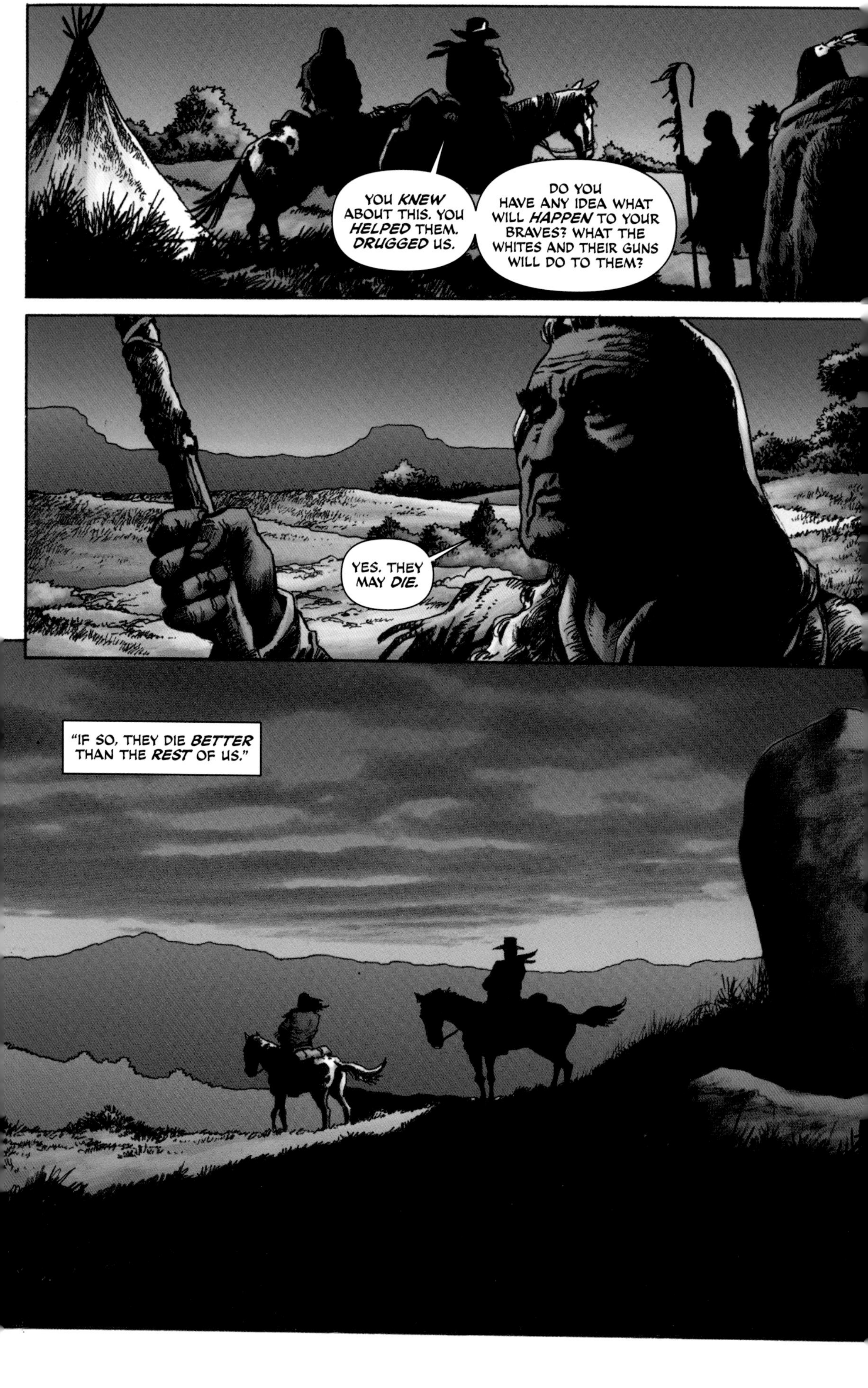
YOU *KNEW* ABOUT THIS. YOU *HELPED* THEM. *DRUGGED* US.
DO YOU HAVE ANY IDEA WHAT WILL *HAPPEN* TO YOUR BRAVES? WHAT THE WHITES AND THEIR GUNS WILL DO TO THEM?
YES. THEY MAY *DIE*.
"IF SO, THEY DIE *BETTER* THAN THE *REST* OF US."

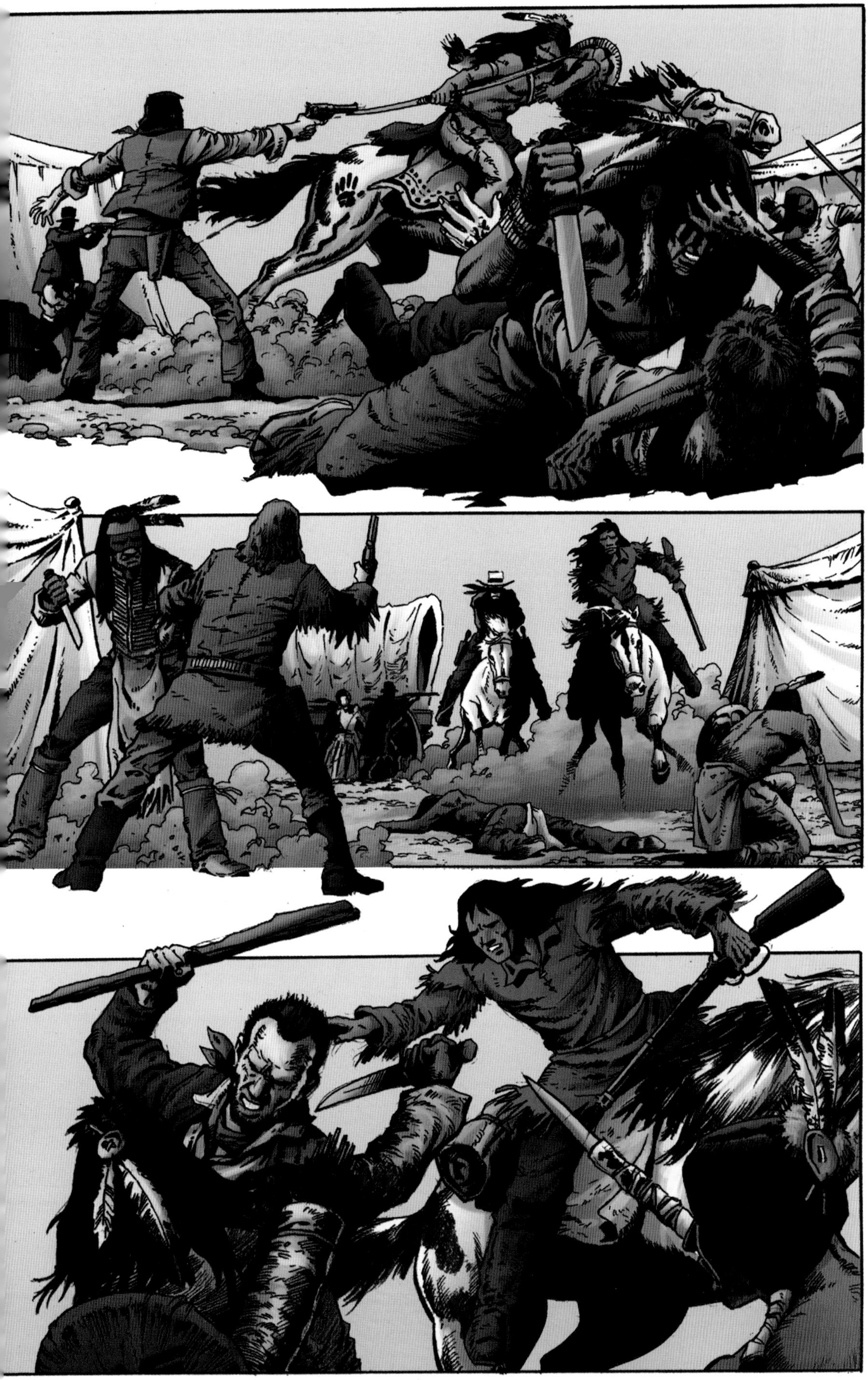

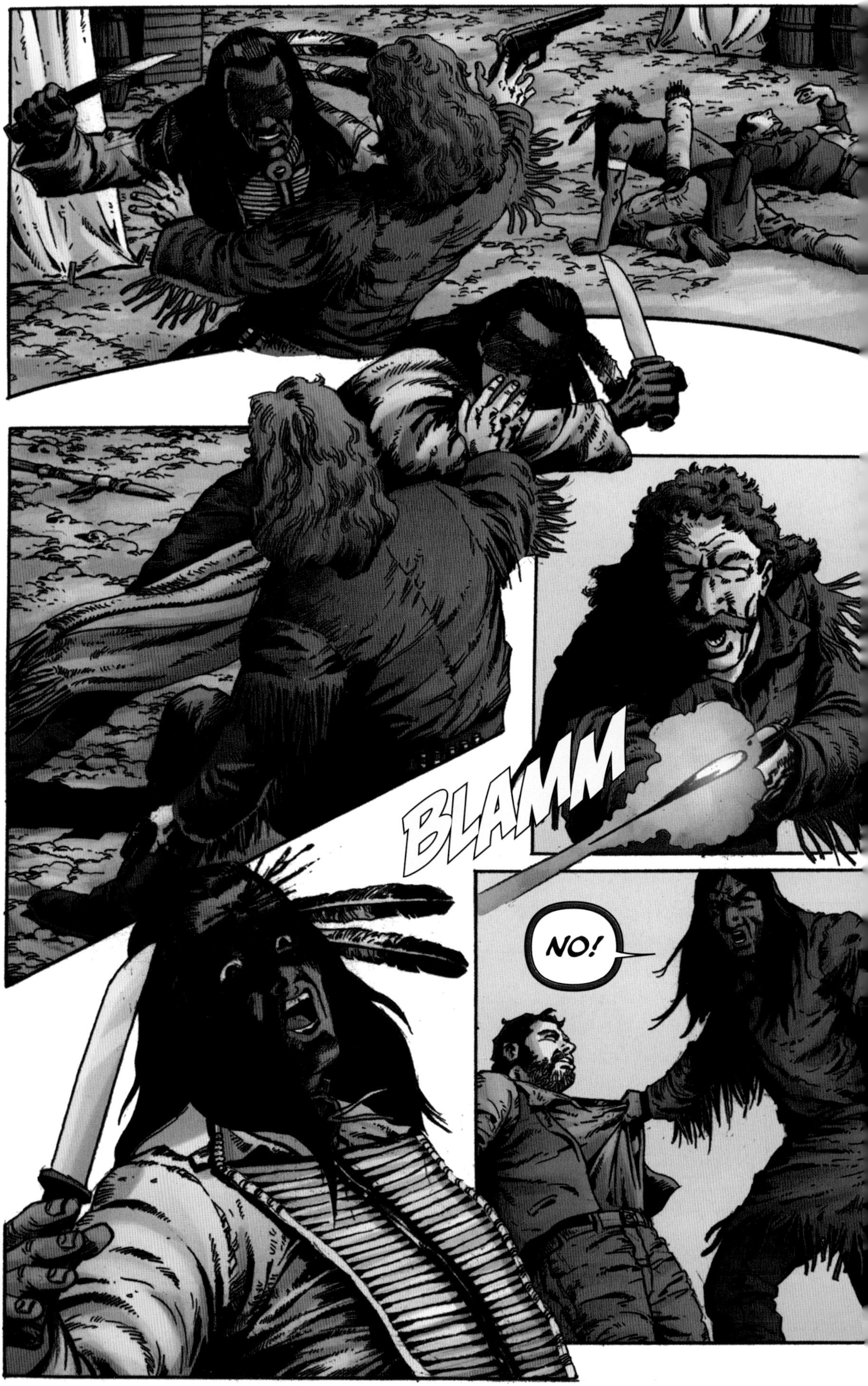
BLAMM
NO!

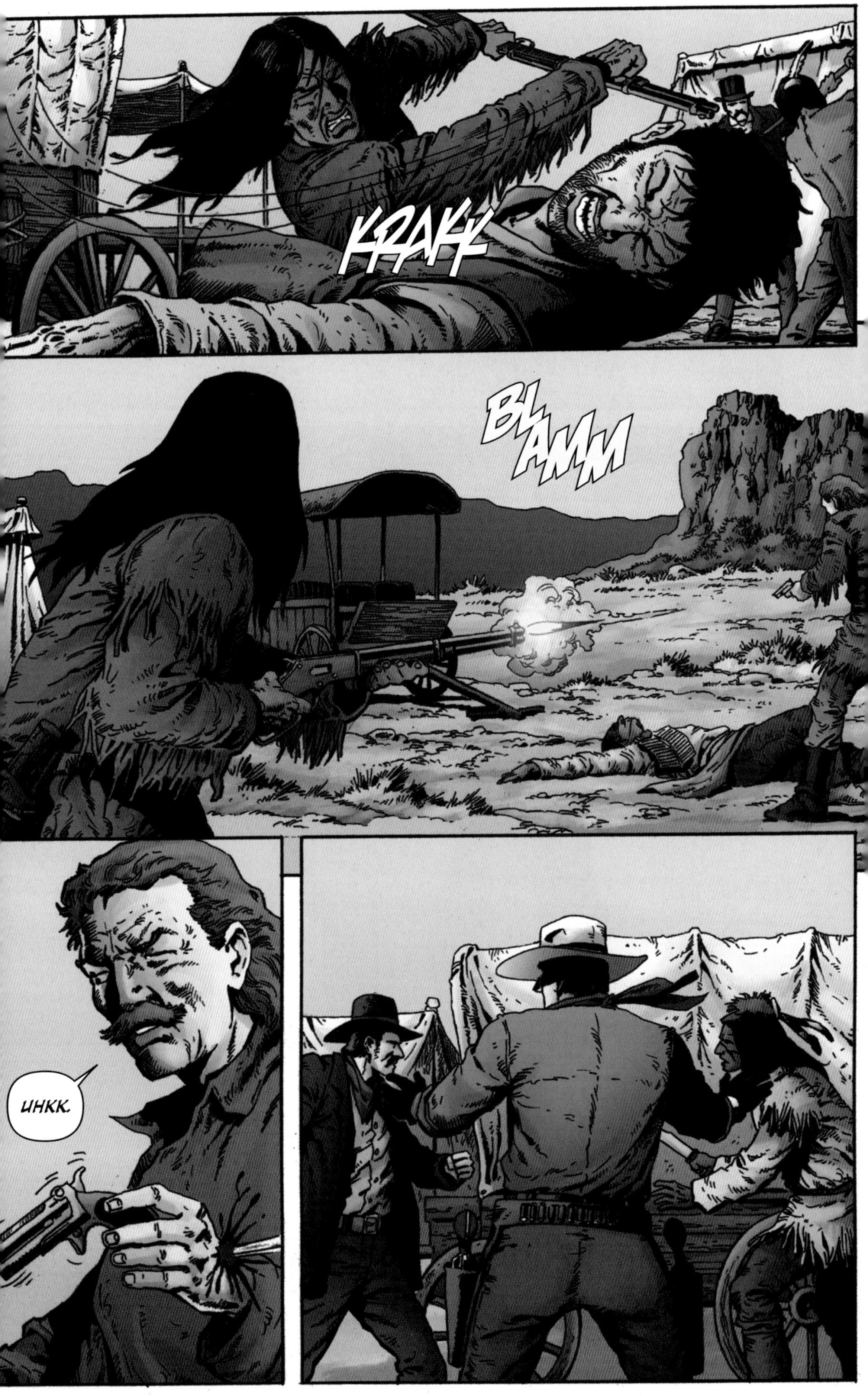
KRAKK
BLAMM
UHKK.

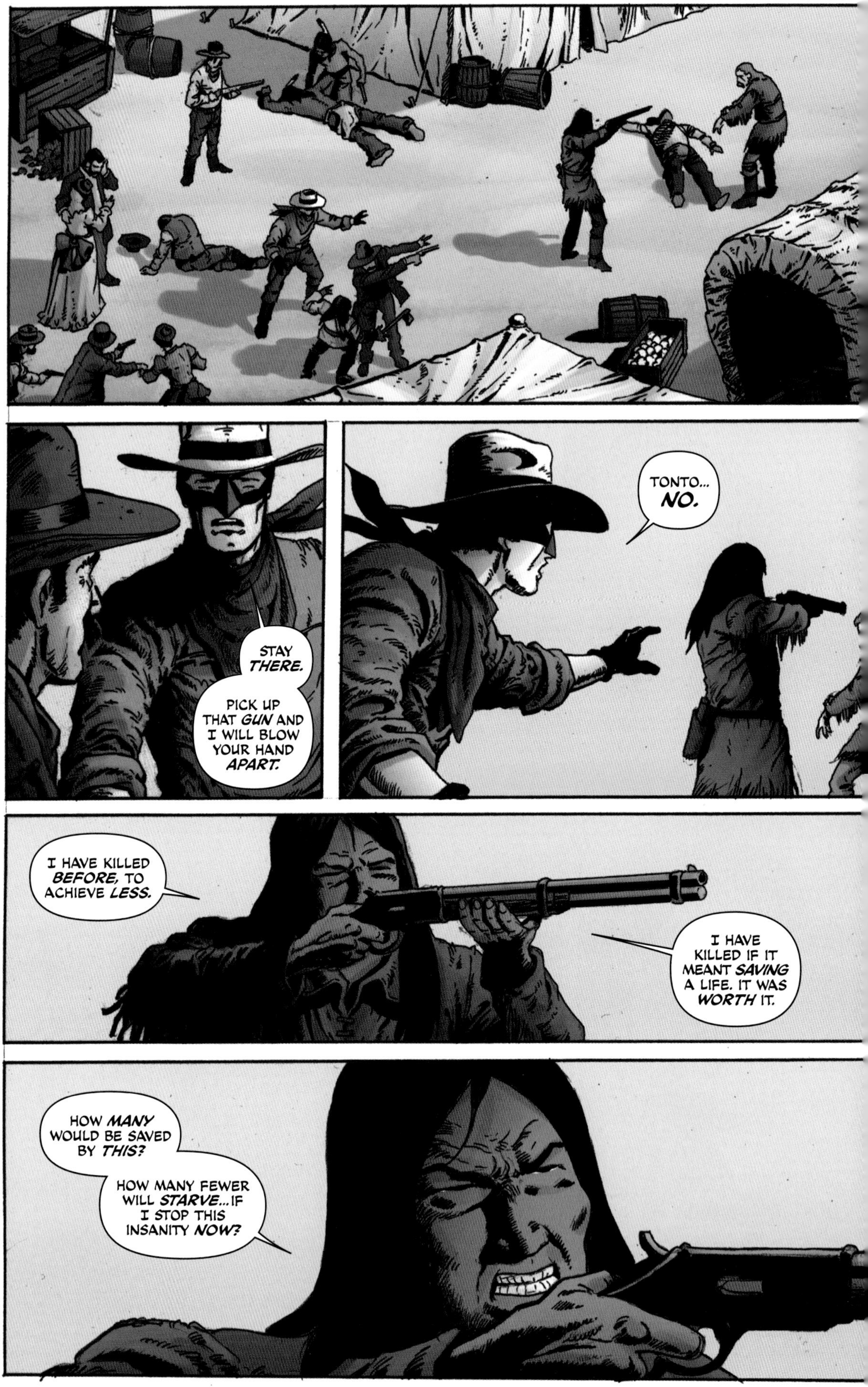
STAY THERE.
PICK UP THAT GUN AND I WILL BLOW YOUR HAND APART.
TONTO... NO.
I HAVE KILLED BEFORE, TO ACHIEVE LESS.
I HAVE KILLED IF IT MEANT SAVING A LIFE. IT WAS WORTH IT.
HOW MANY WOULD BE SAVED BY THIS?
HOW MANY FEWER WILL STARVE... IF I STOP THIS INSANITY NOW?

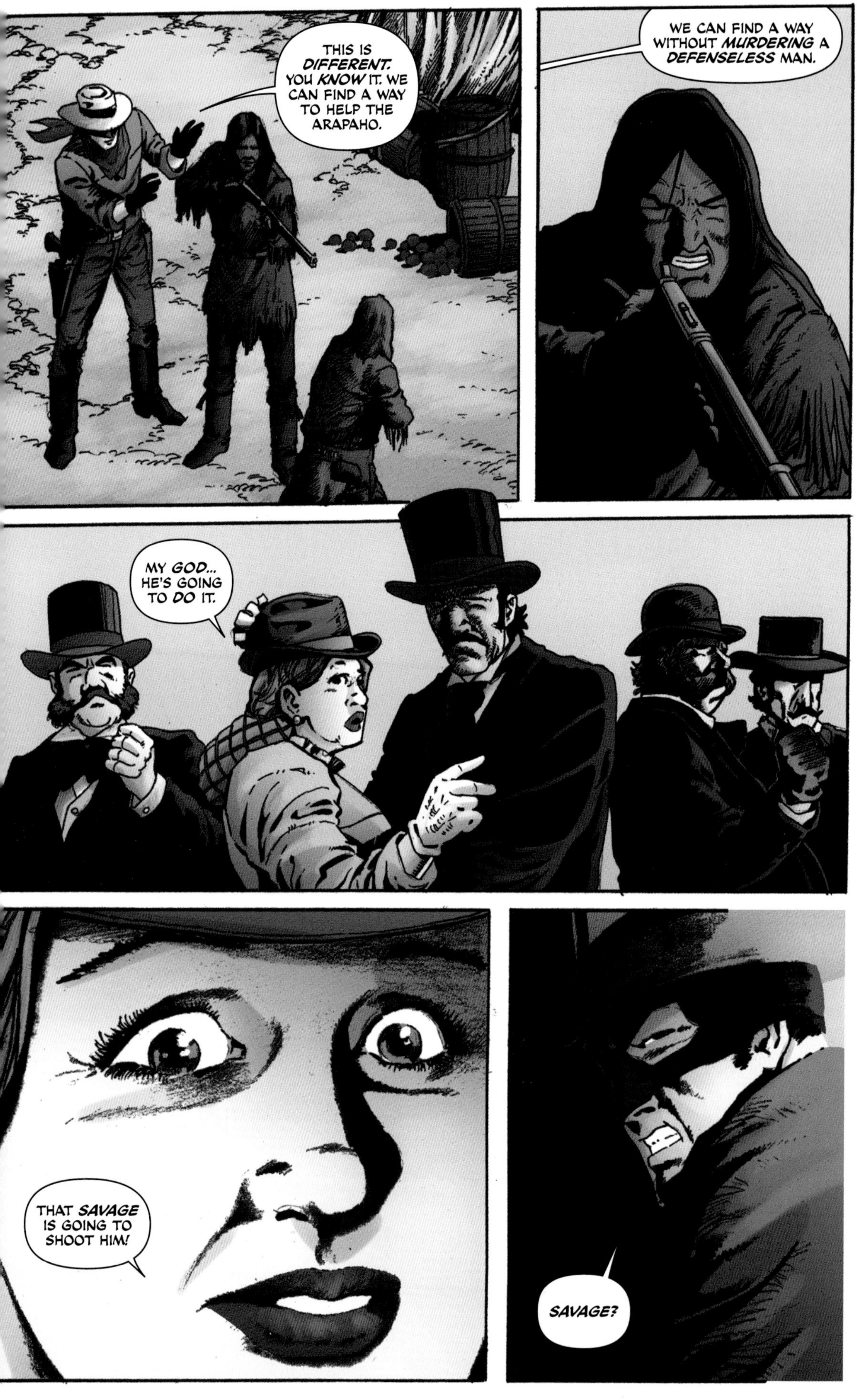
THIS IS DIFFERENT. YOU KNOW IT. WE CAN FIND A WAY TO HELP THE ARAPAHO.
WE CAN FIND A WAY WITHOUT MURDERING A DEFENSELESS MAN.
MY GOD... HE'S GOING TO DO IT.
THAT SAVAGE IS GOING TO SHOOT HIM!
SAVAGE?

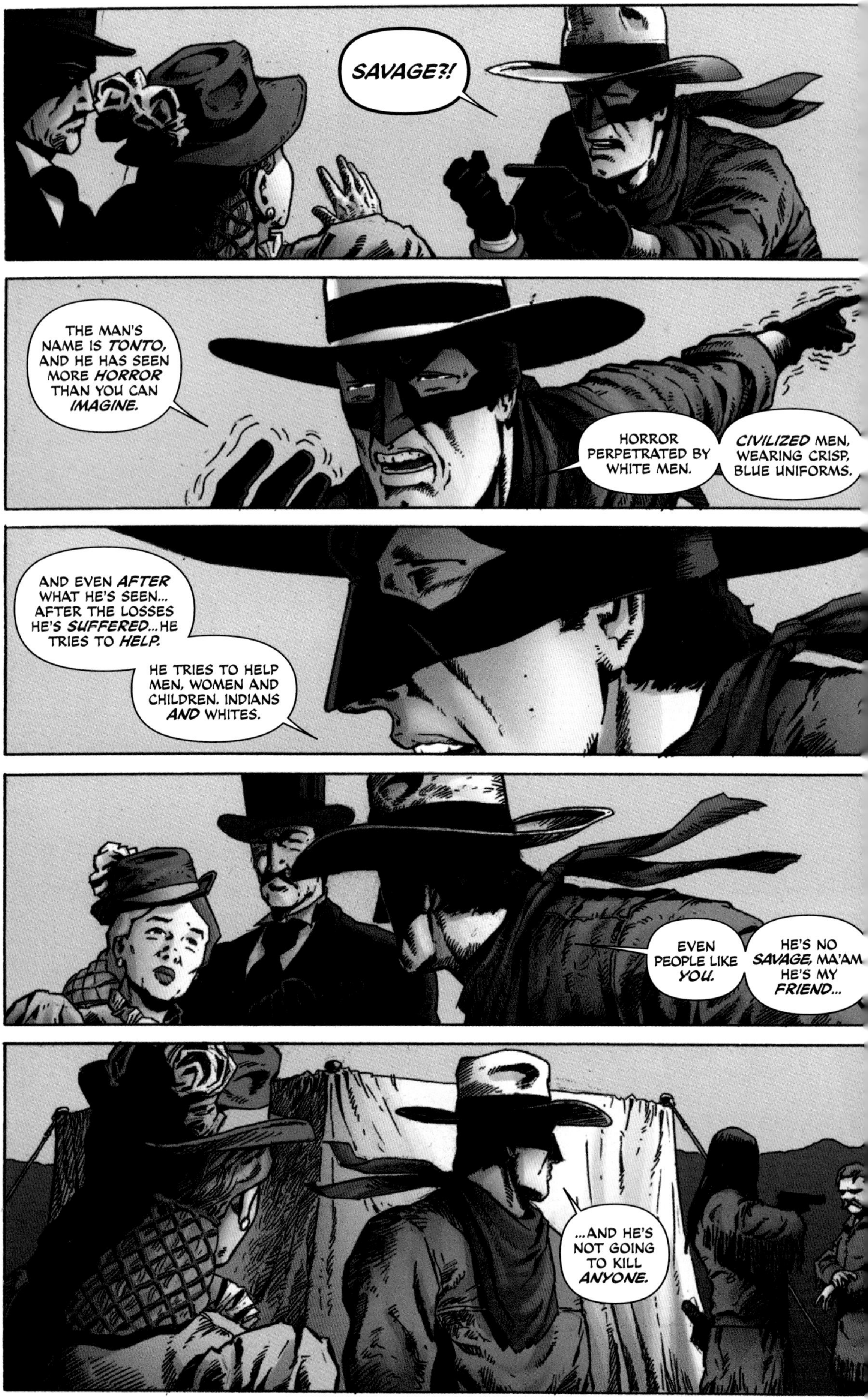
SAVAGE?!
THE MAN'S NAME IS TONTO, AND HE HAS SEEN MORE HORROR THAN YOU CAN IMAGINE.
HORROR PERPETRATED BY WHITE MEN.
CIVILIZED MEN, WEARING CRISP, BLUE UNIFORMS.
AND EVEN AFTER WHAT HE'S SEEN... AFTER THE LOSSES HE'S SUFFERED...HE TRIES TO HELP.
HE TRIES TO HELP MEN, WOMEN AND CHILDREN. INDIANS AND WHITES.
EVEN PEOPLE LIKE YOU.
HE'S NO SAVAGE, MA'AM. HE'S MY FRIEND...
...AND HE'S NOT GOING TO KILL ANYONE.

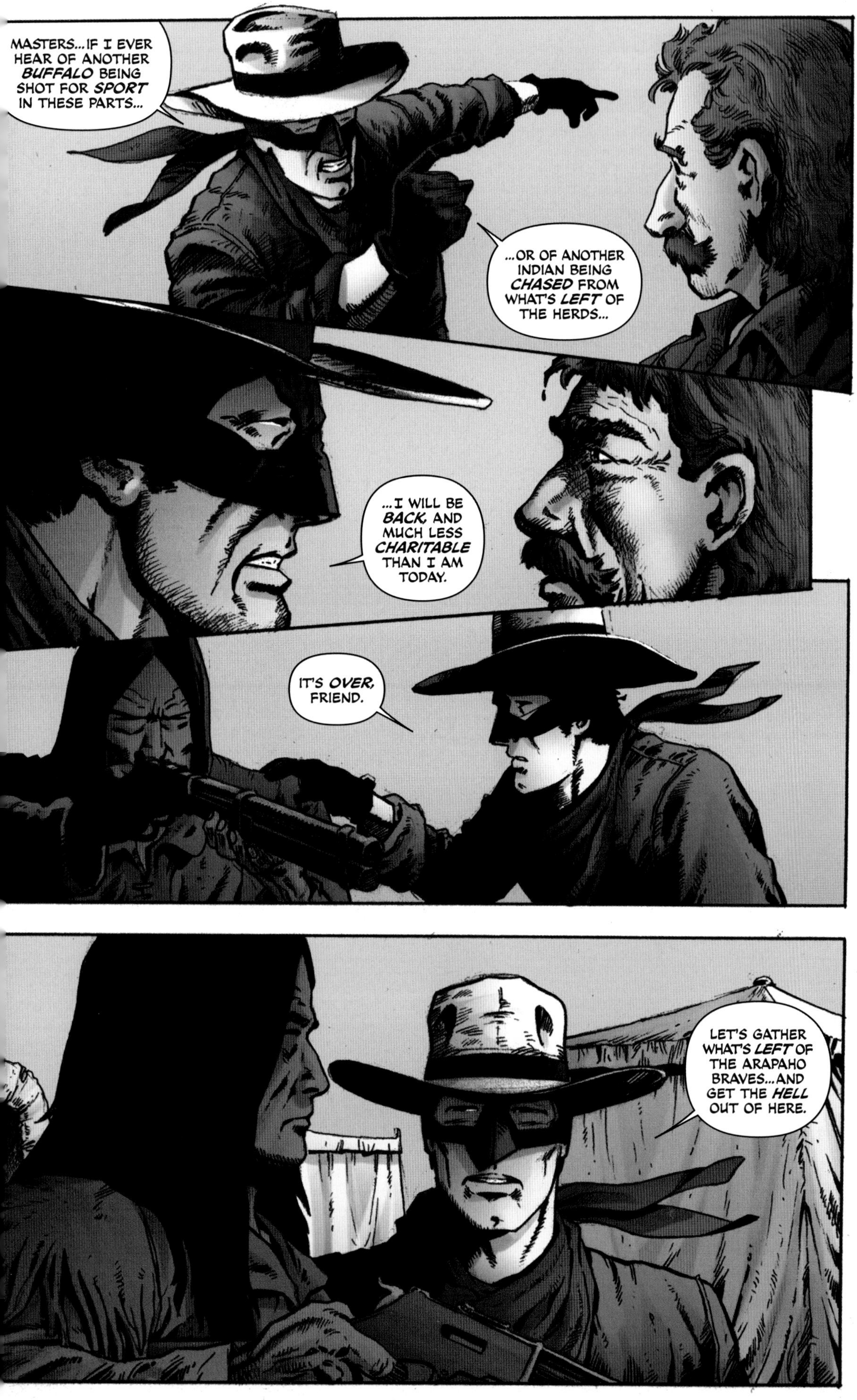
MASTERS...IF I EVER HEAR OF ANOTHER BUFFALO BEING SHOT FOR SPORT IN THESE PARTS...
...OR OF ANOTHER INDIAN BEING CHASED FROM WHAT'S LEFT OF THE HERDS...
...I WILL BE BACK, AND MUCH LESS CHARITABLE THAN I AM TODAY.
IT'S OVER, FRIEND.
LET'S GATHER WHAT'S LEFT OF THE ARAPAHO BRAVES...AND GET THE HELL OUT OF HERE.

The Lone Ranger (see also: Tonto)--

The Ranger, legend has it, was the sole survivor of an ambush, and had been rescued by an Indian brave named Tonto. Today, the legend of the Lone Ranger and his Indian sidekick is regarded as just that: LEGEND.

Pure MYTH, or perhaps a composite of several righteous lawmen of the Old West.

Individual tales have grown out of the myth; stories of people helped in their darkest hour by The Ranger and Tonto.

A family in the Oklahoma Territory, RESCUED from the men who shot down the household's matron in the middle of the night.

A mute widow in Western Kansas, SAVED from a cruel and abusive husband.

MISS DORSEYS HOME FOR WOMEN

She would go on to establish a shelter for similarly abused women-- a shelter that would offer a roof and a fresh start to countless women over the course of several decades.

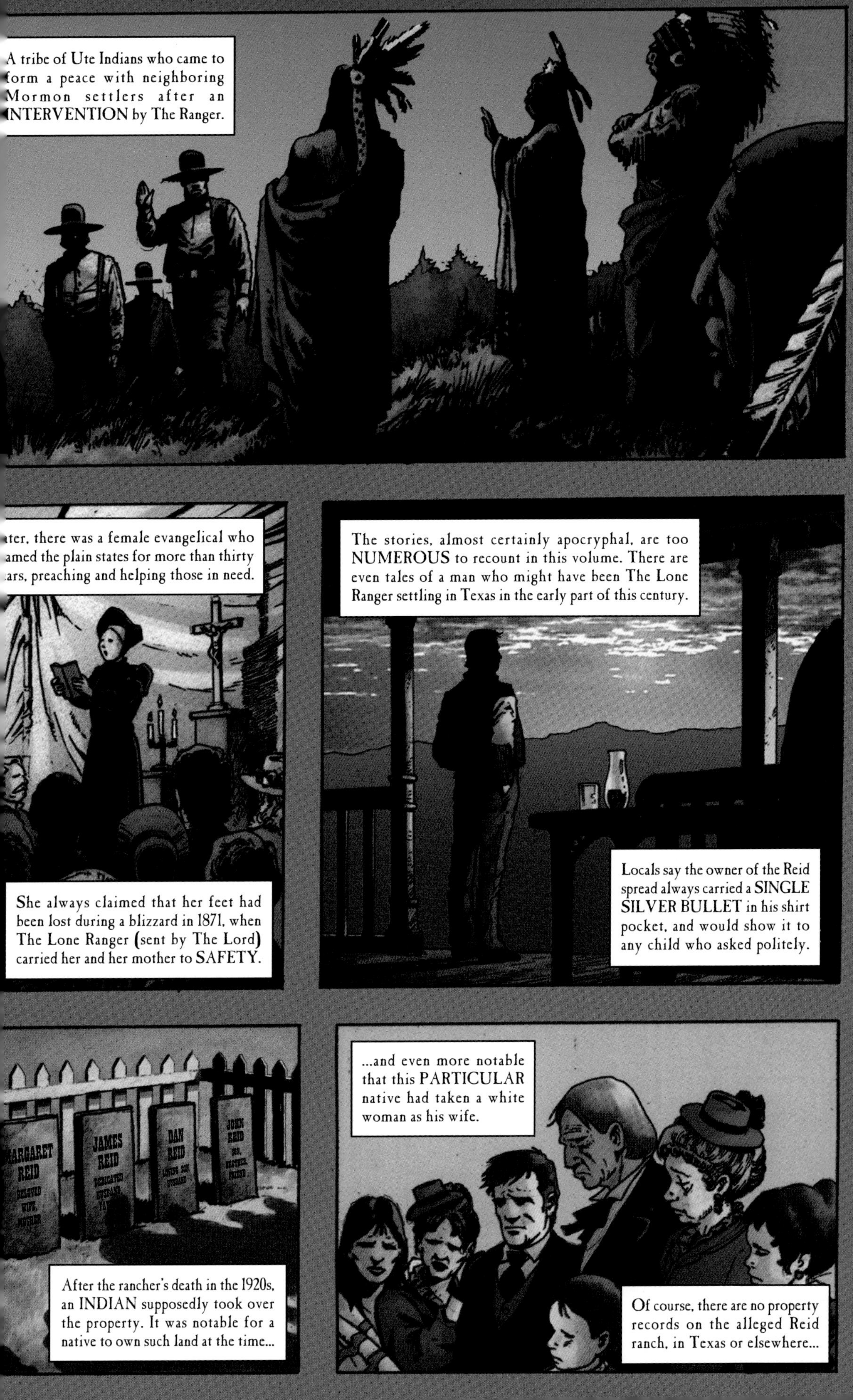

A tribe of Ute Indians who came to form a peace with neighboring Mormon settlers after an INTERVENTION by The Ranger.
ater, there was a female evangelical who amed the plain states for more than thirty ars, preaching and helping those in need.
She always claimed that her feet had been lost during a blizzard in 1871, when The Lone Ranger (sent by The Lord) carried her and her mother to SAFETY.
The stories, almost certainly apocryphal, are too NUMEROUS to recount in this volume. There are even tales of a man who might have been The Lone Ranger settling in Texas in the early part of this century.
Locals say the owner of the Reid spread always carried a SINGLE SILVER BULLET in his shirt pocket, and would show it to any child who asked politely.
ARGARET REID
JAMES REID
DAN REID
JOHN REID
After the rancher's death in the 1920s, an INDIAN supposedly took over the property. It was notable for a native to own such land at the time...
...and even more notable that this PARTICULAR native had taken a white woman as his wife.
Of course, there are no property records on the alleged Reid ranch, in Texas or elsewhere...

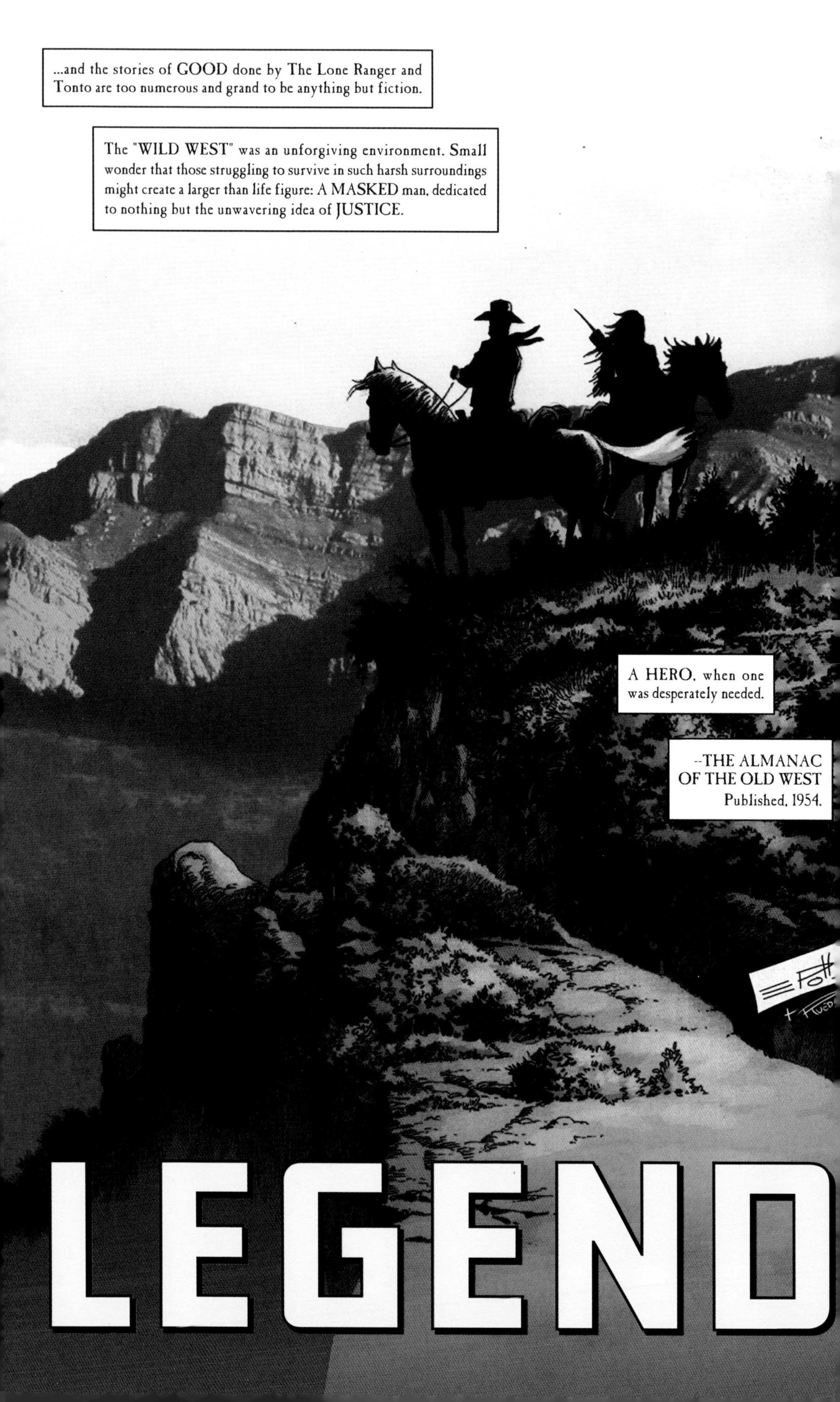
...and the stories of GOOD done by The Lone Ranger and Tonto are too numerous and grand to be anything but fiction.
The "WILD WEST" was an unforgiving environment. Small wonder that those struggling to survive in such harsh surroundings might create a larger than life figure: A MASKED man, dedicated to nothing but the unwavering idea of JUSTICE.
A HERO, when one was desperately needed.
--THE ALMANAC OF THE OLD WEST Published, 1954.
LEGEND

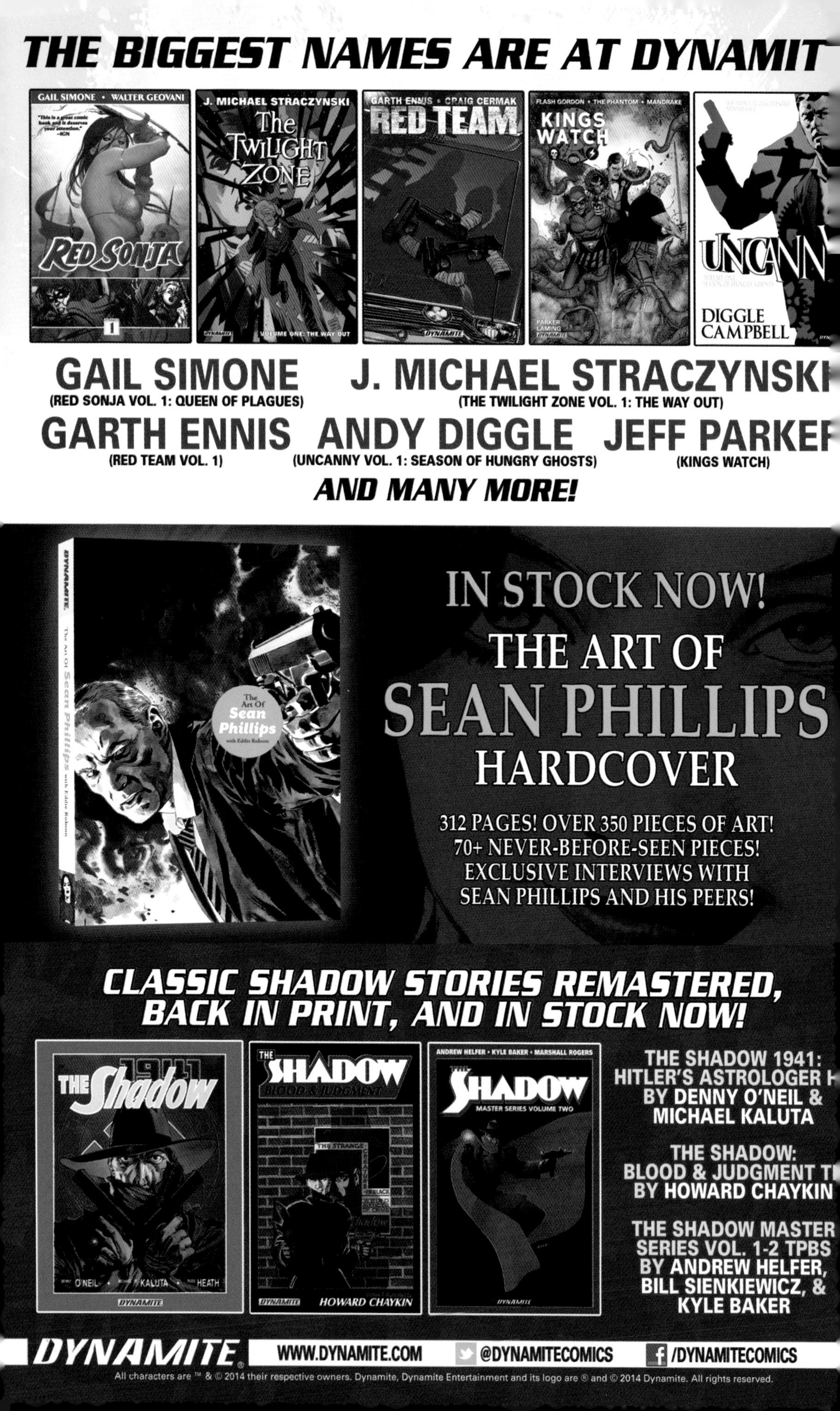
THE BIGGEST NAMES ARE AT DYNAMIT
GAIL SIMONE
(RED SONJA VOL. 1: QUEEN OF PLAGUES)
J. MICHAEL STRACZYNSKI
(THE TWILIGHT ZONE VOL. 1: THE WAY OUT)
GARTH ENNIS
(RED TEAM VOL. 1)
ANDY DIGGLE
(UNCANNY VOL. 1: SEASON OF HUNGRY GHOSTS)
JEFF PARKER
(KINGS WATCH)
AND MANY MORE!
IN STOCK NOW!
THE ART OF
SEAN PHILLIPS
HARDCOVER
312 PAGES! OVER 350 PIECES OF ART!
70+ NEVER-BEFORE-SEEN PIECES!
EXCLUSIVE INTERVIEWS WITH
SEAN PHILLIPS AND HIS PEERS!
CLASSIC SHADOW STORIES REMASTERED,
BACK IN PRINT, AND IN STOCK NOW!
THE SHADOW 1941:
HITLER'S ASTROLOGER H
BY DENNY O'NEIL &
MICHAEL KALUTA
THE SHADOW:
BLOOD & JUDGMENT T
BY HOWARD CHAYKIN
THE SHADOW MASTER
SERIES VOL. 1-2 TPBS
BY ANDREW HELFER,
BILL SIENKIEWICZ, &
KYLE BAKER
DYNAMITE
WWW.DYNAMITE.COM
@DYNAMITECOMICS
/DYNAMITECOMICS
All characters are ™ & © 2014 their respective owners. Dynamite, Dynamite Entertainment and its logo are ® and © 2014 Dynamite. All rights reserved.

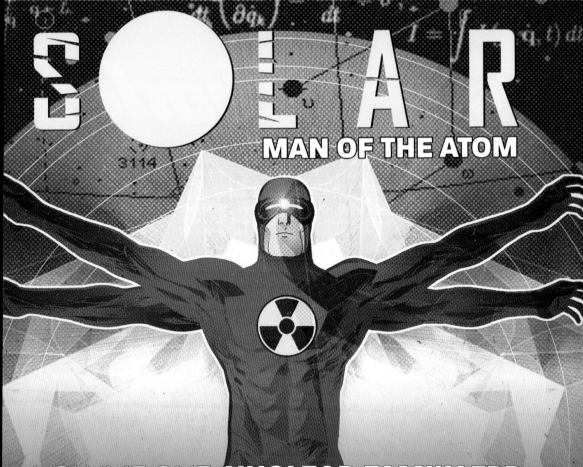
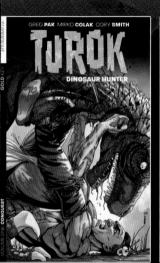
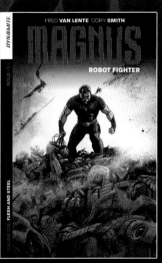

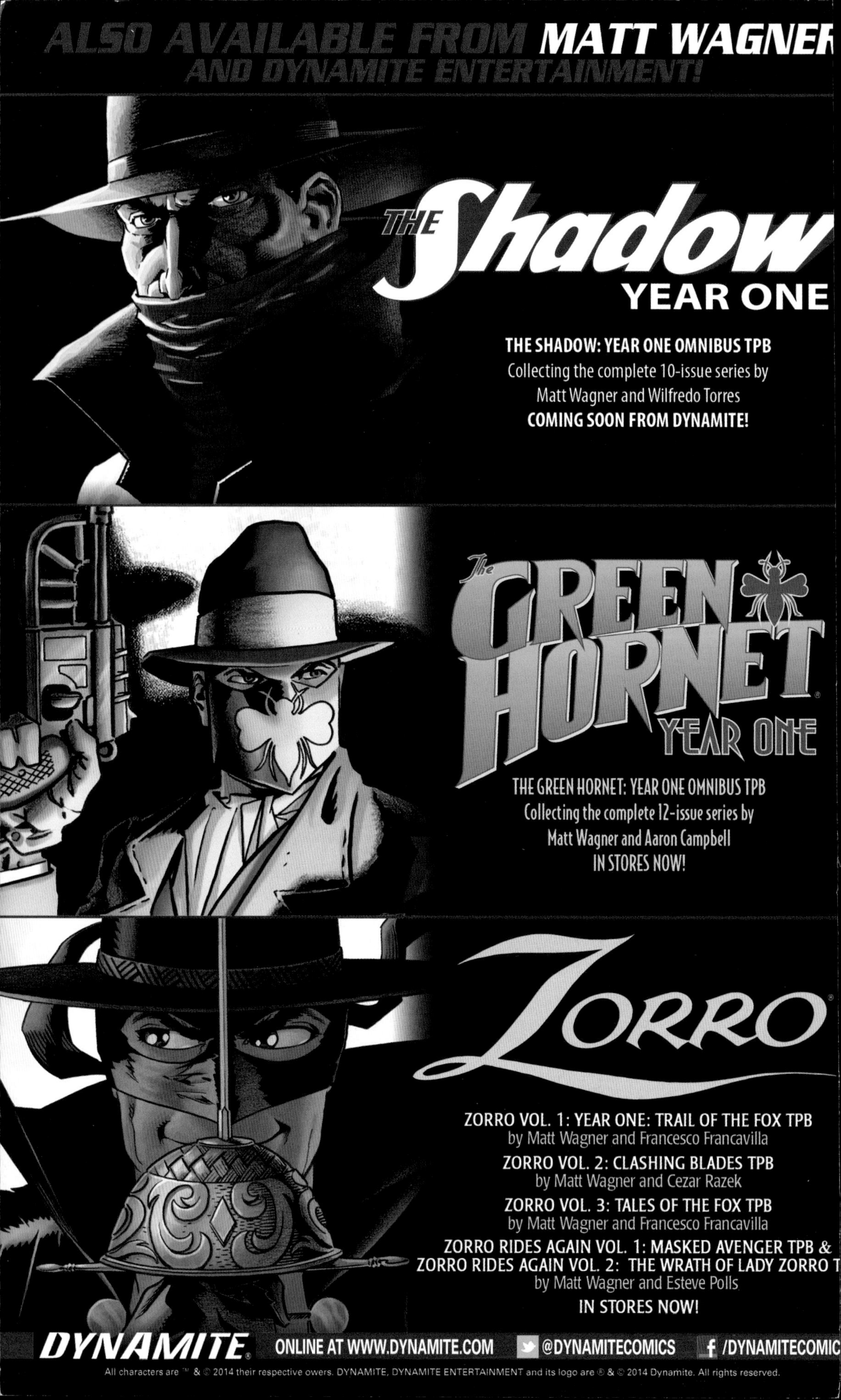
ALSO AVAILABLE FROM MATT WAGNER
AND DYNAMITE ENTERTAINMENT!
THE Shadow
YEAR ONE
THE SHADOW: YEAR ONE OMNIBUS TPB
Collecting the complete 10-issue series by
Matt Wagner and Wilfredo Torres
COMING SOON FROM DYNAMITE!
The GREEN HORNET
YEAR ONE
THE GREEN HORNET: YEAR ONE OMNIBUS TPB
Collecting the complete 12-issue series by
Matt Wagner and Aaron Campbell
IN STORES NOW!
ZORRO
ZORRO VOL. 1: YEAR ONE: TRAIL OF THE FOX TPB
by Matt Wagner and Francesco Francavilla
ZORRO VOL. 2: CLASHING BLADES TPB
by Matt Wagner and Cezar Razek
ZORRO VOL. 3: TALES OF THE FOX TPB
by Matt Wagner and Francesco Francavilla
ZORRO RIDES AGAIN VOL. 1: MASKED AVENGER TPB &
ZORRO RIDES AGAIN VOL. 2: THE WRATH OF LADY ZORRO T
by Matt Wagner and Esteve Polls
IN STORES NOW!
DYNAMITE
ONLINE AT WWW.DYNAMITE.COM
@DYNAMITECOMICS
/DYNAMITECOMIC
All characters are ™ & © 2014 their respective owers. DYNAMITE, DYNAMITE ENTERTAINMENT and its logo are ® & © 2014 Dynamite. All rights reserved.

THE FRENCH BESTSELLER AVAILABLE IN ENGLISH FOR THE FIRST TIME!

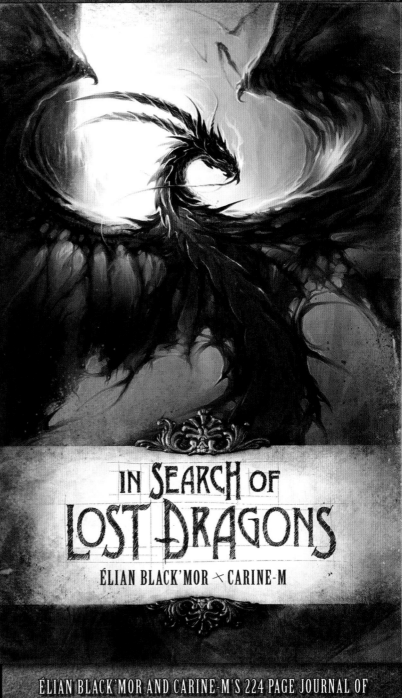

IN SEARCH OF LOST DRAGONS

ÉLIAN BLACK'MOR ✕ CARINE-M

ÉLIAN BLACK'MOR AND CARINE-M'S 224 PAGE JOURNAL OF GORGEOUS, FULLY PAINTED ARTWORK, CAPTURING EVERY MAJESTIC AND FEARSOME VISUAL DETAIL OF THE SCALY BEHEMOTHS, ACCOMPANIED BY SNIPPETS OF LOCAL LORE AS EVIDENCE THAT THESE HIDDEN BEASTS CONTINUE TO SHAPE THE WORLD IN WAYS WE MAY NEVER EXPECT!

OCTOBER FROM DYNAMITE!

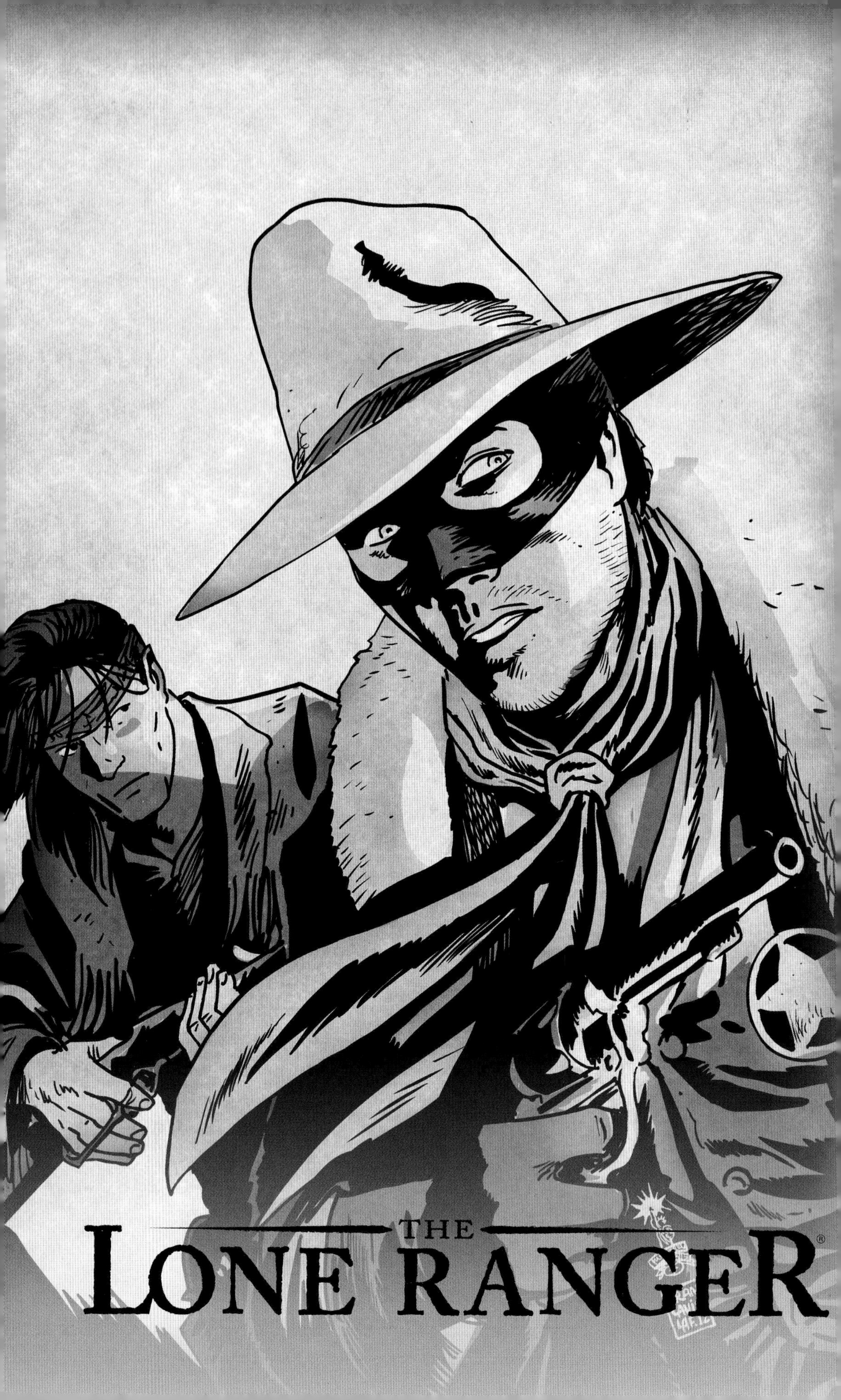
THE
LONE RANGER®